Human Rights Discourse

This book explores the concept of human rights as constructed in language, shedding light on discursive and professional practices at the European Court of Human Rights (ECtHR), as differentiated from other judicial institutions offering human rights defence mechanisms. It unveils the system of genres at the ECtHR adopting a holistic outlook, which caters for an interdisciplinary readership including both language and law professionals. The genres, along with the underlying professional practices and interdiscursive mechanisms, are described following the lifecycle of cases, starting from the initial application to the Court and ending with institutional press releases and execution of judgments, which foster greater democratic participation. The Court is depicted through its plurality of voices and stakeholders, acknowledging the non-monolithic nature of judicial discourse. The work follows the knowledge migration path from national into international justice and traces how national, and linguistically divergent, elements are recontextualized in a supranational context. It problematizes the coexistence of institutional and outsourced legal translation as well as their potential effects on the discourse of human rights. The book covers issues of legal terminology, phraseology, dialogism, pragmatics and knowledge dissemination dynamics. The study will be an invaluable resource for academics, researchers and translators working in the areas of law and language, linguistics, Translation Studies and Genre Studies.

Jekaterina Nikitina is Associate Professor of English Language and Translation at the University of Milan, Italy.

Law, Language and Communication

This series encourages innovative and integrated perspectives within and across the boundaries of law, language and communication, with particular emphasis on issues of communication in specialized socio-legal and professional contexts. It seeks to bring together a range of diverse yet cumulative research traditions in order to identify and encourage interdisciplinary research.

The series welcomes proposals – both edited collections as well as single-authored monographs – emphasizing critical approaches to law, language and communication, identifying and discussing issues, proposing solutions to problems, offering analyses in areas such as legal construction, interpretation, translation and de-codification.

Series Editors

Anne Wagner is Professor of Legal Semiotics and Research Professor at Centre de Recherche Droits & Perspectives du Droit, équipe René Demogue, Lille University, France. She is the Editor-in-Chief of the International Journal for the Semiotics of Law (Springer) and President of the International Roundtables for the Semiotics of Law. She has been awarded the National Research Grant for her research career. Her main research interests include semiotics, verbal and non-verbal sign system analyses, language and law, legal culture and heritage, legal translation, legal terminology, and legal discourse studies.

Vijay K. Bhatia, formerly Professor of English, City University of Hong Kong, is now Adjunct Professor at Chinese University of Hong Kong, and Visiting Professor at the Hellenic American University, Athens (Greece). He is also the founding President of the Languages for Specific Purposes and Professional Communication Association for Asia-Pacific. His research interests include Critical Genre Analysis, academic and professional discourses in legal, business, newspaper, and promotional contexts; ESP and Professional Communication; simplification of legal and other public documents; intercultural and cross-disciplinary variations in professional genres.

Titles in the series

Phraseology in Legal and Institutional Settings
A Corpus-based Interdisciplinary Perspective
Edited by Stanislaw Gozdz Roszkowski and Gianluca Pontrandolfo

Fiction and the Languages of Law
Understanding Contemporary Legal Discourse
Karen Petroski

Law and Imagination in Troubled Times
A Legal and Literary Discourse
Edited by Richard Mullender, Matteo Nicolini, Thomas D.C. Bennett and Emilia Mickiewicz

Social Media in Legal Practice
Edited by Vijay Bhatia and Girolamo Tessuto

Law, Language and the Courtroom
Legal Linguistics and the Discourse of Judges
Edited by Stanisław Goźdź-Roszkowski & Gianluca Pontrandolfo

Ambiguity in EU Law
A Linguistic and Legal Analysis
Sofiya Kartalova

Fair Trial Rights and Multilingualism in Africa
Perspectives from Comparable Jurisdictions
Catherine S. Namakula

Language and Legal Judgments
Evaluation and Argument in Judicial Discourse
Stanisław Goźdź-Roszkowski

The Logic of Legal Argumentation
Multi-Modal Perspectives
Marko Novak

Law and Cognitive Linguistics
A Prototype Theory Approach to Legal Categorisation
Mateusz Zeifert

For more information about this series, please visit: www.routledge.com/Law-Language-and-Communication/book-series/LAWLANGCOMM

Human Rights Discourse

Linguistics, Genre and Translation at the European Court of Human Rights

Jekaterina Nikitina

Routledge
Taylor & Francis Group
LONDON AND NEW YORK

First published 2025
by Routledge
4 Park Square, Milton Park, Abingdon, Oxon OX14 4RN

and by Routledge
605 Third Avenue, New York, NY 10158

Routledge is an imprint of the Taylor & Francis Group, an informa business

British Library Cataloguing-in-Publication Data
A catalogue record for this book is available from the British Library

Library of Congress Cataloging-in-Publication Data
Names: Nikitina, Jekaterina, author.
Title: Human rights discourse : linguistics, genre, and translation at the European Court of Human Rights / Jekaterina Nikitina.
Description: Abingdon, Oxon [UK] ; New York, NY : Routledge, 2025. | Series: Law, language and communication | Includes bibliographical references and index
Identifiers: LCCN 2024044176 (print) | LCCN 2024044177 (ebook) | ISBN 9781032562773 (hardback) | ISBN 9781032562780 (paperback) | ISBN 9781003434788 (ebook)
Subjects: LCSH: Human rights—Language. | Human rights—Terminology. | Human rights—Translating. | European Court of Human Rights.
Classification: LCC K3240 .N547 2025 (print) | LCC K3240 (ebook) | DDC 342.2408/5014—dc23/eng/20240919
LC record available at https://lccn.loc.gov/2024044176
LC ebook record available at https://lccn.loc.gov/2024044177

ISBN: 978-1-032-56277-3 (hbk)
ISBN: 978-1-032-56278-0 (pbk)
ISBN: 978-1-003-43478-8 (ebk)

DOI: 10.4324/9781003434788

Typeset in ITC Galliard Pro
by Apex CoVantage, LLC

Contents

List of tables *xiii*
List of figures *xv*
Preface *xvi*

PART I
The discourse of human rights across institutions 1

1 The discourse of human rights across languages, perspectives and institutions 3

1.1 The discourse of human rights 3
1.1.1 Language and law: legal linguistics 3
1.1.2 Human rights discourse: legal and linguistic perspectives 4
1.2 The discourse of international organizations 7
1.2.1 Institutional multilingualism: linguistic diversity at work 7
1.2.2 Multilingualism and international courts: Comparative Legal Linguistics, Comparative Law and Legal Translation Studies 9
1.3 Methodological toolkit 11
1.3.1 The discourse of human rights and Critical Genre Analysis: methodological perspectives 11
1.4 Human rights discourse across supranational courts 15
1.4.1 Institutional context and professional culture 15
1.4.2 Linguistic regime 19
1.4.3 Discursive practices and genres at the regional human rights courts 22
1.5 Conclusions 24

2 Constructing human rights discourse: insights from legal terminology and phraseology 26

2.1 Introduction 26
2.2 Legal terminology and phraseology: a continuum 27
2.2.1 Legal terminology 27
2.2.2 Legal phraseology 28
2.3 Human rights terminology and phraseology: methodological framework 29
2.4 Human rights terminology and phraseology: findings 32
2.5 Conclusions 39

3 The European Court of Human Rights: context, genres and languages 40

3.1 The European Convention on Human Rights 40
3.1.1 A hope for the future? 40
3.1.2 The living instrument 42
3.2 The European Court of Human Rights: historical background 45
3.2.1 The old Court 46
3.2.2 The new Court after Protocol no. 11, 1998–2009 48
3.2.3 Protocol no. 14: boosting effectiveness 51
3.2.4 Evolving into subsidiarity, margin of appreciation and advisory opinions 53
3.3 Procedure and judicial formations of the ECtHR 56
3.4 Genres at the ECtHR 58
3.4.1 Genre theory: methodological considerations 58
3.4.2 Procedural genres at the ECtHR 61
3.4.3 Derived genres at the ECtHR 66
3.5 The ECtHR discourse: languages and translation 69
3.6 Conclusions 73

PART II
The European Court of Human Rights: inception of cases and the voices of human rights 75

4 Application: the right to individual petition and plain language 77

4.1 The right of individual petition 77
4.2 The application form 80

4.3 The admissibility criteria 81
4.4 Linguistic implications 82
4.5 Generic makeup of an application form 84
4.6 The (plain) language of applications 85
4.7 Conclusions 88

5 Case communication: negotiating supranational terminology through institutional translation 90

5.1 Case communication: a watershed genre 90
5.2 Case communication: genre perspectives 91
5.3 Case communication: translation perspectives 93
5.4 System-bound elements and their translation strategies 96
5.4.1 System-bound elements 96
5.4.2 A quest for equivalence: methodological considerations 97
5.4.3 Translation of system-bound elements at the ECtHR 99
5.5 When national meets supernational: the role of case communications 99
5.5.1 Study design 99
5.5.2 Reliance on case communications 102
5.5.3 SBEs: terminological variation 104
5.6 Case communications and culture-bound elements 107
5.6.1 Freedom of expression 107
5.6.2 Conventions on the translation of unconventional? 108
5.7 Conclusions 115

6 Written observations: the duelling construction of reality 116

6.1 Introduction 116
6.2 The Written Observations Corpus 117
6.3 Written pleadings: genre considerations 118
6.3.1 Communicative situation 119
6.3.2 Linguistic regime: the curious case of written pleadings 121
6.3.3 Conventionalized form 127
6.4 Written pleadings, legal rhetoric and reasoning 133
6.4.1 Legal argumentation toolbox 133
6.4.2 Written pleadings: an argumentative battlefield? 134

6.5 Dialogism in written pleadings 135
6.5.1 Dialogism, polyphony and heteroglossia 135
6.5.2 Dialogical reasoning in written pleadings 137
6.6 Intertextual voicing and reported argumentation 139
6.7 Negation for the duelling construction of reality 145
6.8 Discussion and conclusions 152

PART III
The language of judges at the ECtHR 155

7 Judgment: combining genre, patterning and legal reasoning perspectives 157

7.1 Introduction 157
7.2 The ECtHR judgment: behind the scenes 158
7.2.1 The judgment genesis 158
7.2.2 Deliberation and drafting 159
7.2.3 When no agreement can be reached 161
7.3 The Grand Chamber judgment: genre considerations 162
7.3.1 The RiFT corpus 162
7.3.2 Participation framework 164
7.3.3 Style 165
7.3.4 Length 168
7.3.5 Linguistic regime 170
7.4 The structure 172
7.4.1 The opening section 173
7.4.2 Stating the history and background of the case 174
7.4.3 Justification 176
7.4.4 The operative part 178
7.4.5 The closing section 179
7.5 When argumentation meets evaluation: it is ADJ to-inf/ that *patterns 181*
7.5.1 General overview 181
7.5.2 "It is" *patterns for argumentation: meaning groups 185*
7.6 Conclusions 193

8 Separate opinions: legal, linguistic and pragmatic insights 195

8.1 Introduction 195
8.2 Separate opinions: legal implications 196

8.2.1 Separate judicial opinions across institutions 196
8.2.2 Separate opinions in the literature 197
8.3 Separate opinions: genre considerations 199
8.3.1 Separate Opinions Corpus 200
8.3.2 A genre or not a genre? 201
8.3.3 Types of separate opinions 203
8.3.4 Participation framework 206
8.3.5 Length and organization 208
8.3.6 Style 210
8.3.7 Linguistic regime 212
8.4 Separate opinions: the rationale 213
8.5 "Separatist" discourse: pragmatic considerations 217
8.5.1 A no-compromise land: between dissent and disrespect? 217
8.5.2 Separate opinions: politeness theory 218
8.6 The (im)politeness continuum in SOC 220
8.6.1 Non-politeness markers across different opinion types 220
8.6.2 Politeness markers across different opinion types 223
8.6.3 Impoliteness markers across different opinion types 227
8.7 Conclusions 230

PART IV
The life of cases beyond and after the ECtHR 233

9 **Beyond case-law: disseminating convention-related knowledge** 235

9.1 Introduction 235
9.2 Knowledge asymmetry, specialized communication and popularization 237
9.2.1 Popularization of law 239
9.2.2 Popularization mechanisms 240
9.2.3 Popularization strategies 242
9.3 Knowledge dissemination at the ECtHR 245
9.3.1 Translation and knowledge dissemination at the ECtHR 245
9.3.2 Knowledge dissemination and popularization at the ECtHR: the Press Service 249
9.4 Press releases 251
9.4.1 Institutional press releases at the ECtHR 251

9.4.2 *Newsworthiness* 252
9.4.3 *Press releases: literature review* 255
9.4.4 *Types of press releases at the ECtHR* 256
9.4.5 *GCPR: generic structure* 258
9.5 Conclusions 264

References 266
Index 283

Tables

1.1 Human rights courts: institutional context and professional culture 16
1.2 Linguistic regimes across the human rights courts 19
5.1 Translation couplets of system-bound elements in the ECtHR judgments against Italy 100
5.2 Corpus composition 101
5.3 Case communications 102
5.4 Example of a system-bound element across different genres in *Pīlāgs v. Latvia* 104
5.5 System-bound elements and terminological variation in *Pīlāgs v. Latvia* 105
5.6 Cases dealing with vulgarity 111
5.7 Translation strategies for vulgar culture-bound elements in judgments 111
6.1 The Written Observations Corpus 118
6.2 Rule 38 in the 2024 version of the Rules of Court in English and in French 119
6.3 Introductory section of written pleadings 128
6.4 Beginning samples from the sanitized written pleadings in the English Reference Corpus, the Russian Translation Corpus and the Italian Translation Corpus 129
6.5 The body structure of written pleadings from the English Reference Corpus, the Italian Translation Corpus and the Russian Translation Corpus 131
6.6 Reporting verbs and nouns in the Written Observations Corpus 140
6.7 Prepositions with the function of reference in the Written Observations Corpus 144
6.8 Negation markers in the Written Observations Corpus 148
6.9 Repudiation patterns in the Written Observations Corpus 149
7.1 Composition of the RiFT 96–24 corpus 163
7.2 Structural elements in national and international judgments from Mazzi (2007b: 26–27) 173

7.3 The judgment structure in the RiFT 96–24 Corpus 174
7.4 The opening section in RiFT 175
7.5 Generic makeup of the historical section of the judgment 177
7.6 The Law section from Peruzzo (2019b: 62) 179
7.7 The operative part of the judgment (Peruzzo 2019b: 62) 180
7.8 The Closing section 180
7.9 Top 20 collocates of the introductory *it is* pattern in RiFT 182
7.10 *It is* patterns in RiFT with discoursal function of modality 186
7.11 *It is* patterns in RiFT with discoursal functions of importance, validity and difficulty 189
7.12 *It is* patterns in RiFT with discoursal function of appropriacy and value 193
8.1 Separate Opinions Corpus (SOC) 201
8.2 Separate Opinions Corpus by year and the number of opinions 201
8.3 Separate opinions in the Separate Opinions Corpus and in Rivière (2005) 205
8.4 Authorship of different opinions in the Separate Opinions Corpus 207
8.5 Length of separate opinion in the Separate Opinions Corpus 210
8.6 Typical reasons underlying the creation of separate opinions 215
8.7 Typified non-polite linguistic realizations of the first move across different opinions 221
8.8 Occurrences of non-polite marker *should have* across different corpora expressed as absolute frequencies (AF), normalized frequencies (NF; normalization base 100,000 word) and simple range. 223
8.9 Frequencies of *regret* and *regrettably* across the subcorpora, normalized to 100,000 words. 226
8.10 The use of "in my/our" followed by personal standpoint expressions (view, opinion, etc.) as a hedge across the subcorpora. 227
9.1 Press release categories 256
9.2 The Grand Chamber Press Release corpus composition 257
9.3 Generic structure of a press release in the Grand Chamber Press Release 259
9.4 Comparison of the facts description in the Grand Chamber Press Release and in the Grand Chamber Judgment in the case *Baka v. Hungary* 262

Figures

1.1 Levels of discourse realization 13
1.2 Genres in the regional human rights courts 23
2.1 Terminological-phraseological continuum in supranational human rights courts 31
3.1 The journey of cases in the "old Court" system 47
3.2 Procedural flow after Protocol no. 11 50
3.3 Procedural flow under Protocol no. 14 54
3.4 The system of genres at the ECtHR 62
5.1 Generic structure in case communications 92
5.2 Translation strategies for system-bound terms 100
6.1 Procedural order in written pleadings 121
7.1 Participation framework in the Grand Chamber judgments 166
7.2 Average length of judgments in RiFT over time 169
8.1 Main categories of separate opinions at the ECtHR 204

Preface

The universe of human rights is constructed through language, and this book is an exploration of the discursive and professional practices underlying it. The discourse of human rights is analysed in its natural habitat: the context of supranational human rights courts. Despite the paramount importance of human rights justice, descriptions of its language and translation policies are scant and skewed towards the genre of judgment. The latter is nothing but the final outcome of a stratification of practices distributed along the entire history of the case, which frequently remain hidden from the public eye. What precedes the judgment? How do national cases reach a supranational court? How are they processed from a legal, linguistic and translational point of view? Who is involved in deciding and processing human rights cases, in public and behind the scenes? When do different stakeholders contribute to the formation of human rights discourse? How are different professional practices realized through discourse, and how standardized or idiosyncratic is this discourse? Where does the terminology of human rights come from? What happens when domestic, system-bound concepts underly the complaints?

The *wh*-questions fuelling this book are many, and most are addressed from procedural and linguistic standpoints. Yet, the book is not intended for linguists only. My ambition was to show how the discourse of human rights works across genres, languages and institutions. I strived to resonate with a diverse readership in my exposition of theoretical intricacies, hopefully with brio and human touch. Each chapter can be read on its own as it features multiple focal points that may appeal to diverse readers. Legal professionals may find the contextualizing parts providing descriptions of history, case-law and procedural steps of interest. Language professionals will benefit from the descriptions of genres, their linguistic peculiarities and translation. Different professionals will get an insight into each other's areas of expertise, which may result in a more legally or linguistically informed practice in their respective futures.

The common thread behind the book organization is to follow the lifecycle of cases, analysing genres, professional practices and (inter)discursive mechanisms. The book is organized in four parts. **Part I, The discourse of human**

rights across institutions, outlines the operation of international organizations, zooming in on three supranational human rights courts which form professional communities with distinct professional practices (Bhatia 2015, 2017), reflected in their discursive production. To the best of my knowledge, no prior analyses compare the discursive production across different human rights institutions, and Chapter 1 aims to fill this gap. Chapter 1 endeavours to "demystify, understand, explain, and account for the kinds of professional practices in which specialist users of language are engaged in their everyday professional life" (Bhatia 2015: 14) across three supranational human rights courts: the European Court of Human Rights (ECtHR), the Inter-American Court of Human Rights (IACtHR) and the African Court on Human and Peoples' Rights (ACtHPR), as these are the main international actors contributing to the modern discourse of human rights. The intricacy of the connections between language, institutions and human rights poses considerable analytical challenges, with multiple approaches and perspectives being required to unravel them. To do so, Chapter 1 integrates outlooks from legal linguistics, comparative law, Legal Translation Studies and Critical Genre Analysis. The theoretical discussion ranges from observations on the complexities of defining human rights to acknowledging the opposing perspectives on their universality or cultural specificity as realized through discourse. As international organizations are intrinsically multilingual, I offer considerations of various politics of institutional bi- and multilingualism, describing the linguistic regimes and discourse communities of the three courts. The chapter also offers reflections on the growing importance of English as a lingua franca of human rights, as it is the official language that all the above institutions share.

As different institutions shape the landscape of human rights discourse, it is reflected in their linguistic choices, which are similar but not identical. Chapter 2 continues the cross-institutional exploration of the discourse(s) of human rights, adopting a more linguistically informed outlook of legal terminology and phraseology, and maps the terminological-phraseological continuum across various institutions. This chapter establishes a theoretical-methodological framework for understanding legal terminology and legal phraseology, emphasizing their significance in legal linguistics. The chapter problematizes the diversity of sources contributing to the creation of human rights discourse(s), on a cline of national and supranational dimensions, and proposes a taxonomy of human rights terms and phrases. Whilst decidedly linguistic in its ideational underpinnings, Chapter 2 targets also comparative lawyers as the study of terminology and phraseology of human rights may offer a deeper understanding of its legal mechanisms, too.

After a cross-institutional outlook of the first two chapters, Chapter 3 zooms in on the ECtHR, its context, communicative and linguistic practices. Descriptions of ECtHR language and translation policies are scant (Nikitina 2018a, 2018b; Brannan 2013, 2018, 2021; Peruzzo 2019a, 2019b), hence the chapter offers a systematic overview of an underresearched area. The European human rights discourse derives from and is anchored to the discourse community of the ECtHR, which is depicted through various historical development stages. Central to this exploration is the integration of different discursive and professional practices within the Court. Procedures create social practices. Any exercise of rights is both enabled and constrained by institutional rules which are realized through linguistic and discursive practices and genres. I sketch the system of genres at the ECtHR providing useful distinctions between different genre types and honing in on the natural procedural flow of cases and the participation framework, i.e. all stakeholders involved in the proceedings and creating the discourse of human rights, starting from an initial application to the final judgment. This examination starts from the core genre, the Convention, as a "living instrument", refracting and guiding the evolution of the system. Delving into the general language policy of the Court, I illustrate how, during the case progression, knowledge migrates from the multilingual settings of the 46 Member States of the Council of Europe with potentially 37–40 national and minority languages to the bilingual supranational context. Therefore, the chapter offers also initial considerations on institutional legal translation that are further returned to throughout the book.

Part II, The European Court of Human Rights: inception of cases and the voices of human rights, offers critical genre reflections on the main genres launching the procedure at the ECtHR: application, case communication and written pleadings. In the context of supranational courts, procedures shape their linguistic realizations and, vice versa, language influences the procedures, hence to study the discourse of supranational human rights justice one has to start with the analysis of different procedural steps of a given system. With a view to ensuring democratic participation and streamlining access to supranational justice in multilingual and multicultural European societies, the ECtHR has dedicated significant attention to the initial procedural stages. Chapter 4 focuses on the submission of initial applications. It explores the right of individual petition, tracing its historical development and current realization through the completion of application forms that adhere to the admissibility criteria set forth by the Court. Combining legal linguistics with Critical Genre Analysis, the chapter discusses the linguistic implications of these forms, available in multiple national languages and drafted using the so-called *plain language*, which follows the tenets of informational justice. The study shows how the use of national languages and plain language forms facilitates the right of individual petition – the cornerstone of the ECtHR system – highlighting the interrelatedness of linguistic and procedural aspects.

Chapter 5 investigates the transition from application to case communication, emphasizing the role of covert legal institutional translation in this process. Case communication is identified as a pivotal moment in the transformation of knowledge from national to supranational legal systems, marking the Court's acceptance of the case and guiding subsequent procedures. The chapter highlights the challenges inherent in this process, such as navigating system-bound elements (SBEs) and employing translation strategies that prioritize equivalence. A case study is presented that analyses the movement of SBEs across various procedural genres within the ECtHR. Findings demonstrate how translation choices made at the case communication stage are incorporated into judgments, once again problematizing the interplay between national and supranational dimensions of human rights discourse and the value of language. Additionally, the study sheds light on the translation of culture-bound elements (CBEs), including offensive and vulgar language, getting some methodological insights from forensic linguistics and legal interpreting. Vulgar CBEs are analysed in cases invoking Article 10 – freedom of expression.

Chapter 6 describes another largely underresearched genre: written observations, also known as written pleadings (Nikitina 2018a, 2018b). Written pleadings represent the only opportunity for the parties to engage in a dialogue with the Court duelling for the reconstruction of facts and arguments. Yet, despite being a core genre for the procedure before the ECtHR, it is an "occluded genre" (Swales 1996), since it is not available to general public. This "dark adjudicative matter" (Molbæk-Steensig 2023: 94) is explored through a methodological telemetry of Critical Genre Analysis, dialogism, legal argumentation and Corpus-Assisted Discourse Analysis. The analysis outlines typical structural patterns and moves of the genre, highlighting the challenges faced by non-native speakers of English or French in drafting pleadings in these languages. Consistent with previous research in Translation Studies, the findings suggest a blend of conventional language with some linguistic creativity. When permitted, pleadings may also be submitted in a national language with an accompanying translation. The chapter identifies issues with machine translation practices among Russian parties, noting significant quality challenges. This reveals a general lack of prioritization of translation quality, with translations viewed primarily as informational. Additionally, the chapter explores the dialogical and argumentative nature of written pleadings, underscoring their role in shaping parties' standpoints. Pleadings incorporate intertextual elements and multiple voices from previous proceedings and legislation. Through dialogical techniques such as complex prepositions of reference and the use of reported speech for argumentation, parties engage in a discursive battle to refute opposing arguments and support their positions. This includes leveraging authoritative legal sources and combining reported speech with negation to build persuasive arguments and guide the reader towards a favourable conclusion. The chapter thus provides an indirect guide on the drafting strategies employed in written observations that may be of interest to both lawyers and linguists.

Part III proceeds further along the lifecycle of cases and focuses on **The language of judges at the ECtHR**, as realized through the genres of judgment and separate opinions. Chapter 7 provides an overview of the most widely known genre in the ECtHR system: the judgment. Quintessentially representing a culmination of judicial reasoning and discourse, this is the genre most often associated with it and most often researched. The genre of judgment sets the standard for the discourse of human rights, yet it has to be duly conceptualized within a larger set of professional and discursive practices. Chapter 7 aims at explaining the inherent discursive stratification of the ECtHR judgments, aspiring to provide a behind-the-scenes look into its genesis through the description of drafting and deliberation practices. Using an ad hoc corpus of over 3 million words, the chapter describes judgments issued by the Grand Chamber of the ECtHR on the topic of a right to a fair trial covering 28 years. The analysis provides insights into the discourse community and participation framework, which directly influence the generic makeup of judgments, their length, style and linguistic regime. The findings problematize how legal and linguistic compromises inherent in any international court's operation lead to the conventionalization of discourse. The discourse of human rights may then further influence the way national discourses of human rights develop, taking as a starting point the crystallized norm of the supranational bodies. The linguistic focus of the chapter sheds light on the use of *routines*, i.e. longer stretches of text reproduced verbatim from judgment to judgment as a "linguistic precedent", which contribute to the conventionalization of the ECtHR discourse. Another example is constituted by patterns *it is ADJ that/to-inf*, which are analysed as a case study, combining insights of pattern grammar, legal argumentation and evaluation.

Chapter 8 deals with the genre of separate judicial opinions, forming a stark contrast with the stylized judgment. Written by individual judges to express their unique legal perspectives within a multi-judge panel, separate opinions show that judicial discourse is by no means a monolithic construct. Yet, the discourse of separate opinions has received scant scholarly attention from a legal linguistics standpoint, with few notable exceptions. Within the ECtHR context, separate opinions have been a prominent discursive practice since its earliest days. The chapter employs a multidisciplinary approach, encompassing Critical Genre Analysis, Corpus Linguistics, Discourse Analysis and Pragmatics, to scrutinize the linguistic attributes, rhetorical strategies and discourse structures that underpin the construction of separate judicial opinions. First, separate opinions are conceptualized as a genre, distinct from the judgment by virtue of its communicative goal, positioning, style, organization, length and linguistic regime. Second, the chapter offers a classification of various types of separate opinions, differentiating between dissenting, concurring and hybrid forms, by analysing a corpus of separate opinions generated between 2013 and 2023 in conjunction with earlier data. The analysis encompasses an overview of the principal motivations driving the creation of separate opinions, accompanied by an exploration of the linguistic patterns employed to manifest these moves in discourse. Finally, the chapter adopts a pragmatic outlook drawing on the theoretical-methodological framework of politeness and evaluation to reflect on the dichotomy of respectful versus disrespectful dissent, raised in legal literature but rarely analysed from a legal-linguistic standpoint. The chapter illustrates patterns of politeness, neutral non-politeness – expressing criticism sanctioned by the generic conventions and norms of separate opinions – and impoliteness, hinging on the use of sarcasm, negative evaluation and mixed message devices. The findings illustrate thus the negotiated nature of human rights discourse. The applied goal of this chapter is to inform legal writers of different nuances of politeness in genres of judicial dissent.

Finally, **Part IV, The life of cases beyond and after the ECtHR**, extends the analytical lens beyond the main procedural context of the ECtHR, looking at the professional-discursive practices of different stakeholders that run in parallel with the main proceedings. Chapter 9 explores the mechanisms of knowledge dissemination. The effectiveness of supranational courts often hinges on their ability to communicate decisions and maintain public trust. This study delves into the strategic use of language, translation and genre as a means of achieving these objectives. The chapter starts by outlining the general (r)evolution of law following its digitalization conceptualized as a vehicle for enhancing accessibility. The latter is problematized in terms of (1) interlingual translation, i.e. knowledge transfer across non-official languages of the ECtHR, which arguably has visible political and legal implications; and (2) intralingual translation, i.e. knowledge transfer within the same language but across a variety of stakeholders with different levels of expertise in the field of human rights, known as *popularization*. After describing the overall knowledge dissemination dynamics at the ECtHR through a historical outline of different case-law translation initiatives as well as the creation of the Press Service, the chapter proceeds with the analysis of a quintessential derived genre for knowledge dissemination and popularization purposes: institutional press release. The chapter describes the press release genesis, outlining a theory of newsworthiness for the case selection, which may be of interest to linguists, journalists and communication scholars. It also describes the genre structure and linguistic peculiarities, raising questions about the possible automation of parts of this process. After all, if human rights discourse is a product of negotiations, aspiring at finding a common denominator, automation of certain practices may enhance its standardization, and only time may show whether this is a positive or a negative trend for an international court.

Writing a book on the discourse of human rights would have been a different experience without the humans surrounding me. I thank my academic mentors, Giuliana Elena Garzone and Paola Catenaccio. You lead and inspire by example, showing how it is possible to reconcile personal and professional if you love what you do. I thank you for your wisdom and guidance on this path, as well as for providing precious comments on the first drafts of this book. I would like to thank my family, too – both those who can and cannot read yet – for their love, patience and understanding, and for the lifetime adventure that we share.

Part I

The discourse of human rights across institutions

1 The discourse of human rights across languages, perspectives and institutions

1.1 The discourse of human rights

1.1.1 Language and law: legal linguistics

Lawyers and linguists alike converge on the importance of language *for* law and language *of the* law. Dworkin (1986: 42), for example, acknowledges that "Law is an interpretive discipline, and interpretation is inescapably a linguistic enterprise". Similarly, legal theorist Hart (1961: 117) notes how "[t]he interpretation of legal rules must always depend on some pre-legal understanding of the language in which they are framed", laying the foundation for the exploration of the profound correlation between the nuanced expressions of law and the language that breathes life into its precepts. Even if legal studies wondering about the nexus between law and language do exist, this link has been explored in more detail and more systematically by different branches of linguistics rather than by law itself. Ioriatti (2021: 306), reflecting on the role of language and legal translation in comparative law, noted how these were "initially perceived by comparatists as an instrument of comparative law studies, and not as an object of research. This underestimation originated from the idea of legal concepts being transferable in all languages with the same meaning".

Four branches of linguistics analyse the intersection of law and language: Languages for Special Purposes (LSP), Legal linguistics, Forensic linguistics and Legal Translation Studies (Biel 2024: 94). In LSP studies, legal language is typically represented as a sublanguage, foregrounding its professional field of application: law. General designations, such as legal language or the language of the law, contribute to creating a direct link that foregrounds "the subject matter, the domain in which language is used, i.e. law, at the expense of the linguistic element" (Goźdź-Roszkowski 2011: 11). In contrast to early conceptualizations of LSPs,[1] more modern LSP studies avoid equalling legal

1 Debates on the nature of languages for specific purposes (LSP) have evolved over time. Initially, the discourse in the 1970s–1980s primarily focused on a lexicalized understanding of LSPs, emphasizing specialized terminology. A more recent reanalysis of LSPs has expanded beyond specialized terminology to include various aspects. Chapter 2 will delve into some aspects of terminology in combination with the Critical Genre Analysis perspective.

DOI: 10.4324/9781003434788-2

language with a mere formal written variety filled with a specialist or technical vocabulary. While terminology is crucial in legal texts, it does not capture the full spectrum of their characteristics (Stein 2015: 51).

Legal linguistics, also known as jurilinguistics,[2] has gradually separated into a standalone branch of linguistic research, tracing a demarcation line between law and other professional fields. A modern legal linguist and a prominent advocate of the linguistic turn in law, Galdia (2017: 33) posits that law is "a discursive social practice" wherein language contributes to the creation of law, legal argumentation, interpretation and translation (Galdia 2017: 178–179). Legal linguists apply linguistic methodologies to study the practice and theory of law and to uncover "linguistically relevant parts of legal mechanisms" (Galdia 2017: 35).

Law is not exactly a uniform field, and neither, therefore, is the language of the law. Even a quick and perfunctory overview of multiple book-long studies analysing the language of the law will unravel the variety of labels associated with its different subtypes. Scholars have classified this language by the legal professionals who use it: *the language of judges* (Solan 1993), *judicial discourse* (Maley 1994) or *lawtalk* (Clapp et al. 2011). Other subtypes include taxonomies based on the type of the context (e.g. *the language of the courtroom*, Maley 1994). The diversity within legal language has further been viewed through a genre-based lens, suggesting that legal language comprises a spectrum of interrelated genres (e.g. Bhatia's 1983 legislative or statutory writing, academic legal writing and juridical writing, with the latter including judgments, law reports and case-law), each exhibiting distinct, albeit often similar, lexicogrammar and organization. It is therefore apparent that the language of the law is marked by substantial internal variation due to various subject-matter specializations, which makes it more appropriate to talk about legal languag*es* rather than legal language, or a "a set of related legal discourses", where every set "has a characteristic flavour but each differs according to the situation in which it is used" (Maley 1994: 13). So, "what is routinely referred to simply as 'legal language', represents an extremely complex discourse embedded in the highly varied institutional space of a particular legal system and its respective legal culture" (Goźdź-Roszkowski 2011: 11).

1.1.2 Human rights discourse: legal and linguistic perspectives

The discourse of human rights can be confidently placed within a more general category of legal language. At first glimpse, it has a clear subject-matter specification: human rights. Still, the concept of human rights is elusive; it "defies an exhaustive definition as such" (Salojärvi 2020: 4). Lack of such a definition opens a problem of the legal basis of human rights from the standpoint of international legal order (Pisillo Mazzeschi 2021: 4). Human rights are conventionally viewed through three lenses. The first, *naturalistic*,

2 Especially in Francophone environments.

outlook links them to human nature. The downside of this outlook is a subjective understanding of what makes us human, which introduces subjectivity in defining it universally. For instance, recent biomedical advancements in gene editing, cloning, organ transplants, etc. have further complicated this issue, as they are blurring the core concept of "human".[3] The second lens argues for the *self-evidence* of human rights, but this view is prone to varied interpretations based on cultural differences. The third lens suggests that human rights derive from consensus within a legal system or international community. However, the challenge persists in identifying truly universal human rights established in general international law (Pisillo Mazzeschi 2021: 3–4).

Initially on the fringes of international law in the early 1960s, human rights lacked legal binding and existed in an uncertain position as rules in international law. However, by the mid-1960s, a growing awareness of human rights emerged in international law and relations. The transformative year of 1964 witnessed the publication of the inaugural comprehensive historical analysis of the birth and significance of the Universal Declaration of Human Rights (UDHR), marking a pivotal moment. The global scholarly discourse on human rights had already begun, delving into their history and the profound meaning of the UDHR. By then, the multiword term *human rights* had acquired myriad connotations, rendering its precise meaning and substance beautifully ambiguous (Salojärvi 2020: 117).

Human rights researchers are divided into two opposing groups advocating for the universality of human rights law (and, by extension, human rights discourse) on the one hand, and its cultural specificity or relativism on the other hand (Pisillo Mazzeschi 2021: 14). Proponents of the universality standpoint posit that "human rights are conceptually universal because they derive, by definition, from our common humanity and are (and should be) independent of whatever else divides or distinguishes us from each other" (Agha 2017: 18). Relativists, by contrast, rely on a claim of cultural specificity for the realization and enjoyment of human rights: "Any value which may appear to apply to all or at least to more than one culture or value system must also necessarily be interpreted by each, and this is also likely to result in significant differences" (Agha 2017: 19).

This book concentrates on the *discourse* of human rights rather than on their content; hence I adopt a broad outlook on human rights as "a set of fundamental rights that belong to all human beings simply by virtue of their being human" (Salojärvi 2020: 4).

3 DNA interventions have always created societal and legal tensions, even when those were directed at animals, such as the famous case of Dolly, the first cloned sheep. As most technologies are transferable across different species, they evoked the Frankenstein-fuelled fears. Most recently, with the advent of gene editing, a Nobel Prize-winning biotechnology, it became possible to modify human genome, both in vitro and in vivo, raising a number of challenging legal and ethical questions; see Nikitina (2019a, 2021) for an overview.

In addition to being exposed to potential linguacultural and geopolitical variation, the discourse of human rights is not a chronologically static phenomenon, because human rights can be thought of as both an idea and a law (Salojärvi 2020: 4–5). While the idea of human rights can be both universal and culturally specific, its legal grounding is subject to greater specificity by reason of the existence of national and international legal sources enshrining human rights along with national and supranational judicial mechanisms of human rights protection. Human rights discourse oscillates between "purely legal or more utopian" (Salojärvi 2020: 7) understandings of human rights. Legal doctrinal analysis perceives them as legal rules, whereas legal philosophy applies a more theoretical lens; there is no lack of social and political implications, too.

As concerns the discourse dimension, the conceptualization of human rights as discourse is not foreign to legal scholarship, albeit – paradoxically – the methodologies adopted in legal studies most often exclude Discourse Analysis or other linguistic theories. Research on the human rights *discourse* uses the notion in a broad and not entirely linguistic sense, applying it to the needs of legal philosophy, comparative law or historical overviews. For instance, in his treatment of human rights discourse, Evans (2005: 37–40) discusses its political implications, as well as the substance of human rights law, placing an emphasis on human rights values through a legal philosophy paradigm. Similarly, Beitz (2009: 44) operates with the concept of a discursive practice but does not focus on the language: "an emergent discursive practice consisting of a set of norms for the regulation of the conduct of governments and a range of actions open to various agents for which a government's failure to abide by these norms supplies reasons". Similarly, Flikschuh (2011: 36), while equalling "the language of human rights" to "the lingua franca of normative global discourse", does not provide a linguistic analysis. The metaphor of a global moral lingua franca is further supported in the legal literature on the historical development of human rights discourse (Boot 2017: 3).

Salojärvi (2020: 7) recaps the use of "discourse" and "discursive practices" in legal scholarship on human rights in an explicit way:

> Human rights discourse in legal scholarship may also include elements of philosophical and political discourse. The premises of this discourse are incorporated in the international bill of rights, the substance of which is represented and manifested in discursive practices. Human rights discourse is partly theoretical, partly normative, and it reflects institutional realities. Scholarly discourse mediates the formal substance of law and ideational legal-political goals.

In this book, discourse is used in the linguistic understanding of the term, foregrounding the way the language is used to contribute to the construction and understanding of human rights discourse. To quote Garzone and Catenaccio (2022: 10), my approach is not to "decouple" language and discourse from "what goes on in the real world", but rather to analyse how the world of human rights is encoded in language creating what is referred to here as "the discourse of human rights".

1.2 The discourse of international organizations

1.2.1 Institutional multilingualism: linguistic diversity at work

The Tower of Babel, a biblical story found in Genesis 11:1–9, recounts a narrative where humanity, speaking a common language, attempts to build a tower to reach the heavens. In response, God confuses their language, leading to linguistic diversity and the inability to understand one another.

Linguistic diversity is a defining feature in the realm of international legal organizations. These organizations, often comprising member states with different native languages and legal traditions, face challenges akin to the multilingual confusion depicted in the Tower of Babel story. The diversity of languages within such organizations can pose hurdles in communication, legal drafting, and the interpretation of texts, which makes their discourse a fertile ground for exploration from the perspectives of comparative law and legal (institutional) translation.

While the Tower of Babel narrative emphasizes the potential pitfalls of linguistic diversity, international legal organizations strive to turn this diversity into a strength by fostering mechanisms of cross-cultural understanding and collaboration. As the very name suggests, international organizations exist *inter nations*, i.e. across and above[4] different nations with different national languages.

The national languages of Member States are not to be confused with the international organization's *official language(s)* and *working language(s)*. *Official languages*, typically more than one at the international level, are languages enjoying a special legal status. Publication of acts in these languages produces legal effects, which have to be the same across all official languages, striving to achieve the so-called "equally authentic texts" (see 1.2.2). *Working languages*, on the other hand, are the languages used in day-to-day professional exchanges for internal communication. So, while working languages are chosen based on the considerations of convenience, taking into account the linguistic profiles of lawyers and judges working in international courts, among the official languages, the situation with the latter is more complicated. The selection of official languages in international organizations is the product of political negotiations factoring in budgetary constraints: "even the most inclusive regimes apply pragmatic criteria to reconcile legal obligations with resource and feasibility limitations" (Prieto Ramos 2020: 461). For example, the United

4 There is a distinction between intergovernmental and supranational organizations that concerns the retention of sovereignty in decision-making (intergovernmental) or its devolution to an external body (supranational) in a certain sphere (e.g. judicial, commercial, politics).

Nations have six official languages (English, French, Spanish, Russian, Chinese and Arabic), but one of its bodies, the World Trade Organization, has only three official languages (English, French and Spanish), and "[d]emands by China and the Russian Federation to add their UN official languages to the WTO language regime at the time of their accessions, in 2001 and 2012, respectively, were refused on budgetary grounds" (Prieto Ramos 2020: 461).

Institutional bilingualism is a moderately widespread solution for international courts. Besides the European Court of Human Rights (ECtHR, see 1.4.2), English and French are the official languages of the International Court of Justice (ICJ) and the Permanent Court of Arbitration (PCA), which incidentally share the same building in The Hague. During the operational years of the International Criminal Tribunal for the former Yugoslavia (ICTY, The Hague), it relied on English and French as its official languages, too. Ideally, employees of these organizations have to speak both languages; however, often the staff is more proficient in either English or French, requiring the services of institutional interpreting and translation to guarantee institutional bilingualism. In most cases, these services are offered in the only language combination, i.e. English–French.

The International Criminal Court (ICC) has the same six official languages as its parent organization (UN): English, French, Spanish, Russian, Chinese and Arabic, yet its working languages are limited to the conventional bilingualism of English and French. A similar situation describes the linguistic regime of the Office of the United Nations High Commissioner for Human Rights, commonly known as the Office of the High Commissioner for Human Rights (OHCHR). Most frequently the linguistic regime of the parent institution will influence the languages chosen as the official ones in its different bodies (see 1.4.2 for the description thereof at human rights courts).

Likely the most multilingual court in the world currently is the Court of Justice of the European Union (CJEU) with its 24 official languages. At the inception of the European Union, a policy of multilingualism was adopted, and with the starting number of official languages being four in 1958, it resulted in six possible language combinations, making it a regime similar to the UN. With the wind of change sweeping through Europe, the institution gradually expanded and the number of official languages increased first to six, seven, then 11 in 1995, rising to 20 in 2004, and arriving at 24 in 2013. The beauty of math explored, it becomes clear that the current number of language combinations is set at 552. Is it possible to find language professionals for all these language combinations? Yes. However, it is not always the easiest, the fastest or the most economically reasonable solution. As a result, a pivot translation system (McAuliffe 2017) is used. A *pivot language* is a language used as a bridge between two "unmatched" languages. For example, if there is no translator or interpreter readily available for a combination of languages A and B, a third language can be introduced. This language C becomes the pivot language, around which the other two rotate, providing services from language A into language C and from language C into language B, thus bridging the linguistic gap through linguistic triangulation. The CJEU currently uses five official pivot languages: French, English, German, Spanish and Italian, thus reducing the number of necessary language combinations from 552 to 134. The pivot system is also used by other courts, especially courts having jurisdiction over a large number of multilingual states. For example, the ICC, whose caseload is marked by multiple African cases, frequently relies on African lingua francas as pivot languages.

The practice can extend to drafting: while institutional multilingualism can be "complete" (Koskinen 2014: 485), which involves co-drafting in all official languages, it can also be achieved using translation from a central language, i.e. the pivot system. The Tower of Babel story may be biblical, but modern international courts are living it every day, finding innovative solutions to ensure their multilingualism.

1.2.2 *Multilingualism and international courts: Comparative Legal Linguistics, Comparative Law and Legal Translation Studies*

Since international organizations and courts are multilingual, their discourse (and case-law) cannot be approached from an abstract monolingual perspective. Instead, a comparative approach is needed. This can be provided by Comparative Legal Linguistics, Comparative Law, Legal Translation Studies or any combination of the above.

Legal linguistics started originally as a monolingual discipline; however, the subbranch of Comparative Legal Linguistics quickly gained popularity. Mattila (2013: 16) defines Comparative Legal Linguistics in a relatively restricted way as the study of "the development, structure, and vocabulary of two or more legal languages". General comparative linguistics "compares genetically similar languages from a historical perspective" and is not to be confused with contrastive linguistics, which "usually involves a comparison of two languages to identify similarities and differences for applied purposes" (Biel 2024: 94). So, what comparative legal linguists add to the approach of comparative linguistics is the legal element.

Comparative Legal Linguistics has fuzzy borders with several disciplines, Comparative Law and Legal Translation Studies being the most emblematic. Engberg (2020: 264) draws a parallel between comparative law and legal translation, explaining how both approaches "work across the barriers of languages and legal systems, they intend to create bridges enabling users to see relations between different legal and linguistic settings and understand the unfamiliar, and they rely upon each other in their activities", with the difference that comparative lawyers often pursue more theoretical goals of law harmonization, whereas legal translation scholars are faced with more practically oriented goals (Biel 2024: 91–92). The degree of cross-fertilization between the two disciplines today is undeniable. Legal translation enables "the flow of information between legal systems, facilitating communication and the harmonisation of laws" (Biel 2024: 106). Additionally, "the very experience of translation triggers comparative analysis, due to the need to assess similarities and differences, and helps comparatists 'fine-tune' their findings as 'a kind of language-oriented double-check of the hypotheses'" (Biel 2024: 106, quoting Fuglinszky & Somssich 2020: 767).

The growing influence of international courts on national legal systems, coupled with the establishment of supranational, multilingual judicial systems, has brought about significant transformations in the realm of legal translation, both in terms of process and end product (Peruzzo 2023: 153). One of the most widely used definitions of legal translation recites that it is "an act of communication in the mechanism of the law" (Šarčević 1997: 55). Despite the specificity of legal discourse, Legal Translation Studies (LTS) has been recognized as a separate branch of translations studies relatively of recent. Today, LTS represents one of "the most prominent disciplines of translation studies" (Prieto Ramos 2014a: 261). It has been recognized by both comparative lawyers and translation scholars (Šarčević 2018: 9) and is constantly capitalizing on the developments in the adjacent disciplines of comparative law, linguistics, terminology and corpus linguistics.

Legal translation practiced in international organizations can be defined as institutional legal translation. There are multiple interconnected aspects between the institutional and the legal elements in this domain, with legal elements gravitating towards the content and the institutional towards the context. As Prieto Ramos explains (2020: 455),

> institutional translation is most often associated with translation work conducted by or through institutional language services of national or supranational organizations, regardless of the internal procedural specificities and the level of outsourcing involved in producing the translations for the relevant commissioning institution.

The institutional element provides for "a controlled and regulated environment" (Koskinen 2014: 481), at the same time calling for a certain amount of lingua-political manoeuvring, as "the goals of a translating institution are what determines the general approach taken in the translations it produces" (Mossop 1988: 65). As the multilingual discourse of international organizations is built around political and linguistic compromises, it makes it an example of "droit diplomatique" (Šarčević 2007: 44). Strategic ambiguity and vagueness flourish in the discourse of multilingual organizations, being introduced deliberately to reflect political compromises achieved. Legal institutional translators in this context are sent on a challenging quest to maintain the same level of ambiguity (McAuliffe 2015), which is nearly a mission impossible in a context where multiple languages are involved.

An emblematic example of institutional legal translation is the one carried out by the European Union (EU) institutions, which from a very early stage became a focal point of interest, heralding much of research in this area (see, e.g. Šarčević 2007, 2018; McAuliffe 2015, 2017, 2020; Biel 2014). In a broader sense, and analogously to the examination of legal translation within bi- and multilingual national contexts, the principal focus in this area of research has been on investigating how equivalence is established between texts composed in the official languages of these organizations (Peruzzo 2023: 153). This exploration delves into the mechanisms by which the *principle of equal authenticity* (Šarčević 1997: 64), also known as the *equal authenticity rule* (Cao 2007: 80) or the *principle of plurilinguistic equality* (van Els 2001), is achieved. As Cao (2007: 80) explains, the equal authenticity principle is "a legal fiction" necessary to maintain legal certainty despite the obvious linguistic diversity. It views words and phrases in legal texts as legally and linguistically equal. This approach is consonant with the so-called traditional approach to comparative law, where functional equivalents (similarities) are sought "across legal systems, working under the assumption that legal rules and institutions play the same social function in various systems" (Biel 2024: 92). The so-called postmodern comparative law (Siems 2022: 141–157) abandoned the context-neutralizing method in comparisons, relying instead on a contextual approach, within which comparisons are embedded in the economic, political, cultural and linguistic contexts thus providing a basis for cross-fertilization with other disciplines (Biel 2024: 93).

1.3 Methodological toolkit

While legal scholars focus on the conceptual part of human rights, at times overlooking the inherent discursive elements, linguists may disregard those features that go beyond the discourse level. And yet, human rights and discourse(s) do not exist in isolation from each other or other socio-professional phenomena. This chapter relies on a multi-perspective methodological toolkit drawing inspiration from (comparative) legal linguistics (1.2.2), with particular regard to legal terminology and phraseology (see 2.3) and Critical Genre Analysis (CGA, Bhatia 2015, 2017), to investigate how the discourse of human rights is realized, taking into consideration both text-external and text-internal factors.

1.3.1 The discourse of human rights and Critical Genre Analysis: methodological perspectives

In an early work, Bhatia wondered, "why and how members of specific professional or disciplinary communities communicate the way they do" (Bhatia 1993). This is the question underlying the present exploration of the human rights discourse.

Let's start with the notion of a *discourse community*, defined by Swales (1990)[5] as a group whose members pursue common goals through shared communication mechanisms, genres and particular lexis. The language used by such discourse community is frequently referred to as an "in-group code"

5 Even if Swales analysed academic settings, the concept of a discourse community is highly applicable to ESP context.

used to realize some common knowledge. Cutting (2000: 1) illustrates the concept using an anonymous tale:

> A certain group of prisoners got so bored with hearing each others' jokes again and again that they numbered them from one to a hundred and would amuse each other simply by the way they shouted out the numbers.

This joke aptly illustrates that in a given discourse community much is achieved through shared knowledge, which for the discourse community of human rights may be represented by knowledge of the human rights institution (see 1.4 for supranational human rights courts) and human rights law that comes with the choice of certain lexicogrammatical patterns. In specialized contexts, such as the context of human rights, the notion of a discourse community runs in parallel with what Engberg (2016: 37) defined as the *Knowledge Communication* approach:

> The study of Knowledge Communication aims at investigating the intentional and decision-based communication of specialized knowledge in professional settings (among experts as well as between experts and non-experts) with a focus upon the interplay between knowledge and expertise of individuals, on the one hand, and knowledge as a social phenomenon, on the other, as well as the coping with knowledge asymmetries, i.e., the communicative consequences of differences between individual knowledge in depth as well as breadth.

Discourse is famously conceptualized as "language in social practice". The interaction between linguistic choices, knowledge communication and the professional settings takes on particular prominence in the analysis of the human rights discourse.

Critical Genre Analysis explores the role of discursive practices in the achievement of professional actions, including professional practices and cultures. Bhatia (2017: 5) proposes to analyse discourse at four distinct, yet overlapping, levels, schematized in Figure 1.1.

Zooming in on language use and surface-level text-internal properties (phonological, lexicogrammatical, semantic, organizational and other aspects of text structure), the first layer of analysis in the CGA perspective focuses on *discourse as text*. This layer of analysis tends to exclude a deep consideration of context, emphasizing the construction of the textual product over its interpretation or use (Bhatia 2017: 5–6), perhaps drawing some parallels with *textualism* in legal studies. The banner of legal textualism incidentally includes a range of practices (see, e.g. Grove 2020 for an overview), which makes it challenging to come up with an all-encompassing definition. Simply, the main focus of textualists is – unsurprisingly – on the text in its ordinary meaning, i.e. not necessarily adapting it to context. Linguistic studies focusing on discourse

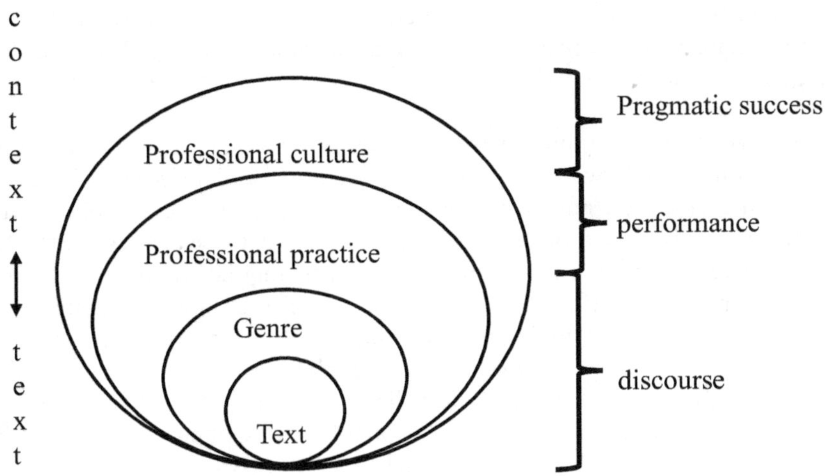

Figure 1.1 Levels of discourse realization
Source: Bhatia (2017: 5).

as text, too, tend to downplay the role of the writer or reader in contributing to the construction or interpretation of the text, along with their knowledge of the world and experiences.

The second layer of analysis, i.e. ***discourse as genre***, goes beyond the textual output to include a broader context, considering how text is constructed, interpreted, used and exploited in various social, institutional or professional settings to achieve specific goals. Genre theories (Swales 1990; Bhatia 1993, 2014) typically involve linguistic, socio-pragmatic, and ethnographic perspectives. A widespread definition of genre typically revolves around several features, summarized by Bhatia (2014: 27) as follows.

> Genre essentially refers to language use in a conventionalized communicative setting in order to give expression to a specific set of communicative goals of a disciplinary or social institution, which give rise to stable structural forms by imposing constrains on the use of lexico-grammatical as well as discoursal resources.

As emerges from this definition, genres do not exist in a vacuum but are embedded in context. When this context and the use of genres are explained, linguists as well as legal scholars (see 1.1.2) frequently operate with the notion of ***discursive practices***, situated at this analytical level. As Bhatia (2017: 6) explains, discursive practices are

> the outcome of specific professional procedures [. . .] embedded in specific professional cultures. Discursive practices include factors such as

> the choice of a particular genre to achieve a specific objective, and the appropriate and effective mode of communication associated with such a genre.

In other words, the way members of a given professional community use discourse is influenced by their *professional practices* and *professional cultures*. Professional practices, naturally, are not confined to discourse only, as they denote the performance of certain actions, too, but these two concepts "are closely related, in that one is significantly instrumental in the achievement of the other" (Bhatia 2017: 7). The operation of international organizations is intrinsically linked to their linguistic regimes and institutional translation practices, which will be included under this label here. Besides the linguistic regime, the professional practices tier defines the use of generic norms and conventions to reach particular professional and disciplinary objectives. For example, the way individuals or states make recourse to a certain human rights court would fall within this analytical layer.

The layer of *professional culture*, first of all, refers to the general discipline of human rights law. It is also inherently linked to institutional and professional identities (see Bhatia 2014), delimiting what can be referred to as the architecture of human rights. Where are human rights institutions situated? What is the legal source lying at the basis of their operation? Who works at such institutions? All these questions should be addressed to describe and define the use of human rights discourse in a professional context- and culture-sensitive way.

The multilayered outlook of CGA, thus, offers to extend the analytical lens "beyond the analyses of textual, intertextual and a number of other semiotic resources used in professional genres in order to understand and clarify professional practices or actions" (Bhatia 2017: 8). This "demystifying" approach is particularly relevant for the exploration of the human rights discourse, since the latter is created and promoted by a range of international organizations with diverging professional practices, cultures, stakeholders, discursive practices, genres and texts.

As an analytical concept, genre has been applied also by scholars operating through the Critical Discourse Analysis (CDA) paradigm, as evident in the works of scholars like Fairclough (2003) and van Leeuwen (2005), who emphasize the connection between genre and ideology. The majority of genre research within CDA has traditionally focused on a text-oriented methodology. This involves analysing various genre-related aspects of texts and other semiotic products, serving as a tool for the identification, critique and potential transformation of ideologies and power relations. (Critical) Genre Analysis, on the other hand,

> is valuable not because it might permit the creation of some kind of taxonomy, but because it emphasizes some social and historical aspects of rhetoric that other perspectives do not. I will be arguing that a

> rhetorically sound definition of genre must be centered not on the substance or the form of discourse but on the action it is used to accomplish.
> (Miller 1984: 151)[6]

Bhatia (2015, 2017) makes a distinction between two aspects of the term "critical" within the analysis of genre. On one hand, "critical" involves drawing on critical social theory in approaches like CDA, aiming to identify, analyse and transform ideological and unequal constructions and positions. On the other hand, "critical" refers to the idea to "demystify, understand, explain, and account for the kinds of professional practices in which specialist users of language are engaged in their everyday professional life" (Bhatia 2015: 14). In this book I integrate broader political, legal and societal considerations of human rights discourse with a thorough examination of discursive and professional practices in supranational human rights courts, as realized through genres.

1.4 Human rights discourse across supranational courts

Building on the theoretical-methodological framework presented in Sections 1.1–1.3, this section will zoom into three supranational regional human rights courts: the European Court of Human Rights, the Inter-American Court of Human Rights and the African Court on Human and Peoples' Rights, tracing the contours of context-sensitive human rights discourse.

1.4.1 Institutional context and professional culture

The European Court of Human Rights (ECtHR or European Court), the Inter-American Court of Human Rights (IACtHR or Inter-American Court) and the African Court on Human and Peoples' Rights (ACtHPR or African Court) are the three best-established regional human rights systems. They are brought together by a common goal of providing a supranational remedy to a human rights violation within their respective member states. The adoption of the European Convention on Human Rights in 1950 signalled the beginning of "the trend to elaborate regional standards" (OHCHR 2003: 72), which continued with the adoption of the American Convention on Human Rights in 1969 and the African Charter on Human and Peoples' Rights, adopted in 1981. The three regional human rights courts called to rule on potential violations of these legal instruments may hear both interstate and individual cases, with the bulk of applications lodged by individual petitioners.[7] Despite

6 Miller did not refer to her approach using the term "Critical Genre Analysis", but her approach is consonant with Bhatia's conceptualization of this method.

7 Hampson et al. (2018: 162) define interstate cases as rare and quote the following statistics, updated by 2018 (note 1): "A handful in the European system (see, e.g., recent cases, Ukraine v. Russia, App. No. 20958/14, and Ukraine v. Russia II, App. No. 43800/14); two cases before the Inter-American system, one rejected by the IACHR (Nicaragua v. Costa Rica, Inter-State Case No. 1/2006, Report No. 11/07 (Mar. 7, 2007)) and one declared admissible

these first-glance similarities, these institutions are surprisingly divergent or even "fundamentally different" (Lambert-Abdelgawad 2010: 11, my translation) in their context and professional culture in the CGA sense.

As Table 1.1 shows, the courts have different seats that reflect their regional nature: Strasbourg (France) for the ECtHR, San José (Costa Rica) for the IACtHR and Arusha (Tanzania) for the ACtHPR. They are the judiciary bodies of, respectively, the Council of Europe (CoE, 46 Member States), the Organization of American States (OAS, 35 Member States) and the African Union (AU, 55 Member States). Despite a comparable number of member states in their "parent" organizations, the three courts, like three sisters, have a different age, weight and story within the human rights family.

Table 1.1 Human rights courts: institutional context and professional culture

	ECtHR	*IACtHR*	*ACtHPR*
Region	*Europe*	*Americas*	*Africa*
Parent organization	Council of Europe (CoE)	Organization of American States (OAS)	African Union (AU), formerly Organisation of African Unity (OAU)
No. of member states[8]	46/46/46	20/35/35	8/54/55
Seat	Strasbourg (France)	San José (Costa Rica)	Arusha (Tanzania)
Treaty/Mandate/ jurisdiction	European Convention on Human Rights (ECHR)	American Convention of Human Rights (ACHR) + American Declaration of the Rights and Duties of Man (OAS member states)	African Charter on Human and Peoples' Rights (ACHPR) + "any other relevant Human Rights instrument ratified by the States concerned" (Art. 3 (I) Protocol ACHPR)
Single or dual mechanism	Single: the Court only since 1998 Dual: Court + Commission between 1959 and 1998	Dual: the Inter-American Commission on Human Rights (IACmHR) and Inter-American Court of Human Rights (IACtHR)	Single: the African Commission on Human and Peoples' Rights (ACHPR) between 1987 and 2006 Dual: the African Court on Human and Peoples' Rights (ACtHPR) since 2006

(*Continued*)

and currently under processing (Franklin Guillermo Aisalla Molina, Ecuador v. Colombia, Inter-State Petition IP-02, Admissibility (Oct. 21, 2010)); and only one in the African system (DRC v. Burundi, Rwanda and Uganda (2004) Afr. Hum. Rts. L. Rep. 19 (ACHPR 2003), decided by the ACHPR".

8 Accepted contentious jurisdiction/ratified the Treaty/total.

Table 1.1 (Continued)

	ECtHR	*IACtHR*	*ACtHPR*
Region	*Europe*	*Americas*	*Africa*
Establishment year (commission/ court)	1959/1959 Since 1998 – only the court	1960/1979	1987/2006
Statistics in 2023[9] (and 2022 for IACtHR)[10]	New applications: 34,650 Inadmissibility decisions: 31,329 Judgments: 1,014 (in respect of 6,931 applications)	New applications (Commission): 2,440 Inadmissibility decisions: 88 New cases sent to the Court: 24 Judgments: 34	New applications: 10 Orders issued: 12 Judgments: 38 (in respect of 38 applications)

The oldest sister, the ECtHR, established in 1959, enjoys a full acceptance and recognition of its contentious jurisdiction, i.e. its authority to hear and decide on disputes involving these states as respondents, by all 46 CoE Member States. The other two have a strikingly different story. The middle sister, IACtHR, although only a year younger (it started functioning in 1960) has been recognized for its contentious jurisdiction only by 20 out of 35 OAS Member States. Such powerful players as the United States and Canada have always kept their distance for political reasons. Contentious jurisdiction of the youngest, African, sister counts only 8 out of 55[11] AU Member State recognitions. In addition to its relatively young age (the African Court started its operation in 2006 only), some of the Member States who originally ceded part of their sovereignty to the ACtHPR opted out at a later stage.[12] As this reluc-

9 Based on the following sources, all accessed on 7 February 2024: ECtHR "Analysis of Statistics 2023", available at https://www.echr.coe.int/documents/d/echr/stats-analysis-2023-eng and ACtHPR statistics https://www.african-court.org/cpmt/statistic.

10 As there were no statistics available for 2023 for the IACtHR, I had to use 2022 data, available at https://www.oas.org/es/cidh/multimedia/estadisticas/estadisticas.html (accessed on 7 February 2024) for the Commission and the Annual Report 2022 for the Court: https://www.corteidh.or.cr/docs/informe2022/ingles.pdf.

11 While encompassing 55 AU Member States, the African continent demonstrates some very reluctant attitude to the Court: 54 out of 55 AU Member States, "with the exception of Morocco, have ratified or acceded to the African Charter and have, therefore, committed themselves to respecting the principles set out therein". Thirty-four out of these 54 ratified the Protocol establishing the Court, and only eight states accepted the Court's contentious jurisdiction (The African Court on Human and Peoples' Rights, "Basic Information", online: https://www.african-court.org/wpafc/basic-information/).

12 As the ACtHPR "About us" website section specifies, Rwanda withdrew its declaration in 2017; Tanzania in 2019; and Côte d'Ivoire and Benin in 2020 (https://www.african-court.org/wpafc/welcome-to-the-african-court/).

tance to fully adhere to the Court's rule shows, frequently the discourse of human rights is directly correlated to the political dimension, "in a historical context in which not only judicialization of international affairs is being generally slowed down but also there is a general 'backlash' against international law institutions" (Rachovitsa 2019: 283).

Different recognition of contentious jurisdiction and the sisters' age gap harbingers different caseload. The ECtHR received 34,650 new applications in 2023, compared to 24 and 10 new applications to the IACtHR and the ACtHPR, respectively. Regarding judgments, the ECtHR generated 1,014 judgments in 2023, and the IACtHR and the ACtHPR produced 34 and 38 judgments, respectively. Even if these figures speak, caution is advised in their interpretation on account of the different structure (single institution vs. dual institution) and historical development of these courts.

In its current version, the European system envisages a single court. Although it has been operating continuously since its establishment in 1959, both its original composition and structure have changed. Initially, a dual or two-tier system was implemented, consisting of two entities: the European Commission of Human Rights and the European Court of Human Rights, both of which were part-time institutions. The former was responsible for receiving, examining and determining the admissibility of applications. They also sought amicable settlements between parties and referred specific cases to the European Court of Human Rights. Acting as a kind of "barrier" or performing a "filtering function" (Peruzzo 2019a: 16), the Commission played a crucial role in discarding inadmissible applications. The "old" system changed in 1998 with the introduction of Protocol no. 11, which streamlined the workflow by abolishing the Commission and transferring its functions to a "new" court (see Chapter 3 for a more detailed description).

In the Inter-American and African systems, a dual system is (still) in place. Similarly to the original setting of the European system, there are two bodies – a commission and a court. The Inter-American Commission on Human Rights (IACmHR or the Inter-American Commission) was created in 1959 and began functioning in 1960 when the Council of the OAS approved its Statute and elected its first members. The Inter-American Court began its operation only 20 years later, in 1979. The Inter-American Commission receives around 2,500 petitions a year, which is a substantial increase compared to the 1990s data (ca. 500 petitions per year), and yet it is still disproportionately few for the Americas and incomparable to the "staggering" European numbers at the parity of their years of existence.

Democratization in some African states laid the groundwork for the creation of a regional human rights protection system in the 1960s. After the African Charter was adopted in 1981, 1987 saw the establishment of the first tier in the dual system: the African Commission on Human and Peoples' Rights (African Commission), which became fully functional in June 1989. Viljoen (2012: 161) notes the scarcity of information about the African Commission's early days of operation until 1994. This was the year when the path towards establishing the African Court began with the first timid discussions of the Protocol on the Establishment of an African Court on Human and Peoples' Rights, adopted in 1998. Finally, the first 11 Judges of the ACtHPR were elected in 2006, effectively completing the creation of a two-tier system, based on the initial "quasi-judicial" filtering mechanism of the African Commission and the judicial resolution of cases of the African Court (Viljoen 2012: 204). Given the strenuous path of its creation, marked at times by "the back-peddling oarsmen of the old guard" delaying the process (Viljoen 2012: 160), the Court has generated a total of 392 decisions (231 Judgments and 161 Orders)[13] by 2023, which amounts to "a drop in the ocean, considering the pool of potential cases" (Hampson et al. 2018: 163).

1.4.2 Linguistic regime

The linguistic regime of any international organization is typically defined in its fundamental treaty or the rules of procedure. For our three supranational human rights courts, the linguistic regime is defined in their Rules of Court, summarized in Table 1.2.

Table 1.2 Linguistic regimes across the human rights courts

	ECtHR[14]	*IACtHR*	*ACtHPR*[15]
Official languages	English and French	English, French, Portuguese and Spanish	Arabic, English, French, Portuguese, Spanish, Kiswahili and any other African language
Working language(s)	English and/or French	Spanish and/or English	English, French, Arabic and Portuguese
Number of national languages in Member States	36[16]	9[17]	1,000–2,000[18]
Number of judges	46	7	11

13 The Statistics section of the African Court's website is available at https://www.african-court.org/cpmt/statistic (last consulted on 8 February 2024).

14 Rule 34 (Rules of Court, 2024, ECtHR) sets forth that "[t]he official languages of the Court shall be English and French".

15 Art. 27 (Rules of Court, 2020, ACtHPR) sets forth "1. The official languages of the Court shall be Arabic, English, French, Portuguese, Spanish, Kiswahili and any other African language. 2. The working languages of the Court shall be Arabic, English, French and Portuguese".

16 Including French and English, see Chapters 3 and 5 for details. If minority languages are counted, the language count may reach ca. 40 languages.

17 This number includes all official languages spoken in the OAS Member States. In other words, I add to the official IACtHR languages also Dutch (spoken in Suriname), Haitian Creole (existing alongside French in Haiti), Quechua and Aymara (used in Peru, Ecuador and Bolivia) and Guaraní (Paraguay).

18 The African continent is marked by the highest degree of linguistic diversity in the world. In fact, African languages amount to approximately one-third of the world languages. Equally fascinating and bewildering, it makes any precise quantification endeavours challenging, to say the least. A range is a necessary concession, based on the African language map on the website of the African Language Program at Harvard University (https://alp.fas.harvard.edu/african-language-map, accessed 9 February 2024).

The figures in Table 1.2 highlight the linguistic diversity of human rights discourse. What emerges is that the European linguistic regime is the slenderest, with only two official languages, coinciding with its working languages and with the official languages of its parent institution (CoE), whereas the African one seems to be the most expansive and inclusive. The previous version of the African Rules of Court indicated that its official and working languages coincided with those of the AU (English, French, Arabic and Portuguese). The 2020 amendment in the rules added Spanish, Kiswahili and "any other African language" among the official languages of the African Court. Due to a long-standing fascination with multilingual meaning-making and communication, much of research in comparative law and legal translation has revolved around the Court of Justice of the European Union (see 1.2). However, since modern linguistics estimates the number of African languages anywhere on a range between 1,000 and 2,000 languages, the inclusion of "any other African language" among the official languages erects this supranational court to be potentially the most multilingual institution in the world.

This linguistic inclusivity testifies to the Court's intention to expand its operation covering a bigger pool of cases. A curious development concerns interpretation or translation: Rule 27 (3) sets forth that the Court will cover the costs when any person appearing before it requires such linguistic assistance. Given the vast linguistic diversity of the African continent, this provision may become a double-edged sword, allowing the court to realize its potential but requiring additional budgetary infusions in the system. So far, the limited number of cases warrants and sustains this inclusive linguistic turn, but is this system sustainable long-term?

Unfortunately, the linguistic regime at international institutions has to take into consideration the financial side of the coin. Talking about the European system, Weston (1988: 679) notes that its bilingualism has a "considerable economic advantage". In 1998, after the former USSR countries joined the ECtHR, the addition of a third institutional language was put up for discussion. The proposed new linguistic entry – Russian – would facilitate the spread of human rights values across these territories. The proposal never left the negotiation table as the negotiators realized that other states might make similar requests (Peruzzo 2019b: 31). Today, the echo of the ECtHR's inclination to a greater linguistic inclusivity is felt in its initiatives concerning the translation of case-law into non-official languages (see 9.3.1). Institutional bilingualism persisted. Moreover, the ECtHR had to switch from a complete to a so-called alternative bilingualism, meaning that its documents can be produced in English or French, and only in a limited number of cases (see 3.5) are both used.

The Inter-American system is blessed by the most linguistically balanced milieu. The region of the Americas is not marked by great linguistic diversity, counting only nine official national languages, four of which are chosen as the official IACtHR languages. However, in practice, the Court most frequently operates in Spanish, one of its working languages. There is hardly any surprise in that. The linguistic regime of a supranational court can be indirectly influenced by its discourse community, i.e. the lawyers and judges who work there, actively contributing to judicial decision-making. The IACtHR is composed of seven judges elected from the OAS countries. Currently, six out of seven judges are native speakers of Spanish, with the remaining judge being a native speaker of Portuguese fluent in Spanish. The contentious jurisdiction of the IACtHR has been recognized by 20 states, the majority of which use Spanish as the official national language. The political reluctance of major English-speaking countries of North America to ratify or adhere to the American Convention results in the linguistic backgrounding of English. And yet, English is the only language in common across the three courts. Should the three sisters decide to communicate, they will likely do it through English, making it the lingua franca of human rights. The idea of using a lingua franca applies not only to the inter-institutional perspectives but also to the intra-institutional communication. As Table 1.2 shows, there are 46 judges[19] at the ECtHR speaking 36 different national languages as their mother tongues. Next to the judiciary, a very ample and linguistically diverse Registry has to be mentioned. When they need to communicate or draft any legal document, sheer statistics will result in this document being prepared by a non-native drafter, thus using a lingua franca. It is again statistically more likely that this language will be English, as the majority of current CoE member states use it (and less frequently French) for communication.

The alternative to using English as a lingua franca could be to rely on the services of legal translators and interpreters. For the latter solution, it is interesting to note that the three sisters have divergent structures. While the ECtHR has an in-house translation and interpreting department carrying out linguistic services (translation and interpreting) between the two official languages (see 3.5), the same cannot be said about the IACtHR[20] or the ACtHPR,[21] which rely on external pre-qualified freelance translators and interpreters.

19 There are as many judges as there are States Parties to the Convention.

20 As one of the freelance interpreters of the Inter-American Court explains in an interview, most services are arranged through the external accredited interpreters, most frequently in the combination English-Spanish and Spanish-Portuguese. She also stresses budget-related challenges for these services (Valoti 2023: 37).

21 A closed tender notice on the African Court's website published in 2022 recites, "In order to update its database, the Court is calling for applications from qualified freelance translators-revisers in Arabic, English, French, Portuguese, Spanish and Swahili, who are nationals of African Union Member countries. [. . .] Freelance translators-revisers are invited to express interest in providing online and face-to-face services (e.g., during sessions and other meetings of the Court). They will be awarded contracts for the translation and revision of documents from the Court" (https://www.african-court.org/wpafc/self-revised-translators-request-for-expression-of-interest-reoi-establishment-of-a-database-of-prequalified-individual-consultants/). A slightly updated notice appeared in 2023, too (https://www.african-court.org/wpafc/request-for-expression-of-interest-reoi-database-of-prequalified-individual-consultants-self-revised-translators/), which means that the Court is still creating its database of language experts.

1.4.3 Discursive practices and genres at the regional human rights courts

Organizational discursive practices are interwoven with and realized through different genres. In a more general context, Bhatia (2006, 2014) outlined a hierarchy of legal genres, dividing them into four groups:

- *Primary genres* occupy the most central position, providing a "reading key" to the rest (legislation).
- *Secondary genres* are designed "to negotiate, document, and report judicial processes and decisions, which are based on appropriate interpretations of legislative intentions" (judgments, cases, courtroom genres; Bhatia 2006: 6).
- *Enabling genres* can be both pedagogic (textbooks, moots, examination papers) and professional (memoranda, essays, pleadings).
- *Target genres* are both the products and the instruments of legal practice (affidavits, client consultation files).

These different genres create a scaffold for discursive practices. Adapting this scaffold to the context of the human rights courts, I distinguish between *core* or *primary, operational, procedural* and *derived* genres, which are graphically represented as a pyramid of human rights genres in Figure 1.2, going from the inner chamber to the outmost one.

For the regional human rights courts, the organization's fundamental treaty is its *primary* or *core genre*. For the three courts in question these are the following treaties:

- European Convention on Human Rights (European Convention or ECHR): adopted in 1950 in Rome (Italy); came into force in 1953.
- American Convention on Human Rights[22] (American Convention or ACHR): adopted in 1969 in San José (Costa Rica); came into force in 1978.
- African Charter on Human and Peoples' Rights (African Charter or ACHPR): adopted in 1981 in Nairobi (Kenya); came into force in 1986.

The beating hearts of the Courts' existence, these treaties permeate the Courts in a capillary way. Similarly to legislation in a national context, they establish each Court's jurisdiction and provide the material framework for its working. They describe its context, enshrine the rights to be protected, etc. From a cross-institutional perspective, these treaties are typically rooted in a "universal" understanding of human rights. While they contain a similar set of human rights (e.g. right to life [Art. 2 ECHR, Art. 4 ACHR, Art. 4 ACHPR], freedom from slavery [Art. 4 ECHR, Art. 6 ACHR, Art. 5 ACHPR]), there are also some significant differences in the interpretation of these rights.

22 OAS Treaty Series, no. 36.

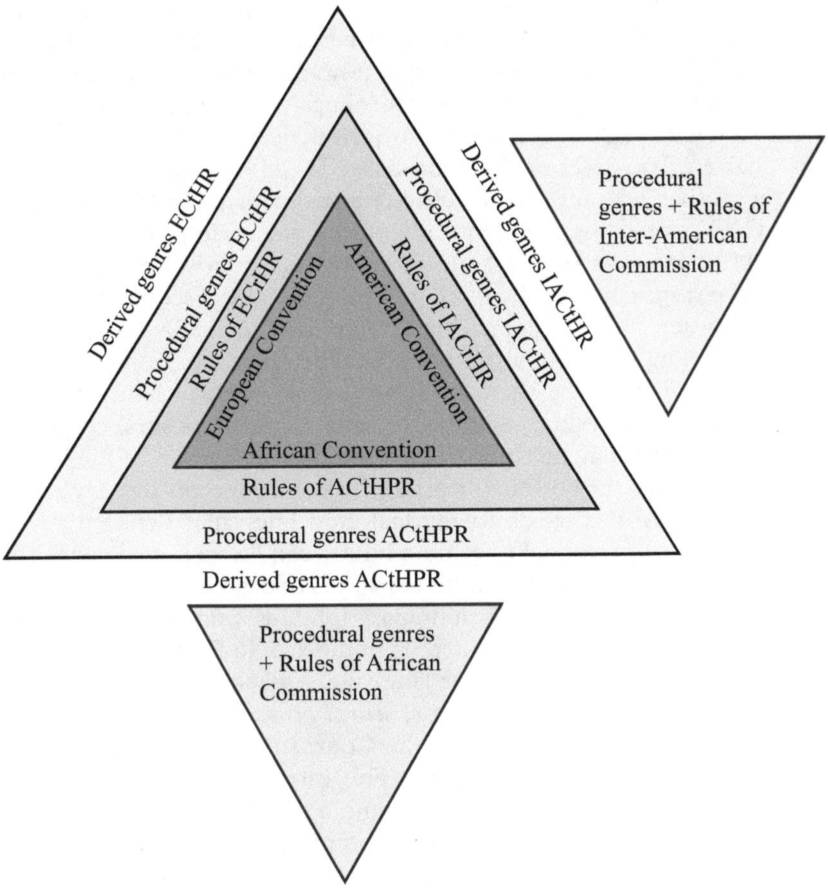

Figure 1.2 Genres in the regional human rights courts

The text of these treaties may look static or outdated, as all of them have existed for quite some time, whereas our societies have undoubtedly undergone some changes. Yet, to quote US Supreme Court Justice Oliver Wendell Holmes: "[a] word is not a crystal, transparent and unchanged, it is the skin of a living thought and may vary greatly in color and content according to the circumstances and the time in which it is used".[23] These conventions are adapted to their geographical and chronological settings through their interaction with operational and procedural genres, showing how "legal meaning is dynamic over time" (Engberg 2023: 27) and space. For instance, the European Convention has been famously labelled as "a living instrument"[24] that "would not be able to survive, had it not been [. . .] constantly developed in the case law

23 *Towne v. Eisner*, 245 U.S. 418, 425 (1918).
24 *Tyrer v. United Kingdom* (Application no. 5856/72), 25 April 1978, Series A No. 26, § 31.

of the Court" (Garlicki 2009: 390). Similarly, Paúl (2017: 54) notices how the IACtHR's case-law has "transformed the American Convention on Human Rights (ACHR) to such an extent,[*sic*] that nowadays it is impossible to grasp its scope without referring to the Court's rulings". The African system's primary genres – with regard to contentious jurisdiction – do not end with the African Charter. Art. 3 (I) of the Protocol to ACHPR extends its jurisdiction to "any other relevant Human Rights instrument ratified by the States concerned" (supported by the identical wording in Article 7 of the Protocol to the ACHPR [sources of law]). In other words, its jurisdictional reach is potentially the vastest among the three, reaching the global scope and making the ACtHPR a new "judicial animal" and "a curious case" (Rachovitsa 2019) not only from a linguistic, but also from a legal perspective.

Next to the primary genre, there are *operational genres*, which include Rules of Court, Rules of Procedure, Statutes or other similarly positioned genres. This scaffolding layer may be compared to the nervous system of the human rights body as it links the abstract or originally static concepts to daily reality. Rules of Court provide a set of operational guidelines: they define the work of the Court and its personnel (e.g. time limits, conditions), its composition and procedure, as well as detailing different stages of proceeding. This genre is further from a core understanding of human rights, as it takes into consideration the specific context of every court, its number of judicial formations, the structure (single-tier vs. dual-tier), the languages spoken, etc.

The third category of genres, i.e. *procedural genres*, comprises the genres that are necessary for the execution of the Court's proceedings. They derive their existence from the Rules of Court. This category includes genres that follow the procedural flow of documents, ranging from the initial application in a one-tier system or the case sent by the Commission in the two-tier system, communication between the parties, any written or oral pleadings, to decisions and judgments of various types, collectively referred to as case-law. As argued above, the interaction between the primary genres and the procedural genres is not unilateral; it is a two-way street, where case-law may leave a significant impact on the understanding of the primary legal source.

Finally, on the outside facets of the human rights justice pyramid, we find *derived genres*. These genres are external to the judiciary mechanisms of human rights protection. Instead, they run in parallel, frequently pursuing wider knowledge dissemination purposes aimed at specialists (e.g. factsheets, legal reports, case summaries) or a wider public (press releases); see Chapter 9.

Human rights discourse is very context-specific, as the diverse and interconnected genres within this discourse adapt and respond to distinct cultural, legal and social settings.

1.5 Conclusions

Law is language, and the fascinating world of human rights is built through discourse of supranational human rights courts. The above pages aimed at exploring, reconciling and interweaving the perspectives of legal scholarship and linguistics, where possible, paying tribute to the elusive and multifaceted nature of the human rights discourse. The multi-perspective analysis incorporated various lenses available to legal linguistics, starting from a general mapping of legal discourse to outline the specificity of its use in international organizations to legal translation as applied to human rights specifically.

Born against the backdrop of World War II, the discourse of human rights developed in similar yet distinct directions across the time and space of the three contexts under analysis. So, can we talk about the discourse of human rights? While a common conceptual core cannot be denied, it would be oversimplistic to claim the existence of *the* discourse of human rights with the melting-pot effect. Despite some instances of reciprocal osmosis among the human rights bodies, I would rather advance the idea of a coexistence of *a number of* human rights discourses, evolved through specific languages, discursive practices, professional cultures and legal genres across different human rights institutions. As concerns their specific realization at a textual level, it can be addressed through the paradigm of legal terminology and phraseology, detailed in Chapter 2.

2 Constructing human rights discourse

Insights from legal terminology and phraseology

2.1 Introduction

The combination of professional culture, professional practices and discursive conventions in supranational courts translates into specific terminological and phraseological choices in human rights texts at the immediate discourse level. To quote Prieto Ramos (2021: 175), "terminology and phraseology are key features of legal discourses, and central aspects of professional practice and research in legal translation", so any discussions of the discourse of human rights should include an insight into the terminological-phraseological continuum of a given discourse. Chapter 1 outlined how context- and institution-specific different professional and discursive practices are; the same holds true for their linguistic codification through the selection of terminology and phraseology that reflects the reality of a given supranational court at a textual level, as it is negotiated out of interactions within the discourse communities of these institutions.

Legal terminology forms the cornerstone of legal language, serving as the lexical foundation upon which legal discourse is constructed. Rooted in centuries of legal tradition and evolving alongside the development of legal systems, legal terminology is among the most distinctive and widely studied aspects of legal discourse (Cao 2007: 53). While legal terminology is undoubtedly expressive of a given legal order, it does not exist in a "vacuum" detached from the rest of textual and discursive practices. In legal discourse, it is important to stay "patterned" (Pontrandolfo 2023) as legal phraseological units cluster around legal terms, forming a continuum with fuzzy borders. This continuum is outlined in Section 2.2, first looking at legal terminology in 2.2.1 and then integrating it with considerations of legal phraseology in 2.2.2. The combined methodological framework of terminology and phraseology as applied to human rights is detailed in 2.3, followed by the taxonomy and findings concerning terms and phrases of human rights in 2.4.

DOI: 10.4324/9781003434788-3

2.2 Legal terminology and phraseology: a continuum

2.2.1 Legal terminology

A widely accepted definition of *terminology* recites that it is "the study of and field of activity concerned with the collection, description, processing and presentation of terms, i.e. lexical items belonging to specialised areas of usage of one or more languages" (Sager 1990: 2). Central to this branch of linguistic inquiry are the notions of *term* and *concept*. In a simplified way, the former is a linguistic designation of the latter. A concept is "a unit of thought that is used to organize people's knowledge and perception of the world around them. Concepts tend to be understood not in isolation but rather in relation to other concepts, in a sort of structured system" (Bowker 2019: 579).

At a first glance, the discourse of human rights might look conceptually homogeneous as it revolves around the understanding of what makes us human and what rights of humankind are to be protected and safeguarded. While there is a certain universal understanding of human rights, as mentioned earlier, concepts "as building blocks of expert legal knowledge are typically openly non-monolithic at any one time" (Engberg 2023: 26) and space (see also Cheng et al. 2014 for the temporal/spatial variation of terms). In other words, legal concepts, including the concepts of human rights, may demonstrate richness and nuance across different legal systems and times. The representation of legal concepts, i.e. legal terminology, is notoriously system-bound, "parochial" (Tiersma 2008: 16), i.e. embedded in a given legal system (Šarčević 1997: 240). It is shaped by the members of its discourse community, according to the linguistic, social and legal settings in place. Legal terminology thus is bound to a specific legal system by its "unique features (e.g., indeterminacy, explicitness, formality, precision, hierarchicality)" (Jopek-Bosiacka 2023: 38).

Legal terminology has elicited an unwavering scholarly curiosity (see Biel & Kockaert 2023 for a recent overview), spanning various disciplines, including linguistics, law, Legal Translation Studies and terminography. Particularly relevant for supranational justice is the research strand revolving around terminology standardization and management. Expectations that "terms, especially legal terms, should preferably not have synonymous, homonymous or polysemous terms" (Cheng et al. 2014: 172) are frequently unrealistic. Indeed, legal terms are subject to variation, across time, space and institutional contexts, and multilingual international organizations invest in ramified terminological departments whose primary function is to manage terminological databases and resolve various issues of terminological variation. Freixa (2006) lists six causes of terminological variation: preliminary causes, dialectal causes (geographical variation, chronological variation and social variation), functional causes, discursive causes, interlinguistic causes and cognitive causes. In the fields of international law and comparative law, the most relevant causes would be of a functional and interlinguistic nature.

Legal terms are "both linguistic units and points of access to complex, open-ended legal knowledge structures activated by individuals for legal communication purposes" (Biel 2024: 98). They constitute systems of signs of a given discourse and professional community, such as that of supranational human rights justice. Legal terminology is regularly scrutinized by lawyers and judges in their legal arguments striving to establish the "ordinary meaning" (Mouritsen 2023). The judicial community provides definitions and redefinitions to a disputed expression (Jopek-Bosiacka 2023).

It is also one of the most challenging aspects of the multilingual functioning of supranational courts, and from the standpoint of Legal Translation Studies (Peruzzo 2019a: 15). In general, research in this area explores the challenges and strategies involved in translating legal terminology while preserving legal accuracy and integrity. Biel and Engberg (2013: 3) list terminological incongruity, the (un)translatability of legal terms and the so-called "terminological bridges", i.e. "strategies for and techniques of establishing equivalence between terms from different legal systems" among the key research brands of legal translation. The intersection of Legal Terminology and Legal Translation Studies, whose most famous offspring is the notion of equivalence, is further explored in multiple sections of this book (see 3.5 and 5.4.2), so it is not detailed here.

Next to single-word legal terms – traditionally placed under the label *terminology* – there are multiword terms (MWT), i.e. terminological phrases consisting of more than one word. MWTs are both terminological and phraseological (Nikitina 2019d: 272) and, along with traditional terms, they act as "depositories of knowledge" (Sager 1998: 259). They convey the knowledge associated with legal terms and systems but are also bound by a certain pattern. The existence of such patterns contributes to a high degree of formulaicity, fixedness and discursive crystallization of legal discourses, which form the tenets of legal phraseology.

2.2.2 *Legal phraseology*

As a moderately young strand of research, legal phraseology has been subjected to a high degree of variation in nomenclature (see, e.g. Pontrandolfo 2023: 127–128 for an overview). There is no unanimous opinion as to what amounts to a phraseological unit. The classical *phraseological* approach employs linguistic criteria to define various types of phraseological units based on transparency and variability. This approach focuses on idioms with non-transparent structures, following the principle of non-compositionality. For example, the idiom "a plaster on a wooden leg" (see 8.6) used in a separate judicial opinion represents a classical phraseological unit.

Next to a purely qualitative definition of phraseological boundaries, the *distributional* or *frequency-based approach* adopts a bottom-up, inductive and corpus-driven analysis of co-occurrences. Some words tend to co-occur, thus forming combinations of two or more words resulting in collocations or larger patterns and routines. In this perspective, the understanding of phraseological units is broadened, with an emphasis placed on contextual patterning and semantic preferences, which extend the meaning beyond individual elements. It is evident that single occurrences of *human* and *rights* do not necessarily mean the same as *human rights*. The distributional approach also considers lexicogrammar, making its applications more diverse and encompassing various study directions such as distributional patterns, structure, functions and use of phraseological units. Since legal terminology is a more established field than legal phraseology, MWTs have been frequently "dismissed as not being phraseological" (Pontrandolfo 2023: 126), left out (Kjær 2007: 507) or subsumed under the umbrella of legal terminology.

The following definition of legal phraseology is applied:

> crystallized lexical and/or morphosyntactic patterns, varying in complexity and internal cohesion, which are "handed down" from texts to texts and become recurrent in specific legal cultures and discourse communities. These patterns frequently co-occur in legal documents as a result of its use by legal professionals who, as part of a specific community of practice, employ them in their daily jargon so that these word combinations represent a discursive pattern typical of certain legal genres. These units may have a specific legal meaning or not, depending on the textual coordinates of the legal genre.
>
> (Pontrandolfo 2023: 128)

In this book, the labels *phraseological unit* or *multiword unit* are used interchangeably as general labels to denote a pattern consisting of more than one element that adds to the formulaic nature of human rights discourse. Next to term-based phraseologies, there are different phraseological, or multiword, units that are not necessarily terminological in a strict sense of the word.

2.3 Human rights terminology and phraseology: methodological framework

The decision-making process concerning the adoption of terms and MWUs in international organizations, "despite its relevance for institutional translation quality, remains largely unexplored" (Prieto Ramos & Guzman 2018: 81). As Brannan (2013: 923) observed, "[t]he legal terminology used by an international court will necessarily be adapted to its specific features", including considerations of its professional culture, discursive practices and genres. While some terminology and phraseology used by supranational courts may be of a general legal nature by virtue of its disciplinary embeddedness in law, other terms and MWUs may undergo conceptual transformations and re-definitions during their migration from a national setting into an international one. New terminology and phraseology may be developed to denote supranational notions at the level of primary, operational or procedural genres.

And yet cases coming to the attention of supranational human rights justice are rooted in unmistakably national systems, bearing traces of their legal order and terminology of origin. The resulting terminological-phraseological gradient presents elements with different degree of interaction between and across the national and supranational dimensions.

To explore this interaction, this chapter builds on the classification of legal terms at international organizations by Prieto Ramos (2014c) and, specifically, at the ECtHR by Brannan (2013, 2018, 2023) and Peruzzo (2019a, 2019b, 2023), supplementing them with phraseological perspectives (Nikitina 2018a, 2018b; Pontrandolfo 2023).

Placing the terminological-phraseological continuum in the supranational human rights courts along the national-supranational axis, three macro-categories can be identified: (1) supranational terminology and phraseology, (2) legal transplants and (3) domestic system-bound terms (see Figure 2.1). Another layer can be added to this category; it is labelled here as *general legal style markers* (Nikitina 2018a). This category stems from the general disciplinary confines of the human rights discourse as a type of legal discourse. While legal style markers may slightly diverge across legal systems, languages and cultures, since they stem from the formal character of legal prose (Tiersma 2015: 29), some lexicogrammatical patterns appear universal. These include complex prepositions, "a striking syntactic feature of legislative writing" (Bhatia 1993: 107), also widely recognized elsewhere in the literature on legal discourse (Mellinkoff 1963; Quirk et al. 1985: 672; Maley 1994; Tiersma 1999, 2015; Nikitina 2018a). Other lexicogrammatical units that contribute to the legal flavour of texts include compound archaic adverbials, such as *hereby, thereto*, etc., Latin expressions, "patterns and lexical bundles which express deontic modality (*shall, must, should, may*), *if-then* mental models of legal reasoning and other conditional clauses (*if, in the event that, in case, unless, otherwise, provided that*), purpose clauses (*with a view to* – ing, *in order to, to this end*), the passive voice and other impersonal structures" (Biel 2014: 179). These markers pertain to the phraseological category of grammatical units (Nikitina 2018a: 178) and are not going to be discussed here in more detail because of their low specificity to the discourse of human rights.

Concerning the national-supranational axis, further subdivisions may be identified within each macro-category, as Figure 2.1 illustrates. These subdivisions concern (1) the origin of terminological and phraseological units and (2) their phraseological type. Relying on an earlier study (Nikitina 2018a: 178–189), I discern between the so-called *term-related units* and other *formulaic patterns*.

- *Term-related units* cluster around terms and include single-word and multiword terms (Kjær 2007: 509), also called "term-forming patterns" in Biel (2014: 180), i.e. terms composed of more than one element, following the structures [Adj + N] or [N + N], e.g. *single judge* or *margin of appreciation*.

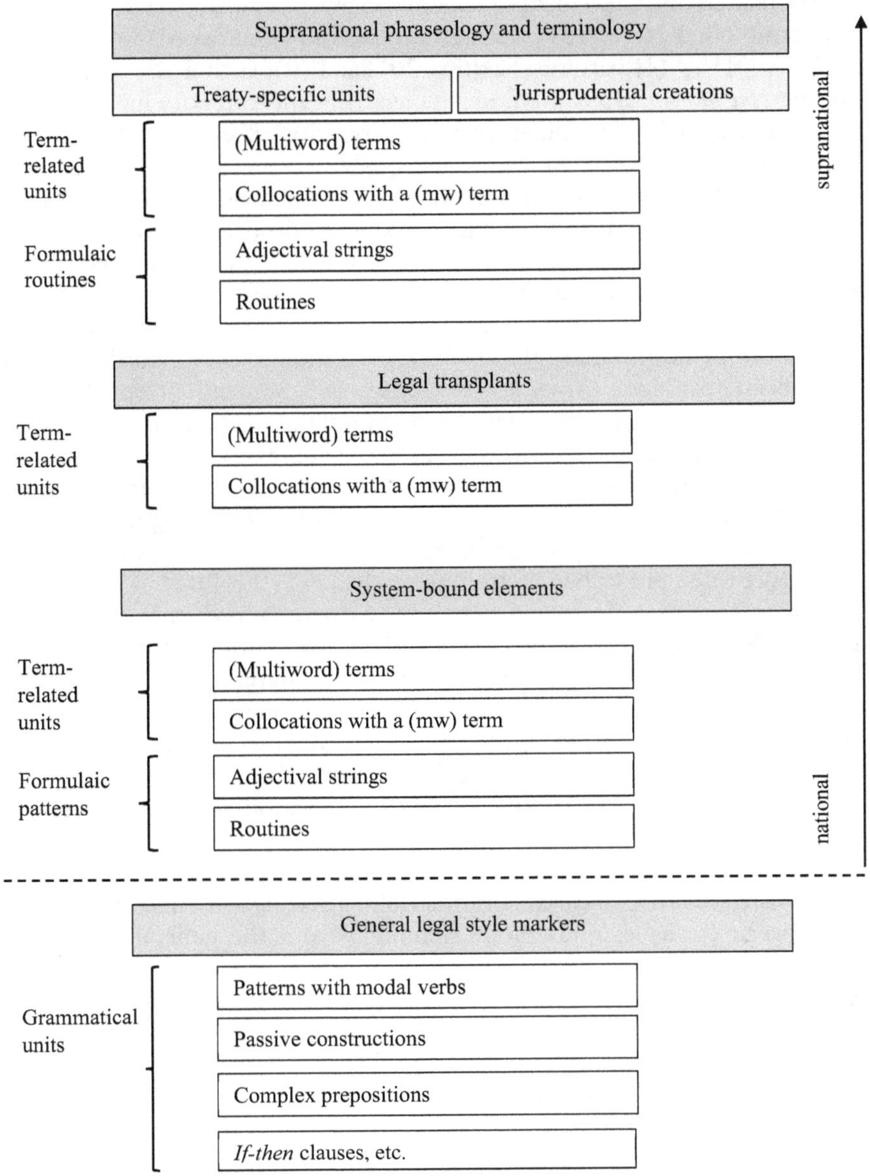

Figure 2.1 Terminological-phraseological continuum in supranational human rights courts

Term-related units also include *collocations with a term* or "term-embedded patterns" (Biel 2014: 181) that revolve around (multiword) terms, in the [N + V]/[V + N] pattern (Nikitina 2018a: 179), such as *the Court holds* or *to strike out an application*. In simple terms, this category includes verbs that collocate with a nominal term in the position of a grammatical subject or object.

- *Formulaic patterns* do not necessarily revolve around terms, and yet divergence in their use "may cause undue inconsistency and confusion" (Brannan 2023: 329). Although some formulaic patterns may derive their existence from the core genre, the treaty, most frequently these pertain to the description of "general principles (but not direct quotations), which have become enshrined in the case-law even though other wording would have been possible or (in some cases) desirable" (Brannan 2023: 329), so in the following description I mention them only under jurisprudential creations. Their use both derives from and contributes to the general formulaicity of the human rights discourse. This category includes *adjectival/ adverbial strings* and *routines*, also known as "text-organising patterns", i.e. larger chunks of text, which often create "repetitive global textual patterns which are often prescribed in drafting guidelines" (Biel 2014: 178), such as *In accordance with Article 45 § 2 of the Convention and Rule 74 § 2 of the Rules of Court, the following separate opinions are annexed to this judgment* (see Chapter 8). These are frequently "used to signpost a part of the text or to transition between different parts [. . .] through the use of a prefabricated pattern, which reduces the effort necessary to process information" (Nikitina 2018a: 178). Formulaic patterns are also known as "habitually routine phrases" (Kjær 1990: 29), whose "variation entails more time to process the meaning but has no legal effects".

Based on previous research, Pontrandolfo (2023: 126) makes a distinction between (a) legal phraseology stemming from the generally formulaic and formal character of legal discourse in a non-content-affecting way and (b) legal phraseology that produces legal effects in a content-affecting way. For instance, *without prejudice to* belongs to type (a) as it can be easily replaced with synonyms, e.g. "without harming or affecting someone". Other instances might include complex prepositions of other grammatical multi-word units that are labelled here as "general legal style markers". At the same time, *to dismiss the appeal* is a type (b) phraseological unit (collocation with a term) since it has a legal effect (Pontrandolfo 2023: 126).

2.4 Human rights terminology and phraseology: findings

The following description arranges the terminology and phraseology of human rights along the supranational-national axis, integrating it with morphological distinctions of different human rights (multiword) units and focusing predominantly on those producing legal effects.

1 **Supranational terminology and phraseology**: As the name explains, these units "transcend domestic realities" (Brannan 2013: 909) and pertain to the supranational dimension. These are the terms and phrases denoting "legal notions that are embedded in the supranational legal system" (Peruzzo 2023: 153) as opposed to the national ones. In a broader context of international organizations, Prieto Ramos (2014c: 128) defined this category as "terms designating shared concepts created in the international system and recognized as established terminology within [its] specific scope of competence". The ECtHR stated famously that in its interpretation it may rely on "any relevant rules and principles of international law applicable in the relations between the Contracting Parties".[1] However, international human rights law "is not a unified concept" (Legg 2012: 2), and caution is advised when approaching discourses and terminologies of human rights generated by different institutions. Supranational terms may be further subdivided into three types.

   a **Treaty-specific (multiword) units** derive their existence from the convention or another treaty upon which the operation of a given supranational court is based. In the ECtHR context, convention-specific terms stem from the text of the European Convention on Human Rights as interpreted and applied by the ECtHR. The IACtHR and the ACtHPR may have different treaty-specific terms that evolved through the courts' interpretations.

      i **Multiword terms**: For example, the multiword term *just satisfaction* is ECHR-specific (Art. 41), *fair trial* appears in both ECHR (Art. 6) and IACHR (Art. 8), and *reasonable time* is featured in all three documents (Art. 5 and 6 ECHR, Art. 7 and 8 IACHR, Art. 7 ACHPR); however, their interpretation may diverge. As treaties and conventions are created to last in time, they frequently abound in the indeterminate language (Lanius 2019), featuring such terms as "reasonable", "fair", "just", etc., which require interpretation by the judiciary. Similarly, the same treaty-based term may have different meanings across the human rights courts. For instance, *subsidiary measures* mentioned in Art. 61 ACHPR denote simply additional measures, whereas *subsidiarity* introduced with Protocol no. 16 to the ECHR has a completely different meaning of a relationship between a Member State and a supranational body, wherein the latter intervenes only when the former has already had the chance to do so, i.e. "repositioning proximate domestic institutions and giving them a more prominent role in the protection and development of human rights" (Madsen 2021: 95). Similarly, all three courts protect the *right to life* (Art. 2 ECHR; Art. 4 IACHR; Art. 4 ACHPR), which along with the *right to liberty* is listed as "two prominent contenders for the primordial

1 *Hirsi Jamaa and Others v. Italy* ([GC] 23/02/2012, § 171).

natural/human right" (Agha 2017: 19). Despite the "primordial" nature of this right, the judicial interpretation of this linguistic label varies across these institutions, especially when it concerns the interpretation of bioethically elusive situations involving the beginning of life (abortion, artificial procreation, embryo donation, etc.) and the end of life (euthanasia, assisted dying, etc.).

ii **Collocations with a term**: A prominent example of a collocation with a term is *to exhaust remedies* (art. 35 (1) ECHR, art. 46(1)(a) IACHR, art. 50 and art. 56 (5) and (6) ACHPR), common to all three systems and thus contributing to the most general understanding of the human rights discourse. Whereas the verb "to exhaust" is used in all three contexts with "remedies", the exact phraseological pattern is subject to some variation: the European pattern revolves around the exhaustion of "domestic remedies", the American one deals with the exhaustion of "remedies under domestic law", and in the African system, it is the exhaustion of "local remedies". Another collocation with a term is *to relinquish jurisdiction*, which is used only in the ECtHR context to denote the transfer of a case to a higher-standing judicial formation, i.e. the Grand Chamber.

iii **Adjectival strings**: An example of an adjectival string used in the European and the American system is *necessary in a democratic society* (Article 8.2 ECHR, Article 16.2 IACHR), typically applied to the description of requirements for the possible limitations of human rights protection. Peculiarly, no such string is used in the African system, and the "ACHPR is silent on the requirements for a restriction on a human right to be lawful under the ACHPR" (Rachovitsa 2020: 4). An adjectival string whose variants exist in all three systems concerns the combination of the following adjectives: "competent", "independent" and "impartial" that collocate typically with "tribunal": *independent and impartial tribunal established by law* (Art. 6.1 ECHR), *competent, independent, and impartial tribunal* (Art. 8 IACHR), *competent national organs* (Art. 7 ACHPR).

b **Jurisprudential creations** are coined by the discursive community in a given supranational context: judges, lawyers and, to a certain extent, translators. When there is "no textual peg on which to hang the doctrine in the European Convention" (Legg 2012: 3), a jurisprudential creation may be needed. A similar situation applies also to the other two courts. As Spano (2018: 478) observed, "Convention rights have [. . .] been developed through language formulated by international jurists and judges".

i **Multiword terms**: An example in the ECtHR context is the multiword term *margin of appreciation*, which pertains to the doctrine of judicial deference, i.e. "the room for manoeuvre that treaty bodies, such as the judicial institutions at Strasbourg, are prepared to accord national authorities in fulfilling their treaty obligations" (Agha 2017: 17). As Spielmann (2012: 4–5) outlines, the concept and the term that denotes it were created by the ECtHR.[2] The term (but not the concept entirely), largely absent from the other courts' case-law, was probably coined under the influence of the French administrative law multiword term *marge d'appréciation*, exploring the mechanisms of the ECtHR's bilingual operation. As Legg (2012: 14) outlines, analysing the judicial practice of margin of appreciation across ECtHR, IACtHR and UN HRC, the latter two do employ it in substance and in a limited way on account of divergent caseloads, but "they do not self-consciously resort to the concepts or labels of the margin of appreciation in the same way as do decisions of the ECtHR". In the ACtHPR, the doctrine was first mentioned in one of its 2013 judgments,[3] drawing on the European case-law. The text of the relevant ACtHPR judgment uses also a variation of the term "margin of manoeuvre".[4] It has been also explicitly referred to in the *Ingabire Victoire Umuhoza* case, where the Respondent State (Rwanda) "had specifically invoked the specificities of its history and asked the Court to adopt a *margin of appreciation* (paras 125–127, 145)" (Rachovitsa 2020: 19). In yet another case, *Kijiji Isiaga*, the ACtHPR explicitly mentioned this jurisprudential creation: it "underscore[d] that domestic courts enjoy a wide margin of appreciation in evaluating the probative value of a [sic] particular evidence",[5] showing how MWTs may migrate from one institution to another, becoming a legal transplant for the receiving institution.

Another jurisprudential creation is the multiword term "objective obligations", used recurrently in the ECtHR case-law since 1961[6] and occasionally employed also by the IACtHR.[7]

ii **Collocation with a term**: An example in the ECtHR case-law is *to strike a fair balance*, applied to "the demands of the general interest of the community and the requirements of the protection of the individual" (Villiger 2017: para. 34). The terms *fair balance*, *balancing test* and *proportionality* are frequently used synonymously in

2 Specifically referring to *Greece v UK* No. 175/56 (1958) (European Commission of Human Rights).

3 In the judgment *Tanganyika Law Society and The Legal and Human Rights Centre and Reverend Christopher Mtikila v The United Republic of Tanzania* (Applications 009 and 011/2011).

4 ACtHPR judgment in the case *Tanganyika Law Society and The Legal and Human Rights Centre and Reverend Christopher Mtikila v The United Republic of Tanzania* (Applications 009 and 011/2011) at para. 31 of the Separate opinion of Vice-President Fatsah Ouguergouz.

5 *Kijiji Isiaga*, para. 65. As Rachovitsa (2020: 19) explains, "The Court's reference to margin of appreciation in *Kijiji Isiaga* was also quoted in subsequent case law (Kenedy Ivan, para 62; Oscar Josiah, para 52). However, the Court never elaborated on whether it formally endorses this doctrine and, if yes, how it contextualises it in its case law".

6 Decision in the *Austria v. Italy* case, ECmHR, pp. 18–19.

7 IACtHR, *Ivcher Bronstein*, para. 42. See Pisillo Mazzeschi (2021: 68–69) for an overview.

legal literature and international case-law (Rachovitsa 2020: 2). They collocate with different verbs. Another verbal string that frequently occurs in cases dealing with freedom of expression is *to offend, shock or disturb*, collocating with "information", "ideas", "opinions", "comments", etc.,[8] in the grammatical subject position (e.g. "comments that offend or shock")[9] but also with "State" or similar in the grammatical object position ("offend, shock or disturb a State or any section of the population").[10]

iii **Adjectival strings**: Very frequently, similarly to convention-specific terms, the human rights discourse relies on indeterminate adjectives, and their consistent use implies consistent construal of their meaning in a sort of a "linguistic precedent" (Weston 2005: 458). Examples of such supranational formulaic expressions in the ECtHR include *practical and effective*. Originally introduced in *Soering v. United Kingdom*[11] as a collocate of "safeguards", it was later used recurrently in the ECtHR case-law as a collocate of "rights" and "guarantees".[12] For instance, in *Airey v. Ireland*, the Court ruled that "the Convention is intended to guarantee not rights that are theoretical or illusory but rights that are practical and effective".[13] Other examples include the strings *manifestly ill-founded* and *well-founded*, which are attributed a "special meaning" in the ECtHR context (Villiger 2017: para. 35), or the adverbial phrase *with full jurisdiction* that entered the ECtHR English under the influence of the French *de plein jurisdiction* (Brannan 2021: 224–225).

iv **Routines** are larger chunks of text, typically contributing to the crystallized character of some genres within and across different human rights systems. For example, judgments of the ECtHR contain the same performative formula at the end: *For these reasons, the Court holds, unanimously, that there have been violations of* [. . .]. Another routine is the judgment-initial formula: *In the case of [. . .], the European Court of Human Rights, sitting as a Grand Chamber composed of [. . .] having deliberated in private on [. . .], delivers the following judgment, which was adopted on the last-mentioned date.*

8 See, e.g. *Handyside v. United Kingdom*, the ECtHR judgment of 7 December 1976, Ser. A No. 24, para. 49. See also IACtHR, *Olmedo Bustos et. al Case* ("Last Temptation of Christ"), Judgment of February 5, 2001, Series C No. 73, para. 69; see also the ACtHPR judgment in the case *Ingabire Victoire Umuhoza v. the Republic of Rwanda*, para. 143.

9 ECtHR, *İ.A. v. Turkey*, (application 42571/98), para. 29.

10 ACtHPR, *Ingabire Victoire Umuhoza v. the Republic of Rwanda*, para. 143.

11 ECtHR, *Soering v. United Kingdom*, (Application no. 14038/88), 7 July 1989, para. 87.

12 It can be part of a longer routine, too: "(the Court finds) in order for the right to a fair trial to remain sufficiently 'practical and effective' . . ., Article 6 § 1 requires that, as a rule, access to a lawyer should be provided as from the first interrogation of a suspect by the police, unless it is demonstrated in the light of the particular circumstances of each case that there are compelling reasons to restrict this right" (example taken from the RiFT Corpus, see Chapter 7).

13 ECtHR, *Airey v Ireland*, 9 October 1979, para. 24.

2 **Legal transplants** (Watson 1974) or **autonomous concepts** (Brannan 2023) compose the second category of the supranational-national axis. These are typically general legal terms (and phraseological units) borrowed from national contexts and redefined in a supranational context so that their meaning is not the same as it was in the legal system of origin. With the rise of English as a lingua franca and a lingua franca of human rights (Flikschuh 2011: 36; Boot 2017: 3), legal transplants have become a very widespread phenomenon. From a linguistic standpoint, this category can be defined as a result of "secondary term formation" (Sager 1990: 80; see also Peruzzo 2012) or semantic redefinition. The Achilles' heel of legal transplants from a translation/comparative law perspective is that while the term itself, i.e. its linguistic realization, can be the same or almost the same across a variety of jurisdictions, the meaning may differ significantly as international organizations reassign it in the operation of "autonomous interpretation" (Peruzzo 2019b: 81). Autonomous concepts in the ECtHR practice have received a fair share of attention in the literature (Malblanc 2019; Brannan 2023). The underlying idea is to interpret the Convention in such a way as to prevent a State from "hiding behind" its domestic terminology (Brannan 2023: 340). Probably the most famous example is the multiword term *criminal charge*[14] as the ECtHR established autonomously what constitutes "criminal" and what constitutes "charge", independently from any national characterizations. Similarly, *expulsion* is an autonomous concept in the ECtHR case-law, with a clearly defined meaning as opposed to near-synonyms *extradition, return* and *removal.* Its adoption and definition have been the product of tailored terminological discussions: the Report on Protocol no. 7 (1984) in describing lawfully resident aliens, referred to it as "an autonomous concept . . . independent of any definition contained in domestic legislation" (quoted in Brannan 2023: 340). The far-sighted terminological awareness of the ECtHR concerning the term *expulsion* (see Brannan 2023) distinguishes it from other autonomous concepts (Malblanc 2019: 76). A well-discussed legal transplant in the IACtHR system is the term *laws*, the meaning of which "cannot be dissociated from the nature and origin"[15] of the "system for the protection of human rights", interpreting as formal laws, namely "a legal norm passed by the legislature and promulgated by the Executive Branch, pursuant to the procedure set out in the domestic law of each State".[16] Another aspect that warrants caution is that the same or almost the same term may be semantically redefined in a different way across different human rights institutions.

14 From *Engel v. the Netherlands*, 8 June 1976.

15 IACtHR, The Word "Laws" in Article 30 of the American Convention on Human Rights, Advisory Opinion OC-6/86 of May 9, 1986, Series A, No. 6, p. 29, para. 21.

16 IACtHR, The Word "Laws" in Article 30 of the American Convention on Human Rights, Advisory Opinion OC-6/86 of May 9, 1986, Series A, No. 6, p. 32, para. 27.

3 **System-bound elements** (SBEs) are term-related units and formulaic patterns "designating culture-bound or *system-specific concepts to be identified as such* in the international context" (Prieto Ramos 2014c: 129, emphasis added). As cases coming to the ECtHR concern violations of the Convention that happened within a *national* context, a number of nationally bound terms inevitably migrate into an international context maintaining their domestic meaning. These terms are used predominantly to refer to national legislation and domestic proceedings. To wit, these are "legal terms and concepts that, in a context requiring comparison, appear to be embedded in one legal system, be it national, regional, or international" (Peruzzo 2019b: 78). SBEs will be discussed in more detail in Chapter 5, but a brief illustration is provided below for the sake of taxonomical completeness.

a **Multiword terms**: An example of a system-specific concept and multiword term is *civil party* (Brannan 2013: 922), which is the literal translation of an Italian concept *parte civile*, which denotes an offence victim who takes part in criminal proceedings with a civil claim to obtain monetary compensation. Similarly, multiword terms may include specific types of judiciary proceedings, names of the institutions or other terms designating system-bound concepts.
b **Collocations with a term**: In the ECtHR system, Peruzzo (2019a: 25) quotes the following example of an Italian SBE that can be classified as a verbal collocation with a term: "to aid and abet the Mafia (*appoggio esterno alla Mafia*)". She notes (2019a: 23) that during the passage from the source language (Italian in this case) to the target language (English of the ECtHR judgments) the system-boundedness is often retained only in the verbal part of the collocation with a verb. For example, the Italian collocation with a term *assume gli elementi necessari ai fini della decisione* becomes "the judge [. . .] shall acquire (*assume*) of his own motion the evidence necessary for a decision to be reached" (*Hermi v. Italy*, Application 18114/02, quoted in Peruzzo 2019a: 23).
c **Adjectival strings**: For example, this case communication features a long adjectival string: "Dissemination through the media and ICT networks, of *socially important information known to be untrue* [*заведомо недостоверная общественно значимая информация*] under the guise of reliable reports [. . .] shall be punishable by an administrative fine of between 30,000 and 100,000 Russian roubles . . ." (*Avagyan v. Russia*, 2020, Application no. 36911/20).
d **Routines**: Peruzzo (2019a: 25) quotes an example of a system-bound Italian routine that migrated to some of the ECtHR judgments as a descriptive paraphrase "On the ground that the alleged facts had never occurred (*perché il fatto non sussiste*)".

2.5 Conclusions

Human rights discourses adapt and transform, shedding old expressions, adopting new vocabulary or redefining the meanings of some pre-existent terms and phrases in a continual process of evolution, shaped by countless factors including cultural shifts, technological advancements and interactions with other human rights contexts and languages. The core legal knowledge is adapted through the mechanisms of legal interpretation to the specific settings. Modern human rights institutions inherited elements from their predecessors, maintaining connections to their linguistic roots while also branching out into novel forms of expression. This chapter did not pursue the goal of providing an exhaustive account of legal terminology and phraseology of human rights. I wanted to provide the reader with an opportunity to don the clothes of a legal linguist, extending the horizons of lawyers and linguists alike, and in the meantime laying the methodological bases for further discussion, centred around the European human rights discourse.

3 The European Court of Human Rights

Context, genres and languages

3.1 The European Convention on Human Rights

3.1.1 A hope for the future?

The roots of human rights as currently understood go back to the period after World War II, the dramatic events of which encouraged Europe to unite and to create mechanisms preventing any future human rights violations (Harris et al. 2014: 3). In pursuit of "lofty ideas of European unity" (Bates 2011: 17), a new organization was created in 1949: the Council of Europe (CoE). This international organization was set up in Strasbourg, France, to promote democracy, human rights and the rule of law. It became home to the Convention for the Protection of Human Rights and Fundamental Freedoms, better known as the European Convention on Human Rights (ECHR or Convention).

At its inception, the "Convention's future was beclouded with doubt" (Bates 2011: 18). The first proposals were not met "with great enthusiasm – far from it" (Bates 2011: 17). It was not seen as "a cause for celebration" but "a source of some acrimony" (Bates 2011: 17), up to the point of becoming a "real disappointment" (Bates 2011: 18) for some, initially.[1]

The Convention was not born out of a vacuum. First, it was open for signature on 4 November 1950, only two years after the proclamation of the Universal Declaration on Human Rights (UDHR). Second, it built on the preexisting concept of human rights. James Fawcett (1967: 125), a British lawyer and a member of the European Commission of Human Rights argued that "the Declarations and Conventions after 1945 are not a wholly new departure, but are logical steps in old and continuing efforts for the protection and enforcement of human rights in many fields around the world". Though the roots of human rights were formally laid post-World War II, the seeds of their conceptualization were sown much earlier, tracing back to the late 19th century and the intellectual enlightenment (Salojärvi 2020: 117). Eventually,

1 Bates (2011: 29) cites a historical anecdote about how the Consultative Assembly's President (Paul-Henri Spaak) announced the signing ceremony for the Convention and its location: "It is not a very good Convention, but it is a lovely Palace!"

DOI: 10.4324/9781003434788-4

some early conceptualizations of human rights may be found even in the Bible, in ancient legal codes like the Hammurabi Code, the laws of Greek cities like Athens and certain precepts from various religions and philosophies such as Buddhism, Confucianism and Hinduism (Pisillo Mazzeschi 2021: 4).

Besides preventing the repetition of tragic events of World War II, the newly established human rights machinery pursued clear political goals of building a Western European "bulwark against communism, which had spread from the Soviet Union into European states behind the Iron Curtain after the Second World War" (Harris et al. 2014: 3). The underlying idea was "to establish a common system that could sound the alarm if genuine democracy was threatened in the member states" (Madsen 2021: 95; see also Bates 2011: 21). The political mood of Europe and the novelty of the human rights idea provided an "unstoppable momentum in favour of creating some type of European human rights guarantee" (Bates 2011: 21).

Today, the European Convention on Human Rights is frequently equalled to "a European bill of rights" (Harris et al. 2014: 4) establishing "a constitutional instrument of European public order" (*Loizidou v. Turkey* 1995: para. 70).[2] This is a reflection of a moderately recent doctrinal theory suggesting that international human rights law should not merely be viewed as a distinct area of international law but as a constitutional dimension within that legal framework, where "human rights treaties would not be 'normal' treaties between States, but would constitute an embryonic form of a *global constitution*" (Pisillo Mazzeschi 2021: 70, original emphasis).

Following the same train of thought, the ECtHR is frequently portrayed as a European constitutional court. In fact, "the ways and methods of the ECtHR's interpretation, as adopted in its case law, may not be very different from the ways and methods adopted by the national courts that deal with constitutional questions" (Garlicki 2009: 391). Some roots of this conceptualization may be found in the original political compromise that saw the birth of the Court: the original text of the Convention in the 1950s "was ambivalent in terms of its mission as either a 'pact for collective action' against totalitarianism or a 'European Bill of Rights'" (Bates 2011: 36).[3] The early narrative on the ECtHR had to account for the difficult political climate of Europe, and the idea of a European Bill of Rights was frequently invoked in a legitimation attempt. Modern proponents of the constitutional theory of human rights,

2 ECtHR, *Loizidou v. Turkey* (preliminary objections), Judgment of 23 March 1995, paras. 70 and 75; *Ireland v. UK*, para. 239.

3 The first President of the ECmHR, Professor C. H. M. Waldock, who said: "If you regard the Convention as a constitutional instrument – as a European Bill of Rights for the individual – then it seems difficult to deny the importance of granting the individual a personal right to place his grievance before the Commission. If, on the other hand, the Convention is regarded rather as a pact for collective action to check the development of any totalitarian methods of government in member countries, then the individual's right of recourse to the Commission may seem less important than that of the Member States. The Convention compromised on the point" (Waldock 1958: 359, quoted in Bates 2011: 36).

who claim that human rights courts perform functions similar to those of constitutional courts in domestic settings (Scheinin 2009: 29–31) define these supranational bodies as "quasi-constitutional", and argue their indisputable link with fundamental moral values that underly every constitutional order, along with addressing individuals (Scheinin 2009: 30).

Yet, despite the widespread nature of such comparisons, "the ECtHR cannot be treated just like one of the constitutional courts", because it "still conserves its nature as a supranational body, created and operating within the realm of international law" (Garlicki 2009: 391). As Spano (2018: 477, original emphasis) observes, "to give life to the Convention's fundamental values, the Court needed to build an elaborate *edifice of human rights*, both at the substantive as well as the methodological levels". Pisillo Mazzeschi (2021: 71) offers an adroit summary of the constitutional theory criticisms:

> It is difficult to argue that conventional human rights norms, which are included in a plurality of normative systems at the universal and regional levels, constitute the expression of a substantive constituent power and give rise to a single system of protection for the individual. Therefore, the argument about the "constitutional" nature of human rights treaties cannot be accepted.

The constitutional outlook is also refuted by Harris et al. (2014), who posit that both states parties and non-governmental organizations (NGOs) "see the Convention as providing a remedy for all individual complaints", without depicting the ECtHR as a constitutional court (Harris et al. 2014: 39, note 299).

3.1.2 The living instrument

The Convention's innovation consisted in crystallizing and rendering binding the rights set forth in the Universal Declaration of Human Rights. Fruit of multiple negotiations, its original text contained "absolute rights which can never be breached by the States" (ECHR 2022: 4).[4] Some of the softer, less absolute, rights, such as the right to education jettisoned by the Nazis through the indoctrination of children at school, or right to property were heavily debated and never made it into the initial text (Bates 2011: 24).

At the time of its entry into force on 4 September 1953, the Convention looked different from what it does today. How did the change happen? Repeatedly conceptualized as "a living instrument which [. . .] must be interpreted in the light of present-day conditions" (*Tyrer v. UK* 1978: para.

4 ECtHR (2022) The European Convention on human rights: a living instrument. Available at https://www.echr.coe.int/documents/d/echr/Convention_Instrument_ENG. Unless stated otherwise, all sources with a hyperlink were last accessed 3 March 2024.

31[5]) to guarantee that "its provisions be interpreted and applied so as to make its safeguards practical and effective" so that its rights are "not [. . .] theoretical or illusory" (*Artico v. Italy* 1980: para. 33), the ECHR evolved into "an instrument designed to maintain and promote the ideals and values of a democratic society" (*Soering v. UK* 1989: para. 87).[6] The "practical and effective" doctrine foregrounded the principle that the protection of the Convention rights is "not an abstract exercise" (Agha 2017: 4). As legal commentators observe, ". . . the Convention would not be able to survive, had it not been regarded as a 'living instrument' and had it not been constantly developed in the case law of the Court" (Garlicki 2009: 390). The Convention constantly undergoes "dynamic interpretation" (Agha 2017: 2) by the Court.

This interpretative approach allows the Court to extend the protection mechanism to "situations that were totally unforeseeable and unimaginable at the time it was first adopted" (ECtHR 2020: 7). Technological advancements of the late 20th and early 21st centuries have modified the fabric of our societies, and it is only reasonable that human rights are protected in the light of these changed conditions. This evolving reading of the Convention allows the Court to apply its provisions to modern issues, such as terrorism, migration, new technologies, bioethics, surrogacy, etc. For example, Art. 8 ECHR (*Right to respect for private and family life, home and correspondence*) extends now to cases of surveillance, phone tapping or data collection, both by law enforcement officers and private individuals,[7] which becomes incredibly relevant given that in modern European societies, much of an individual's private life involves the use of social media. On a similar note, the right to a healthy environment has been included under Art. 8[8] in an interpretative way, even if this right was not explicitly codified in the Convention text.

Provisions of the Convention "are drafted in a general and ambiguous way, and one of the Court's most important functions is therefore to specify the content of the ECHR by weighing and balancing the counterweighing considerations" (Agha 2017: 6). A child of heated debate and political

5 ECtHR judgment *Tyrer v. United Kingdom* (Application no. 5856/72), 25 April 1978, para. 31.

6 ECtHR judgment *Soering v. United Kingdom* (Application no. 14038/88), 7 July 1989, para. 87.

7 For example, ECtHR's Guide on Article 8 (2022: 125) explains that the States now have positive obligations to investigate "the violation of the confidentiality of the applicant's correspondence in the context of domestic violence (*Buturugă v. Romania*, 2020, where the applicant's former husband had improperly consulted her electronic accounts, including her Facebook account, and had made copies of her private conversations, documents and photographs)" and "an obligation to protect the confidentiality of emails exchanged by the applicant on a dating website, produced without her consent by her ex-husband in civil proceedings regarding parental responsibility and divorce (M.P. v. Portugal, § 44)".

8 See the ECtHR Judgment *Hatton and Others v. the United Kingdom* [GC], Application no. 36022/97, 8 July 2003, para. 96.

compromise, the final substantive text of the Convention "was not precise" (Bates 2011: 34):

> Inevitably it was full of general, imprecise notions, frequently referring to non-legal standards and values such as "inhuman and degrading treatment" (Art 3), "respect for private and family life" (Art 8), "within a reasonable time" (Art 5(3)), "in accordance with the law" (Art 8(2)), and "necessary in a democratic society" (Arts 8(2) to 11(2)). It was no doubt for this reason that most of the substantive Articles of the Convention (other than Arts 3 and 4(1)) were crammed with, and in some cases, overloaded by restrictions and "clawback" clauses. These attempted to set out in advance the possible justifications for interference with the rights "protected".
>
> (Bates 2011: 34)

As Garlicki (2009: 391) observes, "neither the Convention nor the Court have one single identity – they rather represent a merger of different traditions arising from different legal systems", and the language of the Convention is a clear indicator of this original plurality. Besides the treaty-based multiword units highlighted by Bates (2011: 34, see Chapter 2), many other provisions contained intentionally indeterminate language. For example, one of the core provisions of the Convention is enshrined in Article 3 (*Prohibition of torture*), which recites, "No one shall be subjected to torture or to inhuman or degrading treatment or punishment". This provision contains the multiword terms *inhuman treatment* and *degrading treatment*, both of which are based on the combination of an indeterminate adjective with the word "treatment". So, rather than fixing the meaning in the Convention, it is left for the Court's interpretation to define what is considered inhuman or degrading.[9]

Besides the dynamic interpretation of its provisions, the Convention has undergone some tangible changes over its 70+ years of existence through the so-called "protocols" that supplemented the text with many rights in addition to those outlined in the original text. As of 2024, the text of the Convention contains the basic version as amended by Protocols nos. 11, 14 and 15. These protocols have altered the text and numbering of the original 1950 text.

Protocols nos. 11, 14 and 16 are also known as the "reform protocols", as they have brough about significant changes in the operation of the ECtHR. Protocol no. 11 created the "New Court" (see 3.2.2), Protocol no. 14 simplified and accelerated the procedure before the Court and Protocol no. 16 regulated the new advisory competence of the Court (Sicilianos 2018: 1).

Seven protocols are not embedded into the main text of the Convention but follow it: the Additional Protocol (the so-called "Protocol no. 1") and

9 The Guide on Article 3 (2022: 6), for instance, explains the threshold criteria that requires the ill-treatment to be of a certain severity on order to qualify for the protection of Art. 3.

Protocols nos. 4, 6, 7, 12, 13 and 16. Hart (2010: 543) illustrates some of the changes brought about by the Convention Protocols in a succinct way:

> Protocol 2 was later integrated into the Convention in its present form as articles 47, 48, and 49. Protocol 4 (E.T.S. No. 46) prohibited imprisonment for debt and guaranteed freedom of movement. Protocol 6 (E.T.S. No. 114) limited the death penalty to wartime. It was signed in 1983 and has been ratified or acceded to by all contracting parties except Russia. The death penalty was finally abolished entirely by Protocol 13 (E.T.S. No. 187) on July 1, 2003. Protocol 7 (E.T.S. No. 117) added a right to appeal in criminal matters, compensation for wrongful conviction, the prohibition against double jeopardy, and equality of spouses.

The history of the Convention is tethered to the history of the Court, and a description of one is impossible without a description of the other.

3.2 The European Court of Human Rights: historical background

Although the European Convention on Human Rights, under which the Court is established (Art. 19), entered into force in 1953, the Court was set up only in 1959, and gave its first judgment on the merits in July 1961.[10] Originally, some Member States even opposed the idea of a Court,[11] too ambitious, risky in terms of potential judicial activism and somewhat superfluous, claiming that a Commission would be enough to guard against the return to totalitarianism (Bates 2011: 25–26). However, the idea of judicial supervision of human rights prevailed.

As with its younger sister courts in the Americas and Africa, the path to the Court's realization was gradual. For a significant time, acceptance of the contentious jurisdiction of this Strasbourg-based court was optional for the Contracting Parties to the Convention. The situation changed in November 1998, when Protocol no. 11 entered into force, making acceptance of the Court's jurisdiction mandatory for all Member States of the Council of Europe (CoE), which currently counts 46 states. Even if there were other significant reforms afterwards, November 1998 was a landmark divisor in the ECtHR history,

10 *Lawless v Ireland*, Judgment of 1 July 1961, Series A No 3; (1979–80) 1 EHRR 15. As White (2009: 1, note 3) explains, the ECtHR "had given a judgment on preliminary objections and questions of procedure in this case on 14 November 1960; Series A No 1".

11 In his overview of the historical development of the Court, Bates (2011: 28) indicated that at the Convention discussion stage, "Seven countries (Denmark, Greece, Netherlands, Norway, Sweden, Turkey, and the UK) declared themselves against; only four were in favour (Belgium, France, Ireland, and Italy). Eight countries were prepared to accept the idea of an optional court (Belgium, France, Greece, Ireland, Italy, Luxembourg, Sweden, and Turkey), but this was not acceptable to the Netherlands or the UK. The idea of an optional court was proposed nevertheless".

dividing its operation into what is traditionally known as the "old Court" (1959–October 1998) and the "new Court" (November 1998–present).

3.2.1 The old Court

In the "old" system, a two-tier mechanism originally existed, making it similar to the other supranational courts of human rights, IACtHR and ACtHPR, which still rely on this structural organization. The two-tier "enforcement machinery" (Harris et al. 2014: 6) in Strasbourg involved two organs: the European Commission of Human Rights (ECmHR or European Commission) and the European Court of Human Rights, to which a third organ was added, the Committee of Ministers.

The European Commission was a "quasi-judicial, quasi-political" (Bates 2011: 35) part-time institution composed of independent experts, "act[ing] in their own capacities, not as representatives of their governments" (Hart 2010: 539). The Commission decided on the admissibility of applications (state and individual), dealt with friendly settlements and created non-legally binding reports on the merits of admitted cases. Remarkably, "there were no qualifications for membership, so Commissioners did not have to be highly qualified lawyers" (Bates 2011: 35). Depending on whether the respondent state accepted or not the Court's jurisdiction, such reports could be "referred to the Court by the Commission or a state with a recognized interest for a legally binding judgment" (Harris et al. 2014: 6, note 37). In other words, within three months of the transmission of the report to the Committee of Ministers, the old Court had to receive such referral by the Commission, the respondent State or the Contracting Party involved (Peruzzo 2019b: 17). Individual applicants could refer a case to the Court only if the respondent State had ratified Protocol no. 9. In such cases, the application went to a three-person panel who "could decide unanimously that the application should not be considered by the Court because it did not raise a serious question affecting the interpretation or application of the Convention" (Rainey et al. 2017: 9). In other words, it went through an additional filtering stage.

In the absence of such referral, under former Article 32 of the Convention, the case was decided by the Committee of Ministers. The Committee of Ministers currently is the political organ of the CoE comprising one representative from each Contracting Party to the European Convention on Human Rights and tasked with monitoring the execution of judgments. In the "old", original, system it reconciled both political and judicial powers. The latter being condensed in its "power to decide, by a two-thirds majority, whether there had been a violation of the Convention" (Foster 2011: 46). Despite this possibility, "the practice of the Committee of Ministers was to endorse the Commission report without any further investigation of the merits of the case" (Rainey et al. 2017: 9).

The procedural journey of a case from an application to judgment went through the three organs of the Convention with "considerable overlap between the[ir] competencies" (Rowe & Schlette 1998: 5); it is illustrated in Figure 3.1 (based on Hart 2010: 541).

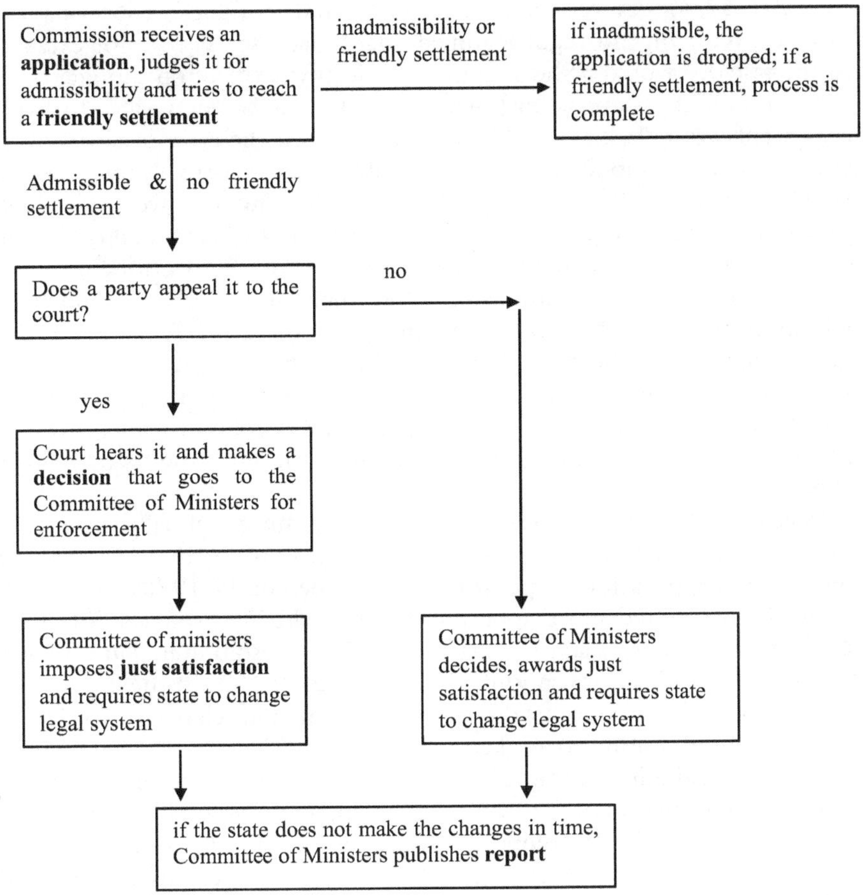

Figure 3.1 The journey of cases in the "old Court" system

Source: Process under the Commission, from Hart, J. (2010) The European Human Rights System. *Law Library Journal*, 102: 541. Reprinted with permission from the American Association of Law Libraries (AALL).

Hart (2010: 541) explains that "[t]he Committee's jurisdiction was the default; the ECtHR's jurisdiction was optional". The Court used to be a part-time organization, too, just like the Commission. The ECtHR's task was to rule on the cases selected by the Commission.

> When hearing cases it was expected that a chamber of seven judges would be convened, but nothing was said as to how a case would be conducted, except that the composition of the Court was to be determined by lot, and a State party to proceedings was entitled to have the judge of its nationality on the bench.
>
> (Bates 2011: 38)

Under Art. 42, judges were paid based on "each day of duty", a sort of a daily allowance, receiving no regular annual salary, because "it was not expected that the caseload would be heavy enough to justify payment on a longer basis" (Hart 2010: 542) as it was imagined to function as "a safety valve for when things went wrong" (Bates 2011: 41). And indeed the early caseload of the ECtHR was quite moderate and comparable with modern numbers in the IACtHR and ACtHPR (see 1.4.1). The initially low numbers were also attributable to the Commission's conservative approach to the admissibility of applications. It pursued the goal of "build[ing] the trust of the governments, which were suspicious of the institutions of enforcement and the right of individual application in particular" (Hart 2010: 543). As the ECtHR judge and former president Robert Spano (2018: 475) stated, the old Court started "from scratch by rendering judgments at the outset into a human rights void where national authorities across the Member States of the Council of Europe, in particular national judges, were not familiar with the legal language of human rights".

There were 138 applications in 1955. This number gradually declined to 104 in 1956, to 101 in 1957 and reached a low of 96 in 1958. Yet, the Commission's approach became steadily more open in the 1970s, "and as the Commission admitted more applications, its credibility grew and the number of applications grew apace" (Hart 2010: 543), resulting in "an explosion of activity under the Convention" (Janis et al. 2008: 22) in the 1980s. The first few years of the Court's work "were performed in relative obscurity, the 'sleeping beauty' waiting to awaken to realise its full potential" (Spano 2018: 475). By the beginning of the 1990s all 22 ratifying states had recognized the contentious jurisdiction of the Court and accepted the right of individual petition, becoming the first portents of a future reform. As Spano conceptualized it, the first 40 years of the Court passed as its "substantive embedding phase" (2018: 475), i.e. in

> a process in which an international court, entrusted by sovereign states with the role of supervising the observation of a collective set of legal norms, by which the states are bound under an international treaty, gives substance to these norms for the primordial purpose of infusing them into the domestic legal systems.

To put it differently, the Court was gradually building the human rights substance and discourse, anchoring these concepts to the legal fabric of Member States.

3.2.2 *The new Court after Protocol no. 11, 1998–2009*

The reform of the Court was a logical consequence of a cultural shift within the Commission and the dissolution of the Soviet Union. When Eastern European communist regimes collapsed, Europe found itself with several new

Western-style democracies, eager to be integrated into the Council of Europe as part of their process of democratization. The democratization of Europe enlarged the pool of potential applicants significantly, which intensified the workload of the original two-tier/three-organ system, where all institutions worked part-time. The European enlargement "was seen as a possible cause of an exponential increase in the number of applications" (Peruzzo 2019b: 19), causing delays in case adjudication. The time was ripe for a reform streamlining the European human rights machinery to process the growing caseload.

The reform path was blazed by Protocol no. 11. On 1 November 1998, Protocol no. 11 abolished the European Commission of Human Rights, lightened the Committee of Ministers of its judicial role, and carved out a new role for the ECtHR, transforming it into the main organ of the Convention. The ECtHR became a permanent and full-time court that could receive applications directly from states, NGOs and individuals. Protocol no. 11 simplified and streamlined the convoluted system of the "old Court" with the overlapping competences of three organs. Another breakthrough of 1998 concerned the right of individual petition (Art. 34), which became an integral part of the Convention system[12] and improved its accessibility. Now individual applicants could apply to the revamped supranational court directly, bringing claims against their governments, and the governments had to accept this scenario without reserve.

Figure 3.2 illustrates the journey of cases from application to judgment under Protocol no. 11, in the period between 1998 and 2009. Each case was assigned a *judge rapporteur*[13] responsible for presenting it to the Court. This rapporteur offered a recommendation on admissibility to a committee of three judges, who then made the initial admissibility decision. Cases unanimously deemed admissible proceeded to a chamber, comprising seven judges, for further admissibility review. The chamber had the authority to rule solely on admissibility or both admissibility and the case's merits. If only admissibility was ruled upon, the case could advance to the Grand Chamber, the highest judicial formation, consisting of 17 judges.

Before long, the "new" Court found itself overwhelmed with an influx of applications. While this was another sign of its ongoing substantive embedding in the national legal systems (Spano 2018), it still forced a reconsideration of the initial optimistic outlook for increased efficiency. Protocol no. 11 improved the delays to some degree, but it did not curb the surge. In just two years, from 1998 to 2000, the pending caseload more than doubled, soaring to 15,900 applications. By 2004, around 50,000 cases were "attributed

12 When the Convention draft was discussed, nine Member States were prepared to include a right of individual petition in the Convention (Belgium, Denmark, France, Ireland, Italy, Luxembourg, Norway, Sweden and Turkey), while three other states (Greece, Netherlands and the United Kingdom) were against it (Bates 2011: 28). Eventually, it was made optional.

13 Note how this multiword term includes the originally French "rapporteur". In fact, many terms in legal English (see Chapter 1) were borrowed from French.

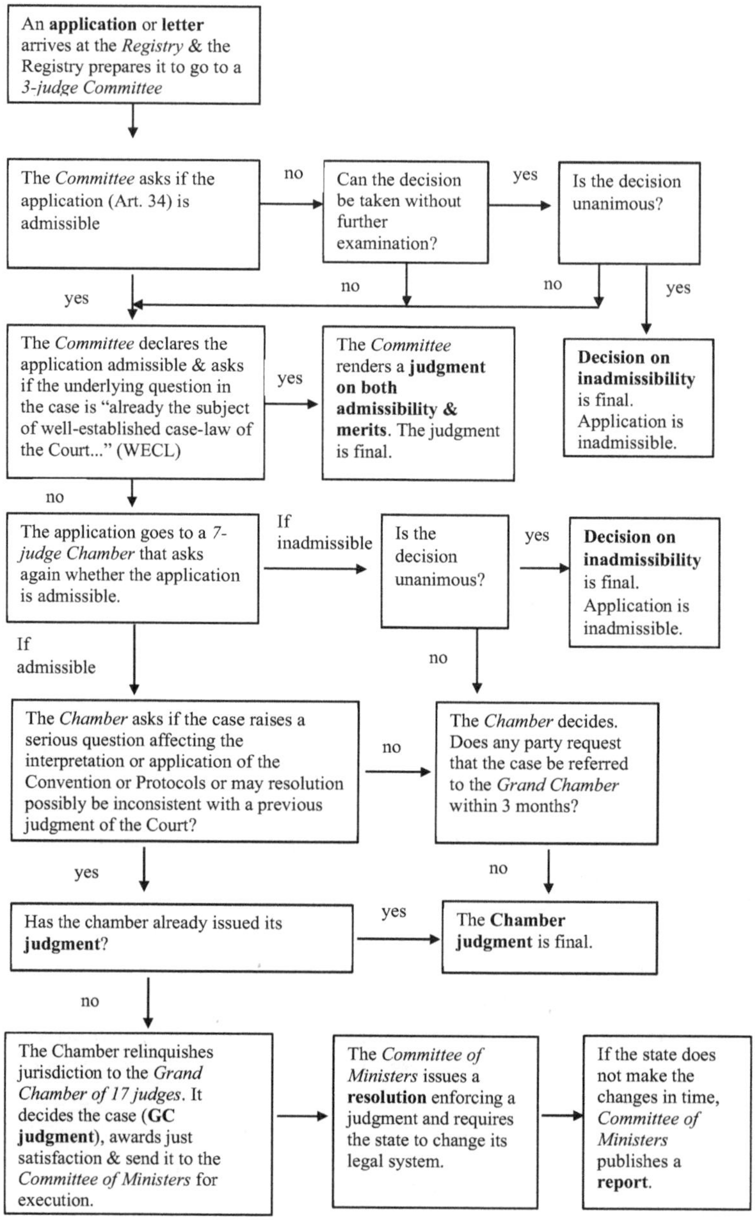

Figure 3.2 Procedural flow after Protocol no. 11

Source: Process under Protocol 11, from Hart, J. (2010) The European Human Rights System. *Law Library Journal*, 102: 547. Reprinted with permission from the American Association of Law Libraries (AALL), with minor typographic changes: the textual products are bolded and the particular judicial formations or other members of the discourse community are italicized.

to a judicial formation", indicating readiness for examination, and this figure excluded over 65,000 cases already lodged but awaiting allocation (Degener 2020). The number of applications continued its relentless climb until 2013 and "soon outstripped the ability of the new institutions to cope" (Hart 2010: 546). Faced with this caseload avalanche, the Court had to generate additional measures to rein it in. Among these, Protocol no. 14 takes centre stage, designed to ensure the sustained efficiency of the ECtHR in the long run.

3.2.3 Protocol no. 14: boosting effectiveness

The changes brought about by Protocol no. 11 had fallen short of the expectations of "unloading" the Court through its restructuring. The Explanatory Report to Protocol no. 14 (CETS no. 194),[14] dated 13 May 2004, explicitly stated that the previous measures "proved inadequate to cope with the new situation", consisting of "a considerable and continuous rise in the number of individual applications" (Council of Europe 2004: 2).

Much of the ECtHR "burgeoning caseload" (Peruzzo 2019b: 19) stemmed from the so-called *systemic problems* generating "repetitive" or "clone" cases fuelled by the same legislative dysfunction, which could be either State-specific or more widespread, such as, for instance, inadequate prison conditions.

In its Position Paper on Proposals for Reform of the ECHR and Other Measures, adopted on 12 September 2003,[15] the Court explicitly warned about the risk of becoming a compensation body for well-founded cases related to a generalized situation already deemed incompatible with Convention standards. Dealing with repetitive cases or systemic violations effectively was identified as one of the primary challenges in the reform process (Degener 2020: para. 14). Protocol no. 14 thus effected change "related more to the functioning of the system rather than to its structure" (Lemmens 2018: 34).

In their own "Clone Wars" the Court had to introduce an innovative mechanism of dealing with repetitive cases. *Nomen omen est*, so instead of calling the new mechanism a "repetitive case procedure", the Court named it the *pilot judgment procedure*, reconceptualizing thus "repetitive" cases as *pilot cases*, i.e. cases that reflected systemic problems. Linguistically speaking, this multiword term is an emblematic case of a jurisprudential creation (see 2.4), i.e. a term created by the discourse community of the Court. Neither the procedure nor the term existed before the Court implemented this procedure to deal with systemic problems, thus "freezing" the flow of repetitive cases. It was exploratory and somewhat experimental, so the term was highly fitting. Inserted under Article 61 of the Rules of Court in 2011, the pilot-judgment procedure

14 Explanatory Report to Protocol No. 14 to the Convention for the Protection of Human Rights and Fundamental Freedoms, amending the control system of the Convention, available at https://rm.coe.int/16800d380f.

15 Position Paper of the European Court of Human Rights on proposals for reform of the European Convention on Human Rights and other measures as set out in the report of the Steering Committee for Human Rights of 4 April 2003 [CDDH-GDR(2003)024].

addresses "large groups of identical cases that derive from the same underlying problem" (ECHR 2009: 1).[16]

The Steering Committee on Human Rights decided against including the pilot-judgment procedure provision in the Convention through Protocol no. 14. On 12 May 2004, as part of measures accompanying Protocol no. 14, the Committee of Ministers adopted Resolution (2004)3 on judgments revealing an underlying systemic problem,[17] inviting the Court:

> as far as possible, to identify, in its judgments finding a violation of the Convention, what it considers to be underlying systemic problem and the source of this problem, in particular when it is likely to give rise to numerous applications, so as to assist states in finding the appropriate solution and the Committee of Ministers in supervising the execution of judgments (Resolution of the Committee of Ministers on judgments revealing an underlying systemic problem, CM/Res(2004)3).

Despite the lack of its formal textual inclusion, the pilot judgment procedure became "a reform measure intended to increase the embedded nature of Convention principles where systemic flaws in national law and practice are found to exist" (Spano 2018: 477).

The original goal of Protocol no. 14 was to enable the ECtHR to cope with "the landslide of cases that threatened to crush it" (Hart 2010: 546). It could only come into force if all the contracting parties acceded to or ratified it. This was not the case with Russia,[18] which ratified it only on 18 February 2010, enabling it to come into force on 1 June 2010. This marked a new era in the Court history. Besides the pilot-judgment procedure, the reform introduced new "filtering" rules and a prioritization policy as well as a new admissibility criterion aimed at trimming down the sprouting of incoming applications: the so-called *significant disadvantage* criterion.[19] As with the original text of the Convention, its newest modifications and jurisprudential creations were keen on indeterminate adjectives, emphasizing the importance of the Court's interpretation to bestow them with meaning.

Another novelty of Protocol no. 14 was the green light given to the European Union (EU) to accede to the ECHR, which became "the most momentous change" (Hart 2010: 550) of Protocol no. 14. Originally established to promote a free market system, the EU soon started to encounter cases dealing

16 ECHR Information note issued by the Registrar (2009), "Pilot-Judgment Procedure", available at https://www.echr.coe.int/documents/d/echr/pilot_judgment_procedure_eng.

17 https://search.coe.int/cm/Pages/result_details.aspx?ObjectID=09000016805dd190.

18 The Russian Federation ceased being a member of the Council of Europe in March 2022.

19 Art. 35 ECHR has been updated to state that the application is deemed inadmissible if "the applicant has not suffered a significant disadvantage unless respect for human rights as defined in the Convention and the Protocols thereto requires an examination of the application on the merits and provided that no case may be rejected on this ground which has not been duly considered by a domestic tribunal".

with human rights in the case-law of the European Court of Justice (ECJ). The logical conclusion was that "the fundamental freedoms of human rights are inextricably bound to the freedom to act as a player in a free market system" (Hart 2010: 550).

The journey of cases from an application to a judgment under Protocol no. 14 is illustrated in Figure 3.3. This is the mechanism that has remained largely unchanged[20] from a procedural point of view as concerns the Court's judicial formations; consequently, these are addressed in a separate section.

3.2.4 *Evolving into subsidiarity, margin of appreciation and advisory opinions*

The adoption of Protocol no. 14 in 2010 and the intergovernmental conferences held in Interlaken, Izmir and Brighton in the period from 2010 to 2012 marked a change in the Court's trajectory towards the so-called "procedural embedding phase" (Spano 2018: 480), with

> the Court taking on a more framework oriented role when reviewing domestic decision making. This review is process-based in the sense that the Court is increasingly examining whether Convention principles have, in fact, been adequately embedded in the domestic legal order and, if so, whether certain material elements allow it to grant deference to national authorities so they can fulfill their duties as the primary guarantors of Convention rights as required by Article 1 of the Convention.

Change, like a river sculpting the landscape, carves pathways for progress, and the Court's evolution has never stopped. The most tangible outputs of the reform were five political Declarations issued by the High Contracting Parties: Interlaken, Izmir, Brighton, Brussels, and Copenhagen. These generated three Protocols: nos. 14, 15 and 16, even if Protocol no. 14 was negotiated before the beginning of the reform.

While the seeds of the majority of the Convention's principles, including "the living instrument doctrine, the principle of autonomy of Convention rights, the principle of effectiveness, and, crucially, the principle of subsidiarity and its functional tool, the margin of appreciation" (Spano 2018: 476) were sown in the 1970s and 1980s by the "old" Commission-Court tandem, officially the last two items on the list were incorporated into the preamble of the Convention through Protocol no. 15. The Protocol was drafted in 2013, effectively opening the Court to an "age of subsidiarity" (Spano 2018: 487), but due to a delay in ratifications it entered into force only on 1 August 2021. Subsidiarity "emphasizes that human rights must be protected above all within the domestic sphere" (Villiger 2017: para. 33).

20 But for the initial application that cannot be done under form of a letter anymore (see Chapter 4), along with different pre-application parameters such as the admissibility criteria changes.

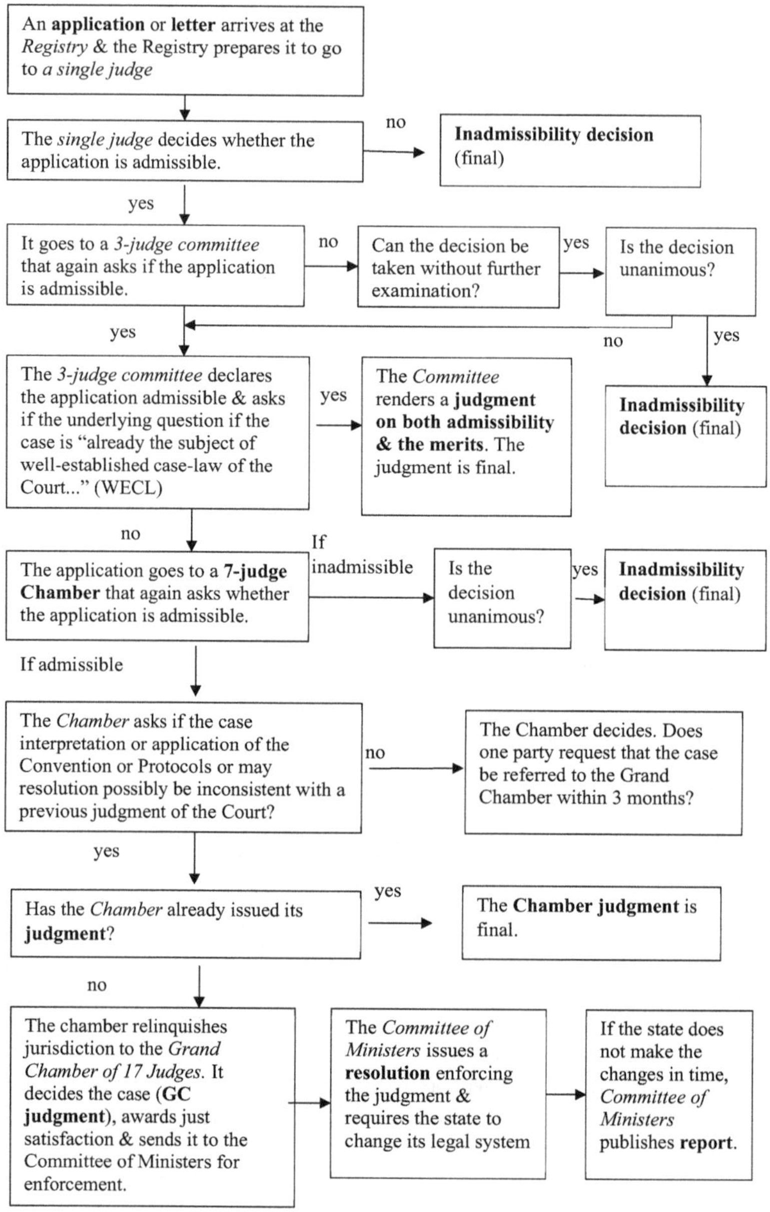

Figure 3.3 Procedural flow under Protocol no. 14

Source: Process under Protocol 14, from Hart, J. (2010). The European human rights system. *Law Library Journal*, 102: 549. Reprinted with permission from the American Association of Law Libraries (AALL), with minor typographic changes: the textual products of the judicial activity are bolded and added where absent from the original diagram; the judicial formations or other members of the discourse community are italicized.

Much legal, political and societal commentary has been dedicated to the duet of subsidiarity and margin of appreciation. Put in simplified terms, these denote room for manoeuvre, state deference, "room for domestic differences" (Madsen 2021: 93) or "elbowroom for states" (Molbæk-Steensig 2023: 85). As can be logically derived, part of the quest for institutionalizing subsidiarity was triggered by political considerations, an emblematic example being the government of the United Kingdom lambasting the ECtHR for what "they saw as expansionist tendencies in Strasbourg at the expense of legitimate domestic institutions, legal as well as political" (Madsen 2021: 95) in the period preceding the Brighton Declaration in 2012.

The Court has steadfastly adhered to the doctrine of margin of appreciation since its earliest days as an expression of subsidiarity. Yet these were external political pressures aiming to redefine the equilibrium between domestic and European institutions, coupled with internal challenges in managing a substantial influx of petitions that have prompted a renewed emphasis on subsidiarity (Madsen 2021: 96).

Peculiarly, the Court has not provided definitions for the above multiword terms, relying again on a certain degree of vagueness and indeterminacy in a strategic way. Studies using statistical methods of corpus linguistics (see, e.g. Madsen 2018 and Molbæk-Steensig 2023) overview the incidence of "margin of appreciation" across the time spanning from 1960 to 2021[21] and its correlation with the newfound principle of subsidiarity, concluding that its use increased along with the increase in cases. This tool is not devoid of criticisms; e.g. it has been defined to be "as slippery and elusive as an eel" (Lester 1998: 75) or "empty" and not necessarily resulting in increased deference (Molbæk-Steensig 2023: 86). It falls beyond the scope of this chapter to delve into the legal details of these principles.

Protocol no. 15 resulted also in some procedural amendments reducing the time limit for applying to the Court after a final national decision was reached from six to four months as part of the so-called admissibility criteria. Finally, during the same year, Protocol no. 16 was also adopted, providing the option for the highest domestic courts and tribunals to seek ***advisory opinions*** from the Court on fundamental questions related to the interpretation or application of the rights and freedoms outlined in the Convention and its protocols. While the advisory opinions in its American and African sister institutions have been practiced for quite some time, for the ECtHR it is a new development.

21 Madsen (2018) uses a more limited dataset of judgments delivered between 2009 and 2015 and counts the incidence of "margin of appreciation" per 1,000,000 words, whereas Molbæk-Steensig (2023) extends it to judgments issued between 1960 to 2021, analysing the recurrence of the MWT per judgment, rather than per a prefixed normalization base. While Molbæk-Steensig's (2023) study is more finely tuned as concerns her analytical methods, both come to consonant conclusions in the period covered by both studies.

The Court is constantly "seeking to balance the quality of its case law with the efficiency of its proceedings" (Keller & Heri 2018: para. 84), striving to achieve a form of zen in all its endeavours and judicial formations.

3.3 Procedure and judicial formations of the ECtHR

Today "the most prolific regional human rights body in the world" (Keller & Heri 2018: para. 1) operates according to the flowchart enacted with Protocol no. 14 (see Figure 3.3). The first judicial formation coming into contact with initial applications are the so-called *single judges* (and not a committee anymore). Protocol no. 14 kept the judicial nature of this filtering stage, but reduced the number of judges to one.[22] Single judges can render final admissibility decisions in individual cases. They are assisted by non-judicial rapporteurs – Registry lawyers – with knowledge of the language and the legal system of the respondent State (see Chapter 5). The underlying rationale was "to release the manpower that is currently tied up by having committees of three judges examine applications for admissibility" (Hart 2010: 548).

The Court's judicial manpower is organized in Sections, "administrative entities made up of either nine or ten judges. [. . .] Sections are formed by the president of the Court, and set up for a fixed period of time by the plenary Court (Art 25 (b) ECHR)" (Keller & Heri 2018: para. 6).[23] Currently there are five sections. As the former President of the ECtHR, Jean-Paul Costa (2021: 319), explains in his didactic memoir:

> Sections, which did not exist prior to 1998, quickly forged a strong sense of identity that has been enhanced by the friendly relations within each one, with activities such as group lunches and dinners from time to time, or the organisation by judges of trips to their home countries or elsewhere. In addition to the nine or ten judges making up each Section there is a Section Registrar and Deputy Registrar, together with two Section secretaries. It is thus a closely-knit and united formation.

The case allocation correlates with the case-processing unit members' language abilities and their knowledge of the respective domestic legal system. As Keller and Heri (2018) note, Registry members need to be familiar with the relevant language and legal system because "the national judge may not necessarily be

22 Ironically, in the "old" system, when the admissibility decision was taken by the Commission, it "originally required the authority of the *whole* Commission" (Bates 2011: 35, original emphasis).

23 They further explain how "Each Section deals with at least one of the Member States from which the most cases come before the Court – as of early 2018, the six highest case-count States were Romania, Russia, Turkey, Ukraine, Italy, and Hungary, which were responsible, respectively, for 18 per cent, 14 per cent, 13 per cent, 13 per cent, 8 per cent, and 6 per cent of the Court's caseload (ECtHR, Analysis of Statistics 2017, 8) – as way of ensuring a fair division of labour" (Keller & Heri 2018: para. 6).

the judge rapporteur on the case in the Chamber proceedings, and is never the judge rapporteur in the Grand Chamber proceedings", in addition to the fact that applicants may initially address the Court in any of the languages of the Council of Europe Member States (Rule 34).

If a case is deemed admissible, it is referred either to a *Committee* of three judges or a *Chamber* comprising seven judges. These judges are selected from a particular Section, the Court's administrative unit. *Committees* have the authority to determine admissibility, and if the decision is affirmative, the committee may then issue a judgment addressing both admissibility and the substance of the case. However, this dual decision is only applicable to cases related to subjects already well-established in the Court's case-law (WECL), i.e. repetitive cases. The Explanatory Report to Protocol no. 14 defines WECL as "[case law] which has been consistently applied by a Chamber", even if by just one judgment "on a question of principle [. . .] particularly when the Grand Chamber has rendered it" (Council of Europe, Explanatory Report to Protocol no. 14, para 68[24]). Committees thus play a decisive role in deflating the amount of "clone" cases on the Court's docket. Unanimity among committee members is required for the decision to be conclusive. The judgments delivered by a Committee are final and cannot be appealed to either a Chamber or the Grand Chamber.

Applications deemed admissible (or not clearly inadmissible) but not falling under the established case-law of the Court are directed to a *Chamber*, composed of seven judges (Rule 26 of the ECtHR's Rules of Court), which decides by a majority. These seven judges include the President of the Section to which the case was allocated, a "national" judge, i.e. the judge whose nationality coincides with that of the Respondent State, and five other judges designated by the Section President. In this case, "[e]ach application is assigned to the case-lawyer (who must have a command of both the language of the application and the legal system of the State in question)" (Garlicki 2009: 393) and "the Section President (acting together with the Section Registrar) appoints the Judge Rapporteur" (Garlicki 2009: 393). Chambers are responsible for making decisions on both admissibility and merits for individual applications. Additionally, in interstate cases, Chambers are entrusted with the initial determination of admissibility and may subsequently decide on both admissibility and merits. It is crucial to note that decisions on these two aspects in interstate cases must be made independently.

The highest judicial body within the ECtHR is the *Grand Chamber*, comprising 17 judges, including the Court President, Vice-Presidents, Presidents of the five Sections, the national judge, and additional judges chosen pursuant to the Court's rules. The Grand Chamber handles a relatively limited number of cases compared to other ECtHR formations. Notably, cases are not directly assigned to the Grand Chamber, and instead, they must be either relinquished by a Chamber (Art. 30 ECHR) or referred to it by any party involved in

24 https://rm.coe.int/16800d380f.

the case (Art. 43 ECHR). In cases previously heard by a Chamber, only the national judge and the Section President sit in the Grand Chamber formation for the same case (Rule 24(2)(d)). If a case is relinquished, the entire original Chamber formation is incorporated into the Grand Chamber formation (Rule 24(2)(c)).

For a case to reach the Grand Chamber, a party must request the referral, and a panel of five Grand Chamber judges will consider the request. The panel will accept the request only if the case raises a substantial question impacting the interpretation or application of the Convention or its protocols, or if it involves a significant issue of general importance. Only under these circumstances will the Grand Chamber rule on the case. Both the relinquishment of jurisdiction and referral to the Grand Chamber are viable options when the case raises a substantial question regarding the interpretation or application of the relevant legal provisions. Relinquishment could also be activated to avoid a situation when the Chamber rules in a way clashing with previous case-law.

Talking about the institutional context, judicial formations and procedures at the ECtHR is challenging without describing its discursive practices and genres. Most of the Court's "production" is gathered today in HUDOC, the ECtHR proprietary database. The database "dates back to the late 1990s and has constantly been developed with the aim of becoming more user-friendly (one aspect being the search refiners or filters)" (Brannan 2021: 218). Available free of charge, as per Rule 104A, HUDOC[25] is accessible through the Court's website and is organized around the Court's genres.

3.4 Genres at the ECtHR

3.4.1 Genre theory: methodological considerations

To talk of legal language in international courts is to talk of "usefully distinguishable" legal genres (Bhatia 1983: 227) embedded in a strictly defined "social-institutional context, including the lawyers and judges who work there and are actively involved in judicial decision-making, and the linguistic realisation of such legal processes" (Nikitina 2018a: 110). Each genre has specific, if often related, features. Genre "comprises a class of communicative events, the members of which share some set of communicative purposes" (Swales 1990: 58). Bhatia (1993: 13) defines genre as

> [a] recognizable communicative event characterized by a set of communicative purpose(s) identified and mutually understood by the members of the professional or academic community in which it regularly occurs. Most often it is highly structured and conventionalized with constraints on allowable contributions in terms of their intent, positioning, form and functional value. These constraints, however, are often exploited

25 http://hudoc.echr.coe.int.

by the expert members of the discourse community to achieve private intentions within the framework of socially recognized purpose(s).

Another discipline-specific definition of genre recites that "genre is conceived as a notion that includes formal aspects (conventionalised forms), sociocultural aspects (social occasions) and cognitive aspects (purposes of the participants)" (Borja Albi 2013: 36). Genre is seen, thus, as "the nexus between an individual's actions and a socially defined context" (Devitt 2004: 31), imbued with "reciprocal dynamic within which individuals' actions construct and are reconstructed by recurring context of situation, context of culture and context of genres" (Devitt 2004: 31). Legal scholars dealing with genres and texts conceptualize the latter as "instruments of knowledge" and the former as "the encasements for those texts" (Rappaport 2014: 197).

Members of a particular discourse community have the knowledge that is needed to communicate successfully. This *genre knowledge* is conveyed through repertoires of "situationally appropriate responses to recurrent situations" (Berkenkotter & Huckin 1995: ix), acquired through communication in the context of a given professional and discourse community.

If "life is a theatre set in which there are but few practicable entrances" (Victor Hugo),[26] in a legal institutional context, these entrances are ensured by legal genres (Rappaport 2014: 204) explored by different stakeholders belonging to the professional and discourse communities, just like a script is explored by theatre performers.

Based on Bhatia's pivotal definition of "genre", the genre analysis grid employed here capitalizes on the broader societal contextualization of the ECtHR and its discourse in Sections 3.1–3.3. The premise is that all genres under discussion are set against the communicative setting – or the "theatre set" – of the professional and discourse community of the ECtHR. The analytical grid, thus, focuses on the following elements.

1 **Genre placement**: macro-category or genre set (core, operational, procedural or derived); genre denomination (in the official languages of the ECtHR); subgenre(s), if any; genre status (public or occluded).
2 **Communicative situation**: purpose/function; participation framework (senders, receivers).
3 **Conventionalized form**: linguistic regime (drafted in English and/or French, translated, etc.); structure (moves and steps, aka "the script"); lexicogrammatical features.

As concerns genre placement, professional and institutional genres do not exist in isolation but rather are intertwined and interrelated. Besides the

26 Hugo, V. Chapter IV: "The back room of Café Musain." *Les Misérables*. http://www.cartage.org.lb/en/themes/BookLibrary/books/bibliographie/H/Hugovictor/LesMiserables/VolumeIII-Marius/book4/ch4.htm.

general genre types, discussed in 1.3, multiple scholars in Genre Studies have devoted significant attention to the description of genre placement and categorizations. From a more general perspective of Genre Studies, Bazerman (1994) distinguishes between the hierarchical concepts of *the genre set* and *the system of genres*. The former represents "only the work of one side of a multiple person interaction" (1994: 98), while the latter stands for "the interrelated genres that interact with each other in specific settings" (1994: 97). The system of genres typically includes genres from multiple genre sets.

Bhatia (2014: 62–63) adds to these categories a third, vaster, level of *domain-specific disciplinary genres*, which in the case of human rights discourse would refer to "a larger set of professional legal genres" in use by the legal professionals in general. In other words, these genres would not be ECtHR specific, but rather derive from the general legal culture. Bhatia (2014: 63) summarizes this three-tier system as follows:

> "Genre set" incorporates a class of typical professional genres that a particular professional engages in as part of his or her routine professional activity (Devitt 1991). "Genre system" represents a complete set of discursive forms that are invoked by all the participants involved in a professional activity. "Disciplinary genres" extend such a system to include all those discursive forms that are invoked in all professional practices associated with a particular disciplinary or professional domain.

As every international court, the ECtHR operates through a system of legal genres that "interact with each other" (Bazerman 1994: 97). Building on Bhatia (2006, 2014), I outlined a taxonomy of genre types in the discourse of human rights courts in Chapter 1, distinguishing between *core* or *primary genres* (as represented by ECHR and other human rights treaties), *operational genres* (i.e. Rules of Court), *procedural genres* (pertaining to the proceedings) and *derived genres* (that do not concern the proceedings but run in parallel with them). These macro-categories can be referred to here as genre sets. Whereas Chapter 1 provided a general description of the hierarchical relationship among these genre types across the three supranational human rights courts, the following sections will outline different genres in the ECtHR context specifically, focusing on procedural and derived genres.

A relevant factor for the operation of any supranational court is the distinction between genres that are publicly available and genres that are hidden from the eyes of stakeholders outside of the institutional community. Researching academic genres, Swales (1996) labelled the latter as "occluded genres" (Swales 1996). This very eloquent term denotes those genres that are somewhat hidden, under-researched and rarely spoken of, as "[o]n the one hand, they are typically formal documents which remain on file; on the other, they are rarely part of the public record", operating "out of sight" of the general public (Swales 1996: 46). In supranational courts, these genres remain "a kind of adjudicative 'dark matter' [. . .] invisible to most scholars and political actors with opinions on the Court" (Molbæk-Steensig 2023: 94). Occluded genres, such as decisions on striking out applications from the list of pending cases under Art. 37, remain "the most invisible part of the already hidden part of the iceberg" (Lambert-Abdelgawad 2018: 8). The following discussion includes both public or open-access genres and occluded genres, shedding light on the latter, where possible.

As concerns the communicative situation, it comprises the notions of communicative goals and participation framework. The communicative goal describes the reasons underlying the creation of a given text. For example, for some of the procedural genres, it can be the inception of proceedings or their advancement to the next phase, whereas for derived genres communicative goals may range from knowledge dissemination to popularization to the lay public. Participation framework is a concept originally developed in sociolinguistics by Erving Goffman (1981). As the term suggests, it deals with a definition of who the participants are based on their ability or inability to act within a communicative event, as well as their rights and obligations to do so in a certain way. For example, a distinction can be made between senders and receivers (Borja et al. 2009: 70), just like theatre actors and public.

The conventionalized form describes a recognizable and fixed structure that genres inherently possess. A theatre play may deal with different subject matters, but it will always be recognized as a theatre play. Along the same lines, a judgment will be recognized as a judgment irrespective of its subject matter. Genre theorists describe this conventionalized form using the concepts of rhetorical moves and steps. *Move* is a term created in the LSP Genre Studies by Swales (1990). It is used to indicate a certain pattern in a text that realizes a given rhetorical function, and *step* is a smaller structural unit within a move which fulfils the communicative function of the move. The total of all the moves serves the overall communicative purpose of the genre. As legal discourse revels in the use of formal, ritualistic formulae, it comes as no surprise that some moves and genres can be described using specific lexicogrammatical patterns.

3.4.2 *Procedural genres at the ECtHR*

Building on Rainey et al. (2017: 17–56) who outline the ECtHR procedure in a detailed way, I supplement their description with a Critical Genre Analysis outlook. As Hart (2017: 1) observed, "it is procedures that create the need to record or communicate. In other words, documents emanate from critical junctures in a process". Figure 3.4 illustrates a number of such critical junctures in the ECtHR procedure, which involves a sequence of actions to be carried out by the Applicant, the Respondent State and the Court itself. These actions translate into a specific procedural genre set. For the sake of convenience, procedural genres will be divided into three macro-categories in this book: genres referring to the inception of cases (dealt in more detail in Chapters 4 and 5), the intermediate or core stage of pleadings (described in Chapter 6) and the final stage of decisions and judgments (outlined in Chapters 7 and 8).

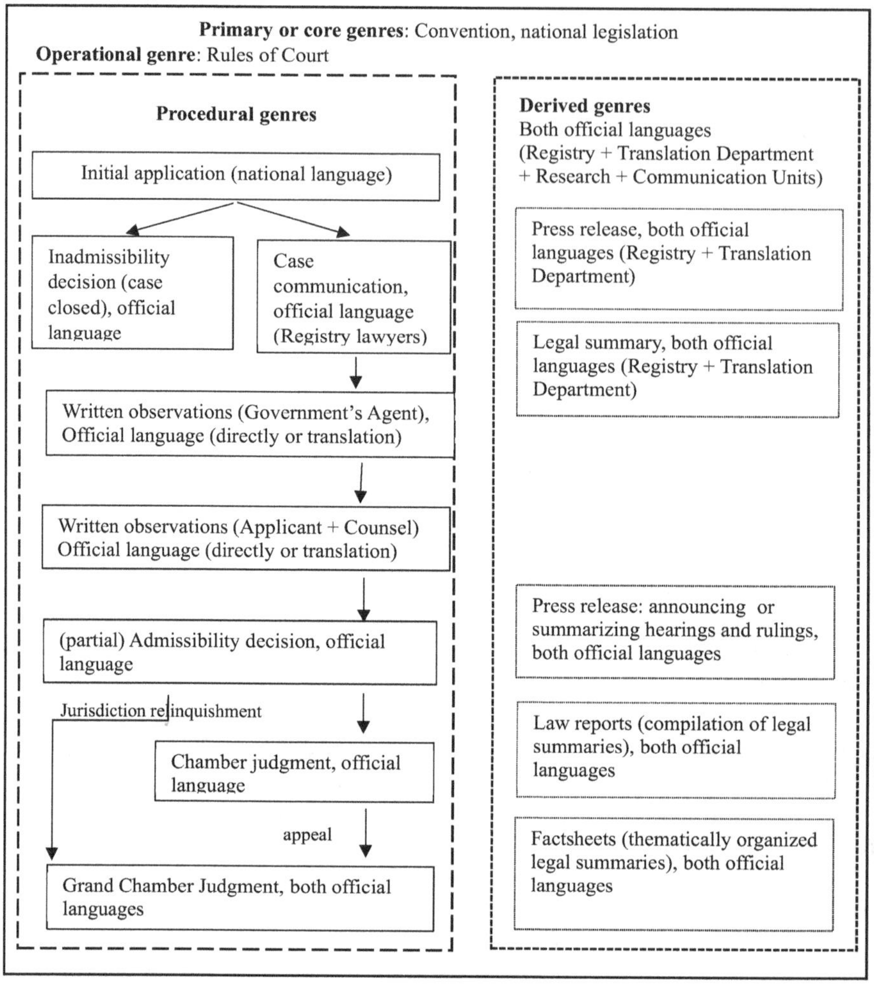

Figure 3.4 The system of genres at the ECtHR

The life of cases at the ECtHR starts with an *application* (*recours* in French). The only way for a case to be born is through the submission of an application. To clarify, the ECtHR lacks the authority to independently initiate cases; instead, it possesses jurisdiction to adjudicate matters related to alleged violations of the ECHR upon receiving applications from individuals or States. The application-derived process may differentiate the ECtHR from some other international jurisdictions. For example, at the International Criminal Court (ICC), the Office of the Prosecutor can start to investigate a situation *proprio motu*. This is not the case with the ECtHR. It used to be possible to make the initial contact with the court through a letter. However, after the publication of Lord Woolf's report in 2005[27] (see Chapter 4), this possibility was abolished, leaving only the genre of the official application form. The latter can be submitted in any national or even minority language of the CoE Member States (Brannan 2018: 171; Nikitina 2018b: 33; Peruzzo 2019b: 35). The application form in itself is a public genre, easily retrievable by anyone with Internet access. However, the way it is filled-in is occluded: filled applications are not publicly available through HUDOC, the Court's database. Upon the receipt of the application, it is "examined by a Registry lawyer who makes the first assessment as to its importance and admissibility" (Garlicki 2009: 393). The Registry currently counts 33 divisions (Peruzzo 2019b: 24), made up of 640 staff members, including lawyers and administrative staff, along with technical staff and translators (ECtHR, ECHR Registry[28]). These divisions may process applications and then assign them to a Section. After this step, the application will be allocated either to a single judge, a Committee or a Chamber based on the type of applicant and the admissibility criteria check.

The second genre in the procedural chain is that of a *case communication* (Nikitina 2022a, 2022b), logically and intertextually deriving its existence from a previous admissibility decision. If the application is deemed admissible, the ECtHR Registry lawyers create a document addressed to the Respondent Government informing them of the case initiated against them and asking them questions that trigger the following written procedure. In contrast to the initial application which can be lodged in any language of the CoE, case communications are drafted in one of the official languages, which involves a significant amount of information processing and re-elaboration across different languages and legal systems. This genre is not occluded in per se, but little is known about its generic makeup which underwent some changes in the recent years (see Chapter 5).

The third distinct genre is called *written observations* (*observations écrites*) or *written pleadings* (Nikitina 2018a, 2018b, see Chapter 6). These occupy the central part of the proceedings. In these documents, the Government answers the Court's questions formulated at the case communication stage and presents its version. Then the Applicant (or rather the Applicant's Counsel) is invited to reply. These documents have to be produced in either English or French, so most Parties whose native language differs from the official ones either recur to a second language (L2) drafting or commission independent translations of a variable quality (Nikitina 2018a). Despite the centrality of this genre for the procedure, it is occluded and not available to the general public, unless a specific request is made to the Registry. Even then, some files will be denied consultation based on their circumstances and priority status.

27 The official title of the report is "Review of the Working Methods of the European Court of Human Rights", available at https://www.echr.coe.int/documents/d/echr/2005_lord_woolf_working_methods_eng.

28 https://www.echr.coe.int/documents/d/echr/Registry_ENG.

Once the written observations from the parties have been received, along with drafts and other documents that may aid the Chamber and its President in carrying out their duties, the judge rapporteur presents a ***report on admissibility***.[29] Little is known about the generic makeup of these reports. Just as written pleadings, this intermediate genre remains occluded (Swales 1996). The occluded nature is partially attributable to the very figure of the judge rapporteur, whose identity is not disclosed to the external world for security reasons (Costa 2021: 319, fn. 11). Much of the report makeup will derive from the situational cognition and professional background of the judge rapporteur. By being the person who normally knows the case the best (Costa 2021: 319–321), they will inevitably rely on their background discursive competence in producing the report. When a case is under consideration by a Chamber, the judge rapporteur typically aligns with "the national judge since he/she has the highest expertise in the national law and in the national context" (Garlicki 2009: 393). Remarkably, the national judge cannot take on the role of judge rapporteur in cases heard by the Grand Chamber.

The next genre in the procedural genre set is represented by ***admissibility*** or ***inadmissibility decisions*** (***décision de recevabilité*** or ***décision d'irrecevabilité***). These are drafted in one of the official languages and, if flagged as key cases, i.e. a selection of the most important judgments and decisions (Brannan 2021: 219), are translated into the other official language. Peculiarly, inadmissibility decisions rendered by single judges are not included in HUDOC (Molbæk-Steensig 2023: 93), making them an occluded genre. Single-judge inadmissibility decisions are unburdened from a deliberation stage, "as the decision issued in such cases is drafted by the non-judicial rapporteur and approved by the single judge" (Keller & Heri 2018: para. 24), up to the point where it was criticized as constituting a mere "rubber stamping" (Shelton 2016). Even if for most legal-doctrinal scholars, these may lack the thrill of innovative interpretations, and although the Court does not refer to these cases in its reasoning in other cases, "[f]or practitioners and potential applicants, however, it is crucial to keep these cases in mind, as more than 90 per cent of all applications will be rejected, struck off the list or declared inadmissible for the same reasons as accorded in these cases" (Molbæk-Steensig 2023: 94).[30] (Partial) admissibility and inadmissibility decisions rendered after the single-judge phrase are part of the public record. In general, separate admissibility decisions are uncommon in the ECtHR practice, as this aspect may be covered also by the judgment on the merits (Villiger 2017: para. 3).

29 As the report is used internally, it is not included in Figure 2.4.

30 She goes on explaining that "[a]nother category of cases which are not made public is those rejected under Rule 47, which came into force with the 2014 changes to the Rules of the Court and the introduction of an online application form. This change enabled the Registry to reject cases at an earlier stage if any information or documents were missing" (Molbæk-Steensig 2023: 94).

Linguistically speaking, the distinction between the terms *judgment* (*arrêt*) and *decision* (*décision*) is relevant to the ECtHR discourse. In general legal discourse, these two terms are treated as synonyms. *Black's Law Dictionary*, for instance, uses one to explain the other.[31] However, in the ECtHR discourse the terms are not synonymous, up to the point that the Court indicated so in its popularizing brochure "The ECtHR in 50 questions"[32] under Question 37: "A decision is usually given by a single judge, a Committee or a Chamber of the Court. It concerns only admissibility and not the merits of the case. Normally, a Chamber examines the admissibility and merits of an application at the same time; it will then deliver a judgment" (ECtHR in 50 questions 2021: 9).

The next procedural genre is *judgment* (*arrêt*), which can be subdivided into three subgenres by the judicial formation delivering the judgment: judgments rendered by Committees, Chambers or the Grand Chamber (see Chapter 7). The "communicative situation may be considered invariable in all the resulting sub-genres" (Peruzzo 2019b: 57). All three may either find or not find a violation. All are open-access public genres. Yet, their linguistic regimes may vary. *Committee* and *Chamber judgments* are normally drafted in one official language and, if selected as key cases, can be translated into the other. *Grand Chamber judgments* by contrast are available in both official languages with equal authenticity, even though in practice one of the language versions is typically a translation (Brannan 2018: 172). Their deliberative process is also formation specific. Committee cases typically bypass voting procedures: instead judges receive a draft judgment or decision prepared by a case lawyer within the Registry, who is well versed in the legal system and language of the country involved. Judges are then given a deadline by which they can express their agreement or disagreement with the proposed text. As a result, Committee sessions generally do not involve meetings or discussions unless one of the three judges requests it. If an agreement cannot be reached, the case will be transferred to the Chamber formation (Keller & Heri 2018: para. 25).

A Chamber or a Grand Chamber judgment, by contrast, is subject to deliberation. Prior to the start of deliberations at the Chamber level, the judges are provided with a substantial dossier from the Registry, including a preliminary draft judgment or decision. Consequently, when the Chamber convenes – always on a Tuesday – the judges initiate their discussions with a specific proposal for resolving the case at hand, which is then examined further. Conversely, in the Grand Chamber, a preliminary draft judgment or

31 *Black's Law Dictionary* defines "judgment" as "the official and authentic decision of a court of justice upon the respective rights and claims of the parties to an action or suit therein litigated and sub- mitted to its determination" (https://thelawdictionary.org/judgment/) and "decision" as "In practice. A judgment or decree pronounced by a court in settlement of a controversy submitted to it" (https://thelawdictionary.org/decision/).

32 Available at https://www.echr.coe.int/documents/d/echr/50questions_eng.

decision is not provided when deliberations begin. Instead, the judges initiate their proceedings based on the rapporteur judge's memorandum and the diverse reports compiled by the Registry (see Chapter 7 for details).

Linguistic studies with a genre element tend to cluster around this most recognizable genre at the peak of the procedural genre set (Weston 2005; White 2009; Nikitina 2019d; Peruzzo 2019a, 2019b), on account of its easy retrievability and comparability with national judgments.

ECtHR judgments may be followed by ***separate judicial opinions***. Their communicative purpose is to convey disagreement with the majority opinion, represented by the judgment, either as concerns the final decision or the reasoning that led to it. In terms of their participation framework, these separate opinions are drafted by individual judges, not organized into judicial formations, and they address other judges on the panel. However, as separate opinions are drafted by judges who are "not bound by the straightjacket of the majority judgement" (Bruinsma 2006: 360), these frequently become enthralling reading material, thus extending the receivers of this genre to general legal scholarship and, at times, even media. Their nature makes it difficult to outline their generic makeup, but some regularities are traced in Chapter 8, along with a description of their style and lexicogrammar.

Finally, a novelty introduced by Protocol no. 16 is the ***advisory opinion***. These opinions do not deal with any active or pending cases in the Court's docket (Art. 47 (2) ECHR), and instead are requested by the Member States' high courts on "questions of principle relating to the interpretation or application of the rights and freedoms defined in the Convention or the protocols thereto" (Art. 1, Prot. 16 ECHR).

3.4.3 Derived genres at the ECtHR

Besides procedural genres, the system includes so-called ***derived*** genres (Nikitina 2019a: 59), i.e. those genres that derive their existence from other genres within the system, but do not pertain to either core, operational or procedural sets. These genres exist in parallel with the other categories, as illustrated in Figure 3.4. Derived genres are public or open-access genres *par excellence*, as they are prepared for knowledge dissemination purposes, "to assist in understanding the Court's Case-law and the official texts" (ECtHR 2023a: 4).[33] In other words, their communicative goal is to reach vaster audiences going beyond the ECtHR boundaries: legal practitioners preparing themselves to apply to the Court, legal scholars analysing the ECtHR case-law, media professionals interested in covering some of the cases, which has been a frequent practice with landmark judgments (***arrêts marquants***), and audience at large, as human rights discourse has acquired increased popularity through Internet-enabled access to previously inaccessible texts.

33 European Court of Human Rights: Finding and understanding the case-law (2023), available at https://www.echr.coe.int/documents/d/echr/clip_finding_understanding_case_law_eng.

In terms of their participation framework, these are prepared by the Court personnel, typically the Registry of the Court, and may aim at intra-specialist, inter-specialist and even popularized communication (see 9.2), marking different levels of scientific and specialized exposition. In contrast to procedural genres, derived genres do not follow a logical flow but rather exist in a cluster.

Case-law information notes (CLIN, *notes d'information sur la jurisprudence de la Cour*) is one of such genres. Prepared monthly by the Registry lawyers and translated by the Court's Translation Department (Brannan 2021: 219), CLIN aimed at providing a thematic list of cases. This genre has been discontinued in 2022, when the Court's Knowledge Sharing platform (https://ks.echr.coe.int/) was launched, which still provides information on legal cases, but in a different way, relying on hypertextual text presentation (see 9.3).

Legal summaries (*Résumés juridiques*) of cases is another derived genre using which the Registry lawyers prepare summaries of judgments, decisions and communicated cases that are expected to spike particular interest. They are organized by thematic criteria – ECHR articles and keywords – and have descriptive headnotes that facilitate their retrieval. The intended audience is composed of legal practitioners, consequently legal summaries are emblematic examples of legal discourse, presenting facts and law in a concise way[34] with emphasis on the legal reasoning of the Court. They are accessible using the Court's database HUDOC. Just like CLIN, legal summaries are translated into the other official language of the Court, if need be, by the Court's Translation Department (Brannan 2021: 219). However, HUDOC also features a collection of legal summaries translated into non-official languages (*NOL Legal Summaries/Résumés juridiques NOL*).

Multilingual factsheets, research reports and case-law guides are examples of mixed target audience genres, aimed at both legal practitioners and laypeople. These are prepared by the ECtHR Press Service and the research department (Brannan 2021: 220). *Factsheets*[35] (*fiches thématiques*) are compiled by the Press Service using thematic criteria: grouping together the Court's case-law and pending cases by topic, such as children's rights, violence against women, expulsion and extradition, reproductive rights, surveillance at workplace, etc. These factsheets are multilingual, as the Court has invested in disseminating information about its case-law in a number of initiatives starting from the 2010s (see 9.3.1). Besides the thematic organization, there are also country-specific factsheets, but those typically denote the execution stage, done outside the Court by the Committee of Ministers, i.e. the body monitoring judgment execution. The CoM country factsheets have links to available information on the status of execution stored in a different database: HUDOC-EXEC.

A fascinating example of a derived genre is the so-called *Case-law guide* (*guide sur la jurisprudence*). As the ECtHR Knowledge Sharing platform

34 An average legal summary will count around 1,500 words.

35 Available at https://www.echr.coe.int/factsheets.

states, "Case-Law Guides provide an overview of Convention case-law on a particular Article/Transversal Theme. Official language versions are updated regularly" (KS-ECHR, online[36]). Translations into non-official languages are available with a waiver that these "are not produced by the Registry of the Court and the Registry does not check their accuracy or linguistic quality, nor is it responsible for their updating" (KS-ECHR, online). Currently, 37 guides address the most frequently invoked ECHR articles,[37] the admissibility guide and some guides that do not concentrate on one article only – also in light of the ECHR's interpretation as a "living instrument" (see 3.1.2) – but instead gather indications on some contemporary rights and transversal themes, such as a guide on data protection, guide on environment, guide on terrorism, guide on the rights of LGBTI persons, guide on mass protests, guide on immigration, guide on prisoners' rights and guide on social rights. These guides are intertextual and interdiscursive in that they rely both on other texts, i.e. case-law (judgments and decisions), but they also appropriate "generic resources, primarily contextual in nature [. . .] across discursive and professional practices as well as professional cultures" (Bhatia 2017: 5) by using some generic features typical of academic genres and didactic genres. Each guide starts with a crystallized "Note to readers", which delineates the communicative purpose of the guides and their contents in a way similar to abstracts in academic discourse. The communicative purpose is "to inform legal practitioners about the fundamental judgments and decisions delivered by the Strasbourg Court", which also clearly specifies the target audience. The "Note to readers" also indicates that "[r]eaders will find herein the key principles in this area and the relevant precedents". Each guide is subdivided into clear sections, with two to three levels of numbering. Their length depends on the case-law in the specific area: the shortest guide counts 5,895 words (Right of appeal in criminal matters, Art. 2 Prot. no. 7), and the longest totals 116,048 (Art. 8, Right to respect for private and family life). The average length of case-law guides is 38,170 words. While case-law guides deal – unsurprisingly – with case-law, their discourse and lexicogrammar is more similar to legal academic genres, illustrating fruitful interdiscursivity.

Another derived genre is *press release* (*communiqué de presse*). As concerns its participation framework, the intended audience of this genre goes beyond legal practitioners and includes media professionals and the public at large. Press releases are typically prepared by the Press Office in collaboration with the Registry lawyers in one of the official languages and are translated by the Court's Translation Department into the other. There are multiple types of press releases overviewing different professional activity and discursive products of the Court. For instance, there are press releases on Chamber

36 https://ks.echr.coe.int/web/echr-ks/all-case-law-guides.

37 Including ECHR Articles 1–15 (with two guides on Article 6 dealing with its civil and criminal limbs respectively), Articles 17–18, Article 46, Articles 1–3 of Protocol no. 1, Articles 2–4 of Protocol no. 4, and Articles 1, 2 and 4 of Protocol no. 7.

judgments, which are generally published at 10 a.m. on Tuesdays and Thursdays, and then there are press releases dedicated to upcoming hearings that are announced at the end of the preceding month. As Brannan (2021: 219) explains, a wider selection of cases is covered by press releases with several functions, ranging from a brief announcement of forthcoming judgments with factual summaries to more detailed press releases, "incorporating a summary of the Court's reasoning, on the day of delivery" (Brannan 2021: 219). As it emerges, interdiscursivity takes centre stage here, too, as press releases stem from other genres in the ECtHR system of genres in a reflection of the interrelated nature of professional and discursive practices thereof. The reader is referred to Chapter 9 for more details on this genre.

3.5 The ECtHR discourse: languages and translation

The number of languages in the CoE countries can "be estimated at nearly 40" (Brannan 2021: 217), and yet the Court's official languages are only two: English and French, under Article 34 of the ECtHR Rules of Court ("Use of languages").[38] Does it make the ECtHR a truly multilingual institution? Probably not, at least, not "in any official sense" (Weston 2005: 448). The Court practices institutional bilingualism, similarly to some other international courts (see 1.2).

Besides providing a general indication of institutional bilingualism, Art. 34 details it following the procedural flow of genres and communicative situations. The initial application under Art. 34.2 can be lodged "if not in one of the Court's official languages, [. . .] in one of the official languages of the Contracting Parties", in fact derogating from the principle of institutional bilingualism in favour of ensuring equal access to supranational justice to the parties coming from 46 Member States. Interestingly, continued use of a language different from the Court's official languages ("the official language of a Contracting Party") may be granted to Applicants for communications concerning hearings, after the case communication stage, at the stage of written pleadings (Art. 34.3(a)) if either the Registry (34.3(b)) or the Applicant (34.3(c)) make the necessary translation or interpretation provisions. A similar leave may be granted also to the Respondent Governments (34.4) and third-party interventions (34.4(d)). The linguistic diversity of applicants coming from the Contracting Parties is further recognized in Art. 34.5, stating that the Respondent Government may be invited "to provide a translation of its written submissions in the or an official language of that Party in order to facilitate the applicant's understanding of those submissions". What emerges is that translation at the early stages of the procedure can be – and most frequently is – outsourced to external translators, commissioned by either the Applicants or the Governments.

38 As amended by the Court on 13 December 2004 and 19 September 2016.

While the Rules specify the provision of translation and/or interpreting services between non-official and official languages for the submission of applications and the presentation of oral and written pleadings, they do not elaborate on the intricacies of the translation and drafting processes, nor on the considerations of translation quality assessment. In the case of written pleadings, for example, "the translations do not undergo any known quality assessment checks", leaving the ECtHR "in a situation where it has to rely on the services provided by unknown translators without any quality guarantees" (Nikitina 2018a: 2).

Finally, as concerns the protection of individual language rights, Art. 34.6 states that

> 6. Any witness, expert or other person appearing before the Court may use his or her own language if he or she does not have sufficient knowledge of either of the two official languages. In that event the Registrar shall make the necessary arrangements for interpreting or translation.

This provision is logically followed by the one on the verbatim record of a hearing in Rule 70.2: "If all or part of the verbatim record is in a non-official language, the Registrar shall arrange for its translation into one of the official languages". The record should provide details about the Chamber's composition, a roster of individuals presented before it, the content of the submissions, questions posed and responses provided, and any rulings issued throughout the hearing. As the language combination is typically different from English-French, in case such translations are commissioned, they are carried out by external translators.

The Court's " 'production' [. . .] may be monolingual, bilingual or multilingual" (Brannan 2021: 218). Translation and its cross-fertilization with comparative law (see 1.2.2) are part of the daily operation of the Court (Popović 2007: 373–374). And yet, the role of translation appears somewhat "marginal" in the Rules, and it "seems to have been almost completely neglected in the literature" (Peruzzo 2019b: 37). The operation of multilingual international organizations is characterized by complex processes of hierarchical institutional translation, or rather "the legal dimension of institutional translation" (Prieto Ramos 2020: 456), with varying degrees of mutual conditioning between the legal and the institutional elements and shifting translation priorities depending on a specific genre and/or purpose of a text to be translated (Schäffner et al. 2014). By virtue of its setting, legal translation at the ECtHR is also an instance of institutional translation. Yet, next to the limited mention thereof in the Rules, it is hard to outline a general institutional policy of translation at the ECtHR. Taking different shapes at different procedural steps, translation at the ECtHR is a gradient of covert and overt operations. Much of the translation at the ECtHR is on the "dark side" of the moon, as it is intrinsic, covert, hidden and not carried out by the Court's translators. It can be outsourced to external translation services at the earlier procedural steps or even rely on machine translation output (see Chapter 6). It can be carried out by the Registry lawyers who process applications transposing national legal realia into the supranational domain (see Chapter 5). It can be carried out by highly trained legal translators working for the Court (see Chapter 7). As this book is organized following the system of genres in the Court, different translational profiles will be detailed in the respective chapters, limiting this discussion to the general organization and legal framework on the use of languages.

Going with the procedural flow, the Rules return to institutional bilingualism in Rule 57 (Language of the decision) and Rule 76 (Language of the judgment), which are nearly identical but for the difference between decisions and judgments, already discussed in 3.4.2:

> Rule 57. Unless the Court decides that a decision shall be given in both official languages, all decisions shall be given either in English or in French. Decisions of the Grand Chamber shall, however, be given in both official languages, and both language versions shall be equally authentic.
>
> Rule 76. Unless the Court decides that a judgment shall be given in both official languages, all judgments shall be given either in English or in French. Judgments of the Grand Chamber shall, however, be given in both official languages, and both language versions shall be equally authentic.

What emerges is a profile of ***alternative institutional bilingualism***, of the *either-or* type in most situations, excluding the discursive products of the Grand Chamber (decisions (Rule 57), judgments (Rule 76) and Advisory Opinions (Rule 88.1(b) and Rule 94.7(b)). The alternative nature is a relatively recent development in the linguistic regime of the ECtHR. It was enacted after 1998 with Protocol no. 11 as a response to the growing caseload of the ECtHR. By contrast, "in the old Court all judgments were delivered in both English and French and the relevant drafts were translated at all stages" (Weston 2010: 77). As Cohen (2016: 505) commented, "the ECtHR's crushing docket has led to rationing bilingualism".

Peculiarly, the ECtHR lacked internal translators until 1987, and the translation workload used to be "split between the Council of Europe's central translation service (which handled the non-confidential material only) and the two native English-speaking and two French-speaking lawyers in the Court's Registry" (Weston 2005: 448, footnote 6). Finally, "in 1986 a request by the Registry for the creation of two posts of senior translator (one into English and one into French) was granted, and since 1987 further posts have been created to cope with the ever-growing workload" (Weston 2010: 77).

Currently, the Court does have a Language Department, separate from the Council of Europe. As there are two official languages, there are two divisions in the Language Department, i.e. the French Language Division (counting five translators, one reviser and four language checkers), and the English Language Division (counting four translators, two revisers and nine language checkers; Peruzzo 2019b: 30). These language divisions typically deal with confidential documents, outsourcing the non-confidential ones to optimize resources (Brannan 2018: 176–177).

From a more general perspective, legal translation can serve three purposes: informative purposes, general legal and judicial purposes, and normative purposes (Biel 2024: 107). Translation for *informative purposes* lacks binding legal force but serves as a source of information for the intended recipients (Cao 2007: 11). Translation of derived genres falls under this category. Dissemination of the Court's case-law through non-official languages (see 9.3.1) is again a type of informative translation, aimed at promoting Convention-related knowledge and making it accessible to national legal communities. Translation for *general legal or judicial purposes* is both informative and descriptive, yet it produces "legal consequences attached to them due to their use in the legal process" (Cao 2007: 12). Procedural genres in the ECtHR system, especially at its early stages, follow this rationale. When the Registry lawyers process applications written in a language different from the Court's official languages, they need to summarize them in either English or French for the benefit of the single judge who does not necessarily speak the national language so that he or she can render an admissibility/inadmissibility decision. As the resulting reports/summaries are used in the following proceedings, it is a clear case of translation for judicial purposes.

Finally, translation for *normative purposes* produces texts with legally binding status. Such texts are equally valid and regarded as "authentic" or "authoritative" legal texts (Cao 2007: 10). This is emblematic of (bi-)multilingual legislation – hence the label "normative" – as in multilingual jurisdictions law is linguistically adapted into an equivalent target speech act, rendering it operative (Galdia 2017: 270). In the ECtHR context, discursive products of the Grand Chamber would fall under translation pursuing normative purposes, on account of their equal authenticity.

The Grand Chamber judgments and decisions are equally authentic in both English and French, distinguishing these ECtHR genres from the same genres at their sister supranational courts: the IACtHR and the ACtHPR. Judgments of the former end with a formula indicating the drafting language, which is Spanish in the majority of cases, e.g. "Redactada en español en San José, Costa Rica, el [date]" or "DONE, at San José, Costa Rica, on [date], in the Spanish language". When translated, these follow informative purposes. The ACtHPR judgments, while being more frequently available in more than one language, end with a formula that clearly specifies that the linguistic regime is not that of equal authenticity, e.g. "Done at Arusha, this [number] Day of [month] in the Year [year], in English and French, the English version being authoritative". These judgments are translated pursuing general legal and judicial purposes of a multilingual institution. At the ECtHR, however, the ending formula highlights the equal authenticity: "Done in English and in French, and delivered at a public hearing in the Human Rights Building, Strasbourg, on [date], pursuant to Rule 77 §§ 2 and 3 of the Rules of Court".

The above formulas illustrate how much translation is incorporated into the highest-level operation of the European human rights machinery. Yet, it is not entirely correct to talk about translation, as there is no source text and no target text. They do not exist de jure. However, de facto the services of the Language Department are employed at the pre-delivery stage, meaning that the judgment is rendered bilingual and equally authentic before being delivered and published. The burden of producing legal translation reaching the threshold of equal authenticity has been frequently addressed in the literature on the European Union, where "translated texts which have *the force of law* must also be considered distinct from other text types, because their translation is concerned with *legal* transfer as opposed to *cultural* transfer (McAuliffe 2016: 9, original emphasis).

Before 2016 when the Court produced official printed law reports, some Chamber judgments and decisions used to be translated into the other official language post-delivery. Now, with the abolition of the printed law reports, "there is no longer any strict obligation" to do so, yet "[s]uch translation is nevertheless completed where they are listed as 'key cases' (Rule 104B), and in a small number of other cases, time permitting" (Brannan 2021: 218–219). "Key Case" is the new label used "to flag the most important judgments and decisions that are selected every quarter (after delivery) by the Court's Bureau upon the recommendation of the Jurisconsult" (Brannan 2021: 219). This label can be applied to different procedural stages. For example, Nikitina (2022c: 118) overviews how certain COVID-19-related *inadmissible* cases were earmarked as "key cases" at the case communication stage, "presumably as a deterrent" of any future applications following their stead.

Translation permeates the linguistic regime of the ECtHR. Whether it is used as a mechanism for ensuring linguistic rights and the right of access to the Court, legal drafting or dissemination purposes, it assuredly contributes to the human rights discourse as we know it today.

3.6 Conclusions

Describing discourses is a perennially challenging area, as professional and institutional discourses resemble echo chambers of the current geopolitical climate. This chapter started from the description of the arid climate surrounding the creation of the European human rights mechanism, following landmark moments in anthropogenic climate change that led to the creation of the modern European discourse of human rights. The underlying idea was to provide the reader with a relatively broad-brush sketch of the Court's context, reconciling legal and linguistic perspectives in the spirit of interdisciplinarity, and to fine-tune it with smaller strokes and details in the following chapters. To venture into a description of a professional discourse without understanding its social, professional and cultural contexts is to venture into it blindfolded, stumbling through language choices without a guiding light. Contextualization serves as a beacon that illuminates the path forward and anchors the European human rights discourse to a certain time, space, discourse community, etc.

Following the idea of contextualization and interlacing, where possible, legal and linguistic perspectives, I wanted to create a kaleidoscopic display of the background, genres and linguistic regime of the European Court of Human Rights. As my primary interest revolves around the way human rights are reflected through discourse, I strived to illustrate here the seamless integration between different discursive and professional practices of the Court through the description of its system of genres. Finally, the general language policy, including translation-related matters, had to be described, laying the foundation for the next chapters of this book.

No single chapter can ever grasp the entirety of actions, practices and changes that happened over three quarters of a century. Indeed, this was not my intention, and the reader is invited to consult other, historically oriented sources for those purposes.

Part II

The European Court of Human Rights

Inception of cases and the voices of human rights

4 Application

The right to individual petition and plain language

4.1 The right of individual petition

Similarly to many international courts, the life of cases at the ECtHR commences with an application (*récours*), as it gives rise to "the introductory stage of proceedings" (Sicilianos & Kostopoulou 2019: 35). What renders the ECtHR unique in comparison to its sister institutions – the IACtHR and the ACtHPR – is that this application can be lodged by any individual directly to the Court. The right to individual petition is enshrined in Article 34 of the Convention:

> The Court may receive applications from any person, nongovernmental organization or group of individuals claiming to be the victim of a violation by one of the High Contracting Parties of the rights set forth in the Convention or the Protocols thereto. The High Contracting Parties undertake not to hinder in any way the effective exercise of this right.

This right has been defined as "the cornerstone of the European system of human rights" (Lambert-Abdelgawad 2018: 8), even though at the origins of the Convention, it was feared this right would become "the rock upon which the Convention as a whole might founder" (Bates 2011: 29). For a political compromise, the right of individual petition was inserted as an optional right in the original Article 25 of the Convention: States could opt out of this right rather than opt in. Its mandatory recognition came around along with the reform of Protocol no. 11 (see 3.2.2) in 1998. It has been defined as "a key feature of the European system, a victory slowly won, and one that is unique in the world" (Costa 2009: 14).The parallel regional mechanisms of human rights protection in the Americas (IACtHR) and in Africa (ACtHPR) do not allow individuals to lodge an application with the respective courts directly; instead, a dual system is in place, consisting of a Commission that sifts through applications and a Court that deals with the admissible applications only (Hampson et al. 2018: 161–163). This reflects the situation which was in place during the "old" ECtHR days, when it could receive cases

> via four referring sources: (1) the Commission; (2) the respondent State; (3) the Member State which had referred the case to the Commission

DOI: 10.4324/9781003434788-6

> in the first place (that is, for an interstate case); (4) the Member State whose national was alleged to be a victim. It will be noted, then, that the individual applicant did not have the ability to refer a case to the Court.
> (Bates 2011: 38)

As right of access to (international) justice "tolerates a broad range of definitions" (Schmitt 2017: 91), the right of individual petition may be conceptualized as one of its facets, along with such elements as the right to effective remedies, right to a fair trial[1] or access to legal aid (Schmitt 2017: 92). In this sense, access to justice has significant overlaps with the concept of legal empowerment (van de Meene & van Rooij 2008: 6). Yet, in its broadest sense access to justice signifies "the possibility for the individual to bring a claim before a court and have a court adjudicate it" (Francioni 2007: 1).

From a cross-institutional human rights perspective, the right of access to international justice in the IACtHR could be understood as part of the right to judicial protection established by the ACHR in Article 25. While Article 44 ACHR[2] mentions individual complaints (directed at the Commission), "it is not clear whether this provision establishes an autonomous and independent right to lodge petitions" (Acosta Lopez & Maya Calle 2009: 15, my translation), leaving thus a grey area in terms of the international responsibility of States.

The rift in the access to justice across these three realms widens, as Article 34 of the ECHR unfolds its interpretation. This article is understood to mandate that all decisions must be rendered solely by a judicial formation, unlike in other regional systems where decisions may be made by a commission in the absence of explicit provisions to the contrary in the Rules of Procedure.

Despite the vast possibilities of access to the ECtHR, it "is not and cannot be absolute, notably when more than 800 million citizens have become potential applicants" (Lambert-Abdelgawad 2018: 8). The boon and bane of the ECtHR, "its force and its weakness" (Costa 2011: 7, my translation), the right to individual petition created a situation when in 2011 90% of cases coming into the Registry – especially, those coming from the five highest-count countries (Russia, Turkey, Romania, Ukraine and Poland) – were deemed inadmissible,[3] i.e. not satisfying the formal admissibility criteria (*critères de recevabilité*). The measure that helped resolve this situation while respecting the need for a judicial decision to be rendered was the creation of the so-called

1 ECtHR, *Golder v. the United Kingdom*, App. No. 4451/70, 1 *EHRR* (1979–1980) 535.

2 Art. 44 ACHR: "Any person or group of persons, or any non-governmental entity legally recognized in one or more member states of the Organization, may lodge petitions with the Commission containing denunciations or complaints of violation of this Convention by a State Party".

3 https://www.echr.coe.int/documents/d/echr/Filtering_Section_ENG. Unless otherwise specified, all hyperlinks indicated in this chapter were last consulted in March 2024.

"Filtering section" and another judicial formation consisting of a single judge. When Protocol no. 14 entered into force,

> the president decided that there should be 20 single judges, serving for one year at a time. Each single judge works approximately 25 per cent of the time on this task, and otherwise continues to carry out his/her other duties within the section to which s/he is assigned.
>
> (Cameron 2013: 33)

As concerns the already mentioned highest-count countries, it was decided to have more single judges for these countries: five judges for Russia, four for Turkey, three for Romania and Ukraine each and two for Poland. The same person could serve as a single judge for three states (two low-count and one high-count state; Cameron 2013: 33).

It would be overly zealous to expect that single judges were linguistically and legally proficient to process applications coming from a mosaic of States. They are assisted by a non-judicial rapporteur from the filtering section, i.e. a Registry lawyer. The section's function

> is to carry out a thorough, accurate and immediate sifting of cases to ensure that all applications are placed on the appropriate procedural track, whether submitted to a Single Judge for prompt decision or sent to await examination by a Committee of three judges or Chamber in accordance with the Court's priority policy.
>
> (Filtering section progress report 2011, online)

In general, "the Registry has several units corresponding either to single countries or to groups of similar countries" (Garlicki 2009: 393). The single judge typically receives a list with "extremely summary information on each case, a sentence or two on what the case is about and the relevant Convention right" (Cameron 2013: 33), based on which he or she will decide whether the case is admissible and should be allocated to a committee or a chamber, or whether it is inadmissible and render an inadmissibility decision. The underlying idea was to enable the system to find the "right balance between maintaining the right of petition and weeding out unfounded applications" (O'Boyle 2010: 197).

This streamlined process allows the Court to maintain the formally judicial nature of the initial analysis of applications, since the eventual inadmissibility decision is always rendered by a judge, as showcased by the Court's "Simplified case-processing flow-chart by judicial formation"[4] (see also Figure 3.3). Yet, a key role in the processing of cases at the Court, as this chapter will show, is carried out by the Registry lawyers. Despite their vitally important mansions, they remain largely unsung and unseen in the literature (Cameron 2013: 34; Nikitina 2022a: 244). When an application is received, particularly if its language is

4 Available at https://www.echr.coe.int/documents/d/echr/Case_processing_Court_ENG.

not accessible to a single judge, its processing hinges upon the bedrock of trust between the single judges and the non-judicial rapporteurs, along with proper training of the latter to ensure the smooth operation of the system.

4.2 The application form

The application form stems from a system of checks and balances: the near-universality of individual petition and the enormous pool of potential petitioners had to be balanced by a clear definition of what can count as an *initial application*. In 2005, the so-called Woolf's Report[5] "recommended changes to the rules of procedure to clarify what constitutes an application and to make clear that there is no application until the receipt by the Court of a completed application form" (Cameron 2013: 28). Before these changes, the applicants would contact the Court first using the most conventional epistolary genre: a letter, which counted as the initial application, engaging the Court in a potentially lengthy and not necessarily efficient correspondence exchange. Lord Woolf (2005: 19) wrote in his report,

> The Convention provides that every individual has the right to apply direct to the Court, and a great many people write to Strasbourg without any legal advice or assistance, and without any knowledge of the Court's conditions of admissibility. As a consequence, approximately 85% of cases arriving in Strasbourg are clearly inadmissible, and 95% are eventually found to be inadmissible. Of the admissible cases, only a fraction raise new questions of human rights law. The remainder are repetitive or "clone" cases. In addition, the Court deals with a considerable amount of correspondence, which I would not regard as being applications.

The Report identified a problem with the petitioners' knowledge about the Court's apparently labyrinthine admissibility criteria. This deficiency contributed, in part, to the burgeoning backlog of cases weighing upon the Court's shoulders like a burdensome mantle. In the spirit of constructive critique, the report not only pinpointed areas for improvement but also proposed solutions, among which was the creation of guidelines. This led to the creation of the Court's "Practical Guide on Admissibility Criteria" (Admissibility Guide), constantly updated in English and French and available in multiple languages as part of the Court's general knowledge dissemination strategy (Chapter 9). Its communicative goal is

> to inform legal practitioners, and in particular lawyers who may be called upon to represent applicants before the Court, about the conditions of

5 The official title of the report is "Review of the Working Methods of the European Court of Human Rights", available at https://www.echr.coe.int/documents/d/echr/2005_lord_woolf_working_methods_eng.

> admissibility of individual applications. This Guide is designed to present a clear*er* and *more* detailed picture of the conditions of admissibility with a view, firstly, to reducing *as far as possible* the number of applications which have no prospect of resulting in a ruling on the merits and, secondly, to ensuring that those applications which warrant examination on the merits pass the admissibility test.
>
> (ECtHR 2023b: 6, emphasis added)

As it emerges from the comparative expressions ("clearer", "more detailed", "as far as possible") used to explain the purpose of the guide, it functions as a supplement to the application form. If the application form is used to photograph and report on a potential human rights violation, the Guide functions as a user's manual explaining the correct settings to maximize the camera's performance. The Guide, as well as other information sheets on each Convention Article "may be particularly useful for applicants and their legal representatives in preparing an application before the Court" (Brannan 2021: 220, cf. Villiger 2019: 457, 461).

The Guide provides additional information on who may lodge an application, explaining and defining the notion of "person" along with subdividing the admissibility criteria – or rather grounds for potential inadmissibility – into three macro-categories: procedural, jurisdiction-related and material. It is thus necessary to look at the synergy of the application and instructions on its filling-in to describe the generic setup and the discursive peculiarities of the application.

4.3 The admissibility criteria

For the application to be added to the Court's list of cases, it has to satisfy the so-called admissibility criteria. The French version of this multiword term – *critères de recevabilité* – provides an eloquent construal of their purpose: their satisfaction allows the Court to *receive* the applications. Jean-Paul Costa, a former president of the ECtHR, notes how the admissibility criteria are "at the heart" of the convention mechanism (Costa 2011: 7, my translation).

Another former president of the court, Linos-Alexandre Sicialianos, along with his colleague Kostopoulou (2019), reflects on the gradual stricture of the admissibility criteria and cautions applicants and their legal representatives to "be very careful when completing the application form and submitting it, together with supporting documents, to the Court's Registry" (2019: 32).

Currently, the admissibility criteria include four main points.

1 **Exhaustion of all available domestic remedies** is the first, procedural, ground for (in)admissibility. Article 35.1 ECHR sets forth, "The Court may only deal with the matter after all domestic remedies have been exhausted, according to the generally recognised rules of international law . . .". In very simple terms, a potential violation of human rights must be examined first in

all available domestic court instances, by virtue of the much discussed principle of subsidiarity (see 3.2.4). Only if no satisfactory redress has been obtained nationally, can an applicant apply to the ECtHR. In recent years, baptized as the era of "procedural embedding" (Spano 2018), the Court has restricted its interpretation of this point: "Applicants have to demonstrate that they have not only pleaded the Convention issue domestically, at least in substance, but done so in a manner that has realistically given the national judge the opportunity to consider the issue through a Convention lens" (Spano 2018: 486).

2 The applicant must lodge the application within a **four-month time-limit** since the date the last national court has issued a ruling (Article 35.1 ECHR). As the Admissibility Guide explains (ECtHR 2023b: 40), the underlying rationale "is to maintain legal certainty by ensuring that cases raising issues under the Convention are examined within a reasonable time, and to prevent the authorities and other persons concerned from being kept in a state of uncertainty for a long period of time". This time limit used to be set at six months, and it was reduced to four months on 1 August 2021, with Protocol no. 15 entering into force.
3 Naturally, **complaints must be based on and compatible with the ECHR,** as this criterion establishes the jurisdiction of the Court. The Guide lists and explains a number of Latin expressions indicating potential grounds for inadmissibility/incompatibility with the Convention (Art. 35.3.a): *Ratione personae*, *ratione loci*, *ratione temporis* and *ratione materiae.*
4 The Applicant must have suffered **significant disadvantage**. This is a moderately new addition to the admissibility criteria, introduced by the Protocol no. 14 reform in article 35.3.b on June 1, 2010. It shifts the focus "from the (objective) insignificance of the *issue* to the (subjective) disadvantage of the applicant". (Cameron 2013: 36, original emphasis)

4.4 Linguistic implications

The application to the ECtHR can be lodged in any official language of the Council or Europe Member States and, eventually, even in minority languages. This is allowed provided that the Registry lawyers handling these applications are fluent in the respective language.[6] Art. 34.2 of the Rules of Court specifies

> In connection with applications lodged under Article 34 of the Convention, and for as long as no Contracting Party has been given notice of such an application in accordance with these Rules, all communications with and oral and written submissions by applicants or their representatives, if not in one of the Court's official languages, shall be in one of the official languages of the Contracting Parties. If a Contracting Party is informed or given notice of an application in accordance with these

6 For example, a Russian-speaking applicant from Latvia may draft an application in Russian, even if Russian is not an official language in Latvia.

> Rules, the application and any accompanying documents shall be communicated to that State in the language in which they were lodged with the Registry by the applicant.

Typically, the Registry lawyer responsible for processing an application not only demonstrates a high level of linguistic proficiency but also holds a law degree from the relevant state (de Salvia & Remus 2011: 59), which ensures their optimal processing of both the national language and legal system. This linguistic regime may continue until the case communication stage. "As long as the respondent State *has not been given notice* of the application under the Rules of Court, applicants may communicate with the Court in writing in the language thus selected" (Siciliano & Kostopoulou 2019: 33, original emphasis).

Drafting an application is a relatively guided process in that it follows a well-defined model: the application form. It would be naïve to expect the right of individual petition to be implemented across the 46 Member States of the Council of Europe if the applicants had to use only the official languages of the Court: English and French. As Brannan (2018: 170) rightly notes, "The right of petition, as it is known, would be meaningless if the applicant were unable to use his or her own language".

To abate potential linguistic barriers to access to the Court, the Registry prepared the application forms in 36 languages of the Council of Europe countries. When a potential applicant opens the webpage "Apply to the Court", he or she may select a language to access the full information package in their language. Interestingly, while applications are always available in all 36 languages, this is not the case with the Admissibility Guide, which explains some very technical criteria. Today the Guide is available in 23 national languages,[7] not counting French and English, whereas for other 12[8] interfaces in national languages, the English version of the guide is loaded. Naturally, the availability of the Guide in a national language increases the chances that a given application is deemed admissible as it explains the technicalities in a more easily comprehensible way. On the other hand, the Guides translated into national languages are not updated as frequently as the ones in the official languages. For example, as of December 2023 the version of the Guide available on the website in English and French was last updated in August 2023, whereas some translated versions date back as far as to 2011. If the applicants are not familiar with the changes brought about by Protocol no. 15 in 2021, cutting the timeframe to lodge an application from six to four months, consulting an outdated but translated version of the Guide could be counterproductive if not

7 Albanian, Armenian, Azerbaijani, Bulgarian, Croatian, Czech, Estonian, Georgian, German, Greek, Icelandic, Italian, Lithuanian, Macedonian, Polish, Portuguese, Romanian, Russian, Serbian, Slovenian, Spanish, Turkish, Ukrainian.

8 Bosnian, Catalan, Danish, Dutch, Finnish, Hungarian, Latvian, Maltese, Montenegrin, Norwegian, Slovak, Swedish.

bewildering. Translations into non-official languages (see 9.3) are a trade-off between considerations of priority and feasibility of a translation effort.

4.5 Generic makeup of an application form

The application form counts 13 pages subdivided into nine blocks (A–I) housing a total of 73 fields to fill in. As any formal document, the initial application must contain the formal details and contact information of the main participants in the participation framework. Applicant's details (name, date of birth, nationality and address) go in field A1 or, if the applicant is a legal person, its full name, date of incorporation or registration, the official registration number (if any) and the official address are to be inserted in field A2. This is very important as the Court does not deal with anonymous applications (Article 35.2 (a) ECHR).

Block B should contain a clear indication of the State against which the application is directed. Blocks C and D are dedicated to the information on the representative(s) of the applicant, if he or she is a natural or a legal person, respectively.

The core moves of the application, however, are to be realized in Blocks E (Statement of the Facts) and F (statement of alleged violation(s) of the Convention and/or Protocols and relevant arguments), followed by Block G (Compliance with admissibility criteria laid down in Article 35.1 of the Convention). Most texts commenting on these fields indicate in a mantra-like fashion that these statements must be "concise and legible", as per Rule 47.1 (e) and (f) of the Rules of Court, see also Sicilianos and Kostopoulou (2019: 34). The use of such intentionally vague or strategically indeterminate adjectives is typical of legal discourse, especially in the common law tradition, amounting to what Lanius (2019: 6) defines a "love-hate relationship with indeterminacy". While "concise" suggests brevity and clarity, what might be concise for one person could be seen as overly brief or insufficiently detailed for another. Similarly, "legible" implies that information should be lucid and easy to read, probably regarding its style, font and handwriting. Rule 47.2 (a) explains that the information referred to as concise and legible "should be ***sufficient*** to enable the Court to determine the nature and scope of the application without recourse to any other document" (emphasis added), using – ironically – another indeterminate adjective. These descriptors take on particular importance if we consider a scenario in which the applicant is not represented by a legal professional (Rule 36.1), adding the dichotomy lay versus legal to the mix. Arguably, a legal professional and a layperson may have a different understanding of "concise", "legible" and "sufficient", by virtue of their divergent discursive and professional background.

As Sicilianos and Kostopoulou (2019: 34) comment, "the purpose of providing all this information in the application form itself is to ensure that incoming cases receive proper consideration and are allocated swiftly by the Court", so it is not acceptable to make simple intertextual references of a "see enclosed" type. As much as the application process is guided by the information package available at the Court's website, the core blocks and fields (moves) in the application (E, F and G) are simple empty pages with lined fields. The only difference concerns that the *Statement of facts* occupies the whole page for a free-flowing narration, for a maximum of three consecutive pages, whereas both *Statement of alleged violation(s)* and *Compliance with admissibility criteria* are subdivided into two columns inviting a more structured information presentation, with the legal details on the left and the explanation/commentary on the right.

Besides the above, little is said about the language to use in the application, but for the caution that it should not be offensive (see also 5.6.2). The Guide explains (ECtHR 2023b: 56) this parameter in the following way,

> 255. It is not sufficient for the applicant's language to be merely cutting, polemical or sarcastic; it must exceed "the bounds of normal, civil and legitimate criticism" in order to be regarded as abusive (Di Salvo v. Italy (dec.), 2007, Apinis v. Latvia (dec.), 2011; for a contrary example, see Aleksanyan v. Russia, 2008, §§ 116–118; X and Others v. Bulgaria [GC], § 146; Gherardi Martiri v. San Marino, 2022, §§ 83–84).

Block H elicits information concerning any other international proceedings, and, finally, Block I is dedicated to the list of appended documents. The final moves are technical in their nature again, being the fields for signatures and confirmation of the corresponding persons.

4.6 The (plain) language of applications

The application form in English counts 1,827 words. The Practical Guide explaining it, in its August 2023 English edition, totals 68,645 words. Apart from the evident contrast in length, these documents exhibit marked discursive distinctions that reflect their disparate target audiences. The application is drafted according to the canons of the so-called Plain Language Movement and is aimed at the vast public. Conversely, the Practical Guide boasts a more intricate and lexically dense discourse, catering specifically to legal practitioners. Before delving into these two documents, a brief explanation of plain language is pertinent.

Attested difficulties of the conventional discursive practices within the legal profession led to the rise of various *Plain Language Movements*, whose aim was to eradicate the elements of "legalese" that render legal English archaic, complex and difficult for non-experts to comprehend (Williams 2011: 139). Originating in the 1970s in the United States, these movements aimed to simplify the language employed in legislation and by legal professionals, and their influence quickly extended to other English-speaking regions, including Australia (Federal Plain Language Guidelines 2011), New Zealand (the New Zealand Parliamentary Counsel Office 2009), South Africa, Canada, and the

United Kingdom (Drafting Techniques Group 2008; Garner 2013). Similar initiatives also emerged within the evolving European legal landscape (European Commission, How to write clearly; the "Fight the Fog" campaign). Williams (2011) observes significant progress in simplifying legal English in the United Kingdom and the United States, where substantive changes were not implemented until 2004, despite initial reform proposals. However, he acknowledges that altering drafting styles in monolingual jurisdictions is less complex than reforming multilingual international and supranational legal systems, such as the ECtHR. In such contexts, modernizing the style of one language can have unpredictable consequences for others (Williams 2011: 149).

Legal writing has been gradually exposed to movements and initiatives aimed at enhancing its comprehensibility and reducing its complexity in line with tenets of informational justice (along with accessibility lately, see Maass 2020), contrasting a standpoint that complex content has to be necessarily expressed using a convoluted lexicogrammar. In this regard, Solan and Tiersma (2012: 4) comment on "a number of regularities in the ways that legal language operates, suggesting that legal orders around the world attempt to harness linguistic regularities in an effort to make language both clear and definitive". The application form to apply to the ECtHR is not an exception.

Traditional legal language, often dubbed as "legalese", displays an array of typical lexicogrammatical features, such as "a highly impersonal style, the consistent use of passive constructions, archaisms and Latinisms, of long and complex sentences, and the lack of emotive connotations" (Sala 2014: 652–653). Among these features, the impersonal and passive constructions stand out prominently, as identified in scholarly discourse (Williams 2007: 36–38). In contrast, embracing the active voice and actively engaging the reader have emerged as hallmarks of a more transparent and accessible writing style.

(1) This form is a formal legal document and may affect *your* rights and obligations. Please *follow the instructions* given in the "Notes for filling in the application form". *Make sure you* fill in all the fields applicable to *your situation* and provide all relevant documents. (ECtHR 2023c: 1)

(2) List of accompanying documents
You should enclose full and legible *copies* of all documents. No documents will be returned to *you*. It is thus in *your interests* to submit copies, not originals. *You MUST*:

a) arrange the documents in order by date and by set of proceedings;
b) number the pages consecutively; and
c) NOT staple, bind or tape the documents. (ECtHR 2023c: 12)

As examples (1) and (2) illustrate, the application form uses recurrently the second-person pronoun to address the intended reader ("you", "your rights", "your situation", "in your interest") in a clear way, increasing thus its chances of being filled-in correctly. In fact, "you" and "your" occur significantly more frequently in the application than in the Guide. Collectively, their normalized frequency[9] in the application is 181 (absolute frequency: 33) as compared to only 0.15 (absolute frequency: 1) in the Guide. The same rationale underlies the use of imperatives ("follow", "make sure") and semantically unambiguous modal verbs ("should", "must") instead of a potentially misleading and unclear "shall", which has become the object of much controversy in legal drafting and legal linguistics (Garzone 2013).

The application form also prefers the active structures ("this form is . . ."). This helps the drafter avoid excessive nominalizations which run in parallel with the passive constructions, wherein a word or phrase from another word class (such as a verb, adjective, or adverb) is transformed into a noun. The application form employs shorter sentences (note also the lettered list in (2) that exploits the graphical potential) that facilitate the information processing. In contrast, the Guide is wrought with passive constructions ("is triggered . . . by", "may be lodged"), use of relative clauses ("where he or she . . .") and otherwise embedded phrases (e.g. adjectival phrase "incompatible with its real functions") and generally longer sentences, as illustrated by (3), (4) and (5).

(3) Supervision by Strasbourg *is triggered* mainly by individual applications, which *may be lodged* with the Court by any individual or non-governmental legal entity *located* within the jurisdiction of a State Party to the Convention. (ECtHR 2023b: 7)

(4) The applicant abuses *the right of application* where he or she repeatedly lodges *vexatious and manifestly ill-founded* applications with the Court that are similar to an application that he or she has lodged in the past that has already been declared inadmissible (M. v. the United Kingdom and Philis v. Greece, both Commission decisions, 1987, 1996). It cannot be the task of the Court to deal with a succession of *ill-founded and querulous complaints or with otherwise manifestly abusive conduct of applicants or their authorised representatives*, which creates gratuitous work for the Court, incompatible with its real functions under the Convention. (ECtHR 2023b: 58)

(5) A finding of lack of jurisdiction *ratione loci* will not dispense the Court from examining whether the applicants come under the "jurisdiction" of one or more Contracting States within the meaning of Article 1 of the Convention (Drozd and Janousek v. France and Spain, 1992, § 90). Therefore, objections that the applicants are not within the "jurisdiction" of a respondent State will more normally be raised as claims that the application is incompatible *ratione personae* with the Convention (see

9 As the size of texts under analysis is different, all frequencies are normalized to 10,000 words, simulating a situation where both texts had equal length to allow a meaningful comparison. In corpus linguistics, absolute or raw frequencies denote the actual number of occurrences of a given item in a given text, whereas relative or normalized frequencies are the "simulated" frequencies that minimize the variable of length to allow comparison.

> submissions of the respondent Governments in Banković and Others v. Belgium and Others (dec.) [GC], 2001, § 35; Ilaşcu and Others v. Moldova and Russia [GC], 2004, § 300; Weber and Saravia v. Germany (dec.), 2006 [. . .]). (Admissibility Guide 2023: 60–61, original emphasis).

The Admissibility Guide employs a range of other "legal style" markers (Nikitina 2018a). To highlight them, a brief explanation of these markers is provided below, supplemented with examples based on the textual material at hand.

In his milestone book on the evolution of legal English, David Mellinkoff (1963: 11–29), who was a *lawyer* and not a linguist, listed key linguistic aspects in legal language, addressing both general features (e.g., precision and deliberate flexibility) and specific elements (e.g., frequent use of archaic and Latin expressions). The former may be linguistically realized using binomials (e.g. "ill-founded and querulous" or "vexatious and manifestly abusive" in (5)) and use of synonyms in general, as well as detailed referencing of relevant case-law. The latter merges clearly in (5) with a range of Latin formulae ("ratione loci", "ratione personae"). Similarly, the famous *linguistic* (and not legal) exploration of legal language by Crystal and Davy (1973) emphasized syntactic complexity, attempts at all-inclusiveness, and the prevalence of conditional structures, non-finite clauses, and lexical repetition in legal documents as markers of legal English. Tiersma (2015 [2006]: 27–28) combining Mellinkoff's classification with his own, created a list of commonly cited linguistic features in legal language. This list encompasses lexical traits (the already mentioned archaic terms and technical vocabulary in general, such as "jurisdiction" in (5) or "lodge an application" and "inadmissible" in (4)) and syntactic characteristics (nominalizations, passive constructions, complex sentences). The list can be enriched with complex prepositions ("within the meaning of" in (5)) and formulaic patterns in general (Nikitina 2018a).

While these classifications may be somewhat dated, they continue to be particularly relevant to the language employed in the Admissibility Guide, explicitly indicating its intended audience of legal professionals. As the Guide aims to assist in navigating the complexities of lodging an application, even for an unrepresented individual applicant, a potential paradox arises. Would an unrepresented applicant find the Guide practically useful, or would they opt for the more straightforward application form, without ever consulting the Guide?

4.7 Conclusions

A significant portion of ECtHR case-law originates from cases brought by individual applicants, and one can discern a strong correlation between the Court's existence and the ability of applicants to lodge applications. Indeed, as demonstrated in this chapter, the Court has devoted extensive legal and linguistic attention to ensuring the effective functioning of the right of individual petition. This has involved accepting applications in national languages and adhering to plain language norms within the application form design. The next procedural step, once the application is deemed admissible, is discussed in Chapter 5.

5 Case communication

Negotiating supranational terminology through institutional translation

5.1 Case communication: a watershed genre

If the application successfully crosses the filtering stage, the procedural flow continues with the case communication[1] genre. As concerns the ECtHR's linguistic regime, this is a watershed genre. While applications are most typically written in a national language, at times by a lay person with no legal background, case communications are prepared by the ECtHR Registry lawyers in either English or French and are typically shorter. As many other procedural genres in the ECtHR system, this genre has not received a fair share of scholarly attention, with few exceptions (Nikitina 2022a, 2022b).

The goal of case communications is twofold: to notify the Respondent Government about the accepted application, i.e. a newly established case (Sicilianos & Kostopoulou 2019: 98), and to launch the exchange of written observations through posing questions to the parties. A manual co-authored by the former president of the ECtHR specifies that

> the notice includes detailed questions for the Government, questions which relate to the main aspects of the case. The Court invites the respondent State to submit written replies to these questions within a period of sixteen weeks or, in priority cases, eight weeks.
>
> (Sicilianos & Kostopoulou 2019: 99)

1 In an earlier study (Nikitina 2022a: 230, note 2), I explained that the term used in the Court's official database HUDOC is "communicated case" or *affaire communiquée* in French, "with the 'communication' element expressed through a premodifying participle. This terminology maintains emphasis on the primary noun, namely the *case*, which is understandably central in legal contexts. However, this section focuses on the act of communication rather than the case itself. To better align with this perspective, the term 'case communication' was coined by reversing the order of the premodifier and the head noun. This label was selected, taking into consideration the language used in Rule 37.1 (Rules of Court), addressing 'communications or notifications'. Its appropriateness was confirmed through an informal inquiry with Registry lawyers". A similar terminological choice is found in Keller and Heri (2018) who define it "communication of cases", but a more synthetic version is preferred here.

DOI: 10.4324/9781003434788-7

This is a watershed genre also from a legal standpoint, because it defines the scope of the case (*l'objet du litige*) before the Court.

> The president of the relevant Section makes the decision regarding the issues to be communicated. Whatever issues are not communicated – because the president declares them to be out of time, manifestly ill-founded, or inadmissible for some other reason – are excluded from the scope of the case from that point onward.
>
> (Keller & Heri 2018: para. 20)

This includes the Chamber and even Grand Chamber proceedings. The decision concerning the case communication has strong and direct repercussions on a case's scope. Inadmissibility decisions may be not communicated at all.

This chapter examines case communication from a critical genre perspective (5.2) and from a Translation Studies perspective (5.3), zooming in on the introduction of national terminology and phraseology into the supranational discourse of human rights at this stage (5.4). The study problematizes reliance on Registry lawyers at the case communication stage (and the behind-the-scenes legal reports and analyses destined for judicial staff) for covert institutional legal translation (5.5). Finally, Chapter 5 includes a case study detailing the creative aspects of this translation in cases dealing with Article 10 violation and the translation of insults (5.6).

5.2 Case communication: genre perspectives

Case communications produce more or less detailed descriptions of the subject matters and statements of facts (Nikitina 2022a). The genre is subject to some variability in terms of its length and contents, which depend on the case complexity and importance, and elude clear-cut analytical explanations. In addition to this initial generic instability, the 2018 reform introduced the so-called ***immediate and simplified communication of application*** (IMSI), i.e. "a very short report which states the object of the case and the questions submitted to the parties. It is up to the parties to present their respective version of the facts and assist the Court in establishing the final version of them" (Sicilianos 2018: 3). Introduced as another "avenue for making the Court more efficient" (Keller & Heri 2018: para. 81), the IMSI "represents an example of the sharing of responsibility between States and the Court" (Keller & Heri 2018: para. 82).

Figure 5.1 illustrates this dichotomy graphically (the moves in italics are optional; A/B are alternatives; the moves in bold are core). The bifurcation occurs in Move 4, dealing with the factual and legal matrix of the text. As I explain elsewhere (Nikitina 2022a: 238), analysing a corpus of 195 case communications dealing with Article 10 violations against Russia, the introduction of case content in the texts showed notable variations, with 62% adopting the label "Subject matter of the case" (4A, i.e. IMSI) and 36% using "Statement

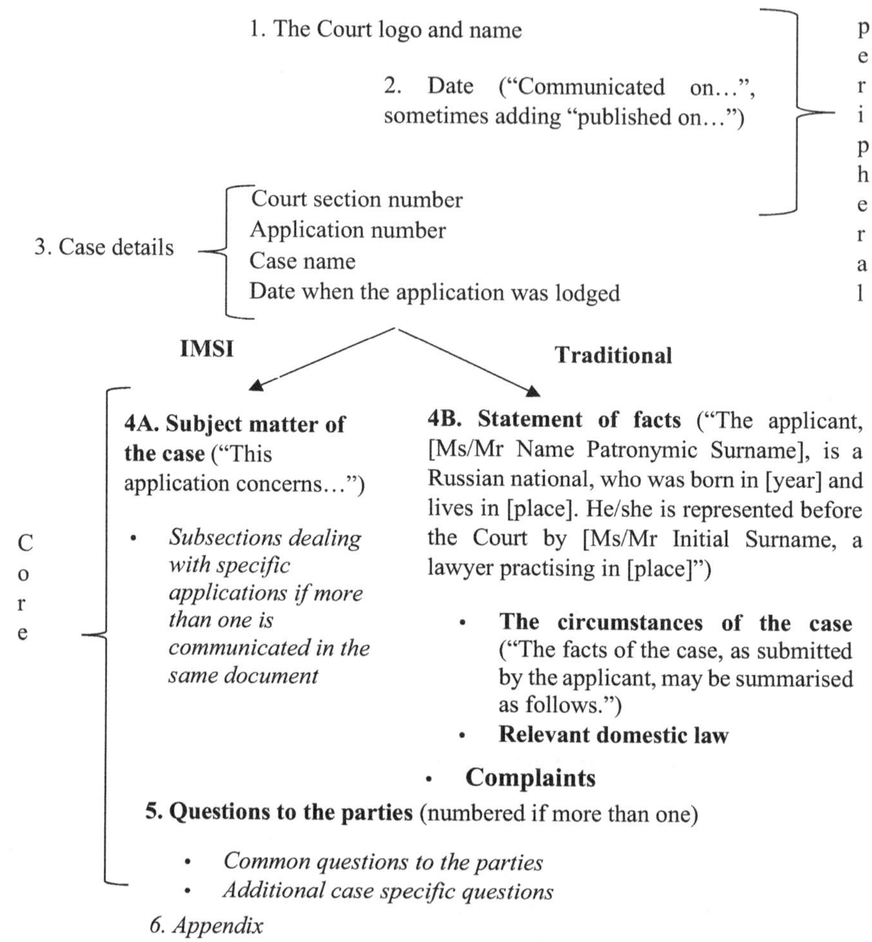

Figure 5.1 Generic structure in case communications
Source: Adapted from Nikitina (2022a: 239).

of facts" (4B, traditional template). The above study analysed case communications drafted between 2016 and 2021, i.e. in the period when the IMSI model was being gradually introduced, hence the ratio of texts following the new and the old formats can find a logical explanation in this transition period. Beyond a mere difference in labels, subtle presentation nuances emerged. The IMSI (4A) texts typically commenced with the phrase "The application concerns . . .", providing a concise case overview, a very "short report" mentioned by Sicilianos (2018: 3). In cases where this formula was omitted, the IMSI introduction started with a depiction of an event or action, emphasizing the foundational actions of the case. Conversely, the case communications following the traditional model introduced the case in 4B with a distinct formula centred on the applicant(s), emphasizing the individuals initiating the application.

Another logical consequence of introducing IMSI – and part of the rationale underlying its creation – concerned the length of texts. The shift to IMSI resulted in shorter texts: with 562 words on average per text in the new model ("half a page noting the case in question and the issue at stake" in Keller & Heri 2018: para. 81) as opposed to 2,150 words in the texts following the traditional template featuring "a detailed analysis of the facts and procedural history of the case as well as the main issues at stake" (Keller & Heri 2018: para. 81).

There were three (2%) texts in the corpus that deviated from the pattern outlined above (Nikitina 2022a: 240). In these texts, Move 4 was substituted by the intertextual formula in (1). Consequently, the focus shifts to the second communicative goal of case communications: to trigger the development of written procedure by asking "Questions to the parties" (Move 5).

(1) The facts and complaints in these applications have been summarised in the Court's Statement of facts and Questions to the parties, which is available in HUDOC.

The "Questions to the parties" core move, common to all texts analysed in the study, invites the parties to provide written observations (or pleadings, see Chapter 6; see also Nikitina 2018a, 2018b) moving along the procedural development of the case. The questions are formulated relying heavily on referential prepositions and short quotations from domestic law (e.g. "Did the national authorities provide any reasoning as regards the statutory requirement of 'exceptional circumstances'?").

Regardless of whether a traditional or a simplified model is used, the resulting text involves extensive knowledge re-elaboration by Registry lawyers, which was also implicitly acknowledged by the ECtHR when they introduced IMSI. As the transfer of knowledge structures from a national into a supranational context occurs, "elements originally embedded in a national legal and judicial system migrate from their natural context into a different environment" (Peruzzo 2019b: 71). Not only are there national elements, but a different type of exposition may also be involved (see 9.2): it is not infrequent to find applications (as one could statistically expect for the highest case-count states) that are drafted by applicants themselves, without any professional legal assistance. In one case against Ukraine, an application was drafted by the applicant's mother who declared to be a cashier in a supermarket, and it lacked the usual legal style markers and instead presented the factual matrix from an informed layperson's perspective (Nikitina 2022b: 95).

5.3 Case communication: translation perspectives

Legal institutional translation at the ECtHR (3.5) is difficult to describe in all-encompassing terms, as it traverses the spectrum of overt and covert endeavours, akin to the light and dark sides of the moon. Reflecting on its nature, Peruzzo (2023) mentions *overt*, or *prototypical*, *translation* (where a source text exists, most frequently used for quotations from legislative or judicial sources) and *covert translation*, which does not correspond to the translation of a whole source text, but manifests itself through "a broader writing or drafting process allowing legal knowledge to circulate beyond national boundaries" (Peruzzo 2023: 159). Brannan (2018: 174–175), as a resident translator, offers a detailed overview of translation activity organization at the ECtHR, primarily focusing on procedural documents at the post-decision stage, including law reports, legal summaries, factsheets, and press releases, all part of a larger system of genres (see 3.3). Translation preceding this stage is rarely institutionalized. Typically, translation at this level is either undertaken by the parties, such as applicants or their counsel, and the government agent's office, as seen in written pleadings (Nikitina 2018a: 167, 2018b: 54; see Chapter 6), or by the Registry lawyers, as with case communications. Consequently, the case communication stage represents a covert or "hidden" layer of institutional translation.

Operating on the "dark side" of the moon, the Registry lawyers process the initial application in a national language, and then summarize (if applicable) and extract relevant fragments from the application directly in one of the official languages of the Court. The resulting document, labelled here "case communication", is then dispatched to the respondent government. Translation procedures at this critical procedural juncture remain somewhat shrouded in mystery. Despite a passing acknowledgment by Brannan (2018: 190) of the existence of such "hidden" translations, accompanied by echoes in Peruzzo (2019a: 36 and 2023: 158), no other linguistic scrutiny has been conducted on this topic. Translation in case communications is of a mixed covert nature, as the target text does not merely mirror the source text in a different language but emerges from complex re-elaboration and knowledge mediation, intended as a fluid phenomenon that is shaped through various forms of communication (Engberg 2022).

Similarly to the judges at the ECtHR, whose proficiency in languages is deemed "one of the most important non-binding substantive criteria" (Kosař 2015: 133; also cited in Brannan 2018: 175), language skills hold significant weight in the selection of Registry lawyers.[2] However, notably, formal translation or linguistic training is not mandatory. In addition, as the majority of Registry lawyers are non-native speakers of English or French (Weston 2005:

2 "A typical vacancy at B1-B3/A1-A3 level requires the candidates to know at least one of the CoE languages, i.e. English or French, and knowledge of the other language is desirable. No minimum CEFR level is indicated; however, given the fierce competitiveness of the selection procedure, only proficient candidates are likely to be pre-selected. Knowledge of one's mother tongue and the national judicial system is a tacit requirement, because candidates in respect of a given country need to hold a university degree issued in that country, assuming their fluency in that national language" (Nikitina 2022a: 236, note 6).

457), when they process applications and draft case communications, they engage in L2 drafting, i.e., drafting in a language other than their native one.

Informal dialogues with Registry lawyers suggest that the selection of knowledge transformation and translation methods often rests in the hands of the involved legal practitioners. As I have suggested in a previous study (Nikitina 2022a: 236), the choice of official language appears to be tacitly determined "based on the active working languages of the legal professionals involved". Parties from the former Soviet bloc as well as Scandinavian parties seem to gravitate towards English in their communication, whereas parties coming from countries whose national languages belong to the neo-romance language group, such as Italy or Romania, tend to prefer French. The Registry lawyers dealing with these national situations also frequently display the same linguistic preferences.[3] Like the CJEU *référendaires* drafting judgments, the ECtHR Registry lawyers drafting case communications "are not only constrained by their own legal language(s) in the reasoning they employ but are equally 'reined in' by the framework of the institutional language in which they work. The layers of 'hidden' translation thus go far beyond simply finding terminological equivalents" (McAuliffe 2020: 72).

While the initial stages of proceedings may not prioritize translation concerns, any oversights or inaccuracies could seep into the judgment, following the currents of these concealed translation mechanisms. The Registry lawyers not only process the application, but also collaborate on the judge rapporteur's draft of the following decision or judgment. Costa (2021: 325) foregrounds the importance of judges' trust into Registry lawyers who must be "totally reliable, so as not to lead the rapporteur astray with his/her superior linguistic and/or cultural knowledge, and to be a faithful 'translator' of the file, in all senses of the word (many documents are in languages other than the Court's two official languages)".

A "substantial amount of 'covert' translation from a third language" (Weston 2005: 449) is recognized as existing in decisions and judgments covering cases against non-English- or French-speaking states. The very wording of judgments may incorporate excerpts from preceding procedural documents. Typically, it concerns descriptions of national legislation (Brannan 2018: 178) and the domestic legal order. The importance of underscoring the scrutiny of terminological-phraseological choices made at this pivotal stage is evident. The ECtHR in-house language professionals work with the court's official languages only, i.e. in a French-English linguistic combination. Most frequently, they will be native speakers of either or both languages. Their ability to intervene substantially in elements linked to the realm of hidden translation from languages they do not speak is restrained.

3 Nikitina (2022a: 236) notes, "Russian-speaking lawyers and the Russian Government's agents appear to prefer to communicate in English, whereas Italian-speaking lawyers and Government agents most frequently seem to rely on French".

As outlined in 2.4, the terminological-phraseological continuum in international organizations typically includes three categories: (1) supranational terms and phrasemes, (2) legal transplants whose meaning has been autonomously reinterpreted by the organization in question and (3) system-bound elements (SBEs), i.e. elements pertaining to the domestic legal order that must remain marked as such. The latter most typically are introduced into the discourse of the ECtHR at the stage when information from applications is processed into case communications through translation. Peruzzo (2019a, 2019b) researching SBEs in the ECtHR judgments against Italy from a Legal Translation Studies standpoint identified a number of translation strategies for their rendition that are detailed in the following section.

5.4 System-bound elements and their translation strategies

5.4.1 System-bound elements

The multiword term "system-bound elements" is not to be confused with "culture-bound elements". Both may initially appear self-explanatory, just as the concepts of system and culture might. A brief explanation of the latter is needed before proceeding with the former, as they lay the theoretical framework for Sections 3.5 and 3.4, respectively. As Peruzzo (2019b: 71) observes, the "cultural turn in translation studies" (Bassnett & Lefevere 1990: 1–13) resulted in a proliferation of studies focused on addressing the challenges posed by transferring culture-bound elements (CBEs) from one language and culture to another. A victim of its popularity, CBEs lack a universally agreed-upon definition or terminology. Translation studies have employed various terms to refer to culture-specific elements (Peruzzo 2019b: 71):

> namely "cultural words" (Ivir 1987: 36; Newmark 1988), "cultural categories" (Newmark 1988: 95), "culture-specific concepts" (Baker 1992: 21, although she also uses "culture-specific items" and "culture-specific words"), "cultural references" (Mailhac 1996; González Davies and Scott-Tennent 2005), "culture-specific items" or "CSIs" (Aixelá 1996; Cómitre Narváez and Valverde Zambrana 2014), "culture-bound terms" (Díaz-Cintas and Remael 2007: 200; Harvey 2000; Schäffner and Wiesemann 2001: 32), "culture-bound or culture-specific phenomena and terms" (Schäffner and Wiesemann 2001: 32), "realia" (Robinson 2003; Florin 1993; Leppihalme 2001), "culturemes" (Whithorn 2014: 160; Nord 1997: 34; Katan 2009: 79), "cultural referents" (Santamaria 2010), "culture-bound elements" (Hagfors 2003), "allusions" (Leppihalme 1997), and "extralinguistic culture-bound references (ECRs)".
>
> (Pedersen 2005: 2)

A logical consequence of the above richness of labels is the smorgasbord of their definitions and classifications. These classifications tie into the very concept of culture, a definition of which lies beyond the scope of this book.[4] What is important for our discussion is to recognize that law, and especially human rights law, is part of a culture. Being "entirely created by humans", law is a social phenomenon as it is closely linked to the culture of a given society (Mattila 2013: 105–106). As Peruzzo (2019b: 77–78) summarizes, "Legal concepts and norms are human constructions that are bound to a specific legal system and that such a legal system is, in turn, the product of a specific culture".

Just as there are differences across different cultures, there are differences across legal systems, with "variable degrees of comparability of legal systems in general and of legal concepts in particular, depending on the relationship between the legal systems and the respective legal families and their historical development" (Peruzzo 2019b: 78). Scholarship on culture-bound elements following the Translation Studies logic converges on the fact that the more culturally embedded a given word or expression is, the harder it is to translate. Similarly, much research on legal translation ponders the (un)translatability of certain legal terms linked to system-specific legal concepts (e.g. Šarčević 1997: 232). The "untranslatables" (Biel 2024: 97) are placed next to other "problems" of legal translation, such as legal transplants, implications of legal texts and subjectivity of meaning. Competence in legal culture is listed by the International Organization for Standardization among the requirements of legal translation[5] as "the ability to understand the distinction and cultural and factual implications behind different legal systems and approaches" (ISO 20771:220: 7). As legal systems are generated by different societies and cultures, "the legal terms of each legal system are also a type of culture-bound element" (Peruzzo 2019b: 78). System-bound terms, thus, are those terms that are embedded in the national legal system. They retain their clear national flavour when introduced into the supranational discourse of human rights, either for reasons of untranslatability or because they must be distinguished from supranational MWUs and legal transplants. Given that the ECtHR operates in only two official languages, English and French, but applications may be drafted in a number of languages nearing 40, whenever case communications are drafted, the Registry lawyers processing them may be faced with translation of system-bound elements. This makes them enter the unchartered territories, "a kind of no man's land which is outside the borders of established disciplines" (Husa 2017: 264), to overcome both the linguistic and the systemic barriers.

5.4.2 *A quest for equivalence: methodological considerations*

Tiersma (2008: 16) accused legal terminology of being "extremely parochial", as it is deeply rooted in the jurisdiction of its origin, bound to the system.

4 Peruzzo (2019b: 77, note 3) mentions, "As far back as 1952, Kroeber and Kluckhohn compiled a list of 164 definitions of 'culture'".

5 ISO 20771:2020 *Legal translation – Requirements*. Geneva: International Organization for Standardization.

System-bound elements, especially those pertaining to the phraseological domain, do not receive adequate support from legal dictionaries, making the idea of "off-the-shelf, all-purpose binary 'equivalents'" (Prieto Ramos 2014b: 15) a utopia of legal translation. And yet, when information exchange is unviable without legal translation, as is the case of supranational courts with multiple and multilingual Member States, a solution has to be found to achieve some sort of equivalence.

A "migrant" from mathematics and logics, where it denotes the relationship of an absolute "one-to-one correspondence" (Šarčević 1997: 234), in Translation Studies this term does not necessarily refer to the untenable heights of absolute equivalence. To put it differently, "if X and Y are said to be equivalents, this simply means that X can be used to translate Y and vice versa, without implying that they are identical at the conceptual level" (Šarčević 1997: 234–235). Equivalence is intended as a gradient. One of the tools to define the degree of equivalence is the conceptual analysis which distinguishes between core characteristics of terms (*essentialia*) and additional characteristics (*accidentalia*) (Šarčević 1997: 237). Achieving *absolute equivalence* is like hitting the bullseye with a perfect arrow shot: every detail matches precisely between the source and target texts. *Near equivalence*, on the other hand, is like hitting the target just outside the bullseye; while it may not be a perfect match, it is close enough to convey the intended meaning effectively between source language and target language concepts, when the respective terms "share all of their essential elements and most of their accidental characteristics" (Šarčević 1997: 238). *Partial equivalence* is the most common type for functional equivalence in legal translation; it occurs when source language and target language concepts "share most of their essential elements and only some of their accidental characteristics", landing the arrow somewhere closer to the outer ridge. Finally, *non-equivalence* characterizes situations when the arrow misses the target entirely, i.e. when source language and target language concepts share only a few or none of their essential elements.

Most studies in legal translation advocate for the pursuit of the so-called *functional equivalence* (Šarčević 1997: 236), also known as *legal equivalence* (Beaupré 1986: 179), *dynamic equivalence* or even *cultural equivalence* (Biel 2024: 103). A functional equivalent – the term used both by translation scholars and comparative lawyers, and the preferred term here – is a term or a MWU "designating a concept or institution of the target legal system having the same function as a particular concept of the source legal system" (Šarčević 1997: 236). To put it differently, it caters both for the content and legal effects and is "the closest natural equivalent" (Šarčević 1997: 235, quoting Nida & Taber 1974: 13). A frequently quoted example of functional equivalents is the French *hypothéque* and the English *mortgage*. Yet, functional equivalents are not a panacea as they may be insufficiently accurate, misleading or just absent, leading to the development of "terminological bridges" or compensation strategies aimed at addressing legal asymmetry and establishing equivalence between terms from different legal systems (Biel & Engberg 2013: 3).

5.4.3 Translation of system-bound elements at the ECtHR

Overviewing system-bound terms in ECtHR judgments against Italy, Peruzzo (2019a: 24–25) identifies several recurrent translation strategies. She relies on Šarčević's (1985, 1997) classification of *translation strategies*, distinguishing among source language and target language-oriented techniques. The former include *transcription*, *phonological/graphological translation* and *loan translation*. The latter comprise such techniques as *adaptation* and *lexical expansion*. In adaptation, functional equivalents are used to cater to the expectations of the receiver. As outlined above, functional equivalents are most frequently of a partial equivalent nature, which amounts their use to adaptation. In lexical expansion, supplementary information is either integrated into the text itself or provided in a glossary or marginal notes. "By expanding or delimiting the sense of functional equivalents, the lexical expansions [. . .] modify concepts of the target legal system, making them artificially correspond to the source concepts or vice versa" (Šarčević 1997: 251). The inclusion of additional information in the text often results in the creation of what are known as "translation couplets or triplets" (Šarčević 1985: 131) or combinations of two or three translation techniques within the same section of translated text.

Peruzzo (2019a: 25–27) lists the following translation strategies, ordered by their frequency, that characterize the introduction of Italian system-bound terms into the ECtHR case-law, examining directly the judgment stage (see Table 5.1).

Peruzzo (2019a: 26–27) mentions that most of these strategies involve the use of loanwords or borrowings, maintaining the original Italian multi-word unit or term. These loanwords are graphically separated, either using italics or inverted commas, and may be placed in brackets or after dashes. Statistically, loanwords occur more frequently after the "main" translation strategy, i.e. descriptive paraphrase, functional equivalent, literal translation or transposition. However, loanwords may occur also before the main translation strategy as summarized in Figure 5.2. Besides translation couplets, Peruzzo (2019a: 28) identifies also translation triplets, falling under one of the first three strategies followed by an acronym, most typically in the source language.

5.5 When national meets supernational: the role of case communications[6]

5.5.1 Study design

This section presents a case study aimed at analysing the role of case communications in the movement of SBEs across various procedural genres of the

6 An earlier version of this section appeared on pages 97–104 in Nikitina J. (2022b) The discourse of the European Court of Human Rights: the role of case communications in the introduction of system-bound elements, in Ločmele, L. (ed.), ***Language for International Communication: Linking Interdisciplinary Perspectives: Language for Specific Purposes in***

Table 5.1 Translation couplets of system-bound elements in the ECtHR judgments against Italy

Translation strategy	*Definition*	*Examples*
Descriptive paraphrase + loanword	Descriptive paraphrases "spell out the intended meaning in neutral language that can be understood by lawyers worldwide" (Šarčević 1997: 252) Loanword or borrowing is a case of zero-translation, i.e. the retention of the source term or MWU.	Admission of fresh evidence (*integrazione probatoria*) On the ground that the alleged facts had never occurred (*perché il fatto non sussiste*) A dangerous Mafia organization (the *n'drangheta*) An alternative measure to detention (*semilibertà*)
Literal equivalent + loanword	Literal equivalents are instances of word-by-word translation which are used for semantically transparent terms or MWUs (Šarčević 1997: 259)	Preliminary investigations judge (*Giudice per le indagini preliminari*) By means of a reasoned decision (*con decreto motivato*)
Functional equivalent + loanword	Functional equivalents "designat[e] a concept or institution of the target legal system having the same function as a particular concept of the source legal system" (Šarčević 1997: 236).	Aiding and abetting the Mafia (*appoggio esterno alla Mafia*)
Transposition + loanword	Transpositions stands for "the substitution of one grammatical category for another, on the basis that both may be fairly said to possess the same semantic weight or equivalent semic density" (Alcaraz Varó & Hughes 2002: 181)	Guilty of having sexually abused (*atti di libidine violenti*) An objective situation effectively permitting every individual to be aware of the acts in question (*situazione oggettiva di effettiva conoscibilità, da parte di tutti, degli atti medesimi*)

Source: Adapted from Peruzzo (2019a: 25–27).

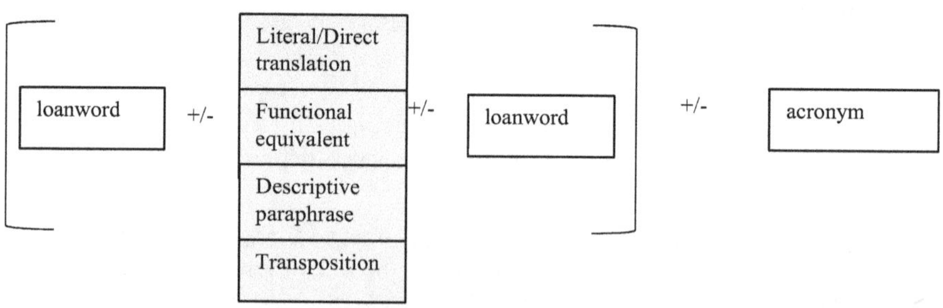

Figure 5.2 Translation strategies for system-bound terms

ECtHR. Do linguistic choices made by case communication drafters "migrate" further into other genres in the ECtHR system? Are there any country-specific differences?

In order to answer these research questions, an ad hoc corpus of four cases (against Latvia, Ukraine, Russia[7] and Italy) was compiled (see Table 5.2). These texts were gathered using the HUDOC database, i.e. the official database of the ECtHR case-law. There were four selection criteria: (1) time, (2) language, (3) Respondent State and (4) subject matter.

The temporal criterion concerned the date of the final judgment: all judgments were delivered between 1 February 2022 and 3 March 2022, covering a period of 31 days. The second criterion related to the language in which the final judgment was rendered: only judgments in English were selected. As regards the third criterion, four different Respondent States with four different languages of the initial applications were chosen. Finally, the fourth criterion was the subject of the case: only cases dealing with violations of Article 6 ECHR (right to a fair trial) were selected to ensure thematic consistency.

After collecting all the materials available in HUDOC in open access, access to initial applications and written observations (see Chapter 6) has been requested. These are referred to using Swales' notion of ***occluded genres*** because they remain "out of sight" of general public and are intended

Table 5.2 Corpus composition

Case name	*Martynenko v. Ukraine*	*Pīlāgs v. Latvia*	*D'Amico v. Italy*	*Kramareva v. Russia*
Application no.	40829/12	66897/13	46586/14	4418/18
Judgment date	24/02/2022	17/02/2022	03/03/2022	01/02/2022
Application	ca. 6,000	ca. 4,000	n/a	n/a
Case communication	1,903	1,025	221 (French)	629
Observations by the Government	2,745	4,728	n/a	n/a
Observations by the Applicant	1,746	ca. 4,900	n/a	n/a
Additional observations by the Government	–	1,739	n/a	n/a
Decision	–	–	–	–
Judgment	1,632	1,596	4,129	8,122
Press release	–	–	–	131
Legal summary	–	–	653	–
Total texts	5	6	3	3
Total tokens	14,026	17,988	5,003	8,882

the Era of Multilingualism and Technologies. Volume 4. Riga: University of Latvia Press. It is reproduced here with permission of the publisher and minor modifications.

7 The corpus was compiled before 16 March 2022, when Russia was still a CoE member. The findings are nonetheless valid and potentially future-oriented as Russian is used in a number of other CoE Member States, and the ECtHR continued hearing cases against Russia in 2023.

for "specific individual or small-group audiences" (Swales 1996: 46), see Chapter 3. Despite the final judgment had been already rendered, access to the Italian and the Russian applications and written observations was not granted, but they may become available for consultation at a later stage.

Texts belonging to the occluded genres were provided as graphical files (.jpg, .tif and .pdf) and required optical recognition. Unfortunately, it did not manage to recognize successfully Cyrillic characters in Ukrainian and diacritics in Latvian, so parts of these documents had to be retyped. As a result, mainly the graphical files were used for the analysis, with an approximate number of characters indicated in Table 5.2 (marked "ca.") for informational purposes. Finally, the case communication in *D'Amico v. Italy* was drafted in French, which is the most frequently chosen language by the Italian Registry lawyers, but it was kept for the analysis of SBEs.

5.5.2 *Reliance on case communications*

Three out of four case communications in the corpus follow the traditional format and range between 16% and 32% of the original application in terms of their length (see Table 5.3), whereas the fourth amounts to ca. 5% of the original application, which shows an extensive amount of summarization as part of the translation/entextualization/recontextualization process.

Despite the IMSI format is available since 2018 "to shift the burden of factual reconstruction onto the Governments and *prevent factual objections*" (Sicilianos & Kostopoulou 2019: 100, emphasis added), only *Martynenko v. Ukraine* applied it. The Government in their written observations "respectfully ask[ed] the Court to supplement its exposition of the factual matrix of the present case with the following facts" (*Martynenko v. Ukraine*), showing how Governments indeed object to factual reconstruction. Yet, when the facts sections across various genres were compared, it emerged that the judgment used a verbatim account of the case communication (see examples (2) and (3) that differ only by the spelling of *eyewitnesses*, emphasis added).

Table 5.3 Case communications

Case name	*Communication year*	*Format*	*Proportion to the original application (%)*
Martynenko v. Ukraine	2020	Traditional	32
Pīlāgs v. Latvia	2015	Traditional	26
D'Amico v. Italy	2019	IMSI	16*
Kramareva v. Russia	2019	Traditional	5*

Note: * Data marked with an asterisk represent an estimated value which was calculated based on statistics available in several previous studies that analysed similar corpora (Nikitina 2022a, 2022b).

(2) According to the police reports on *a test purchase of drugs*, on 12 and 30 January 2009 the applicant sold a small quantity of cannabis to his acquaintance P. used by the police as their undercover agent. The supposed purchases took place in the apartment house where the applicant lived, in the absence of any *eye-witnesses*. (*Martynenko v. Ukraine*, case communication)

(3) According to the police reports on *a test purchase of drugs*, on 12 and 30 January 2009 the applicant sold a small quantity of cannabis to his acquaintance P. used by the police as their undercover agent. The supposed purchases took place in the apartment house where the applicant lived, in the absence of any *eyewitnesses*. (*Martynenko v. Ukraine*, Judgment)

Interestingly enough, potentially system-bound elements in the Ukrainian case are not rendered through the use of translation couplets featuring any loanwords. In no texts (besides the application written entirely in Ukrainian by the applicant's mother) are there any loanwords or otherwise non-translated elements. The SBEs present are somewhat domesticated using functional equivalents (such as *a test purchase of drugs* in (2) and (3) for *оперативна закупка*) or translated literally (e.g. *Criminal Code of Ukraine* for *Кримінальний кодекс України* or *appeal and cassation proceedings* for *апеляційне та касаційне провадження*).

A similar scenario appears in *Kramareva v. Russia*, another case using Cyrillic. Despite multiple references to national legislation and proceedings in the judgment, no words are left in Russian. The names of numerous judiciary bodies mentioned are translated literally with the transliteration of the toponym (*the Preobrazhensky District Court of Moscow*), which undoubtedly maintains its system-bound character. In contrast to the Ukrainian case communication, the case communication in *Kramareva v. Russia* applied the strategy of translation couplets, introducing both a literal translation and a source expression in brackets (the Preobrazhenskiy District Court of Moscow (*Преображенский районный суд г. Москвы*)) or even transliterating an acronym followed by a proper name (GUP Mosecostroy (*ГУП 'Мосэкострой'*)). At the same time, a type of a legal entity (AO) was translated with a functional equivalent (JSC), followed by the loan acronym (Mosinzhproekt JSC (*АО 'Мосинжпроект'*), which indicates a hybrid translational strategy. Nevertheless, none of the loanwords migrated into the final judgment, where the drafters chose to maintain only the translations.

In *D'Amico v. Italy*, in line with Peruzzo's (2019a) findings, a translation couplet with a loanword was introduced both in the case communication (*l'indemnité intégrative spéciale* (*'indennità integrativa speciale'*)) and in the judgment (*a special supplementary allowance* (*indennità integrativa speciale – 'the IIS'*)), with the only difference concerning the use of quotation marks in French versus English and the introduction of a loan acronym in the judgment, making the expression a translation triplet.

Table 5.4 Example of a system-bound element across different genres in *Pīlāgs v. Latvia*

Judgment	*Case Communication*	*Government's Observation*	*Applicant's Observations*
the Bureau for the Prevention and Combating of Corruption (*Korupcijas novēršanas un apkarošanas birojs* – "the KNAB")	the Bureau for the Prevention and Combating of Corruption (*Korupcijas novēršanas un apkarošanas birojs* – "KNAB")	the Office for the Prevention and Combating of Corruption ("the KNAB")	the Corruption Prevention and Combating Bureau (*Korupcijas novēršanas un apkarošanas birojs*) (hereinafter referred to as the KNAB)
Translation triplet: literal translation + loan multiword term + loan acronym	Translation triplet: literal translation + loan multiword term + loan acronym	Translation doublet: functional translation + loan acronym	Translation triplet: literal translation + loan multiword term + loan acronym with an introductory phrase

In *Pīlāgs v. Latvia*, as Table 5.4 illustrates, the judgment adopts the same multiword term as proposed in the case communication, again signalling the almost verbatim reliance on this source, as the only difference between these two texts is in the use of the definite article before the loan acronym *KNAB*.

The Applicant opted for a very similar strategy in his observations selecting a translation triplet composed of a literal translation (maintaining even the same nominal structure) followed by a loan multiword term with a loan acronym and an introductory phrase. At the same time, the Government offered a different strategy: they changed the head noun in the multiword SBE from a phonologically closer "Bureau" to its functional equivalent "Office" and omitted the loanword. As the SBE at hand is an administrative body with probably an existing official English translation of its name known to the Government, it is remarkable that the judgment chose to rely on the translation provided by the Registry lawyers and not the Government.

5.5.3 SBEs: terminological variation

The Court frequently refers to its previous judgments in similar cases or in relation to the same legislation (Peruzzo 2019b: 99), thus in a case on undercover operations in one member state, other case-law dealing with the same issue in relation to another state is often quoted. Moreover, different national laws may interpret and define undercover operations in a different way. In other words, the same term may have different legal consequences across different systems. This highlights the importance of system-bound terminology adopted in judgments. As the evidence adduced in this study suggests, these choices tend to migrate with little modifications from case communications.

Table 5.5 illustrates the terminological variation concerning the SBE *operatīvais eksperiments* in *Pīlāgs v. Latvia* (the numbers in brackets indicate the number of occurrences).

Already in the application drafted in Latvian two similar multiword terms are used, which are both maintained in the case communication as translation couplets ***undercover operation*** (*operatīvais eksperiments*) and ***operational investigation*** (*operatīvās uzskaites lieta*). After the first mention of the translation couplets, the case communication goes on by using only the translated part in English, which in the second case presents a small inconsistency (operation*al* vs. operat*ive*). The Government in its observations uses two translations without any loanwords: ***the special operative experiment*** and ***the special investigative experiment***, which seem to be variants of the same concept. The Applicant in his observations, which are drafted in L2 English or translated by his own means in accordance with the rules concerning written pleadings, refers to the concept using a different translation couplet: ***investigative test*** (*operatīvais eksperiments*). Finally, the judgment replicates the translation couplet used in the case communication, again demonstrating full reliance on this genre as concerns the rendition of SBEs.

Table 5.5 System-bound elements and terminological variation in *Pīlāgs v. Latvia*

Application	*Case Communication*	*Government Observations*	*Applicant's Observations*	*Judgment*
operatīvais eksperiments	undercover operation (*operatīvais eksperiments*) undercover operation (3); operations (1) operational investigation (*operatīvās uzskaites lieta*), operative investigation (2)	the special operative experiment the special investigative experiment	investigative test (*operatīvais eksperiments*)	undercover operation (*operatīvais eksperiments*), undercover operation (6); operation (4)
operatīva darbība (slepenu) nolūkā iesaistīt mani noziedzīgu darbību veikšanā	incitement claim; incitement; allegation; KNAB officials had incited him (2)	incitement plea	repeated investigative test (incitement)	incitement (11); incitement plea (2)
				entrapment (2); plea of entrapment (1)

There are altogether four Latvian cases in the ECtHR case-law that deal with *operatīvais eksperiments*: *Baltiņš* (2013), *Taraneks* (2014), *Meimanis* (2015), and *Vinks and Rubicka* (2020). Curiously, the two earlier cases render it in their judgments as *investigative test* (*operatīvais eksperiments*) (same as the Applicant's version), while the two later cases use *undercover operation* (*operatīvais eksperiments*), i.e. the multiword term with a loanword used in the case communication and in the judgment. As *Pīlāgs v. Latvia* was communicated in 2015, it is possible to hypothesise that the current version of the SBE was consolidated in 2015, when, probably, the Latvian lawyer of the Registry changed. This illustrates how terminology in a supranational court is still very much subject to human factors, especially when SBEs are involved, which deserves future inquiry.

Finally, Table 5.5 shows that along with translation couplets a functional equivalent *police incitement* was used by all the parties, with grammatical variants *to incite* and multiword terms *incitement plea* and *incitement claim* to render *operatīva darbība (slepenu) nolūkā iesaistīt mani noziedzīgu darbību veikšanā*. The ECtHR provided a definition of *police incitement* in *Ramanauskas v. Lithuania* (judgment of 5 February 2008 at paragraphs 54–55) as a situation

> where the officers involved – whether members of the security forces or persons acting on their instructions – do not confine themselves to investigating criminal activity in an essentially passive manner, but exert such an influence on the subject as to incite the commission of an offence that would otherwise not have been committed, in order to make it possible to establish the offence, that is, to provide evidence and institute a prosecution.

Peculiarly, in the *Pīlāgs* judgment another term appears: *entrapment*, showing that a number of different people worked on the judgment's drafting. It is used as a synonym for *police incitement*. Guide on Article 6 (Council of Europe & ECtHR 2024: 52, note 6) states that "The terms entrapment, police incitement and agent provocateurs are used in the Court's case-law interchangeably". A quick HUDOC search yields 68 hits of *entrapment* (most cases against Russia (18), Romania (10), United Kingdom (9), the Republic of Moldova and Lithuania (6)) and 346 hits of *police incitement* (most cases against Russia (71), Turkey (56), Romania (20), Ukraine and the Republic of Moldova (17), Azerbaijan (16) and Lithuania (11)). At the same time, the already mentioned *Guide on Article 6* (Council of Europe & ECtHR 2024) – prepared by the CoE personnel and drafted originally in English – clearly prefers *entrapment* (38 hits) over *police incitement* (21). The UK cases also demonstrate a preponderance of *entrapment*. It may be hypothesized that the latter term appeared in the *Pīlāgs v. Latvia* judgment as a result of heteroglossia inherent in the ECtHR system, which requires further investigation from a terminological standpoint.

5.6 Case communications and culture-bound elements

5.6.1 Freedom of expression

As Section 5.4 illustrated, much of the translation choices between non-official and official languages in the ECtHR case-law is made at the case communication stage. Searching for legal equivalents resembles at times a wild goose chase, which requires a high level of expertise in comparative law, legal translation as well as the knowledge of professional and discursive practices in the source legal system of a given state and in the supranational system of the ECtHR. As Peruzzo's (2019a) and Nikitina's (2022a) work illustrated, frequently SBEs revolve around the classical descriptions of legal processes and institutions. In addition to these intrinsic difficulties of dealing with different legal systems, the Registry lawyers are exposed also to more general types of culture-bound elements (CBEs) that do not necessarily belong to the legal field. Despite their general nature, such CBEs may pose additional challenges at the case acceptance and notification stage.

Traditionally, legal translation is depicted as a deeply technical and specialized endeavour. While there is room for a degree of creativity in legal translation, especially concerning syntactical and stylistic changes, the extent of tolerated creativity in legal translation without endangering the uniformity of interpretation and application is not clear (Šarčević 1997: 116); and anyway, it pales in comparison to the artistic liberties often taken in literary translation having to deal with linguistic creativity.

All languages stretch between conventionality and creativity. Conventionality gravitates towards formulaic phrases and standardized institutional contexts, shaping familiar and repetitive linguistic structures guided by grammar rules and societal norms. The conventional end of the continuum manifests itself through reliance on genres and crystallized legal patterns. Conversely, creativity emerges through departures from these linguistic norms and regulations, manifesting in unconventional word usage, bending of rules, formation of irregular compounds and unique linguistic patterns (Nikitina 2019b: 314). While it is atypical for institutional legal translation to face cases of linguistic creativity, in the ECtHR discourse – by virtue of the rights safeguarded by the Convention – some highly creative scenarios emerge.

Article 10 of the ECHR safeguards the freedom of expression, affirming the right to hold opinions and share information without government interference, transcending geographical boundaries.[8] While many cases invoking Article 10 involve risks to image or reputation and defamation claims stemming from media publications, some also centre on unconventional forms of expression, such as altered drawings of political figures, posters and videos, which

8 Article 10.1 ECHR specifically recites: "Everyone has the right to freedom of expression. This right shall include freedom to hold opinions and to receive and impart information and ideas without interference by public authority and regardless of frontiers. This Article shall not prevent States from requiring the licensing of broadcasting, television or cinema enterprises."

face similar legal scrutiny. While the pictorial cases are undoubtedly curious, this book does not pursue the goals of multimodal exploration of discourse, so the primary focus will be placed on unconventional forms of expression.

A significant part of Article 10 cases deals with language-based harassment, the legal regulation of which is frequently quite blurred across the CoE Member States. The right to freedom of speech typically does not protect against or authorize insults, untruthful language (perjury, fraud, defamation), language used to incite or execute crime (solicitation, provocation, threats) and trolling, although the latter is quite hard to define (Hardaker 2020). So frequently, Article 10 cases revolve around balancing the right to free speech with the need to prevent harm or offence to individuals or society. National courts often consider factors such as the context in which the speech occurred, the intent behind the speech, the social value of the expression and the potential harm caused by the language. While freedom of expression is a fundamental right protected by many legal systems, it is not absolute. The interpretation of what constitutes offensive language and where the boundary lies between freedom of expression and harmful speech is subject to ongoing legal debate and may evolve over time in response to societal norms and values.

5.6.2 Conventions on the translation of unconventional?

As I have noticed in a previous study, several case communications dealing with Article 10 abundantly used creative language which ranged "from colourful epithets to straightforward taboo lexis" (Nikitina 2022a: 243). Some applications in Article 10 cases contain highly culture-bound expressions that would be lost on judges – who do not necessarily speak every national language or master their less conventional layers of expressivity – without the linguistic and cultural mediation of the Registry lawyers processing these cases.

Determining what constitutes offensive expressions, including obscenity and profanity, especially in defamation cases, falls under the purview of forensic linguistics, where it is acknowledged that "prosecuting crimes based on offensive linguistic behaviour is considered notoriously difficult" (Hardaker 2020: 700). As already mentioned in 4.5, to be considered offensive, language "must exceed 'the bounds of normal, civil and legitimate criticism'" (ECtHR Admissibility Guide 2023b: 56, para. 255). Works on insults and impoliteness in legal context include also the dimension of intentionality (Culpeper 2005: 38; Culpeper & Hardaker 2017; see also 8.5–8.6). For a statement to be considered offensive, its producer has typically to pursue the goal of insulting the receiver(s).

While an average user of language has an intuitive understanding of what counts as insulting or even obscene, it must be subject to more definitive rule in a legal context. For instance, in the United States, reliance is made on the so-called Miller test (*Miller v. California* 1973) where it is defined "as something that is sexually salacious and/or scatological, and that also lacks serious literary, artistic, scientific or political value" (Hardaker 2020: 699). It is important to distinguish between the concepts of offensive language and vulgarity. As the Court stresses in *Atamanchuk v. Russia* (para. 47),[9]

> Offensive language may fall outside the protection of freedom of expression if it amounts to "wanton denigration", but the use of vulgar phrases in itself is not decisive in the assessment of an offensive expression as it may well serve merely stylistic purposes. Style constitutes part of communication as the form of expression and is as such protected together with the substance of the ideas and information expressed.

This section will focus predominantly on vulgar expressions and issues of style, as their culture-bound nature is hard to dispute. A typical understanding of linguistic vulgarity includes expressions pertaining to sexuality, including both sexual intercourse and genitalia, as well as scatological references or other bodily functions. McEnery (2006: 30, his examples) categorized "bad" language by its "scale of offence" into five categories: (1) very mild (*bloody, crap*); (2) mild (*arse, bitch*); (3) moderate (*arsehole, shag*); (4) strong (*fuck*) and (5) very strong (*cunt*). Obviously, the ranking of offence may take a different scale across cultures, but typically sexual and scatological references remain vulgar, even when used as in-group identity markers for "mock impoliteness". In this paper, vulgarity, besides clear thematic reference delineated above, subsumes the idea of being expressed using taboo or slang words. In other words, neutral and scientific terms denoting the same areas (e.g. "anus") and actions (e.g. "copulate") do not qualify as vulgar, even if they can be equally offensive depending on their usage. In addition to straightforward taboo (Allan 2019) or obscene expressions (strong and very strong in McEnery's (2006)[10] taxonomy), I include under vulgarisms dysphemisms[11] and slang expressions with the same referents of the mild-moderate spectrum.

Translating insults poses pragmatic challenges due to their culture-bound nature. As Mateo and Yus observe (2000: 100), "insults are [. . .] culturally bound. The cognitive drive which impels people to insult one another is the same for everyone, but the tools employed differ (sometimes radically) from one language to another". Offensive language often relies on specific cultural references, wordplay and social dynamics that may not directly translate into other languages. Moreover, the impact and severity of an insult can vary significantly depending on the cultural background and social context of the target audience. Insults may even function as discourse markers of solidarity (Culpeper et al. 2017), thus not being intended to offend. The challenge

9 Application no. 4493/11, Judgment (Third Section) of 12 October 2020 (final).

10 McEnery's (2006) gradient may be perceived as typically British, and is not necessarily applicable in a cross-linguistic perspective. It is quoted here to acknowledge that vulgarity may have a different offensive load.

11 As Allan (2019: 2) observes, "dysphemism is typically impolite because it is offensive; orthophemism ('straight-talking') is polite and so is euphemism ('sweet-talking')".

of accurately and effectively translating offensive expressions from one language to another is well documented, particularly for legal interpreters, who must possess advanced pragmatic skills (Hale et al. 2020), striving to maintain the intended tone, impact and level of offence conveyed by the original insult. Another area of research tackling the translation of insults applying the paradigms of Translation Studies and pragmatics is audiovisual translation (Avila-Cabrera 2023). For institutional legal translation carried out by lawyers, and not linguists, this issue seems to be a relatively new and underresearched avenue.

When the Registry lawyers have to notify cases revolving around offensive language and vulgar CBEs to the Respondent Government as well as make them understandable to the ECtHR judges who do not speak the national language, it requires the highest level of pragmatic competence (Hale et al. 2020: 388) and translation experience (Hale et al. 2020: 387), going well beyond a comparative law perspective, typically required of lawyers.

Some of the CBEs translated by the Registry lawyers during the case communication (CC) stage included insults reproducing jail jargon (Nikitina 2022a: 242); see (4), which is included under the category of "vulgarity".

(4) On 31 May 2012 in a speech delivered during a parliamentary session, the applicant – who was then a parliamentarian in the Pskov Regional Parliamentary Assembly (*Псковское областное Собрание депутатов*) – addressed another parliamentarian (Mr S.) with the following phrase: "But you've been G.'s stooge, always – the whole region knows that!" ("А вот то, что Вы были "шестеркой" Г., всегда, – это тоже знает вся область!") (CC, Savitskiy v. Russia 2017, underlining added for emphasis)

While the source insult *шестерка* was translated using the functional equivalent "stooge" with a similar derogatory pragmatic force, it lost all connotations of the prison jargon in translation, somewhat mitigating the general pragmatic effect. Curiously, the wording of the Chamber judgment in the case *Savitskiy v. Russia* (2022: para. 10)[12] used a different functional equivalent (10), "errand boy", losing the pragmatic marking of vulgarity in the expression itself but adding it as a premodifying gloss. A possible explanation may derive from the fact that judgments (in contrast to case communications) are subject to linguistic revision provided by non-Russian speaking experts, which may have generated the pragmatic mitigation.

(5) As to the content of the impugned statements, there must be a clear distinction between criticism and insult. In the instant case, the applicant used a vulgar expression "errand boy" (*шестерка*, Russian word for "six" used to indicate a lackey to an authority in prison slang). (*Savitskiy v. Russia*, Judgment 2022)

12 Application no. 35839/13, Third Section Judgment of 8 November 2022.

In legal interpreting (Hale et al. 2020: 373), the primary approach to translating vulgar or offensive expressions involves introducing a functional equivalent, just as it happened in (4) and (5), because an insult becomes such only if it produces the desired pragmatic effects of offending the target audience.

HUDOC search for Article 10 case-law featuring vulgar expressions (additional search word "vulgar") produced 36 results. I sorted these cases discarding those that did not deal with language (such as graphical vulgarity) or did not use language with sexual or scatological innuendos. The resulting corpus contains 12 cases, for all of which judgments and case communications were gathered, see Table 5.6. As more than one vulgar CBE could be the object of the case, I manually extracted all of them from judgments, cross-checking the translation solutions in case communications, using a spreadsheet. Next, I analysed how vulgar CBEs were rendered into English, reporting the results in Table 5.7.

Peculiarly, the most widespread solution included literal translation, used in 51% of CBEs collectively. In (6), a Hungarian scatological insult involving a hedgehog is translated literally, i.e. using the same metaphorical mapping, which, although semantically transparent in its unpleasant sensory implications, does not convey the constructional meaning of disdain or contempt towards someone, which is the functional intention.

(6) People like this should go and shit a hedgehog and spend all their money on their mothers' tombs until they drop dead. ("Azért az ilyenek szarjanak sünt és költsék az összes bevételüket anyjuk sírjára, amíg meg

Table 5.6 Cases dealing with vulgarity

Genre	*Texts*	*Tokens*	*Types*
Judgment	12	148,414	10,652
Case communication	12	20,647	3,993

Table 5.7 Translation strategies for vulgar culture-bound elements in judgments

Translation strategy	*Number of vulgar CBEs*	*%*
Functional equivalent + loanword	2	5
Functional equivalent	10	25
Loanword + gloss	4	10
Loanword	2	5
Descriptive paraphrase	1	3
Descriptive + gloss	1	3
Literal translation	13	33
Literal translation + gloss	1	3
Literal translation + loanword	6	15

nem dögölnek.") (Magyar Tartalomszolgáltatók Egyesülete and Index. Hu Zrt v. Hungary)[13]

The popularity of literal translation may find an explanation in the limited number of referents, as the number of taboo physiological functions or organs is typically universally restricted by human nature.

Functional equivalents were used in 30% of cases, with most standalone cases coming from a single case: *Delfi AS v. Estonia*,[14] about a news portal not deleting insulting comments. As (7) illustrates, the graphically modified "fcking" was used as a functional equivalent to reinforce the negative epithets attributed to L. In (8) again a relatively "standard" English-language amalgam vulgarism pertaining to the sexual domain was used to render a more creative Russian compound featuring a modified version of "bitch" and the abbreviation of an insult inviting the recipient to "go to male genitalia".

(7) If there was an ice road, [one] could easily save 500 for a full car, fckng [L.] pay for that economy, why does it take 3 [hours] for your ferries if they are such good icebreakers, go and break ice in Pärnu port . . . instead, fcking monkey, I will cross [the strait] anyway and if I drown, it's your fault. (*Delfi AS v. Estonia*)

(8) "I hate the cops, for fuck's sake" ("Ненавижу ментов, сцуконах") (*Savva Terentyev v. Russia*)

It appears that whenever functional equivalents are employed, they result in the overall flattening or conventionalization of vulgar expressions.

To preserve the original style, some cases relied on translation couplets with loanwords, used in 35% of cases, similarly to the tendency identified by Peruzzo (2019a) for SBEs (see 5.4.3).

(9) His comment on the second video read: "Russia gifted $30 million to Kyrgyzstan. Putin is a fairy-tale dumbwit." The expression "fairy-tale dumbwit" (*сказочный долбоёб*) was first used to describe the hapless Prince Myshkin in the 2001 Russian comedy film Down House, a spoof of Dostoyevsky's novel *The Idiot.* Since then it has become a popular way of describing people who are so stupid that they could not possibly exist in the real world. (CC, *Kartyzhev v. Russia*, 2020)

In (9), for example, the functional equivalent "dumbwit" with a literally translated epithet "fairy-tale" is coupled with a zero-translation, i.e. a loanword multi-word insult *сказочный долбоёб* and an explanation providing cultural background for the sake of the extended participation framework, i.e. judges and lawyers coming from different contexts. This translation demonstrates

13 Application no. 22947/13, Judgment (Fourth Section) of 2 May 2016 (final).

14 Application no. 64569/09, Judgment (Grand Chamber) of 16 June 2015.

pragmatic mitigation. Whereas the compound "dumbwit" denotes only the stupidity of the subject, based on the combination of words "dumb" and "wit", the source insult belongs to the taboo layer of language, as the compound *долбоёб* features both the idea of "dumb" (*долбо-*) in the first part and a deverbal noun coming from the verb denoting sexual intercourse in the second part (*-ёб*). In other words, the vulgar marking of the insult was entirely lost in translation. As I noticed in an earlier study (2022a: 243), "The hesitation with straightforward taboo equivalents is comparable to many cases in legal interpreting, where obscenities are toned down (Felberg Radanović & Šarić 2017) as interpreters feel responsible for saying them. It is understandable that putting such equivalents in writing in a supranational context would require even a greater effort".

This tendency is well observed in examples (10)–(13), underlining added. Examples (10) and (12) are extracted from case communications, i.e. these translations are produced by the Registry lawyers, whereas examples (11) and (13) are extracted from the judgments of the same cases, i.e. at the procedural stage where court documents undergo linguistic revision by experts without any knowledge of the national language.

(10) What will you do to us? There are millions of you, sheeple (*быдло*), and two thousands of us, people. (CC, *Moseyev v. Russia* 2017)[15]

(11) What will you do to us? There are millions of you, scum («быдло»), and two thousand of us, human beings. (Judgment, Third Section, *Moseyev v. Russia* 2022)

(12) The second applicant (Mr Makarashvili), whilst standing peacefully among other protesters, was holding a banner with an inscription identifying the Panorama project with a human penis, using the lewdest synonym available in the colloquial Georgian language for the latter: "Not the Panorama but a cock" ("პანორამა არა (*)ლე") (CC, *Peradze and others against Georgia* 2016)

(13) The second applicant (Mr Makarashvili), whilst standing still among the other protesters, held a banner with an inscription likening Panorama Tbilisi to a human penis, using the lewdest synonym available in the colloquial Georgian language for the latter: "Panorama, my cock!" ("პანორამა არა, ყლე!"). (Judgment, Fifth Section, *Peradze and others against Georgia*, 2023)

In (12) the vulgar Georgian expression (loanword in parenthesis) was mitigated using an asterisk in the case communication, eliminated in the judgment (13) along with some minor stylistic adjustments. In (10) a less conventional insult was proposed as a functional equivalent, which successfully rendered the source insult's etymology (a mass noun to refer to cattle), while remaining derogatory. It underwent a lexical change at the judgment stage (11), losing

15 Application no. 78618/13.

its animalistic origins but increasing the pragmatic value of an insult, getting closer to the original CBE, in what Avila-Cabrera (2023: 78)[16] defined as "toning up" of the semantic-pragmatic load.

Finally, in 16% of cases the strategy of providing a gloss, i.e. a brief explanation in a note or in parenthesis, was used. As with functional equivalents, the distribution of glosses was skewed as it was used mainly in one case: *Klein v. Slovakia*.[17]

(14) I. As is generally known, the Earth is a flat board. Even if it is not a flat board, the Sun turns around it. Even if it does not turn, the church dignitary made love to his mother[1]. [1] The verb "trkať" was used which is a slang and unofficial term for, inter alia, having sexual intercourse (The Dictionary of Slovak Slang by B. Hochel, HEVI 1993: 164). (Klein v. Slovakia)

Example (14) illustrates how a descriptive paraphrase without any vulgar marking ("omitted transfer" of insult in Avila-Cabrera (2023: 78)) was used along with a gloss explaining that the source expression indeed had a sexual innuendo.

Returning to the conceptual analysis discussed in 5.4.2, it is curious to apply the idea of core (*essentialia*) and additional (*accidentalia*) (Šarčević 1997: 237) elements to insult translation in the legal field. In general insult translation, the semantic components are closer to the category of *accidentalia*, whereas the pragmatic ones take on the role of *essentialia*. The legal field, however, requires an increased precision in translation, which results in the reliance on such compensation strategies as translation couplets with a loanword and glosses.

Translation of vulgarity is extremely challenging and deserving a more extensive analysis than the one provided on these pages. The idea behind this brief overview was to illustrate the complexity of covert institutional translation, including the translation of insults, which frequently falls short of reproducing the same pragmatic effect. A sentence found in the case *Szanyi v. Hungary*,[18] para. 25, is emblematic of these translation difficulties: "the Government added that an English translation of the interpellations did not fully

16 Avila-Cabrera (2023: 78) distinguishes between successful and unsuccessful translation of insults. When the meaning or tone of the source text (ST) is effectively conveyed in the target text (TT), it indicates successful transfer. He categorizes it into three types: "toned up" when the TT intensifies the meaning compared to the ST, "maintained" when the meaning remains balanced, and "toned down" when the meaning is softened due to linguistic or temporal constraints. Conversely, instances where the semantic or pragmatic load of the ST is not fully transferred to the TT are divided into two categories: "neutralized" when the chosen TT lacks the offensive or intense meaning of the original, and "omitted" when the meaning or tone of the ST is not maintained in the TT.

17 Application no. 72208/01, Judgment (Fourth Section) of 31 January 2007 (final).

18 Application no. 35493/13, Judgment (Fourth Section) of 6 March 2017 (final).

reflect their original vulgar tone". Probably, on account of these observations the judgment contained a footnote specifying that translation was carried out by the Registry. While most judgments do not feature such authorship indications, based on the analysis of different procedural genres it is clear that translations of such CBEs, similarly to legal SBEs, falls on the Registry lawyers' shoulders shortly before or at the case communication stage.

The need to keep the same level of derogatory connotations along with legal precision decidedly places the Registry lawyers tasked with drafting case communications in a position requiring the highest level of translation expertise, not frequent even in literary translation, debunking to a certain extent the myth that legal institutional translation is a dry and purely technical enterprise.

5.7 Conclusions

This chapter delved into the role of covert institutional legal translation, which, though overlooked and undervalued, is fundamental to the Court's operation. The flow of applications in different national languages necessitates extensive covert institutional translation during the crucial stage of case communication. This juncture serves as a critical point in the transformation of knowledge from national to supranational legal systems, marking the Court's acceptance of cases and initiating the subsequent written procedure.

By adopting the methodological outlook of Legal Terminology and Legal Translation Studies, this chapter reflected on the role of covert translation in addressing challenging linguacultural hurdles such as system-bound elements (SBEs) and culture-bound elements (CBEs). The findings underscore the expertise of Registry lawyers who facilitate this linguistic and cultural exchange within the European human rights machinery, thereby enabling the smooth progression of procedural steps, starting with the genre of written pleadings discussed in Chapter 6.

6 Written observations

The duelling construction of reality

6.1 Introduction

In contrast to many domestic settings where oral hearings reign, the procedure before the European Court of Human Rights (ECtHR) is predominantly written. Once an application is declared admissible and the case is communicated, the parties to the case may submit further observations and evidence in writing. As the Court's popularizing brochure "The ECHR in 50 questions" states under question 30, "The Court basically has a written procedure but occasionally decides to hold public hearings in specific cases".[1] The Court's pinnacle genre, the judgment, too, is typically delivered in writing, with public hearing delivery being an exception.[2]

The standard procedure is carried out through the genre of *written pleadings* (*observations écrites*). Codified in Rule 38 of the Rules of Court, written pleadings stand for an exchange of submissions and observations between the parties and the Court. Not much is known about this genre. In the ECtHR system of genres (see 3.4), written pleadings remain *occluded* (Swales 1996) as they are not accessible to the general public, unlike the oral courtroom pleadings in national proceedings and similarly to the context of the International Court of Justice (ICJ), where the respective stage is termed "written proceedings" (Bedjaoui 1991: 33). And yet, they form part of "the mass of materials which, in the course of the proceedings, accumulate in the depot known as the case file, pending their transfer into the processing plant, i.e. the deliberation" (Bedjaoui 1991: 29). Despite the significant role played by written pleadings in ECtHR procedures, the academic community paid almost no heed to this genre, with few exceptions (Nikitina 2018a, 2018b). This chapter intends to bridge the information gap on this genre, which can be of potential interest not only to linguists but also to legal professionals. The latter may feel inspired by some conventional knowledge structuring, text-organizing patterns and

1 *European Court of Human Rights: The ECHR in 50 questions*, Available at https://www.echr.coe.int/documents/d/echr/50questions_eng. Unless otherwise indicated, all links cited in this chapter were last consulted in April 2024.

2 European Court of Human Rights, "Delivery of judgments, Available at https://www.echr.coe.int/delivery-of-judgments.

DOI: 10.4324/9781003434788-8

argumentation strategies that can be replicated or used as a foundation for further inquiry.

In a Critical Genre Analysis vein, the chapter describes the genre, its structure and typical moves (see Section 6.3) using a corpus of written observations drafted by parties from different Member States (see Section 6.2). Written observations represent a dialogical exchange (Bakhtin 1981, see Section 6.4) between the two duelling parties – the Applicant and the Respondent Government, and are marked by frequently oppositional argumentation (see Section 6.4). The chapter analyses a range of dialogical argumentative patterns, paying particular attention to the incorporation of different voices for dialogical purposes and the use of polemic negation as a main mechanism of the refutation of the opponent's standpoint.

6.2 The Written Observations Corpus

The challenge of working with "adjudicative dark matter" (Molbæk-Steensig 2023: 94) is the general unavailability of these texts to the public at large, which impinges on the researcher' freedom. Written pleadings are an occluded genre, in that they remain part of the case file but – not being produced by the Court – they are not available via HUDOC, and special requests must be made in order to get access to these files. To cast some light on this occluded genre, this study relies on the Written Observations Corpus (WOC). WOC contains authentic written pleadings drafted in the period between 2002 and 2021 by parties coming from different Member States of the Council of Europe: Russia, Ukraine, Latvia, Italy, the United Kingdom and Malta. The pleadings from non-English speaking countries are translations (Russia, Italy)[3] and instances of L2 drafting (Latvia, Ukraine), whereas pleadings from English-speaking countries (United Kingdom, Malta) were written by native or near-native speakers of this language. As the overarching concept behind this chapter was to unshroud this genre from the mystery surrounding it, I had to accept some methodological concessions, the biggest being my lack of control over the selection of textual material. The corpus was created only thanks to the kind assistance of the Registry personnel, whose contribution is recognized and acknowledged here with gratitude. WOC was collected over different periods of time. A part of it was collected in 2014–2015 as part of my PhD project, which culminated in the publication of two books (Nikitina 2018a, 2018b). Another part was added during the COVID-19 pandemic. The general idea behind the corpus collection was that it had to reflect the general flow of pleadings and applications against the abovementioned countries in the indicated period.

3 I have managed to secure also the source texts for most pleadings, but these are left in the static .pdf form, so no statistical data are provided with regard to the source texts.

Table 6.1 The Written Observations Corpus

Corpus	*Texts*	*Tokens*	*Percentage*
WOC	49	277,677	
Government's Observations	32	168,981	61% (tokens), 65% (texts)
Applicant's Observations	17	108,696	39% (tokens), 35% (texts)

WOC totals 277,677 running words (tokens) in 49 texts with 13,262 types; see Table 6.1. It is slightly skewed towards written observations drafted by the Governments, responding to the Applicants' initial applications.

In addition to the tantalizing text-retrieval quest, the pleadings were not machine-readable at the beginning. Originally all texts in the corpus were static documents (.jpg or scanned .pdf), and their optical recognition was a most time-consuming and challenging process, as some documents had to be retyped partially or in whole. WOC is supplemented by two corpora of source texts for the pleadings that were marked as translations: the Russian Source Corpus (RUSC) and the Italian Source Corpus (ITSC). These corpora were left unaligned and in their static formats for comparative purposes, where necessary, hence no statistical data thereof are reported here.

6.3 Written pleadings: genre considerations

Oral pleadings have received their fair share of scholarly attention from both linguists (Shuy 2007; Chaemsaithong & Kim 2018) and lawyers (Richardson 2006) as part of courtroom genres, most frequently being conceptualized as "a parallel genre related to written judgment" that is realized through negotiation of justice in the courtroom (Bhatia 2006: 5). *Written* pleadings are, unsurprisingly, part of the *written* procedure, which is the default mode before the ECtHR, and scholarship on this genre is in its budding phase only. Oral pleadings and hearings are more of an exception than a rule in the ECtHR, and may happen when the case is heard by a Chamber[4] (Rule 55.5, Rules of Court): "the Chamber may decide, either at the request of a party or of its own motion, to hold a hearing if it considers that the discharge of its functions under the Convention so requires", or by a Grand Chamber (Rule 71, Rules of Court).

The ECtHR discourse is marked by a mild terminological variation between the terms *written pleadings* and *written observations* that coexist and are used interchangeably in the Rules, "the English version of which utilises the former for titling and the latter generally in the text" (Nikitina 2018a: 49); see Table 6.2.

4 A case may be examined by a single judge (Rule 53), who rules mostly on questions of admissibility, by a Committee (Rule 54), by one of five Chambers of equal standing (Rule 55), and in exceptional cases it may be relinquished in favour of (Rule 72) or referred to (Rule 73) a Grand Chamber.

Table 6.2 Rule 38 in the 2024 version of the Rules of Court in English[5] and in French[6]

Rule 38 – Written pleadings	*Article 38 – Observations écrites*
1. No *written observations* or other documents may be filed after the time-limit set by the President of the Chamber or the Judge Rapporteur, as the case may be, in accordance with these Rules. No *written observations* or other documents filed outside that time-limit or contrary to any practice direction issued under Rule 32 shall be included in the case file unless the President of the Chamber decides otherwise.	1. Il ne peut être déposé d'*observations écrites* ou d'autres documents que dans le délai fixé par le président de la chambre ou par le juge rapporteur, selon le cas, conformément au présent règlement. Les *observations écrites* ou autres documents déposés en dehors de ce délai ou en méconnaissance d'une instruction pratique édictée au titre de l'article 32 du présent règlement ne peuvent être versés au dossier, sauf décision contraire du président de la chambre.

It can be hypothesized that some linguistic interference from French leaked into the English-speaking discourse community, resulting in the multiword term *written observations.* In addition, the term "pleading" has been an object of some controversy. For instance, in the United Kingdom, under the influence of Lord Woolf's innovation, it was suggested that *pleadings* be replaced with *statements of case* (Galdia 2017: 165). In this book, I use these terms interchangeably reflecting the autochthonous ECtHR dichotomy.

Critical Genre Analysis (see 1.3 and 3.4.1) draws inspiration from the evergreen questions "who", "what", "where", "when" and "how". Chapter 3 outlined the institutional context of the ECtHR ("where"), with Chapter 5 suggesting the "when" of written pleadings (after the case communication). Subsection 6.3.1 explores their communicative situation, focusing on the participation framework ("who?") and the communicative goal ("why?"), with the "how?" addressed in 6.3.2 with regard to the linguistic regime of pleadings and in 6.3.3 as concerns their generic markup.

6.3.1 Communicative situation

Unlike initial applications, where applicants can forgo legal representation, the drafting of written pleadings is the prerogative of legal professionals representing the involved parties. Although the pleadings are addressed to the Court, their immediate recipients are lawyers from the ECtHR Registry, who typically are proficient in a/the national language of the Respondent State, as well as have a degree in law of this state.

While inter-State applications are permitted under the ECHR, they are infrequent in the ECtHR practice. This study primarily focuses on written pleadings in individual cases, where the parties are represented by their lawyers

5 Available at https://www.echr.coe.int/documents/d/echr/rules_court_eng, emphasis added.
6 Available at https://www.echr.coe.int/documents/d/echr/rules_court_fra.

(Rule 36, Rules of Court) and the Respondent Government is represented by their Agent (Rule 35, Rules of Court). There is no requirement for the Applicant's representative to share the same nationality as the Applicant or Respondent, but in many cases, at least one member of the legal team will have the same nationality as the Applicant.

The procedural organization of the ECtHR bears a strong resemblance to the ICJ, with which the ECtHR is often compared as concerns its modus operandi and style (Brannan 2021: 21). As a former ICJ judge, Bedjaoui (1991: 34) explains,

> The inception of a case by a unilateral application lends a systematically adversary character to the procedure as it takes its course. It thus begins with an attack, in which the applicant elaborates in a Memorial the allegations outlined in the application, and continues with a defence, in which the respondent devotes a Counter-Memorial to refuting the contentions of its opponent.

The communicative purpose of written pleadings under Rule 38 (Rules of Court) is to address the Court's inquiries formulated in the case communication (see Chapter 5) by restating the facts, presenting legal arguments and by responding to the opposing party's submissions, if necessary. After the introduction of IMSI in case communications (see 5.2), the burden of preparatory work concerning the factual and legal reconstruction of domestic proceedings has been shifted to the Parties, mainly the Respondent Government. It gave more breathing space to the Registry lawyers who used to bear the burden of reconstructing the case resulting in a hefty amount of work. At the same time the respondent governments received a loophole to reconstruct the case "from the point of view of one of the parties", with a "potential to be one-sided" (Keller & Heri 2018: para. 82).

As Figure 6.1 illustrates, the Parties take turns in responding to the Court's questions (Q1, Q2 and Q3).[7] The Respondent Government, or rather its Agent, answers the Court's questions first (A1, A2 and A3 in Figure 6.1). Then the Applicant (or rather the Applicant's Counsel) is given an opportunity to reply, maintaining the adversarial spirit of the proceedings or, as Bedjaoui (1991: 34) remarked, trying "to tear the Counter-Memorial to shreds". As the Applicant will have seen the Government's answers, his or her reply will typically include references both to the Court's questions and to the Government's answers. Hence, the Applicant's reply consists of counter-answers (CtA).

A second round of exchange may then be ordered by the Court, when the Government may submit further observations, replying to the Applicant's pleadings in part or in whole "to demolish" (Bedjaoui 1991: 34) them, which can be followed by the Applicant's reply to the Government's further observations (shapes in dotted lines in Figure 6.1). Either before or after this step, the

7 The number of questions in Figure 6.1 is indicative and intended for procedural flow illustration purposes. There may be more or fewer questions at each stage.

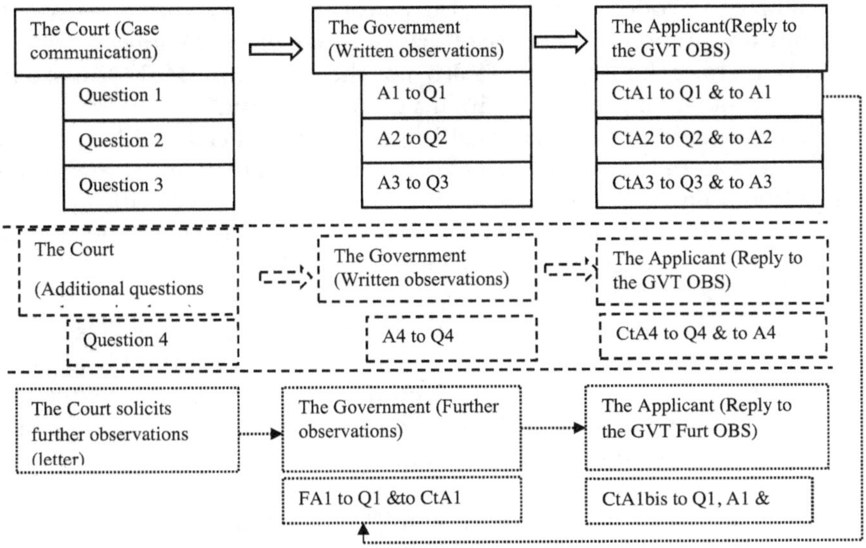

Figure 6.1 Procedural order in written pleadings

Court may formulate additional questions to the parties (dashed line), which may generate another round of pleadings exchange. The back-and-forth movement along these procedural steps produces a dialogical setting of a *discours* and a *contre-discours* (Plantin 2005), which are developed using argumentation with claims and counterclaims (Feteris 2017), bestowing on written pleadings a flavour of a lengthy adversarial prelude.

While in the ICJ context this duel is "a useful if sometimes leisurely way of clearing the ground so that the war horses will have room to manoeuvre in the forensic tilting of the oral proceedings" (Bedjaoui 1991: 34–35), in the ECtHR context it may be the only moment for the said war horses to trot, as oral proceedings may not follow at all, unless the case reaches the Grand Chamber. Written pleadings "are always distributed to the judges before the deliberation, both in the Chamber and Grand Chamber formations. The only exception applies in Chamber proceedings where an applicant has made submissions in his or her native language, where this language is not an official language of the Court" (Keller & Heri 2018: para. 33).

6.3.2 *Linguistic regime: the curious case of written pleadings*

In contrast to the ICJ written proceedings, where all documentation – at times anecdotally lengthy and heavy[8] – has to be translated in *both* English and French by the Registry, in the ECtHR written pleadings have to be produced in *either* English or French. Moreover, the Registry is unburdened from any

8 Bedjaoui (1991: 36–37) mentions a case with paper pleadings weighing 25 kg and totalling 60,776 pages.

translation endeavour at this stage. Occasionally, permission may be granted to exchange observations in *a* or *the* official language of the Member State (art. 34.3(a)), if either the Registry (34.3(b)) or the Applicant (34.3(c)) make the necessary translation provisions within a given time limit.[9]

While translation from a national language into either English or French is quite widespread, there are cases that mention translation being commissioned from English or French into the national language, i.e. with a reversed directionality. For instance, in the case *Martynenko v. Ukraine*,[10] the Government argues in its cover letter to the pleadings (2021):

> Therefore, the Government are of the opinion that, unless the President of the Chamber duly grants leave to use the applicant the Ukrainian language in the proceedings, provided the applicant files such request, the Government should not bear additional burden of preparation of a Ukrainian translation of their observations.

Time is of essence in every professional field, and filing an observation in a national language followed by translation at a later stage saves time and prevents language-related lengthening of the proceedings. As established in a previous analysis of written pleadings in Russian and in Italian (Nikitina 2018a: 58), roughly a month passed between the transmission of the original pleading in the national language and its translation. For the stepwise fashion of the pleadings transmission, illustrated in Figure 6.1, saving a month is a considerable gain. How is it possible? Written pleadings are processed by the Registry lawyers who share the same nationality or mother tongue with the drafting party. These lawyers are often selected from the Registry Division that handles applications against the relevant State, ensuring familiarity with the parties' cultural and legal backgrounds (see Chapter 5).

Given the linguacultural alignment between the transmitters and the recipients of pleadings, their translation seems to pursue mostly *informative purposes* (Cao 2007: 11), rather than general legal, see Section 2.5, of which examples (1), (1a) and (1b) are emblematic.

(1) Ни одного случая *короны* в Краснодаре и крае НЕ БЫЛО. Ни один пациент с этим диагнозом не получил на руки анализы с подтвержденным вирусом. Думайте зачем это нашим властям. . .Никто не скажет об этом, иначе уволят, а то и убьют. И то, что деньги предлагают чтоб в свидетельстве о смерти написать умер от короны тоже все знают. . .(Application, *Avagyan v. Russia*[11])

(1a) There has NOT been a single case of *corona*[*virus*] *infection* in the Krasnodar Region. No patient who tested positive has received a document

9 Rule 34.4(b) states (emphasis added), " If such leave is granted, it shall be the responsibility of the requesting Party.

10 Application no. 40829/12.

11 Application no. 36911/20.

showing ***a confirmed virus infection***. Think why the authorities would need it . . . No one will talk about it, for fear of being fired or killed. Money is being offered for agreeing to list the corona[virus] as a cause of death in the death certificate, everyone knows it . . ." (Case communication and APPS OBS, §27)

(1b) There was NOT a single case of ***a corona*** in Krasnodar and in the region. No patient with this diagnosis has received ***tests with a confirmed virus.*** Think why our authorities need it . . . No one will say about it, otherwise they will be fired, or even killed. And the fact that the money is offered to write in the death certificate that the person died from the corona also everyone knows . . . (GVT OBS)

These examples are taken from the case *Avagyan v. Russia*, lodged by a woman from Krasnodar (Russia[12]) who, at the beginning of the COVID-19 pandemic, made an Instagram post claiming that there was no coronavirus in Krasnodar (reproduced in the author's grammar and style in (1)). She was fined – allegedly disproportionately – for disseminating fake news. The case was communicated to the Respondent Government using the translation of the post reproduced in (1a), which was prepared by the Registry. Translation in (1a) shows a combination of different strategies (e.g. addition of "corona[*virus*] *infection*" or "confirmed virus *infection*", lacking in the source text because of its colloquial style and an overall creative attitude to grammar, along with a number of shifts, condensations and deletions) resulting in a text that reads natural in English and is comprehensible even to non-speakers of English. The Government's observations were first filed in Russian and then a copy of its English translation was transmitted, containing (1b). Finally, the Applicant's pleadings came, copying verbatim the version used in the case communication (1a).

Upon a closer look at the Government's version (1b), it becomes apparent that it is a literal translation of (1). However, this results in decreased readability in English. As I sought to provide a literal translation for example (1), I used one of the most widely available machine translation (MT) services, Google Translate. The output was identical to (1b), suggesting that the Government used the same service for its observations.

MT translation traces resurfaced in multiple cases in the Russian subcorpus of WOC, in both parties' pleadings. For example, in the Applicant's observations on the just satisfaction claims in the case *Kashcheyev v. the Russian Federation*,[13] the Applicant's surname *Кащеев* is rendered in an unharmonized way due to an unstable transliteration conventions from Russian (Kashcheev vs. Kashcheyev). Moreover, the same surname is maintained in the genitive case (see examples (2) and (2a)), as the MT service mistook it for the female version of the surname *Кащеева*. These errors, which would have been clear to a human translator, serve as evidence of the limitations of MT.

12 Russia was still a member of the Council of Europe in 2020.
13 Application no. 15468/13.

(2) The court checked the dismissal procedure *Kashcheeva G. V.* to reduce staff and reasonably disagreed with his arguments that the *defendant was violated* his preferential right to remain in the service. [. . .] In the course of the hearing from November 1, 2011 in *Brotherly city court*, the representative of the defendant *shut the T. A.* showed that the *performance* of the first dismissal signed by an employee, *in respect of which made the view because the view can be clerical*, and employee needs after reviewing the submission, point out inaccuracies, then the submission shall be signed by the chief of UMVD of Russia on the city of Bratsk [. . .] (Kashcheyev v. Russia, Applicant's Observations 2019)

(2a) Суд проверил процедуру увольнения Кащеев*а* Г.В. по сокращению штатов и обоснованно не согласился с его доводами о том, что *ответчиком было нарушено* его преимущественное право на оставление на службе. [. . .] В ходе судебного заседания от 1 ноября 2011 г. *в Братском городском суде*, представитель ответчика *Шуть Т.А.* показала что *представление к увольнению* сначала подписывает сотрудник, *в отношении которого вынесено данное преставление, поскольку в представлении могут быть описки*, и сотрудник должен ознакомившись с представлением, указать на неточности, потом уже представление подписывает начальник УМВД России по г. Братску [. . .] (source text)

(2b) The court reviewed the procedure for dismissing Kascheyev G.V. due to staff reductions and reasonably disagreed with his arguments that the defendant violated his preferential right to remain employed. [. . .] During the court hearing on November 1, 2011, at the *Bratsk City Court*, the defendant's representative *T.A. Shuti* argued that the dismissal notice is to be first signed by the employee to whom it applies, because there may be errors in the notice. The employee, after reviewing the notice, should point out any inaccuracies before the head of the Russian Ministry of Internal Affairs for Bratsk signs it. (my translation)

Example (2) illustrates how proper names and legal terms were incorrectly understood by the MT, generating a moderately comical effect. The "brotherly city court" is far from a friendly or affectionate utopia. The source pleading (2a) mentioned the city court of Bratsk, a city in Russia, using its adjectival form Bratskian (*Братский суд*). Incidentally, the same adjective can be translated as "brotherly", which was the MT solution. Immediately after that the proper name *Шуть Т.А* became the enigmatic "shut the T.A.", followed by cryptical mentions of "the performance" (*представление*). The source term is a polysemic word, which can indeed stand for "a performance", "a show" or "a view" (as it was translated later in (2)), but in the legal context it denotes "a dismissal notice". Last, but not least, the clause "in respect of which made the view because the view can be clerical" eludes any logical sense-making attempts as the Russian legal discourse – presenting some punctuational and phrasal challenges in the source text – was treated as general language, resulting in an incorrect understanding of semantics. Despite improvements in MT after the introduction of neural mechanisms, there is still a large consensus that MT cannot provide "the quality and polish expected of a trained, expert human translator without extensive post-editing" (Groves & Mundt 2021: 2), which catches the eye in examples (1) and (2). To wit, using MT services without post-editing shows the parties' perception that the translation of their pleadings is a formality.

Consideration of the extended participation framework takes on particular importance. It is crucial to recognize that Registry lawyers who speak the source language are not the sole recipients of these observations. At later stages, these documents are reviewed by other Court members who may lack proficiency in the source language, relying on translations for legal reasoning, thereby assuming a significant role in the process.[14] Translation in (1a), done at the case communication stage, shows emblematically the target-oriented approach, which enables a single judge or a committee to understand the implications of the statements made in the post. It would be naïve to insist on human only translation, especially in cases against high case-count countries. In fact, starting in 2022, the Registry lawyers have access to one of the widely known commercial machine translation services, which they have been authorized to use to assist them in these translations. Given the burgeoning caseload of come Registry lawyers, reaching up to 100 new applications per day and having to prepare legal analyses and "language checks" for ca. 1,000 applications as a general workload in some high case-count countries, reliance on machine translation is more than understandable, yet it is never used without any subsequent post-editing.

When parties from non-English- or French-speaking States decide to draft their written pleadings directly in one of the Court's official languages, such documents may be prone to linguistic interference (Toury 1995) and discourse transfer (Toury 1986; Nikitina 2018a). Interference, defined as the impact of one's native language and culture on their performance in cross-cultural and cross-linguistic communication, has intrigued interlanguage researchers for many years. In Translation Studies, interference, interpreted as the influence of the source text on the translation process, has generally been accepted as a reality. Early Translation Studies adopted a prescriptive approach, discouraged and cautioned against interference. However, descriptive Translation Studies recognized interference as a distinguishing feature of translated language, alongside other linguistic features (Garzone 2015: 62). Given that the exchange of pleadings occurs in English or French between parties and Registry lawyers of the same linguistic background, successful communication is likely facilitated by shared language and legal knowledge, streamlining the process of legal interpretation, despite any linguistic interference.

(3) Moreover, with reference to the alleged applicants' "inactivity" for the period in which the Administration omitted to reorganise, *it is hereby highlighted* that the Public Administration is obliged to proceed with the reorganisation whereas no duty lies on the private individuals, as

14 Written pleadings may be quoted in the judgment or in separate opinions.

confirmed by the established case-law of the *Administrative law judge*. (*Odeschalchi and Lante della Rovere v. Italy*,[15] 2012, APPL OBS)

(3a) In secondo luogo, quanto alla pretesa "inerzia" dei ricorrenti per il tempo in cui l'Amministrazione ha omesso di ripianificare *si ribadisce* che sussiste un vero e proprio obbligo della pubblica amministrazione di procedere alla ripianificazione mentre nessun onere grava in capo ai privati in tal senso, come confermato dalla giurisprudenza consolidata del *Giudice Amministrativo*.

For instance, in (3a) the Italian Applicant refers to "Giudice amministrativo", which is translated literally as "Administrative law judge" in (3). A regional administrative court (*tribunale amministrativo regionale, TAR*) in this case is personified and metonymically referred to as an "administrative law judge". Such periphrastic constructions are listed among "peculiarities of Italian judicial drafting" (Peruzzo & Scarpa 2023: 125). Rather than general linguistic interference, these pertain to the discursive practices of the source legal system. In their TrIACLE project aimed at facilitating legal interlinguistic translation in immigration and asylum settings by first working on intralinguistic translations, i.e. improving the input quality of source texts, Peruzzo and Scarpa (2023: 125) illustrate this phenomenon as follows (original emphasis),

> a lexical trait which provided a challenge for the translators is the use of different variants to denote the same concept within the same decision: in Order No. 17954/2020, the Turin Court of Appeal (*Corte d'Appello di Torino*) is in fact referred to by as many as seven different terms (*Corte cisalpina, Corte distrettuale, Collegio subalpino, Collegio piemontese, Collegio cisalpino, Corte subalpina* and *Corte territoriale*), in compliance with the low level of tolerance to lexical repetition typical of the Italian rhetorical style, opting instead for semantically ambiguous synonymic variation.
>
> (Peruzzo & Scarpa 2023: 125)

Such *legal discourse transfer*, understood as "the introduction of higher-level discursive and linguistic patterns from the source system into the target system" (Nikitina 2018a: 131) may be mitigated by the Registry lawyers' knowledge of the source legal discourse.

These transferred patterns coexist with some increased *conventionalization* in translation, i.e. "the overuse of institutionalised repertoremes" (Nikitina 2018a: 129). Known also as the *law of growing standardization* (Toury 1995: 267–268), *normalization* (Baker 1996: 176–177), *textual fit* (Biel 2014), it is the "tendency to overuse and exaggerate typical TL style markers and patterns, either by converting the source text discursive and linguistic patterns into TL prefabricated units or by adding the latter at the stage of translation without any ST stimuli" (Nikitina 2018a: 190).

15 Application no. 38754/07.

(4) The applicants should *hereby* like to comment on the Government's answers, as well as to answer the questions put by the European Court before the Government. (Shokkarov and others v. Russia 2008, APPL OBS)[16]

(4a) В настоящем документе заявители *считают необходимым не только* представить некоторые комментарии ответов Правительства *Российской Федерации*, но *и со своей стороны* ответить на вопросы, поставленные перед властями *Российской Федерации* Европейским Судом *по правам человека*. (source text)

(4b) In the present document the applicants *consider it necessary not only to provide* some comments to the answers of the Government *of the Russian Federation, but also* to answer questions posed to the authorities *of the Russian Federation* by the European Court *of Human Rights*. (literal translation)

Along with a number of deletions (italicized in the source text (4a) and its literal translation (4b)), example (4) introduced an English legal style marker "hereby" under the tendency to conventionalize translations (see also (3)). This shows how translated or L2 written pleadings introduce a mix of discourse transfer and conventionalization. There is a lack of fixed institutional guidelines for translation of written pleadings, coupled with a lack of translation quality controls, as "these translations are essentially left unattended within full discretion of the parties" (Nikitina 2018a: 117).

6.3.3 Conventionalized form

As with every professional genre, written pleadings have a distinct structure, outlined in the *Practice Directions*[17] issued by the ECtHR Registry. The specific form and content requirements in Article 15 show a three-move macro-structure, followed by an optional fourth move if the case includes just satisfaction claims:

15(a) The parties' pleadings following the admission of the application should include:

- (i) a short statement confirming a party's position on the facts of the case as established in the decision on admissibility;
- (ii) legal arguments relating to the merits of the case;
- (iii) a reply to any specific questions on a factual or legal point put by the Court.

(b) An applicant party submitting claims for just satisfaction at the same time should do so in the manner described in the practice direction on filing just satisfaction claims.

16 Application no. 41009/04.

17 Available at https://www.echr.coe.int/documents/d/echr/pd_written_pleadings_eng.

The introductory pleading section follows a crystallized structure outlined in Art. 10 and 11 of Practice Directions, schematically represented in Tables 6.3 and 6.4.

Table 6.3 Introductory section of written pleadings

Introduction	*Move*	*Example*
	the addressee	*IN THE EUROPEAN COURT OF HUMAN RIGHTS*
	the application number and the name of the case, typically consisting of the Applicant's name(s) and the name of the respondent State	*Application No. xxxxx/20* *[Applicant's name] v. [State]*
(optional)	a date (optional), placed under or above the address or title, included in the title or visible in the headnote after the transmission via fax	*observations . . . dated [. . .]*
(optional)	an indication of the translated nature of the document	*Translation from Russian; Translation from Italian*
	Document title indicating the nature of the content	*Observations on admissibility [and the merits]; reply to the Government's/the applicant's observations on admissibility [and the merits]; observations on the merits; additional observations on admissibility [and the merits]; Further observations of [. . .] on the admissibility and merits of the case*
	a note/statement as to the object/purpose of the pleading, which is usually to answer either the counterpart's or the Court's questions	*The Government respectfully submits* *By letter of the 13 July 2021, the Court invited Government to submit further written observations on the admissibility and merits of the case.*
(optional)	A note/statement clarifying the translated nature of pleadings. In some cases it is structured as a separate cover letter.[18]	*Please find attached a copy of the English translation of the Memorandum of the authorities of the Russian Federation [RUTC].* *I send, on behalf of the plaintiffs, the observations concerning the above mentioned file and the attached four documents [ITTC]*

18 Some sanitized samples of such cover letters are available in Nikitina (2018b: 65).

Table 6.4 Beginning samples from the sanitized written pleadings in the English Reference Corpus, the Russian Translation Corpus and the Italian Translation Corpus

English Reference Corpus	*Russian Translation Corpus*	*Italian Translation Corpus*
IN THE EUROPEAN COURT OF HUMAN RIGHTS Appln No. 24089/05 BETWEEN: (1) SUE SARANDON (2) JOHN SMITH Applicants – and- UNITED KINGDOM Respondent REPLY TO OBSERVATIONS OF THE RESPONDENT	20 September 2009 10001/09 EUROPEAN COURT OF HUMAN RIGHTS MEMORANDUM Application no. 10001/09 Ivanova v. Russia	HONOURABLE EUROPEAN COURT OF HUMAN RIGHTS APPLICATION no. 38754/07 MARINI AND RODARI V ITALY COUNTERCLAIMS TO THE COMPLEMENTARY REMARKS OF THE ITALIAN GOVERNMENT AND ON THE JUST SATISFACTION
This reply should be read with the full application. Since the respondent has not dealt with all the matters raised in the application on a point by point basis and it is not always clear which paragraphs of the application the respondent is alluding to, it has been necessary in this reply sometimes to re-state and expand upon what is in the application.	On 3 June 2010, the European Court of Human Rights (hereinafter – "the European Court") informed the Russian Federation authorities of application no. 10001/09 Ivanova v. Russia lodged with the European Court by a Russian national Larisa Petrovna Ivanova under Article 34 of the European Convention for the Protection of Human Rights and Fundamental Freedoms (hereinafter – "the Convention"), as well as invited them to submit their observations and answer the following questions.	In reply to the Italian Government's remarks of 30 May 2010, the applicant has the honour to submit the following remarks to the attention of this Honourable Court.

Source: Nikitina (2018a: 60).

The initial page may contain other identification elements:

- Name, title and full address of the law firm/legal professional(s) representing the applicant(s), either added as a stamp or visible on the headed paper.
- Name, title and full address of the Agent representing the Respondent Government, typically under form of letterhead.
- Name, title and full address of the person from the ECtHR Registry, who receives the pleading.

Sections 11 (f) and (g) of the Practice Directions set specific requirements as to the content and form of the body part of written pleadings, which should

(f) be divided into chapters and/or headings corresponding to the form and style of the Court's decisions and judgments ("Facts"/"Domestic law [and practice]"/"Complaints"/"Law"; the latter chapter should be followed by headings entitled "Preliminary objection on . . .", "Alleged violation of Article . . .", as the case may be);
(g) place any answer to a question by the Court or to the other party's arguments under a separate heading;

Analysing the body part in the Three-Part Comparable Corpus of Written Pleadings, consisting of two translated corpora of pleadings originally drafted in Russian and Italian with respective source texts and one reference corpus of pleadings drafted in English, I schematized (Nikitina 2018a: 63) the body part of pleadings as shown in Table 6.5.

The concluding section of the pleading is discursively realized through a range of "closing formulae" (Nikitina 2018b: 69), i.e. standardized expressions that recap the party's stance and/or solicit further action based on the arguments and justifications presented in the preceding sections. In its use of verbs and expressions with performative value it bears some resemblance to the final parts of judgments (see 7.4.5).

A typical closing formulae contains two main elements (Nikitina 2018b: 70), the so-called *intertextuality routines*, i.e. those routines that refer to other sources and texts, and *performativity routines*, i.e. those routines that contain a verb conveying the illocutionary point of the utterance (Austin 1962).

1) ComplexPrep$^{\text{cause or reference}}$ + *foregoing/aforesaid*: intertextuality routine
2) *I submit* + *I ask/I request*: performativity routine

These routines are reproduced, with reasonable variations, in most pleadings analysed. The topic of intertextuality will be further addressed in sections dealing with dialogism, whereas the performativity routines are explained below.

(5) *By virtue of the foregoing*, representing the interests of the Russian Federation according to the Provisions on the Representative of the Russian Federation at the European Court of Human Rights, approved by the Decree of the President of the Russian Federation dated March 29, 1998 No. 310, *I SUBMIT: [. . .] I ASK THE HONOURABLE COURT* [. . .] (*K.M and Others v. Russia*,[19] GVT OBS)
(6) *Based on the above stated*, representing the interests of the Russian Federation in accordance with the Regulation on the Representative of the Russian Federation at the European Court of Humans Rights approved

19 Application no. 46086/07.

Table 6.5 The body structure of written pleadings from the English Reference Corpus, the Italian Translation Corpus and the Russian Translation Corpus

English Reference Corpus	
Government's Observations	**Applicant's Observations**

• INTRODUCTION
• [containing questions]
• PART I: THE FACTS
  ◦ The applicant
  ◦ The [name of the political party]
  ◦ [name of the case]
• PART II: DOMESTIC LAW AND PRACTICE
• [subtitles referring to different sections and acts]
• PART III: THE ISSUES UNDER ARTICLE 35 OF THE CONVENTION
• PART IV: THE ISSUES UNDER ARTICLE 11 OF THE CONVENTION
• [subsections referring to specific notions of article 11]
• PART V: CONCLUSIONS
	• Introduction
	• Preamble
	• The applicants' legal advice: response to para. 3.18 of the Respondent's Observations
	• Witnesses and other evidence that the Applicants would have called: response to para. 3.15 of the Respondent's Observations
	• [with subsections]
	• Response to Respondent's summary of the facts – Part I of the Respondent's Observations
	• Relevant domestic law and practice [with subsections]
	• Substantive Issues Arising.
	• [subsections]
	• Conclusion

Italian Translation Corpus	
Government's Observations	**Applicant's Observations**

• Introduction
• Objectives of the reference to the grand chamber
• The law
  ◦ The admissibility of the complaint alleging a violation of the reasonable time requirement
  ◦ Substance
  ◦ The fairness of the proceedings
  ◦ The violation of article 1 of the first protocol (upsetting the fair balance)
  ◦ Just satisfaction
	• Receivability
	• On merit
	• Fair compensation: moral damages
	• CONCLUSIONS

Russian Translation Corpus	
Government's Observations	**Applicant's Observations**

• The circumstances of the case important for the proceedings
• Reasons why the present case should not be considered on the merits by the European Court, to the Government's opinion
• Facts
• Applicable legislation
• Analysis of grounds of the applicant and answers to questions of the European Court
• [questions, numbered and quoted entirely]
	• General Statements
	  ◦ Application of Rule 54 A of the Rules of the Court
	  ◦ Whether the application is well-founded and who shall carry the burden of proof
	• Applicants' position on the merits of the questions posed by the Court
	• [rephrased numbered questions, afterwards quoted entirely]

Source: Nikitina (2018a: 63).

by the Decree of President of the Russian Federation dated March 29, 1998, No. 310, *I SUBMIT [. . .]* (*Karimov v. Russia*,[20] GVT OBS)

(7) *In the light of the foregoing considerations*, the Italian Government has the honour *to ask* the Court to dismiss the application as ill-founded. (*Scoppola v. Italy*,[21] GVT OBS)

(8) *In the light of the foregoing*, the Italian Government have the honour of *asking* the Court to declare the application inadmissible or to dismiss it as manifestly ill-founded. (*Scoppola v. Italy*,[22] GVT OBS before GC)

(9) *This being the case*, the plaintiffs as represented and defended above, *request* that the European Court of Human Rights grants the following CONCLUSIONS [. . .]. (*S.A. and Others v. Italy*,[23] APPL OBS)

(10) *As a result, in light of this and following on* this Court's well-established case law on the matter, Government *considers* that the applicant should not be awarded any compensation in the case of a finding of a violation of the Convention. The Government of Malta *humbly submits* these observations for the learned and distinguished consideration of the Honourable European Court of Human Rights. (*Fenech v. Malta*,[24] 2021, GVT OBS)

(11) *It is respectfully submitted* that the sums claimed by Ms Eweida and Ms Ladele are excessive and disproportionate, seeking high sums of costs for cases that have (at least so far) been considered on the papers. (*Eweida, Chaplin, Ladele and McFarlane v. UK*,[25] 2012, GVT OBS)

(12) *On the basis of the foregoing*, the Applicant *is requesting* the European Court 1) to recognize the application *Tovsultanova v. Russia* as admissible on the merits; 2) to find a violation of Articles 2, 3, 5 and 13 of the Convention; 3) to award the Applicant just compensation for non-pecuniary damage, and also costs and expenses. (*Tovsultanova v. Russia*,[26] APPL OBS)

Examples (5) and (6) contain *explicit performatives* (Austin 1962: 32), composed of a verb that denotes the illocutionary point of the utterance in the present indicative active with the first-person singular pronoun (Austin 1962: 5, 56). In the other examples the agents refer to themselves in the third person, the so-called transposed third person, which satisfies the conditions for the verb to be adjudged explicit performative (Austin 1962: 57).

The performative value of the performativity routine, i.e. its potential to do things with words, may be diluted by hedges. In linguistics, hedges are used

20 Application no. 54219/08.
21 Application no. 10249/03.
22 Application no. 10249/03.
23 Application no. 158/12.
24 Application no. 19090/20.
25 Application nos. 48420/10, 59842/10, 51671/10 and 36516/10 *Eweida, Chaplin, Ladele and McFarlane v the United Kingdom*.
26 Application no. 26974/06.

to mitigate the force of the statement, placing additional distance between the author of the statement and its contents. For instance, examples (7) and (8) mitigate the performative value of the statement by "has the honour"; a similar effect is achieved in (10) by "humbly". These hedges are introduced for reasons of politeness (Kurzon 2001; see 8.5–8.6).

Whereas example (9) is still undoubtedly an explicit performative, even if the agent is referred to in the third person ("the plaintiffs"), examples (7) and (8) are the so-called *implicit performatives*, as they are "reducible, or expandible, or analysable into a form with a verb in the first-person singular present indicative active (grammatical)" (Austin 1962: 61–62). Example (11) contains a pattern typical of the English Reference Corpus built around the passive form of the verb with a performative value after the introductory "it" – "it is submitted". As Austin acknowledges, "person and voice anyway are not essential" (Austin 1962: 57). Finally, example (12) uses a grammatical deviation in the progressive form, which could be attributed to linguistic interference, as normally the progressive form is dissociated from performativity "because the action is conceptualized as punctual, i.e. as beginning and ending at the time of utterance or of writing" (Williams 2007: 59). Despite some variation in the form of these routines, their function remains undoubtedly performative: to do things with words, i.e. to request that the Court adopts a certain course of action.

6.4 Written pleadings, legal rhetoric and reasoning

6.4.1 Legal argumentation toolbox

Argumentation in judicial texts has been approached from a variety of perspectives (see Goźdź-Roszkowski 2024 for an overview), including research targeting "the linguistic constituents of argumentative discourse within judicial texts" (Mazzi 2007b: 22). Legal argumentation scholars, such as Plantin (1996, 2005, 2022), Sartor (2002), Prakken (1993, 2005), Feteris (2017), have elaborated extensive theories, focusing on the reconstruction of legal arguments from a logical standpoint (see also 6.5.2). Analysing any legal argument without building on this impressive body of research (see, e.g. Feteris 2017 for an overview) would be counterproductive. Yet, my main focus is on the discursive and textual realization of legal reasoning, rather than on its logical tenets, so I draw inspiration from the Pragma-dialectical approach, which reconciles rhetoric with argumentation, supplementing it with elements from legal argumentation, where appropriate (Feteris 2015, 2017).

The pragma-dialectical theory of argumentation, developed by Frans van Eemeren and Rob Grootendorst (1992), offers a comprehensive framework for understanding and evaluating argumentative discourse, of which judicial discourse is an emblematic example and a fruitful field of application. At its core, the theory views argumentation as a means of resolving differences of opinion through reasoned dialogue, which is highly applicable to written pleadings as this genre is realized as a reasoned dialogue, or even a polylogue (see Figure 6.1). Pragma-dialectics emphasizes the importance of rational persuasion within a dialectical context, where participants engage in cooperative and critical discussion to achieve resolution or understanding.

According to this theory, arguments are analysed in terms of structure, strategies, and underlying assumptions, with particular attention given to the rules and norms governing acceptable discourse. Central to the pragma-dialectical approach is the notion of a critical discussion stage, wherein interlocutors present, defend, and critically assess their positions using logical reasoning and relevant evidence. This theory also highlights the significance of maintaining procedural integrity, ensuring that discussions proceed according to mutually agreed-upon rules of engagement, such as relevance, non-fallacious reasoning and sincerity.

Van Eemeren (2010) extended the classical, argument-centred, theory of pragma-dialectics by elaborating the notion of *strategic manoeuvring*. It stands for the deliberate and strategic use of argumentative moves to achieve rhetorical goals in communication, getting the abstract models of argumentation closer to real-life argumentative discourses. These discourses, of which written pleadings are very representative, pursue a twofold goal of achieving effectiveness and reasonableness in a balanced way. In other words, the arguing parties manoeuvre between argumentation and persuasion. It involves the selection and deployment of arguments, language and the so-called presentational devices, i.e. "the communicative means used to present the argumentative moves constituting a piece of strategic manoeuvring" (van Eemeren 2010: 118) to persuade or influence an audience. Strategic manoeuvring acknowledges the context-dependent nature of argumentation and recognizes that successful persuasion often requires more than just logical reasoning. As Goźdź-Roszkowski (2024: 16, original emphasis) stated, "the scholar of argumentation is interested in the *what*, whereas the linguist is interested in the *how*", and the concept of strategic manoeuvring allows the analyst to look at the *how*, without discarding the *what*.

6.4.2 *Written pleadings: an argumentative battlefield?*

Judicial proceedings at any level, domestic or supranational, aim at resolving differences of opinion. Transposing Feteris's (2017: 218–219) outline of differences of opinion in domestic proceedings to the supranational context of the ECtHR, the following differences of opinion can be identified:

1 The applicant(s), i.e. the party initiating the procedure as a *protagonist*.
2 The Respondent Government as an *antagonist*.
3 The Court as an institutional catalyst.

As the Applicant makes the first claim (in the application), the Court processes it and asks critical questions addressing both parties (in the case communication). The Respondent Government then challenges the Applicant's claim by submitting their answers or counterclaims that refute or undercut the position articulated in the application (in written pleadings). In a national context, Feteris (2017: 2018–2019) defines the Court's role as that of an "institutional antagonist", who "must both check whether the claim is acceptable in light of the critical reactions of the other party and in light of certain legal starting points and evaluation rules which must be taken into account when evaluating arguments in a legal process". The ECtHR's role is better described through the metaphor of *institutional catalyst*, a neutral party who cannot side with either the Government or the Applicant, and instead advances the proceedings through critical yet neutral interventions. While advancing their standpoints, both parties react to or anticipate the Court's critical reactions, making written pleadings a fertile ground for a critical discussion "in which a protagonist defends a standpoint against the anticipated or actual reactions of an antagonist" (Kloosterhuis 2013: 73).

As the pleadings at the ECtHR typically occur after the case has exhausted all available effective domestic remedies, the dialogical standpoint reconstruction is nuanced and articulated. While the ECtHR "subjects the institutions of the state to outside scrutiny" (Cameron 2013: 59), it is not an appeal court or a "fourth instance" (ECtHR Questions and answers 2014: 6)[27] in that it does not rehear cases, revise, revoke or otherwise modify domestic decisions. It relies on the facts and decisions as re-constructed by the Parties, including the original difference of opinion between the Applicant and the State authorities at the domestic level that remained unresolved, to which any national appeal proceedings are added, with potential differences of opinion between the trial and the appeal judges and the parties. Yet, it is an international court of last resort, and it is the parties' last opportunity to defend their standpoints. The resulting argumentative structure is complex, interdiscursive and intertextual, and, to quote Saïd et al. (2013: 239 in Galdia 2017: 330), "it starts with the enthymeme as a part of court pleadings". The protagonist and the antagonist engage in the reasoned dialogue of written pleadings challenging each other's representation of the situation through critical discussion, leaving the domestic proceedings sometimes as an unstated assumption, and at the same time weaving facts, legal points and voices of the domestic proceedings into their dialogical reconstruction of reality in written pleadings. As Bedjaoui (1991: 35) noticed for the parallel ICJ situation of written proceedings, "A number of well-defined contentions and arguments emerge within the opposing perimeters, while it not seldom happens that once seemingly impregnable positions appear in ruins after this battle of the printed word".

6.5 Dialogism in written pleadings

6.5.1 Dialogism, polyphony and heteroglossia

Bakhtin (1984) originally distinguished between different types of dialogism, acknowledging at the same time that these are difficult to discern in stylistic

27 Available at https://www.echr.coe.int/documents/d/echr/guide_echr_lawyers_eng.

analysis. Bres (2001, 2020) elaborated on his distinctions and categorized three types of dialogism: *interdiscursive, interlocutive* and *intralocutive*.

Interdiscursive dialogism, also conceptualized in the literature as "manifest intertextuality" (Fairclough 1992: 117), occurs when several utterances are related by virtue of a common topic; i.e. the dialogic relationship is established not between the interlocutors but between the contents of the utterances (*le même objet* in Bres 2020: 40). Within written pleadings, dialogism is not necessarily realized as a sequence of turns in a dialogue, but can occur through "an inherent enunciative duality within the same syntactic unit (cf. [. . .] Bres/Nowakowska 2005: 140)" (Garzone 2016: 4). Roitman (2015: 22) notes how legal discourse is rich in "refutations representing interdiscursive dialogism [which] include – and refute – previous 'real' arguments and arguments resumed from the interlocutor's discourse" (Roitman 2015: 22). For instance, in *Burmistrova v. Russia*,[28] the Government in its additional observations notes how "the applicant's observations in whole consist of disagreement with the stance embodied in observations of the Government of the Russian Federation and repeat arguments of the initial application", which is a clear description of interdiscursive dialogism.

In *self-dialogism*, or *intralocutive dialogism*, the internal dialogue is built on itself, where the enunciator[29] is also the primary interlocutor (Bres 2020: 41). This type of dialogism, which can be illustrated by Shakespearean soliloquys, such as "to be or not to be, that is the question" is not widespread in the ECtHR genres, where the interlocutors tend to be different from the enunciators.

Finally, the third type of dialogism, *interlocutive dialogism*, is characterized by the situation when "the locutor anticipates the reaction/response an addressee may have to the utterance (Bres/Nowakowsa 2005: 139)" (Garzone 2016: 5; see also Bres 2020: 40). This is the classical understanding of dialogism, where the dialogic relationship is established *ad personam*. This has been also referred to as "recipient design" in that it "involves anticipating recipients' interpretations when formulating turns at talk" (Deppermann 2014: 16). As Roitman (2015: 22) explains, "interlocutive dialogism [may] include – and refute – virtual, hypothetical, (possibly) future responses or arguments".

Dialogism is inherently linked to the idea of *heteroglossia* (Russian *raznorečie*), a Bakhtinian neologism that denotes a coexistence of different

28 Application no. 73740/14.

29 Ducrot (1984) explains the phenomenon of dialogism/polyphony, using a tripartite distinction between three speaking subjects (*sujets parlants*): the locutor (*le locuteur*), the enunciator (*l'énonciateur*) and the empirical producer of the utterance (*le producteur empirique*). The locutor is responsible for the utterance act, or as Dendale (2006: 7) puts it, whose pronouns are indicated. The enunciator is the one to whom standpoints expressed in the utterance are attributed. Finally, the empirical producer is the one who is materially responsible for the utterance, regardless of its authorship.

voices and opinions in any discourse, its inner pluralism of "the speaking personality, the speaking consciousness" (Bakhtin 1981: 434). These voices represent different perspectives and points of view, and typically refer to the diverse enunciative sources present in discourse. Dendale (2006: 9) referred to it as "the simultaneous presence of at least two distinct discursive entities holding differing points of view and/or representing different individuals". Next to coining – yet using in a very limited way – the term *heteroglossia*, Bakhtin (1984) borrowed the musical concept of polyphony to analyse Dostoevsky's polyphonic novel (*polifoničeskij roman*), where the authorial voice coexisted on equal terms with the main character's voice. The theory of polyphonic discourse has gained popularity in linguistic research, particularly among French scholars (Ducrot 1984; Bres 1999; Bres & Nowakowska 2005; Bres 2020), who have expanded its application beyond literary studies. Garzone (2016: 4) highlighted the subtle differences between polyphony, often linked to Ducrot (1984), and Bakhtin's dialogism, noting that dialogism emphasizes interaction, while polyphony involves the layering of different voices. When protagonists in written pleadings incorporate fragments from the antagonist's pleadings and vice versa, or answer the Court's questions, this is a dynamically dialogical interaction, whereas embedding other voices, such as quoting legislation, experts or other elements are instances of polyphony. However, the distinction is very subtle and not universally recognized, so these terms are used here interchangeably.

6.5.2 *Dialogical reasoning in written pleadings*

Scholars of legal argumentation have long recognized the dialogical nature that underpins judicial writing and courtroom interactions. For instance, Prakken (1993) created a logical framework for analysing arguments for conflicting positions. In subsequent works, Prakken and Sartor (1996) expanded on the dialogical approach by introducing the concept of challenging an undesirable or unacceptable argument. Similarly, Sartor (2002) refined theory-based argumentation through the dialectical exchange of opposing theories. These challenges are executed through rebuttal or undercutting (Prakken 2005), which essentially negates the validity of the opponent's stance through negative responses to critical questions. Feteris (2017: 39) noted, in applying legal reasoning models to AI, that "legal reasoning and argumentation have a dialectical nature, involving a claim, counter-claim, arguments, and counter-arguments". Another prominent proponent of dialogical reasoning, Plantin (1996, 2005, 2022), posited that argumentation in general is a discursive and dialogical phenomenon revolving around the exchange between a *discours*, which is critically questioned or opposed through *contre-discours*.

Analysing how COVID-19-related cases were debated before the ECtHR, I noted in a previous study (Nikitina 2022c: 114) the dialogical representation of different positions in written pleadings, where the government's standpoint "is built dialogically – in an oppositional sense of the word, as a rebuttal of the applicant's story". The Government does not grope in the dark for a construction of an appropriate position. Rather than feeling anxiety to leave no stone unturned, the Governments forge their pleadings in opposition to the applications as they "take the word, and make it [their] own" (Bakhtin 1981: 292). At the same time, the Applicants refute the Governments' observations, advancing their own standpoints and exploiting any perceived chinks in the Governments' armour. The exchange of pleadings results in "a dialogical scaffolding or clustering of frames" (Nikitina 2022c: 118), with an intricate interplay of refutation, rebuttal and undercutting mechanisms.

The textual manifestation of argumentative patterns, viewed as "the sum of the dialogic devices used in the discourse" (Roitman 2015: 22), has garnered its fair share of academic interest. Bourcier and Bruxelles (1995), for example, analysed how the expression *c'est-à-dire* ("that is to say") was used by the French Supreme Court's judges for the explanation of reasons underlying their decision through clarification and paraphrase. Mazzi (2011) directed his scrutiny at reformulation markers (*in other words, rather, instead*, etc.) in judgments of the Court of Justice of the European Communities and Ireland's Supreme Court, showing how these patterns served clear argumentation purposes allowing the judges to "characterise, refine or grade reported arguments/interpretations or they wish to make their reasoning more solid and convincing" (Mazzi 2011: 22). Similarly, Garzone (2016) highlighted the argumentative potential of syntactic negation in her study of the UK Supreme Court judgments (see also Nikitina 2025, forthcoming) and analysed negation as a marker of dialogical reasoning in separate judicial opinions.

"All forms of dialogism [. . .] are associated with lexicogrammatical clues that signal the presence of two or more enunciative instances" (Garzone 2016: 5). French scholars (Bres 1999; Bres & Nowakowska 2005) have analysed a number of dialogical markers, including irony, various forms of negation (including escalating construction, e.g., *not only . . . but also*; rectification, e.g., . . . *not* . . . *but* . . .), confirmation, concession, opposition, presupposition, interrogation (like rhetorical questions), comparison, cleft sentences, extraposition (such as right- or left-dislocation), manipulation and adaptation of proverbs, echo-utterances, autonymical modalization, reported speech, and in the French language, the use of the conditional mood with hearsay value. Notably, some of these discursive features – such as speech reportage or "language representations", presupposition, negation, and irony – are highlighted in Fairclough's work (1992: 117–118) as indicators of "manifest intertextuality" (Garzone 2016: 6).

The following sections analyse reported speech and negation as textual realizations of argumentation and dialogism in written pleadings.

6.6 Intertextual voicing and reported argumentation

Dialogism and polyphony can manifest linguistically by integrating another author's speech into a new text. Different voices are incorporated through reported speech, either direct or indirect. Reported speech, or "the practice of intertextual voicing" (Chaemsaithong & Kim 2018: 39) has been extensively studied in a variety of contexts, and works in the legal field typically focus on their recurrence in judgments (Mazzi 2007a, 2007b) and in courtroom interaction (Matoesian 2000; Rosulek 2010; Felton Rosulek 2015; Chaemsaithong 2018; Chaemsaithong & Kim 2018). Analysing a genre with some parallels to written pleadings, i.e. opening statements, Chaemsaithong (2018: 91) illustrates "how voices can be instrumental in each side's creation of a persuasive, plausible discourse, culminating in two competing versions of reality despite similar basic events and characters in their narratives". Reporting speech is also a key tool for shaping judicial arguments in discourse maintaining the dialogical exchange and overview of opinions (Mazzi 2007a). Reported speech in the duelling reconstruction of reality may blend the reporting voice with the voice of the reported speaker, giving statements emotional and evidential weight (Matoesian 2000). As a result, courtroom interactions are characterized by frequent and dexterous voice-switching to adopt multiple perspectives.

The main parties to written pleadings, Applicants and Governments, must consistently engage with what has been written before (e.g. in the initial application, in the case communication or even earlier, in domestic proceedings) and respond to the Court's questions and the other party's observations. As a result, written pleadings become polyphonous, multi-perspectival and interactionally dialogical. Reported speech in written pleadings revolves around taking a previous segment of speech/text from one context and placing it into the current context, creating thus an intertextual connection between the two speech events.

These embedded voices can be textually traced through several lexical cues such as reporting verbs (*claim*, *argue*, *submit*), reporting nouns (*submission, claim*), quotation marks and other graphical means (the use of italics, formatting as a block quotation), as well as connectives with the function of reference and reformulation. A frequent co-occurrence of the main parties to pleadings, "the Applicant(s)" and "the Government" with such reporting verbs as *claim, seek, contend, state, argue, ask, refer*, etc., which introduced different standpoints and voices into the discourse of written observations has been already highlighted (Nikitina 2018a: 349). A combination of manual reading and corpus-assisted analysis illustrates a high degree of polyphony in WOC. Table 6.6 reports the most frequently used reporting verbs and nouns, retrieved through lexical search using #LancsBox 6.0.

Table 6.6 Reporting verbs and nouns in the Written Observations Corpus

Reporting verb or noun[30]	*Absolute frequency*	*Normalized frequency (100,000)*
submi*	511	224
claim*	315	138
complain*	268	118
stat*	229	101
argu*	225	99
request*	220	97
report*	217	95
belie*	182	80
hold*/held	131	58
ask*	108	47
answer*	106	47
declar*	104	46
assert*	94	41
say*/said	91	40
accus*	80	35
reply*/replie*	72	32
reject*	62	27
contend*/contention*	49	22
describ*/description*	42	18
deny*/denie*	40	18
remark*	24	11
outlin*	17	7

The qualitative part of the study – through the analysis of concordance lines – shed light on the differences in the pragmatic functions with which these intertextual voices were used. Reported speech performs a variety of pragmatic functions, realized through "full of snatches of other texts which may be explicitly demarcated or merged in, and which may assimilate, contradict, ironically echo, and so forth" (Fairclough 1992: 84). Mazzi (2007b: 24), analysing reported verbs in judgments, elucidated how these are "used in particular to introduce a statement, by attributing it to someone else as the current writer or speaker, but also to express self-references". He stressed how connectives and meta-argumentative expressions (such as *reason, to follow, to hold, ground, to accept, argument, conclusion, to conclude, to justify, to dismiss* essentially perform the function of incorporating different argumentative voices for the purposes of legal argumentation (Mazzi 2007a: 384).

Chaemsaithong and Kim (2018: 39), building on Rosulek's (2010) research, distinguish four main functions of reported speech: *narrativization* ("verbal action" in Rosulek 2010), *legitimation, (re)contextualization* and *deconstruction*. As the communicative goals of opening statements and closing arguments are consonant with those of written pleadings, i.e. to promote a

30 All items on the list were checked in the concordance lines to avoid reporting false positives, such as when "state" is used to denote a Member State or a mental state. The wildcard (*) allows to search for different word forms, e.g. *denie** captures both *denies* and *denied*.

preferrable outlook on the facts and legal issues at hand, this taxonomy appears to be applicable also to the analysis of reported speech in written pleadings. As the authors explain, "legitimation provides evidence for an assertion, while deconstruction provides evidence against it. Narrativizing and (re)contextualizing voices allow the reporter to strategically evaluate or convey attitudes, explicitly or implicitly, concerning the original speaker or the reported utterance" (Chaemsaithong & Kim 2018: 39).

The most frequently used reporting item – *submit** and *submission* – owns its popularity in part to the communicative situation of written pleadings. As already mentioned in 6.3.2, every pleading ends with the so-called performativity formula, which is frequently realized using *submit**. In addition, the parties refer to each other's *submissions* as in (13).

(13) The construction of s. 174 which the applicant then proposed (without reference to Article 11 ECHR) did not correspond with the *submission* it makes in this application as to its rights under Article 11. On the contrary, its *submission – that it was entitled to rely on any of Mr Lee's activities over and above the mere fact of membership of the BNP* – was a limited one which went no further than was (in its view) necessary for it to succeed in the circumstances of Mr Lee's case. The EAT accepted that *submission*. (*A.S.L.E.F. v. the UK*, 2006, GVT OBS)

As (13) shows, *submission* here is used for a combination of narrativizing ("submission it makes", "accepted that submission") and recontextualizing functions ("its submission [. . .] was a limited one"). The applicant's (a legal entity) voice is integrated into the government's reconstruction of the events at hand, using indirect speech and positioning the submission in question against a new context, fitting the Government's version of the events.

(14) The judge *stated* the following reasons of his decision: Mr Bordikov was accused of perpetration of grave offences and state of his health allowed to keep him in custody. In compliance with the information of the Russian Federation Supreme Court this decision has not been appealed against. (*Bordikov v. Russia* 2006, GVT OBS)

Another verb, which is used most frequently in its narrativizing function is the verb *state* (14) or its noun version *statement*, which is functionally close to *assert* and *assertion* (15). Next to narrativizing functions, these verbs are routinely used to recontextualize events reported by the other party. Other lexical cues of recontextualization are represented by reformulation markers (Mazzi 2011), such as *in other words*, *instead*, *rather*, the so-called "graders" (Lo Cascio 2009: 204), see (15) and (16).

(15) The Government's *claim* that the Applicant was also kept in isolation to reduce "the risk that someone may attempt to communicate with him

and attempt to, in any way, hinder the important investigations being carried out at the time into the assassination of Mrs Daphne Caruana Galizia" should also be dismissed. ***Had there been any truth in these assertions,*** the prison authorities would have conducted a detailed risk assessment both at the time of the Applicant's incarceration or at the time of his move into a mixed dormitory. At a minimum, this would have involved (i) an assessment of the risk to the Applicant of moving the Applicant to the general prison population (and a revolving number of prisoners into his cell); and (ii) a review of the investigation (still ongoing at the time of the move to a mixed dormitory and today). ***Instead,*** no such assessment was conducted. (*Fenech v. Malta* 2021, APPL OBS)

(16) ***The applicants wish to submit*** for the Court's examination actions of a general nature and thus the term "practice", which refers to repeated conduct by the Italian State, is ***mentioned*** several times. ***In other words, they are asking*** the Court for a judgment that will regulate this area. This last request ***is supported*** by the third-party interveners, ***notably*** Columbia Law School – Human Rights Clinic. The United Nations High Commissioner for Refugees has also ***expressed*** his general interest. The same ***position has been taken*** by the other third-party interveners: Aire, Amnesty International and the International Federation for Human Rights. ***In spite of*** these general aims, the subject-matter of the application implies examination of events which took place on a single day. This limited subject-matter emerges clearly from the ***facts indicated*** in the application, the Court's statement of facts and the resulting "questions to the parties", which are limited to the events of 6 May 2009. ***Thus, there is*** a major gulf between the factual basis of the dispute and the applicants' cited objectives, supported by the third-party interveners, in the fairly complex field of sea-based immigration. (*Hirsi and others v. Italy,*[31] 2011, GVT OBS)

These reformulating illocution markers "take up the core of a reported statement about the interpretation of the issue to be settled in order to precise its scope" (Mazzi 2011: 19) in an argumentative way. In (15), ***instead*** is used to lend evidence to a dispreferred development of the situation in a dialogic reversal of the argumentative orientation. The applicant refutes the Government's argument ("had there been any truth") and replaces it by their own: an assessment should have been conducted. Thus, the voice is used for argument deconstruction purposes. In (16), after the narrativizing use of ***submit*** collocating with the opposing party – "the applicants" – the writing party reformulates the opposing standpoint by using ***in other words,*** which is followed by a series of legitimizing voices incorporating supporting positions by third-party interveners, only to be followed by the Government's counterargument, marked by the concessive ***in spite of.*** The alternative voice marker

31 Application no. 27765/09.

in other words ("preciser" in Lo Cascio 2009: 201; NF = 5.76; R = 29%) and the graders *rather* (NF = 16.57; R = 35%) and *instead* (NF = 10.44, R = 33%) are used recurrently in written pleadings in combination with reporting items in a wider co-text (17).

(17) The Court would further *emphasise* that the essence of such a violation does not so much lie in the fact of the disappearance of the family member *but rather* concerns the authorities reactions and attitudes when the situation is brought to their attention. It is especially in respect of the latter that a relative may *claim* to be a direct victim of the authorities' conduct. (*Shafiyeva v. Russia*,[32] 2010, GVT OBS)

(18) The first Tribunal decision mentions the issue of human rights in a single paragraph (§47), and there is no hint that the applicant had *contended* that s. 174 should be given a limited construction, pursuant to s. 3 of the Human Rights Act 1998 ("HRA"), in order to comply with Article 11. (*A.S.L.E.F. v. the UK*, 2006, GVT OBS)

Reporting verb *claim* is used to perform the deconstruction function (17), similarly to *contend* (18). It belongs to the class of the so-called "metapropositional verbs" (Coulthard 1994: 305–306), because they mark the reporter's interpretation of the original speaker, as opposed to "metalinguistic verbs" that merely convey prosodic descriptions. *Claim* is semantically loaded to include a connotation of the speakers disagreement with the statement, making its use highly dialogical and argumentative. In WOC *claim* – as a verb and as a noun – collocates with the party having expressed a view that contrasts the writing party's argument, i.e. with the Applicant in the Government's observations and with the Government in the Applicant's observations. In an earlier study of written pleadings (Nikitina 2018a: 249), I identified a collocational pattern where complex prepositions of contrast (*in violation of*, *contrary to*) frequently co-occurred with *submissions* and *claims*, performing thus the deconstruction function.

Besides reported speech, polyphony in legal texts is enhanced by prepositions with the function of reference (Nikitina 2018a: 241), most emblematically complex prepositions. They refer to legal sources, such as domestic acts, statutes, laws, case-law and the European Convention, incorporating thus a variety of voices into written pleadings that are not necessarily oppositional to the writing party, but frequently serve the legitimizing function, i.e. lending support to the writing party (see the use of "pursuant to" in (18)). Bhatia's (1998) definition of these devices as "signalling textual authority" reflects their fundamental idea, i.e. to demonstrate linguistically compliance with legal sources or near-legal sources of authority. Building on Nikitina (2018a: 241),

32 Application no. 49379/09.

Table 6.7 gathers together complex prepositions with the function of reference and a simple preposition ***under*** when it is used in the same function.[33]

The bigram "under article" is very frequent (AF = 211; NF = 76), widespread (CV = 1.05; R = 73%) and strongly associated (LL = 1501.55) in WOC.

(19) The present case should be analysed as one of interference with the applicant's rights ***under Article*** 11§1 which must be justified ***under Article*** 11§2. (*A.S.L.E.F. v. the UK*, 2006, GVT OBS)

Other, slightly less frequent collocates of ***under*** to the immediate right (R1-R2) are "articles", "rule(s)", "provision(s)", "section(s)", "sub", "domestic", "law", "Convention", "CPR", etc. These are also shared with other complex preposition in the table. By providing the established legal framework for the textual claims, these intertextual references carry out the legitimating function and represent instances of interdiscursive dialogism (Bres 2020).

The analysis of concordances of different markers of dialogism and polyphony shows that they are inserted in sequences of ***reported argumentation*** combined with ***proponent's argumentation*** (Mazzi 2007a: 394). The writing party (***sujet parlant*** in Ducrot 1984) reports the other party's arguments, to whom the authorship of the standpoint actually belongs (***énonciateur*** in Ducrot 1984), in a "polyphonic and asymmetrical game of opinions" (Mazzi 2007a: 395).

(20) As for the Article 2 claim, the ***Maltese government argues*** in paragraph 59 of its written observations, that the Applicant is not a "victim" and his claim is "hypothetical" since there has not been any Covid-19 case within the Corradino Correctional Facility till date. As explained in the

Table 6.7 Prepositions with the function of reference in the Written Observations Corpus

	AF	*NF*	*R*	*CV*
Under	487	175	92%	1.05
according to	203	73	80%	1.03
in accordance with	160	58	71%	1.37
in compliance with	35	13	33%	1.44
in conformity with	29	10	18%	3.08
in line with	8	3	12%	3.58
in pursuance of	2	1	2%	6.92
with accord to	1	0	2%	6.92
pursuant to	90	32	49%	1.49

33 Cases where ***under*** is part of a composite predicate (e.g. "come under responsibility", "be under detention") and fixed expressions (e.g. "under circumstances", "under-age", "under oath") are excluded from the analysis.

> preceding paragraphs, the ***Applicant's claim*** relating to his continued detention during Covid-19 is ***not*** that his rights under Articles 2–3 of the ECHR have been violated because he has contracted Covid-19 owing to the actions or omissions of the Maltese authorities, ***but*** that his Articles 2–3 rights have been violated as a result of the Maltese authorities' demonstrable and complete failure to address his medical situation and put into place an appropriately tailored protective regime. (*Fenech v. Malta*, 2021, APPL OBS)

In (20), the applicant reports the government's argument (after the lexical cue "the Maltese government argues"), giving also a precise intertextual reference which culminates in several instances of direct speech flagged by inverted commas. This reported argument is followed by the applicant's own argument (***proponent's argumentation*** in Mazzi 2007a), introduced by "the Applicant's claim". Peculiarly, this pattern of reported argument and the proponent's counter-argument is marked by the presence of a negative correlative pattern *not . . . but*, which will be further explained in the next section.

6.7 Negation for the duelling construction of reality

Laurence Horn (2010: 1) famously posited, "negation is what makes us human, imbuing us with the capacity to deny, to contradict, to misrepresent, to lie, and to convey irony". Studied from a variety of perspectives (see, e.g. Horn 2001, 2010; Zeijlstra 2004, 2023), in legal genres that stem from a battle of perspectives, such as written pleadings, opening and closing statements between the prosecution and the defence in court interaction or the majority and minority opinions in judgments (Nikitina 2025, forthcoming), negation vehiculates alternative standpoints promoting misalignment and/or disagreement with previous discourses or interlocutors. If argumentation is viewed as a global speech act with local textual manifestations, it is reasonable to expect counter-argumentation to unfold through negation at a local text level.

As Martin and White (2005: 118) conceptualized,

> negation is a resource for introducing the alternative positive position into the dialogue, and hence acknowledging it, so as to reject it. Thus in these dialogistic terms, the negative is not the simple logical opposite of the positive, since the negative necessarily carries with it the positive, while the positive does not reciprocally carry the negative, or at least not typically.

This dialogical and argumentative potential of negation makes it highly recurrent in legal argumentative texts as opposed to other genres and contexts (Garzone 2016: 10; Nikitina 2025, forthcoming). Negation is not necessarily argumentative at inception. In his works on dialogism, Bakhtin illustrated how the negative statement "Life is not good" does not become automatically dialogical to "Life is good" (Bakhtin 1984: 183), showing indirectly how "affirmatives are psychologically less complex than negatives" (Just & Carpenter 1971: 248–249, quoted in Horn 2001: 154). The dialogical relationship between the two utterances is activated when both correlate with distinct opinions corresponding to diverging speaking positions (e.g. commentary, retort, rejoinder, qualification; Etxabe 2022: 477). If the negative statement is produced "to predicate a state of things, and its author does not present it as opposing a contrary opinion/assertion" (Garzone 2016: 7, building on Ducrot 1974: 173–174), it constitutes the so-called *descriptive negation*. Conversely, if negation "aims to contrast a contrary/adverse opinion, which is incorporated in the clause" (Garzone 2016: 7), we talk about *polemic negation*. In later works, Ducrot (1984: 218) problematized this dichotomy, presenting polemic negation as the primary form and demoting descriptive negation to a derivative of polemic negation. He advocated that negation inherently involves a certain level of contradiction or denial of an opposing proposition, indicating a distinct underlying point of view or enunciation (Anscombre 1990: 59 in Garzone 2016: 8). As Horn (2001: 426) observed overviewing this distinction, "metalinguistic or polemic negation corresponds to a special negative speech act – a way of rebutting a previously uttered affirmation".

Deppermann (2014) applied the conversation-analytic concept of "recipient design" to the dialogical uses of negation when it is used to constrain unacceptable interlocutor interpretations either in a retrospective or anticipatory way. Despite "recipient design" in the classical conversation analysis understanding is circumscribed to the actual ratified participants (Goffman 1981), and the Bakhtinian dialogism envisages a much wider heteroglossic context, this conceptualization is pertinent to the context of written pleadings. Recipient design refers to practices of discursive constructions informed by the metacognitive knowledge of a "partner model" (Deppermann 2014: 19).

The line between descriptive and polemic negation can be fuzzy and dependent on contextual pragmatic factors, i.e. on the "illocutionary complex" of the statement (Garzone 2016: 11). By incorporating negative statements, even those based on facts, into the dialogic framework of written pleadings centred around the idea of a "mutually destructive" (Bedjaoui 1991: 45) narrative, instances of descriptive negation can don a contentious motley and engage argumentation strategies (Nikitina 2025, forthcoming).

(21) Accordingly, given that the applicant's status of the State official as such did *not* preclude him from performing other activities, the Government firmly maintains that he could *not* have been "incited" to engage into afore-mentioned activities as they would *not* amount to "the commission of an offence". *Nevertheless*, the applicant's administrative liability was established, *but* it was *not* based on his involvement in civil contractual relationships, *but* on his failure to obtain prior permission pursuant to relevant provisions of domestic law and internal regulations of the State Revenue Service. Namely, the actions of the authorities did *not*

> go beyond the ordinary conduct which is normally expected of parties in civil contractual relationships and it was up to the applicant to respond in a lawful manner and to obtain permission and inform his superiors about his engagement in cash transfer. The applicant has ***never*** complained that he had been specifically asked or requested by V. ***not*** to undergo the internal authorisation procedure. ***On the contrary***, the applicant decided to ***forego*** this procedure and to ***ignore*** the requirement on his own initiative, whereas the actions of undercover agent did ***not*** go beyond the conduct which could be normally expected in the course of lawful civil contractual activity. (*Pīlags v. Latvia*,[34] GVT OBS)

Multiple instances of morphologically expressed negation ("not", "not . . . but", "nevertheless", "never") coexist with semantically negative words ("on the contrary", "forego", "ignore") in (21), all of which refer to the reconstruction of facts, i.e. to the establishment of the epistemic reality. Had they occurred in a context-deprived vacuum, they could have been interpreted as descriptive. Yet, the argumentative and dialogical context of written pleadings endows these voices with a polemic value. These statements aim at refuting and rebutting the Applicant's claims in what was earlier referred to as a deconstructing voice, resulting in the so-called ***interpretation dialogue*** (Feteris 2017: 158, original emphasis, quoting Aarnio 1987), involving "a ***disagreement*** between a person A and a person (or group of persons) B about a particular interpretation". The coexistence and frequent correlation of the opposing voices with negation results in a situation where the predominant function of reported speech in written pleadings becomes that of *explicit deconstruction* (Chaemsaithong & Kim 2018: 44), coupled with some pragmatic deconstructing implicatures. For example, mentions of "lawful manner" or "obtaining permission" implicitly invite a conclusion that the applicant did not carry out these actions, which is rendered explicit in the last sentence of the example.

From a pragma-dialectical perspective, example (21) shows how negative statements are stratified into two alternative points of view (pov1 for the Applicant and pov2 for the Government) (Roitman 2015: 20).

Premise: the State Authorities incited the Applicant to commit an offence
pov1: the authorities went beyond the ordinary conduct
pov2: the authorities did not go beyond the ordinary conduct, it was the applicant's duty to inform his superiors (so, pov1 has to be refuted)
Conclusion: the State Authorities did not incite the Applicant to commit an offence.

In argumentation terms, "schemes resulting in opposite conclusions can be regarded as rebuttals, while negative answers to critical questions about

34 Application No. 66897/13.

exceptional circumstances correspond to undercutters" (Feteris 2017: 38). The Government continued to develop its undercutters in the second part of example (21) by stressing how the Applicant "did not undergo"/"forego"/"ignore" the authorization, inviting a conclusion which is dialogically opposite to the Applicant's position.

From the grammatical perspective, negation is realized through various categories (cf. Quirk et al. 1985: 798–799; Huddleston & Pullum 2002: 843–849), among which there are determiners (*no, neither*), pronouns (*none, neither, nothing, nobody, no one*), adverbs of place (*nowhere*), time (*never, no more, no longer*), manner (*in no way*), degree (*no, none the*), etc. Different word classes can be transformed into their negative counterparts by adding negative prefixes (*probable–improbable, likely–unlikely*, etc.). In addition to these classical categories there are also words that are negative semantically but not morphologically (Quirk et al. 1985: 780), such as *seldom, rarely, scarcely, hardly, barely, little, few*, or verbs that imply a negative lexical component, such as *overlook, ignore, strike out, rule out, set aside*, etc. Focusing predominantly on morphological markers of negation, this section ponders their use for purposes of duelling construction of reality on written pleadings.

Table 6.8[35] reports the morphologically and semantically marked uses of negation for single-standing markers, highlighting their recurrence in WOC, while Table 6.9 illustrates negative correlatives with a *repudiatory* function (Quirk et al. 1985: 935, 941), in that they contrast and refute the content of the first conjoin – explicitly or implicitly attributed to the other party in the pleadings.

Table 6.8 Negation markers in the Written Observations Corpus

Negation marker	*Raw frequency*	*Normalized frequency (100k)*	*Simple range (R)*	*Dispersion (CV)*
No	1,294	466.01	100%	0.641
Not	1,982	713.78	100%	0.385
Cannot	148	53.3	76%	0.895
Any	708	254.97	98%	0.747
Anything	13	4.7	22%	2.10
Anyone	9	3.2	10%	3.31
Neither	48	17.29	43%	1.41
Either	35	12.60	51%	1.30
Nor	73	26.3	53%	1.26
None	23	8.3	31%	3.06
Nobody	3	1.1	6%	4.07
Never	47	16.9	39%	1.53
Nonetheless	13	4.7	16%	2.57

35 Simple Range (R) is a lexical dispersion measure that indicates how many texts in the corpus feature the search word. Coefficient of variation is another dispersion measure that "describes the amount of variation relative to the mean relative frequency of a word or phrase in the corpus" (Brezina 2018: 50); the closer to zero it is, the more even the distribution of the search word is in the corpus.

Table 6.9 Repudiation patterns in the Written Observations Corpus

	Absolute frequency	*Normalized frequency (100,000)*	*Log-likelihood*[36]
not . . . but	253	91	2164.54
not only . . . but	44	16	509.65
not only . . . but also	35	13	389.24
and * not	82	30	110.73
neither . . . nor	37	13	581.44
either . . . or	28	10	263.93

In the pattern *not . . . but*, see (20, 21), the second conjoin, marked by the "connective of counter-argument" (Mazzi 2007a: 387) *but* introduces *rectification* (Bres 2005): an alternative version, or a counterargument. The adversative connective *but* (as a single-standing token: NF = 120; R = 84%; CV = 0.95) is very strongly associated with the particle not (NF = 714; R = 100%; CV = 0.385), producing a log-likelihood value of 2164.54, showing the statistical relevance of this pattern in WOC. As Garzone (2016: 16–17) expounded,

> [w]hile in a standard instance of negation a positive utterance attributed to a non-specified opponent is negated, and beyond that nothing is said specifically about the author's view and the reader is left to infer it from the context, in rectification, by contrast, the locutor's view is also specified, often introduced by *but*.

This double-standpoint presentation performs specific argumentative purposes, as the first, refuted, conjoin signals a need for another argumentative move, present in the second conjoin.

Other negative correlative pattern identified as statistically relevant for WOC is *not only . . . but* (LL = 509.65) and *not only . . . but also* (LL = 389.24). These patterns have been baptized "renchérissement" (Bres 1999), "reinforcement" (Dendale 2006; Garzone 2016) and "escalating repudiation" (Nikitina 2025, forthcoming) in the literature on the dialogic uses of negation. As Quirk et al. (1985: 941) explain, in this pattern "the content of the first conjoin is framed as surprising, with 'but also' enhancing the content of the second conjoint as even more surprising", see (22) and (23).

36 Log-likelihood measures how probable a set of observed data is under a particular model or set of parameters. In this case, the threshold was set at 6.63, which is the critical value for a chi-squared distribution with one degree of freedom at the 0.01 level of significance (Brezina 2018: 114). In other words, any co-occurrence above 6.63 is considered statistically significant; the higher the LL value is, the stronger the collocation is. All collocations in the table are much more common in the data than could be expected by chance. Comparing the log-likelihood values, *not . . . but* is the strongest collocation, followed by *neither . . . nor* and *not only . . . but*.

(22) As concerns the applicant's detention from 4 January 2020 onwards, the applicant once again makes allegations that are ***not only unsubstantiated but*** are, in some cases, ***completely fallacious***, as will be explained below. (*Fenech v. Malta* 2021, GVT OBS)

(23) The Applicant could have pursued this argument at the second hearing before the House of Lords. *Not only* did it choose ***not*** to pursue this argument at that time, as recorded in the judgment of Lord Hoffmann (quote above), the argument the Applicant did advance before the House of Lords accepted the premise that it was open to the Government to choose to fund access to justice in this way. For this reason, the Court should reject these parts of the Applicant's case. (*MGN Ltd v. the UK*,[37] 2009, GVT OBS)

Examples (22) and (23) illustrate the grading, or escalating, potential of this dialogical pattern. In (22) it leads to an oxymoronic combination of a mitigated ("in some cases") and boosted ("completely") assertion of fallacy. The sentence-initial placement of the formula in (23) adds to the dramatically escalating effect. It is worth mentioning that both examples feature double negatives ("not unsubstantiated" and "not did not pursue"), which are quite common, even if somewhat disputed, in judicial writing (Ondelli & Pontrandolfo 2016).

Another form of repudiatory escalation is represented by the patterns *neither . . . nor* (24) and *either . . . or* (the latter in combination with a negation marker, see (25)). When used as negative correlative conjunctions, *neither . . . nor* pattern serves a reinforcing purpose (Quirk et al. 1985: 935), similar to the additive meaning of *both . . . and* (Quirk et al. 1985: 938).

(24) In the present case there is ***neither an allegation nor any evidence***, submitted by Government, that the 1st instance court judge or appeal court judges had been impartial. Even having doubts about the applicant's guilt, the domestic courts made ***no attempt*** to eliminate these doubts [. . .]. *Nevertheless*, Government, ***with no arguments in support***, keep stating that "it follows from the case file against the applicant that the courts ***did not*** assume the function of supporting of prosecution" (see paragraph 61 of the Government's observations). (*Avagyan v. Russia*,[38] 2021, APPL OBS)

(25) Although the vessels which took part in the operations on 6 May 2009 come under Italian jurisdiction, they ***did not exercise either absolute or exclusive control*** in the rescue and assistance operation involving the applicants, in compliance with the obligations arising from the provisions of the international law of the sea. (*Hirsi v. Italy*, GVT OBS).

37 Application no. 39401/04.
38 Application no. 36911/20.

These can be used as negative additive adverbs to expand on the previous – either explicitly or implicitly – negative clause or phrase. Remarkably, *nor* is not synonymous with "not" + "or" but is instead equivalent to "not" + "and" (Quirk et al. 1985: 937), enhancing the escalation effect. This can be observed in the phrase "Nor does she suggest . . ." in (26), which has the same meaning as "and she does not suggest".

(26) It is impossible to see *any* distinction with Ms Ladele's case and *none* is suggested by her. *Nor* does she suggest that Pichon was wrongly decided or *is no longer* good law (and indeed it has been applied in recent cases: see Sahin §121 and RR v Poland (2011) 53 EHRR 31 §206). (*Eweida, Chaplin, Ladele and McFarlane vs. UK*,[39] 2012, GVT OBS)

Finally, WOC displays a significant number of *and*-prefaced negation. Table 6.9 reports the combination "and" + "not" in the 2R[40] range (getting thus both "and not" and "and does not"). With the increase of the collocation window to 10R, the pattern *and * not* takes on additional relevance (AF = 440, NF = 158; LL = 1350.95), demonstrating the widespread reliance on this escalating/additive effect of the pattern, which is typically inserted in a series of negative statements, as exemplified by (27) and (28), with refutation purposes.

(27) [. . .] why Martynenko S. A. was *refused* a comparative examination of drugs based on the suggestion that "possibly" the applicant had various drugs; why the facts of damage to packages containing material evidence *were not taken* into account (the cause of the damage (eaten by small rodents) *is not reliable, as it was hypothetical and not verified by the Court*); why the court denied the applicant's and the lawyer's request to demand the register from the district police department as material evidence; why the Court, having all the grounds, *did not* question the testimony of witnesses; statement of the witness Zaika Yu.; V. *why there are no* audio recordings of the court hearing (*Martynenko v. Ukraine*,[41] 2021, APPL OBS).

(28) [. . .] in order to determine whether a retroactive law and its capacity to harm acquired rights are compatible with the Convention, it is necessary to compare the effects of the retroactive rule with those which would have proceeded from the application of the rule in force at the time when those facts occurred (*and not, on the contrary*, with the rule in force at the time when the individual decides to initiate legal proceedings) (*Scordino v. Italy*, GVT OBS)

39 Application nos. 48420/10, 59842/10, 51671/10 and 36516/10 *Eweida, Chaplin, Ladele and McFarlane v the United Kingdom*.

40 Two words to the immediate right.

41 Application no. 40829/12.

6.8 Discussion and conclusions

As a concept, legal institutional translation is detached from "the internal procedural specificities and the level of outsourcing involved in producing the translations for the relevant commissioning institution" (Prieto Ramos 2020: 455). What comes as the first logical assumption when one hears "outsourcing", "legal translation" and "supranational court" is the idea of a high-quality external service, probably a translation agency. This is not the case with written pleadings, as the present analysis shows. For obvious budgetary and human resources constraints, translation of written pleadings is left on the outskirts of the translation hierarchy and beyond the radar of institutional translation quality controls.

The long-fought victory of a universal right of individual petition created a most curious linguistic regime at the ECtHR. To render the right of individual petition truly effective, applicants were allowed to apply in their national languages. This generated the need to employ a significant number of Registry lawyers who spoke the said national language and could process these applications, especially in the high case-count states.[42] Another logical consequence of this system affected the next link in the procedural chain: written pleadings. Sometimes it was more expeditious to allow pleadings in the national language, shared and understood by the applicants, the governments and the Registry lawyers. Yet, the ECtHR is not multilingual in a classical understanding, as it practices alternative bilingualism, so any part of the procedure, besides the initial application, has to be available in an official language. The question of translation quality control thus clashes with resource prioritization. How important is translation, if the case has been already or is being processed in a national language?

Written pleadings shape parties' standpoints and engage in oppositional legal argumentation. Traditionally, judicial discourse is seen as polyphonous and argumentative. This study takes a critical genre perspective, exploring how the extended participation framework affects written pleadings' discursive markup.

The dialogical and argumentative nature of written pleadings, influenced by the Court's questions during case communication, makes them highly intertextual. Parties use "manifest intertextuality" (Fairclough 1992), involving references and reported speech to activate dialogism. This integration of voices

42 For instance, as of May 2024 there are ca. 50 case-processing lawyers in the Turkish division of the Registry (38 staff and 11–12 seconded officials, i.e. externally founded by the State) and some 20 secretaries; ca. 30 case-processing lawyers in the Italian Division (22 staff and 7–8 seconded officials); 33 case-processing lawyers in the Ukrainian Division (32 staff and 1 seconded official); 12 case-processing lawyers in the Polish Division. States with a relatively low case-count have fewer case-processing lawyers. For instance, there are 6 lawyers in the Armenian Division and 5 lawyers in the Latvian Division (4 staff and 1 seconded official). There are even some single-lawyer divisions, e.g. there is only one, seconded, case-processing lawyer for Andorra).

serves refutational legal argumentation. Patterns of metapropositional lexis alternate between the opponent's and proponent's arguments, using negation to present opposing viewpoints and enhance polemic value. The use of authoritative sources and negation techniques strengthens arguments, guiding readers towards favourable conclusions for the writing party. These findings enhance understanding of case construction and presentation in the ECtHR system, impacting adjudicative outcomes, as discussed in Part III of this book.

Part III

The language of judges at the ECtHR

7 Judgment

Combining genre, patterning and legal reasoning perspectives

7.1 Introduction

Judgment is the pinnacle genre in every international court's system of genres. Defined as "the official and authentic decision of a court of justice upon the respective rights and claims of the parties to an action or suit therein litigated and submitted to its determination" (*Black's Law Dictionary*[1]), it is *the* genre, the logical peak of month- or year-long proceedings before the Court. It comes as no surprise that this genre is most frequently associated and equalled with the Court, its discourse community and discourse practices.

The representativity, legal significance and easy retrievability of judgments has generated a substantial amount of research on judgments, from a variety of perspectives. Scholarship on the judgment as a textual genre can be divided, based on their context of origin, into studies dealing with national contexts, studies dealing with international contexts and studies comparing different contexts. The "national" research strand (see, e.g. Goźdź-Roszkowski 2011; Bletsas 2015), as can be logically expected, is embedded in a specific legal framework, monolithic and monolingual. The "international" research strand embraces the hybridity intrinsic of international courts and their multilingualism (Peruzzo 2019a, 2019b; Brannan 2013, 2021, 2023; McAuliffe 2015, 2020). The "comparatists" engage in the analysis of judgments across at least two systems, which can be both national (Goźdź-Roszkowski & Pontrandolfo 2013; Goźdź-Roszkowski 2024) or national and international (Mazzi 2007a, 2007b, 2011).

Scholars dealing with judgments of international and supranational courts display a clear fascination with judgments of the European Court of Justice. Its multilingual jurisprudence, pursuing the quest for saying the same thing in all its official languages, has elicited strong curiosity among scholars interested in the relationship between law and language for the creation of ECJ case-law (Sousa Domingues 2017), the implications of multilingualism (Wright 2018; McAuliffe 2020), and the role of translation (McAuliffe 2015, 2016) at the ECJ (see Peruzzo 2019b: 54 for an overview). Literature on judgments of

1 Available at https://thelawdictionary.org/judgment/. Unless otherwise specified, all links were last accessed in May 2024.

DOI: 10.4324/9781003434788-10

other international courts is less saturated, and legal linguistic studies of the ECtHR judgments are comparatively few (Weston 2005; Brannan 2013, 2018, 2021; Peruzzo 2019a, 2019b).

This chapter offers a look behind the scenes, outlining the process of drafting and deliberation behind the creation of judgments within the discourse community of the ECtHR (Section 7.2), both at a Chamber and a Grand Chamber level. Next, using an ad hoc corpus that focuses specifically on Grand Chamber judgments (Section 7.3.1), I describe this genre following the Critical Genre Analysis framework, delving into its participation framework, length, style and linguistic regime, as well as providing a detailed description of its structure in 7.4. Continuing the description of argumentation in judicial writing set out in Chapter 6, this chapter describes the genre of judgment as argumentative and evaluative. The linguistic focus is, thus, placed on patterns of argumentative evaluation, exploring inputs from pattern grammar and legal argumentation studies: *it is ADJ to-inf* and *it is ADJ that*.

7.2 The ECtHR judgment: behind the scenes

Legal literature on judgments in international courts frequently mentions their "manufacture" (Bedjaoui 1991), or *confection* in French (Berger 1992), or similar metaphors portraying an almost industrial landscape concealed behind the scenes. So, how are judgments in international courts crafted? The "manufacturing" process can be described using two elements: drafting and deliberation. As mentioned in 3.4.2, this process is formation-specific: while the Committee stage is not burdened by a deliberation/voting stage, both Chamber and Grand Chamber judgments go through the complete manufacturing cycle. The question of what comes first, drafting or deliberation, resembles the philosophical enquiry into the chicken and the egg, so while the following sections try to delimit the two issues, the reader is invited to bear in mind that the distinction is beyond blurry.

7.2.1 The judgment genesis

Linguistic literature frequently forgoes the judgment genesis, which is crucially important for the understanding of this genre from a critical genre standpoint. For Chamber formations, the process is relatively streamlined by the Registry, who send a "thick file" to the judges before their Tuesday meetings along with a judgment draft. This draft is co-created by lawyers from an administrative unit of the Registry and the so-called *judge rapporteur*, a judge who is designated by the president of the relevant Section (Rule 49 (2)). The identity of the judge rapporteur is never disclosed (Keller & Heri 2018: para. 38). So, when the Chamber members meet,[2] they already have a text to work

2 Former ECtHR president Costa (2021: 315) overviewing his time as a Third Section member defines its atmosphere as "warm and invigorating". He also explains that Section members are

on. Moreover, at the Chamber level, the "drafting process is informed by the observations of the Jurisconsult, who draws up a document concerning the Court's case law to support the preparation of the draft" (Keller & Heri 2018: para. 39).

This is not the case at the Grand Chamber. No judgment proposal is circulated among the Grand Chamber judges before deliberation, typically on Wednesdays. What happens in that time? Little is known about the process preceding formal deliberation. Keller and Heri (2018: para. 31) mention "an informal rule" according to which Chamber judges receiving a draft and finding themselves in disagreement with it would "notify their colleagues of this a few days before the deliberations take place [. . .] by e-mail" to allow the judge rapporteur and the other judges "to adequately prepare themselves for the deliberations". A *rapporteur's note* is prepared then with the assistance of the Registry. The note "usually serves as a source of background information and provides an overview of the existing case law as well as an indication of where modifications of the jurisprudence may be necessary" (Keller & Heri 2018: para. 34). The national judge might craft a similar note, albeit without the comforting embrace of the Registry's assistance. In the Chamber, the national judge's note may include additional arguments, whereas in the Grand Chamber it hews to domestic law and practice, ensuring that the judge rapporteur – never coinciding with the national judge at the Grand Chamber level – has accurately understood the domestic law and practice.

The judges may rely on a comparative or international law research report, typically commissioned of the Research Division by the judge rapporteur in case some specific comparative law questions arise. Once completed, the report is circulated among judges whose home legal systems have been examined. Additionally, there may also be reports on the Court's previous case-law if deemed necessary (Keller & Heri 2018: para. 36).

7.2.2 *Deliberation and drafting*

At the Chamber level, deliberations are coordinated by the Section president, subjecting the process to a set of procedural rules and customs. The President first grants the floor to the judge rapporteur, to pass it later to the national judge (if the latter does not act as the judge rapporteur). Following this, the remaining Chamber judges join the ensemble and share their views on the draft. "Each judge will speak in the official language of his or her choosing, but interpreters – and it gives me pleasure to say that they are outstanding – provide simultaneous translation" (Costa 2021: 381). There is no predetermined sequence for these interventions, and judges may speak multiple times. Their remarks are then followed by a vote, which serves as the basis for the Registry to refine the draft (Keller & Heri 2018: para. 40). When possible, the draft

"are appointed for a three-year period based on a geopolitical balance and with an equal number of male and female judges" (Costa 2021: 317–319).

is adopted by a majority vote at the same meeting (Villiger 2017: para. 13). Chamber deliberations' length may vary depending on the case complexity,[3] but "usually [they] last half a day, sometimes more if there is a full agenda" (Costa 2021: 379). Deliberations are private; and are "lively" and with a "totally collegial" decision-making process (Costa 2021: 383), resulting in "a courteous and even friendly, rarely tense" atmosphere (Costa 2021: 385).

While the input for Chamber deliberations is predominantly written, i.e. a draft judgment or decision, the Grand Chamber may rely also on an oral input delivered at the Grand Chamber hearing, a rare opportunity for the judges to interact with any party through questions (Rules 62 (2) and 71 (1)). So, the process is somewhat inverse: the Grand Chamber first meets at a hearing; then, properly inspired, its members retire to begin their first round of deliberations, and only after do they prepare the first draft.

As in the Chamber, Grand Chamber deliberations begin with the judge rapporteur and the national judge presenting their arguments. Then, the other judges express their opinions. Unlike in the Chamber, judges without special roles (president, judge rapporteur or national judge) can speak only once and cannot rebut arguments from colleagues speaking later. Thus, judges must choose strategically when to speak. The national judge and judge rapporteur may speak again at the end, while the president leads the deliberation (Keller & Heri 2018: para. 50).

Judge rapporteur and national judge constitute a system of checks and balances for Grand Chamber deliberations. The role of the national judge in this context is "little known and often poorly understood in the outside world" (Costa 2021: 327); it resembles that of the Advocate General of the European Court of Justice in that he or she "is called upon to present their view on the case, to analyse the Rapporteur's opinion, to supplement it, and possibly even to disagree with it" (Villiger 2017: para. 12).

Grand Chamber deliberations can take up to 4–5 hours, as it is expectedly challenging to find consonant trends when 17 different voices are concerned. Typically there is more than one round of deliberation. In the first deliberation, judges "may abstain from voting if they provide reasons for doing so" by identifying the points of potential misalignment, disagreement or doubt. Different personal and judicial temperaments may emerge at this stage, too. The abstaining judges reserve "their vote for the second deliberation, at which point the draft text of the judgment will be available" (Keller & Heri 2018: para. 51). All judges must cast their votes in the indicative vote at the beginning of the second deliberation.

As there are 17 judges, a tie is impossible. However, due to abstentions in the first round of deliberations, there could be cases when judges are divided into two fractions, one for finding a violation and the other for not finding

3 Judge Costa (2021: 397) indicated a timespan ranging between a few minutes to ten minutes per case on average.

it. In such cases, two draft judgments are prepared and acknowledged at the beginning of the second round of deliberations.

> In controversial cases, the president will commence the second deliberation by noting that two drafts have been prepared, and determining which draft is preferred by the majority by taking an indicative vote. As noted above, judges cannot abstain from this vote [. . .]. If, on an indicative basis, a clear majority of judges prefers one alternative, then the judges proceed to go through that draft and deliberate on its content paragraph by paragraph. Once an agreement has been reached on the text – or a near-agreement, as there may still be a need to apply the pigeonhole procedure [. . .] to some issues – a definitive vote takes place. (Keller & Heri 2018: para. 52)

At the end of the first deliberation session, the national judge and the judge rapporteur summarize the discussions and pose questions for the judges to vote on, as determined by the president based on the rapporteur's proposal. After this, the president selects several judges who voted with the majority, including the judge rapporteur, to form a drafting committee. This committee, usually five judges, drafts the judgment more efficiently than if all 17 Grand Chamber judges were involved. The national judge assists but cannot vote within the committee. If there is a divided majority, representatives of different opinions are included in drafting, and multiple drafts may be prepared. Following the first deliberations, a second meeting with the judge rapporteur, the Registrar and the case lawyer guides the preparation of the draft judgment, which takes about six weeks. The drafting committee then reviews and amends this draft, meeting around six to seven weeks later to finalize it. The committee's composition is decided by the president and aims to include those judges with the best arguments, reducing the judge rapporteur's drafting burden (Keller & Heri 2018: paras. 53–57).

In contrast to Chambers' monolingual procedures – "the judges receive the case file about two weeks in advance, in English or French depending on the case – but not in both of the official languages" (Costa 2021: 37) – the draft judgment of the Grand Chamber is translated by the Registry's translation unit into the other official language of the ECtHR and the translation is circulated among the judges. A second deliberation is held to present and discuss the draft judgment, culminating in a final vote. Judges may change their votes from the first to the second deliberation, though significant changes are rare (Keller & Heri 2018: paras. 58–59).

7.2.3 When no agreement can be reached

Deliberation and drafting may result in a varying "scope of the interventions", which are all "useful", and "may range from the acutest of accents to the gravest of questions" (Bedjaoui 1991: 53). Nothing is taken for granted, and in general while the ECtHR judge's work is "intellectually and morally gratifying, and also well paid, it is arduous, tiring, demanding and sometimes frustrating, and generally voluminous" (Costa 2021: 371).

If the intervention concerns the wording, but not the substance, the Court may capitalize on the so-called *pigeonhole procedure*, when the Registry is invited to devise an amenable formulation in the text of individual paragraph(s), the so-called *pigeonhole* (Keller & Heri 2018: para. 61), to resolve a linguistic conflict in a draft. The recommended formulation is shared via e-mail. This approach lightens the judges' burden of preparing "a publication-ready text in a language that is often not their native one" (Keller & Heri 2018: para 62).

When the apple of discord is the wording, the pigeonhole procedure allows for "the harmonization of conflicting demands" saving the time and effort of the case lawyer and the judge rapporteur. "It may therefore also improve the draft text by allowing, for example, for the identification and removal of contradictions between different paragraphs" (Keller & Heri 2018: para 63). Regardless of linguistic fine-tuning, "the judges clearly have the last word" (Brannan 2021: 224).

If the judges are misaligned on the substance that goes beyond any linguistic loopholes, the Court may adjourn and prepare a new draft, going for the second round of deliberations. If the judges do not agree with the second draft, extensive discussions may occur. If agreement on controversial paragraphs cannot be reached, the pigeonhole procedure may be applied again, because the Court has a strong preference towards having a clear majority, as explained by Garlicki (2009: 396):

> The level of unanimity cannot have any impact on the binding effect of judgments. It may, however, influence their persuasive authority: a judgment adopted by a tiny majority indicates that there are divergent positions within the Court. That is why, particularly on the Grand Chamber level, there is a clear preference for drafts that are able to attract a clear majority of participating judges.

Finally, if the judges do not feel represented by the majority judgment, and there is no way to sway their votes by paraphrasing challenging paragraphs, they vote against it and may append subsequently a separate opinion (Chapter 8).

7.3 The Grand Chamber judgment: genre considerations

7.3.1 The RiFT corpus

To analyse a given discourse/professional practice, the analyst must select appropriate materials, authentic and representative of the chosen context. For judgment description, as the Court has a notoriously "burgeoning caseload" (Peruzzo 2019b: 19) coupled with its "prolific" output (Keller & Heri 2018: para. 1), I had to delimit the corpus using the judicial formation criterion and the thematic criterion. This study focuses on judgments delivered by Grand Chamber formations on cases dealing with Article 6 ECHR, "Right to a Fair Trial". The corpus of judgments on the right to a fair trial, hence RiFT, was collected using the Court's database HUDOC, filtered by formation: Grand Chamber, language: English, article: 6. The search yielded 200 results, the main statistical data for which are reported in Table 7.1.

Without a predetermined timeframe, RiFT collects all Grand Chamber (GC) judgments dealing with Article 6. Incidentally, the first judgment in the corpus dates back to February 1996 and the last one to April 2024, for the total of 28 years. Peculiarly, no Article 6 judgments were issued in 2021, and 19% of texts in RiFT refer to 1999, following the reform in 1998 (see 3.2.2), when the Court merged with the former European Commission on Human Rights, and the Grand Chamber "inherited" the task of ruling on applications for which the Commission issued a report (see 3.2.1) resulting in unusually high "production" rates. The greater or lesser amount of judgments per year thus reflects the Court's dynamic.

Table 7.1 Composition of the RiFT 96–24 corpus

Timeframe	*Texts*	*Percentage of texts*	*Tokens*	*Types*
1996–2024	200	100	3,165,243	77,257
1996	8	4	68,458	12,148
1997	5	2.5	46,220	8,531
1998	6	3	67,358	11,710
1999	38	19	318,312	61,218
2000	17	8.5	160,089	28,076
2001	12	6	160,639	24,544
2002	5	2.5	36,451	7,196
2003	6	3	86,840	13,457
2004	5	2.5	78,479	11,239
2005	6	3	127,841	17,509
2006	19	9.5	294,378	42,335
2007	4	2	70,413	9,972
2008	5	2.5	47,132	8,310
2009	7	3.5	92,667	14,646
2010	6	3	108,788	15,211
2011	4	2	69,276	9,266
2012	3	1.5	52,092	7,948
2013	2	1	33,125	4,844
2014	2	1	70,164	9,998
2015	4	2	69,951	9,489
2016	8	4	213,614	25,559
2017	7	3.5	241,796	39,702
2018	10	5	242,850	30,624
2019	2	1	43,751	5,789
2020	2	1	69,574	6,947
2022	2	1	81,122	7,470
2023	3	1.5	107,658	10,660
2024	1	0.5	106,205	8,249

Article 6 is a polyhedric article, having both a civil and a criminal limb. Jackson (2022: 101) summarizes the criminal limb case-law as concentrating on "fair trial standards for criminal proceedings such as the presumption of innocence, the protection of the accused against abusive coercion, the right to examine witnesses and the need for 'equality of arms' and an 'adversarial procedure' between the investigating or prosecuting authorities and the accused", whereas in the civil context it mainly revolves around the concept of "civil rights and obligations" (Art. 6 §1 ECHR) coupled with the existence of a "dispute" (*contestation*).

Since I decided to treat separate opinions annexed to judgments as a separate genre (explained in 8.3.2), I was faced with a challenge of removing them from the files containing judgments. HUDOC does not have a category for separate opinions, so they exist on the margins of judgments. Yet, as the analysis will show, their structure, composition and style are too different from the judgment to place them together. Resolved to treat them as a distinct genre, I went through the analyst's delight of separate-opinion-ectomy, manually cutting out separate opinions from the texts of 200 judgments. The structure of judgments in RiFT is reported in 7.4.

7.3.2 *Participation framework*

Gerards (2017: 267–268) acknowledges the challenge of determining "the audience of the Court's judgments". She identifies several readers, including the parties involved in a specific case (both the Applicant and the Respondent Government), national authorities (including those of other States) and domestic courts. Similarly, Goźdź-Roszkowski (2024: 12) states that judgment "audiences may range from fellow judges ('the bench') to lower court justices, litigants, the legal community, legislators and government officials to news outlets and the public at large". In a world of eight billion inhabitants, with ca. 740 million inhabitants in the Council of Europe Member States, connected and empowered by the digitalization of justice (see 9.1), it is increasingly difficult to outline the participation framework of a supranational court's judgments.

Kurzon (2001: 67–68) described the participation framework in the national contexts of the high courts in the United States and the United Kingdom indicating among the audience (or addressees) (1) fellow judges sitting on the same bench, (2) judge(s) at a lower appeal level, (3) judges of courts of first instance, (4) counsel appearing in front of judges and (5) audience at large.

Despite the different context, some similarities with the ECtHR emerge (see Figure 7.1). The judges tasked with applying Convention law in their respective jurisdictions are undoubtedly primary recipients of the Court's case-law (Brannan 2021: 221). Similarly to other international contexts, such as that of the International Court of Justice (ICJ), the judgments of the ECtHR go through an "impressively lengthy period of gestation" (Bedjaoui 1991: 29), which involves several preliminary drafting rounds, where the text of the judgment is discussed and perfected within the discourse community of the Court, typically involving all judges sitting on the bench, some of whom form part of the drafting committee along with the Registry representatives. This is the stage when some "warning shots [are] fired to announce the impending battle of the votes" (Bedjaoui 1991: 52) signalling a probable insurgence of separate opinions at a later stage (see Chapter 8).

Other judges of the ECtHR, who did not form part of the panel, might constitute another group of addressees of a published judgment. Cases may reach the Grand Chamber following one of two paths: either at the request of one of the parties following a Chamber judgment (Art. 43 ECHR), or due to a Chamber relinquishing the case (Art. 30 ECHR). When a request for referral is made under Article 43 ECHR, a five-judge Grand Chamber Panel evaluates whether it raises significant questions regarding the Convention's interpretation or application, or addresses issues of general importance. If deemed so, the request is granted, and the case is referred to the Grand Chamber (Art. 43 (2) and (3) ECHR). Relinquishment occurs when the Chamber handling the case concludes that it raises crucial questions about the Convention's interpretation or application, or if there is a potential conflict with the Court's well-established case-law (aka WECL, Art. 30 ECHR).

The 17 members of the Grand Chamber are usually "selected by the drawing of lots mere days after the Grand Chamber is seized in a case, and work on the case begins almost right away, with a first orientation meeting between the case lawyer, the Registrar, and the judge rapporteur" (Keller & Heri 2018: para. 47). The participation framework, thus, includes also some behind-the-scenes participants of the ECtHR discourse community: the Registry personnel, who is actively involved in its production both from the legal standpoint (draft preparation, pigeonhole procedure, etc.) and the linguistic standpoint (Grand Chamber judgments are bilingual, translated by the in-house team of translators, see 7.3.5).

The parties to the case, the Government's Agent and the Applicant's Counsel, are also among the judgment recipients. Additionally, national and international legal scholars, practitioners – judges and counsel alike – and researchers interested in the court's jurisprudence form another addressee group. For instance, researchers dealing with the ECtHR sister courts – the IACtHR and the ACtHPR – may be listed among the recipients of the ECtHR judgments, too, by virtue of their interest in supranational human rights justice. Moreover, as the ECtHR case-law broaches socially sensitive topics empowering individuals to seek redress at a supranational level, it may address a broader public, which can be potentially equalled with the legally capable population of the CoE Member States.

7.3.3 Style

Judgments of supranational courts are "composite" texts (Bedjaoui 1991: 49) as a logical consequence of a collegial drafting process. These documents are

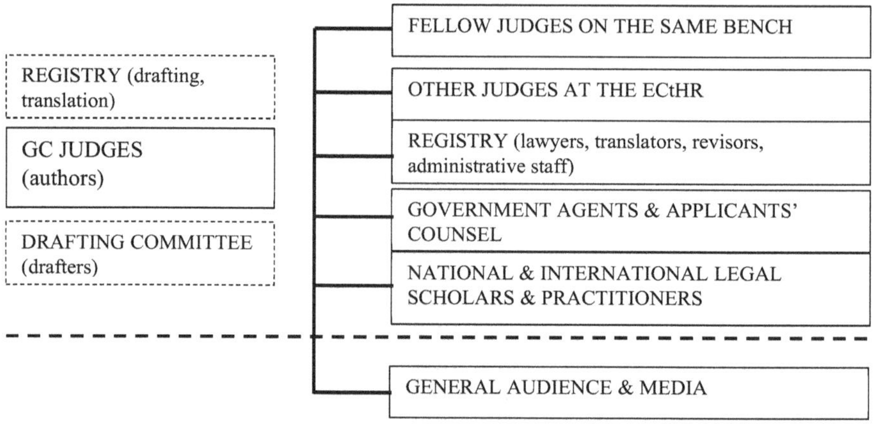

Figure 7.1 Participation framework in the Grand Chamber judgments

not produced in "one fell swoop by a single pen" (Bedjaoui 1991: 50). Cohen (2016: 513) finds Strasbourg judgments to be "longer and more discursive", while nevertheless following a "French-like format". Villiger (2017: para. 22) contrasts this view, stating that despite the judgments being written in English and/or French, their style "does not resemble that of judgments of the United Kingdom or France. Rather, the style is highly idiosyncratic; as such, it has been developed over a period of nearly 60 years. It is best described as a European human rights style". The style is "disciplined but also quite elaborate" (Garlicki 2009: 391), reminiscent of constitutional courts in terms of methodology "oriented towards explaining and convincing [rather] than simply issuing dry commands". Far from a Frankenstein-esque combination, this style is "born out of the wish to engage national courts and authorities", this being "the key to successful implementation of the Convention" (Senden 2011: 21). Despite the best efforts, sometimes this style is perceived by national judges as difficultly phrased and conveying an "alien line of thinking" (Kjær 2011: 328). These "somewhat heterogeneous in character" (Bedjaoui 1991: 56) texts are the product of lengthy discussions and compromise of the 17 judges of the Grand Chamber.

Brannan (2021: 222) has defined the ECtHR judgments as "somewhat comparable to the style of the International Court of Justice (ICJ), which inspired its functioning at the outset and has the same working and social languages, maintaining a similar parallelism in its bilingual texts". The ICJ judge Bedjaoui (1991: 50) wondered, "How can the lapidary, laconic or even elliptical style of one Judge be seamlessly welded to the highly decorative, rhetorical and parenthetic style of another who may, moreover, be using the other language of the Court?" The ECtHR found a more or less formalized solution to such a situation: the pigeonhole procedure, "demanding no less cunning than tact [. . .] to ensure homogeneity". Less enthusiastic commentators have defined the resulting style as "stilted", "unidiomatic for native speakers of

English", "flat" and built around "certain almost ritualistic formulae" (Merrills 1993: 30, 36, quoted in Brannan 2021: 225).

For Brannan (2021: 224), "[t]he style of the original draft will depend to some extent on the novelty of the case (Grand Chamber judgments are thus particularly 'elaborative'), but the cutting and pasting of passages from relevant case law ('authorities') is commonplace". Additionally, one must remember that regardless of the extent of passages copied from previous case-law or drafting from scratch, the judgment "will be deliberated upon by a collegial panel of judges from diverse legal traditions" (Brannan 2021: 224), which may result in some peculiar lexicogrammar and "convoluted sentences as a result of juxtaposing segments of previous judgments to formulate a general principle" (Brannan 2021: 224). For instance, Brannan (2021: 225) reports how "rules of law" evolved into "legal rules" to avoid confusion with the "rule of law".

While in general language phraseologies may draw their existence from the so-called "acoustic inertia of the language" (Parks 2014: 220), simply because they "sound good" (MacKenzie & Kayman 2016: 1), the discourse of human rights judgments has to deal also with legal and interlinguistic considerations. As the style of judgments is frequently the fruit of linguistic compromise, some "successful" formulations migrate from judgment to judgment verbatim, transforming into *routines* (see 2.4), i.e. longer stretches of text that are reproduced without changes and that contribute to the formulaic character of judicial discourse.

(1) Freedom of expression constitutes one of the essential foundations of a democratic society and one of the basic conditions for its progress and each individual's self-fulfilment. Subject to paragraph 2 of Article 10, it is applicable not only to "information" or "ideas" that are favourably received or regarded as inoffensive or as a matter of indifference, but also to those that offend, shock or disturb; such are the demands of that pluralism, tolerance and broadmindedness without which there is no "democratic society". Freedom of expression, as enshrined in Article 10, is subject to a number of exceptions which, however, must be narrowly interpreted, and the necessity for any restrictions must be convincingly established.
(2) The Court finds that this complaint is not manifestly ill-founded within the meaning of Article 35 § 3 (a) of the Convention. *It further notes* that it is not inadmissible on any other grounds. It must therefore be declared admissible.

Example (1) is a 144-word routine found in 23 out of 200 RiFT texts, the first of which dates back to 1997 and the last to 2017, covering the period of 20 years, over which this routine has been consolidated in the European human rights discourse. Originating from a Turkish case, it has been applied to cases from Italy, France, Finland, Switzerland, Hungary and Liechtenstein. Example (2), featuring "only" 44 words, is reproduced verbatim in 8 out of 200 judgments, the earliest issued in 2008 against Hungary and the latest in

2023 against Turkey. If minor variations are taken into account, the overall number of cases using (2) rises to 11 out of 200 including cases against Hungary, Russia, Bosnia and Herzegovina, Portugal, Ukraine, Belgium, Romania, Turkey and Italy.

There are some routines that are substantive in that they apply to legal principles elaborated on a particular topic. For instance, example (3) shows a routine formulated in the famous case *Salduz v. Turkey*[4] in 2008 and currently appearing in six cases in RiFT (against Turkey, Russia, Croatia, Bulgaria, Belgium and the United Kingdom).

(3) (the Court) finds that in order for the right to a fair trial to remain sufficiently 'practical and effective'. . . Article 6 § 1 requires that, as a rule, access to a lawyer should be provided as from the first interrogation of a suspect by the police, unless it is demonstrated in the light of the particular circumstances of each case that there are compelling reasons to restrict this right.

On account of the institutional context and drafting and deliberation peculiarities outlined in 7.2, the ECtHR judgments – at least as represented by RiFT – include an impressive inventory of formulaic patterns. Once an agreement on a given routine or expression is reached, it is reasonable to expect this routine or expression to permeate the ECtHR case-law across space and time. As "prefabricated" patterns reduce processing effort and optimize the drafting process, they are very recurrent in institutional contexts.

7.3.4 Length

The length and a near-religious attitude to detail in the ECtHR judgments may "render the style somewhat cumbersome or long-winded, but arguably for good reason" (Brannan 2021: 226). The average length of judgments in RiFT is 133,044 words, with *Mikulski v. Poland*[5] being the shortest (1,202 words) and *Burmych and Others v. Ukraine*[6] being the longest (138,569 words). Curiously, both have been struck out of the list,[7] although for varying reasons: friendly settlement in the former and not justified continued examination for the latter. Villiger (2017: para. 23) explains how initially "ECtHR judgments tended to be highly detailed and lengthy. By the 1990s, as the workload increased and repetitive cases abounded, the judgments became shorter". Looking at RiFT in time, an upwards time-length tendency can be observed (Figure 7.2), which contrasts with Villiger's perception.

4 Application no. 36391/02, GC Judgment of 27 November 2008.

5 2000, Application no. 27914/95. Conclusion: struck out of the list (friendly settlement).

6 2017, Application nos. 46852/13;47786/13;54125/13;56605/13;3653/14. Conclusion: Struck out of the list (Art. 37) Striking out applications-{general}; (Art. 37–1) Striking out applications; (Art. 37–1-c) Continued examination not justified.

7 See Lambert-Abdelgawad 2018 on the ECtHR practice of striking out applications.

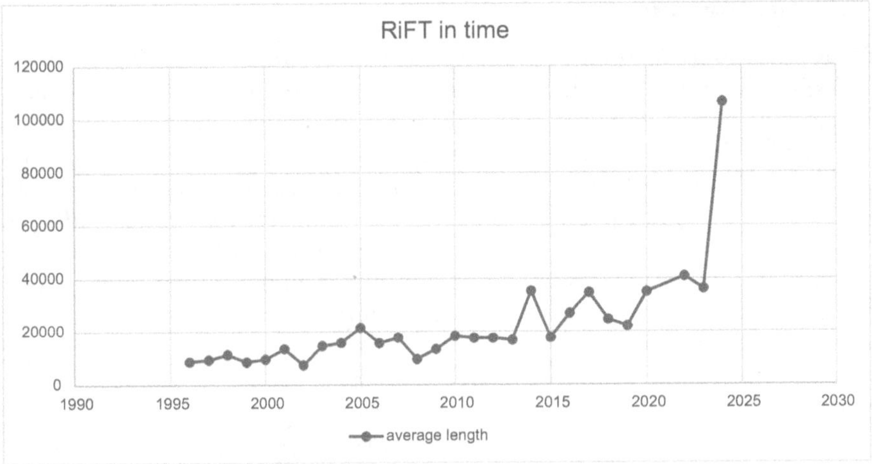

Figure 7.2 Average length of judgments in RiFT over time

The length factor in the RiFT corpus of judgments increases with time, instead of decreasing. Naturally, RiFT is a thematic corpus covering the period between February 1996 and April 2024 and is not indicative of all ECtHR judgments, which may present divergent tendencies. Even if the 2024 outlier is not considered (there is just one "long-winded" 2024 judgment in RiFT), Figure 7.2 shows how the average length of judgments[8] gradually increased after 2014. A possible explanation may derive from the turnover of judges facilitated by the Court's age limit, grafted onto judges with Protocol no. 11, which resulted in a changed discourse community in the 2010s.

In his comparison of English and Irish judgments with judgments of the European Court of Justice, Mazzi (2007b: 27) found the latter shorter. The ECtHR judgments are "on the whole [. . .] relatively lengthy, certainly longer than those of the ECJ" (Brannan 2021: 222). The length of supranational judgments, of which the ECtHR judgments are quite emblematic, derives from the need to incorporate portions of domestic proceedings next to multiple "hidden quotes", i.e. "the reproduction of previous findings (especially on general principles) without quotation marks but followed by numerous references" (Brannan 2021: 224). It seems logical that the more the Court relies on the principle of subsidiarity and the more case-law it accrues, the longer its judgments become. Hence, another possible explanation for the lengthening of judgments in RiFT could be the Court's entering its "age of subsidiarity" (Spano 2018: 487) trailblazed by Protocol no. 15, which involves embedding major portions of national legislation and case-law.

8 Calculated as a simple mean value: the length of all judgments in RiFT delivered in a given year divided by the number of judgments.

7.3.5 Linguistic regime

Before the Court merged with the European Commission of Human Rights in 1998, all ECtHR judgments were published in both official languages. Today, Chamber judgments are published in only one language. In contrast to Chamber judgments that stride along the path of alternative bilingualism (Rule 76 (1), Rules of Court), Grand Chamber judgments are fully bilingual, with both languages equally authentic. Since both Grand Chamber judgment versions are legally authentic, insisting on the existence of a source text and a translation is de jure incorrect. Once both (or even more than two) versions of a legal text are declared authentic, the source text in its Translation Studies understanding disappears. In this sense, the phenomenon of a vanishing original is common to both the ECJ and the ECtHR. In Grand Chamber cases translation occurs before the delivery of the judgment, in other cases (e.g. "key cases") translation may follow delivery for the purposes of publication (Brannan 2018: 171). In Chamber proceedings, the relevant documents are generally translated into one of the official languages, where necessary, and before the Grand Chamber they are made available in both official languages.

Insider perspectives, however, shed additional light on this bilingually idyllic landscape. In reality, the drafting language – English or French – "will depend on the appointment of the Judge Rapporteur ('Rapporteur') and their preference" (Villiger 2017: para. 9). Brannan (2021: 220) states that statistically speaking, "most Strasbourg judgments are now drafted in English", by virtue of the Court's composition, where most judges' preferred working language is English.

Bilingual and equally authentic judgments at the Grand Chamber level impose a significant burden on translators due to their profound legal implications. Despite the rarity of cases challenging language discrepancies in Grand Chamber judgments – an indirect testament to the high quality of translations – the notion of equal legal authenticity in multilingual texts has been deemed "utopic" (see 1.2). A single authentic text is a more common and straightforward solution in international courts (e.g. ICJ or IACtHR), as it minimizes risks to legal certainty that multilingualism might introduce. Brannan (2018: 173) cites the case *Salduz v. Turkey*,[9] which upon being analysed by the Supreme Court of the United Kingdom was criticized for discrepancies between the French and the English version:

> The language [of the English text] might seem to suggest that in Salduz the Grand Chamber was innovating and laying down a rule under which restrictions [on legal assistance] for good cause would now be treated differently. [. . .] The language of the French text of para 52 is different and gives no support for any such inference.
>
> (Lord Rodger in *Cadder v. Her Majesty's Advocate* (Scotland) [2010] UKSC 43)

9 Application no. 36391/02, Grand Chamber judgment of 27 November 2008.

Eventually, the UK Supreme Court explored the bilingual loophole and leaned on the French version in its conclusions as closer to its own line of thinking "without considering that the French might have been the translation and that the English was possibly more accurate" (Brannan 2018: 173).

Similarly to ICJ, where both versions are authentic and shall be "taken for original texts", the version which is a translation in practice should "not stray too far afield from a style which is perhaps uniquely characteristic of the other language" (Bedjaoui 1991: 50). A degree of linguistic compromise, inevitable to reach an intra- and interlinguistic consensus, may result in "convoluted language, nuancing, complementing or truncating previous wording", which poses additional challenges for translators (Brannan 2021: 224).

The bilingualism of the ECtHR discourse has inevitable influence on the language of judgments. The "French capture" (Cohen 2016: 513) has blessed or plagued many international courts, such as the ICJ, the ECJ and the ECtHR, even though their judgments "tend to be longer and more explanatory than the typical terse French opinion" (Cohen 2016: 513). Brannan (2021: 226) adds that Gallicisms are more visible in ECJ judgments, which are drafted in French. Yet, some French fleur may be traced in the ECtHR, too. Besides the jurisprudential creation *margin of appreciation*, already discussed in 2.4, an adverbial string "with full jurisdiction" may be cited as an example. RiFT features nine occurrences of this string used in three cases (against Switzerland, Belgium and Portugal).

(4) The applicant submitted that his right to a fair trial had been infringed in view of the fact that his conviction by the Assize Court had been based on a guilty verdict which did not contain reasons and could not be appealed against to a body *with full jurisdiction*. (*Taxquet v. Belgium*[10])

(4a) Le requérant soutient que son droit à un procès équitable a été méconnu, en raison du fait que l'arrêt de condamnation de la cour d'assises était fondé sur un verdict de culpabilité non motivé, qui ne pouvait faire l'objet d'un recours devant un organe *de pleine juridiction*.

Example (4a) is the French version of (4), which reads quite naturally, whereas in (4) a "body with full jurisdiction" is a Gallicism, introduced to reduce potential discrepancies between the language versions. Once the translation constitutes a linguistic precedent, it may give rise to a repeated use in other judgments and even perpetuate errors. In fact, legal and institutional translators approach their tasks not only as a question of terminology, but also of phraseological conventions. Brannan (2018: 179) quotes an example of *due diligence* incorrectly introduced in several English judgments as a functional equivalent of the French *la diligence requise* "referring more to the notion of promptness or expedition in English", see (5), which in this case is a false friend. This translation created a Gallicism, which "probably should have been

10 Application no. 926/05, Grand Chamber Judgment of 16 November 2010.

corrected over the years". In RiFT, it is used in this Gallic sense 11 times over the period ranging from 1999 to 2024 in cases against France, Poland, Russia, Turkey and Switzerland. As 7.3.3 illustrates, once a routine – or an adverbial string such as *with due diligence* – migrates from French into English, it starts spreading across the Court's case-law as a "linguistic precedent".

(5) As regards the judicial authorities' conduct, the Commission also considered that the case had been handled differently according to the period under consideration. On the one hand, it had been conducted *with due diligence* until 22 June 1994, the date on which an investigating judge at the Versailles tribunal de grande instance was appointed. (*Selmouni v. France*[11])

Research has already identified a correlation between the translated nature of law and its increased formulaicity (Biel et al. 2019), showing how translations develop their own formulaic profiles, a finding which seems to be true also for the ECtHR context. Arguably the reciprocal osmosis between the two official languages of the Court contributes to some linguistic hybridization of the European human rights discourse, increasing its idiosyncratic quality (Villiger 2017: para. 22). Besides the official languages, the linguistic regime of judgments is exposed to covert translation from other languages of the Council of Europe, which frequently results in the embedding of system-bound fragments in languages different from English and French, already discussed in Chapter 5.

7.4 The structure

Despite the common idea of providing a resolution to a dispute, the structure of judgments varies across different courts and jurisdictions. Peruzzo (2019b: 60–63) draws on Caliendo (2004: 297–298) and White (2009: 3–4), and outlines six macro-sections in the structure of the ECtHR Grand Chamber judgments: the opening section, the procedure section, the facts section, the law section, the operative part of the judgment and the closing section. The judgment is subdivided into sections and subsections to reflect the typical visual organization that "delivers the sentence in packages, so to speak, making it easier for the mind to grasp the whole. It does visually what the reader would do mentally without it" (Driedger 1982: 78).

As Rietiker (2013: 44) pointed out, the ECtHR judgments follow a hybrid style, combining civil law formalism with common law length and detail. This detail can be perceived in the organization of the judgments' structure. Bhatia's (1993) milestone book on professional genres conceptualized judgments as faithful records of the factual matrix of a case, the judge's decisions as well as arguments underlying it, since judgments "are generally

11 Application no. 25803/94, Grand Chamber Judgment of 28 July 1999.

Table 7.2 Structural elements in national and international judgments from Mazzi (2007b: 26–27)

Irish and English judgments	*ECJ judgments*
1. Identifying the case	1. Identifying the case
a. Establishing facts of the case	2. Identifying the scope of proceedings before the Court
b. Arguing the case	3. Retrieving relevant Community and/ or national legislation
2. Stating the history of the case	4. Stating history of the case
3. Identifying the conflict of categorization	5. Arguing the case
4. Presenting arguments	a. Arguments of the parties
5. Deriving ratio decidendi	b. Arguments of the Court
6. Pronouncing judgment	6. Settling costs
	7. Pronouncing judgment

used as evidence in favour of or against a particular line of argument or decision" (Bhatia 1993: 119). To create a comparative baseline, studies examining judgments in other contexts should be quoted. Analysing two different contexts, Mazzi (2007b: 26–27), drawing on Bhatia's pivotal work (1993),[12] identified the following generic structure of judgments (see Table 7.2). Based on the above taxonomies, supplemented by Villiger's (2017) overview of the "contents" of judgments, the structure of judgments in RiFT is outlined in Table 7.3.

Former ECtHR judge Villiger (2017: para. 21) describes this structural approach as "syllogistic", as it starts with a tacit premise of domestic proceedings. At the same time, a predetermined template makes the judgment "easy to navigate" (White 2009: 15, 17).

7.4.1 *The opening section*

The opening section, also known as the introductory unit, aims at identifying the case and contains "the title of the judgment, the case application number and date of delivery, followed by the list of judges composing the Chamber" (Caliendo 2004: 298). The case identification typically includes the application number and the applicant's surname, sometimes preceded by name in earlier judgments and judgments from high case-count countries. "All judgments are drafted in a manner that allows the identification of the names and

12 Bhatia (1993) identified the following structure:
- a) Identifying the case
- b) Establishing facts of the case
- c) Arguing the case
  - i. Stating the history of the case
  - ii. Presenting arguments
  - iii. Deriving ratio decidendi
- d) Pronouncing judgment

Table 7.3 The judgment structure in the RiFT 96–24 Corpus

Function/structural part	*Moves*
The formulaic bracketing	1) Opening section
Stating the history and background of the case	2) The Procedure 3) The Facts a) The circumstances of the case b) Describing relevant domestic law and practice c) Outlining other provisions: comparative national and international law (*optional, can contain more than one subsection*)
Justification	4) The Law a) Acknowledging the Government's preliminary objections (*optional*) b) Establishing the admissibility of the application (*optional, if contested*) c) Identifying the conflict of categorization i. The parties' submissions (application, applicant's submissions, Government's submissions) ii. Submissions of third-party interveners (*optional*) iii. The Chamber judgment (*if applicable*) d) The court's assessment (deriving ration decidendi) e) Establishing the application of article(s) 41 and 46 of the ECHR (just satisfaction claims, i.e. settling costs) (*optional*)
The operative clause	5) Pronouncing the judgment
The formulaic bracketing	6) Closing section

the position taken by all participating judges", but the judge rapporteur's identity is never disclosed in contrast to some constitutional and supreme courts (Garlicki 2009: 396).

Earlier judgments (before Protocol no. 14) feature the "old" Council of Europe logo and may present bilingual titles of cases, but most RiFT judgments use the current logo of the Court and single-language titling only. The opening section is a typified template, with some variable data (underlined in Table 7.4).

7.4.2 *Stating the history and background of the case*

In contrast to judgments in other contexts (Irish, ECJ; see Mazzi 2007b), the next structural element in the ECtHR Grand Chamber judgments is dedicated

Table 7.4 The opening section in RiFT

Structural element	*Communicative goal*	*Examples*
Opening section	Identify the case, including the context, the active participation framework and the time.	/Logo/ GRAND CHAMBER **CASE OF X v. MEMBER STATE** ***(Application no. XXX/XX)*** JUDGMENT STRASBOURG Date *This judgment is final.* OR *This judgment is subject to editorial revision [before its reproduction in final form in XXX]* **In the case of surname/initials v. Member State,** The European Court of Human Rights, sitting [IN EARLIER JUDGMENTS: *in accordance with Article 27 of the Convention for the Protection of Human Rights and Fundamental Freedoms ("the Convention"), as amended by Protocol No. 11, and the relevant provisions of the Rules of Court,*] as a Grand Chamber composed of: (title,) name and surname, *President,* (titles,) names and surnames, *judges,* and (title,) name and surname, *XXX Registrar,* Having deliberated in private on date(s), Delivers the following judgment, which was adopted on (the last-mentioned) date:

to issues of procedure and not facts, and it is the section where the judgment paragraph numbering begins. Comparable to "Identifying the scope of proceedings before the Court" in the ECJ judgments, it describes "the proceedings that have taken place up to the adoption of the judgment: lodging of the application (and a brief summary of the applicant's complaints); allocation of the case to a Chamber/the Grand Chamber; exchange of pleadings ('memorials'); hearing, if any" (Weston 2005: 452).

The procedure section is followed by the Facts section, subdivided into a description of the circumstances of the case – most typically copied verbatim from the case communication if it does not follow the IMSI format (Nikitina 2022b), – description of relevant domestic law and practice and of other provisions in comparative national and international law. Typically, there is a summary and citations of relevant domestic law, along with extracts from relevant national case-law, such as judgments of the Supreme or Constitutional Court. As Peruzzo (2019b: 66) expands, "the relevant source may be invoked and its content summarised [. . .], or extracts of the invoked source are quoted in inverted commas". The law and practice of other States "may be important in order to establish 'an emerging European consensus' in respect of a new right, for example the legal recognition of same-sex couples (*Schalk and Kopf v Austria*, 2010: paras 27–34 and 105)" (Villiger 2017: para. 27).

Both facts and procedure create the "anamnesis" of the case, its historical background (see Table 7.5). "The content of these sections is drawn from the materials gathered and research carried out by the Registry" (Keller & Heri 2018: para. 64), hence their authorship is mixed.

7.4.3 Justification

The next structural section is "divided into a variable number of subsections according to the peculiarities of the case at hand" (Peruzzo 2019b: 66). It provides the "reasons in point of law [. . .] preceded by a summary of the ECtHR's case law on the particular issue" (Villiger 2017: para. 18). Bedjaoui (1991: 40) ironically baptized this part as a transformation of a "gargantuan repast into digestible pap". This is probably the most heteroglossic part of the judgment, as it has to report on frequently conflicting views of the parties and third-party interveners,[13] along with any previous judgments.

In his work on Irish and English judgments, Mazzi (2007b: 26) reflects on one of their structural moves: *Identifying the conflict of categorization*, a move through which

> the judge explicitly acknowledges that his categorisation of the facts of the case, i.e. his interpretation of them under the appropriate pre-determined legal category (e.g. murder v. manslaughter), clashes with an alternative categorisation proposed by other subjects such as the representatives of a party in the dispute, another judge of the same bench or another court of the jurisdiction.
>
> (Mazzi 2007b: 26)

This happens also in the ECtHR judgments. These voices must be diligently reported, because "if the Court gives too clear an indication of what it considers relevant, it may create the impression that it is inclined towards the party most sharing its view of that relevance and lay difficulties in store in the event that the deliberation evolves so as to cast doubts on the Court's first appraisal of the case" (Bedjaoui 1991: 44). Garlicki (2009: 395) portrays the main idea behind this section as "show[ing] what legal norms (precedents) are governing the outcome of the case and how those norms (precedents) find application to the facts of the case".

13 See Keller and Heri (2018: para. 37) for a description.

Table 7.5 Generic makeup of the historical section of the judgment

PROCEDURE 1. The case originated in an application (no. XXX) against Member State lodged with the Court/the European Commission of Human Rights ("the Commission") under Article no. of the Convention for the Protection of Human Rights and Fundamental Freedoms ("the Convention") by no. national(s), Mr/Ms surname ("the applicant(s)"), on date. 2. The applicants (applied to the Court through Mr/Ms surname and) are represented by Mr/Ms XXX, a barrister practising in XXX/of the XXX Bar. The XXX Government ("the respondent Government/the Government") were represented by their Agent, Mr/Ms XXX, and by their co-Agent, Mr/Ms XXX/assisted by Mr/Ms XXX, Deputy Co-Agent. 3. The applicant(s) alleged a violation of Article XXX of the Convention/ alleged that there had been a breach of Article XXX of the Convention on account of XXX/complained in particular of a violation of Article XXX of the Convention, as a result of XXX. 4. The application was allocated to the XXX Section of the Court (Rule 52 § 1 of the Rules of Court). [. . .] X. On date the (XXX) Government (and the applicant) requested, in accordance with Article XXX of the Convention and Rule XXX, that the case be referred to the Grand Chamber. On date a panel of the Grand Chamber accepted that request. X. The composition of the Grand Chamber was determined according to the provisions of Article 27 §§ 2 and 3 of the Convention and Rule 24. X. A hearing took place in public in the Human Rights Building, Strasbourg, on date (Rule 59 § 3). There appeared before the Court: (a) *for the (respondent) Government* Mr/Ms XXX, *deputy co-Agent/Co-Agent;* Mr/Ms XXX, *Adviser;* (b) *for the applicant(s)* Mr/Ms XXX, of the XXX Bar/Lawyer, *Counsel;* Mr/Ms XXX, *Adviser;* (c) *for the third-party intervener* Mr/Ms XXX, *Third-party intervener,* Mr/Ms XXX, of the XXX Bar/Lawyer, *Counsel.* (d) *for the Government of XXX* Mr/Ms XXX, *Agent,* Mr/Ms XXX, *Adviser(s).*) The Court heard addresses by XXX. [. . .]	**Procedure section**
THE FACTS I. THE CIRCUMSTANCES OF THE CASE In case of one applicant: X. The applicant was born in year and lives in place (country). In case of more than one applicant: X. The no. applicants are citizens of country. [For every applicant the year of birth and the place and country of abode are specified afterwards.] [. . .] II. RELEVANT DOMESTIC LAW AND PRACTICE [can be further subdivided into subsections] X. OTHER RELEVANT PROVISIONS	**Facts section**

Source: Peruzzo (2019b: 61–62).

Occasionally, if the case was not relinquished, this section will report on the findings of the Chamber judgment. "The Court is of the opinion that consistence of its jurisprudence constitutes one of the legitimizing factors for its – sometimes quite extensive – interpretation of the Convention", and it "always attempts to place its new judgments within the context of the already existing case law" (Garlicki 2009: 395). Yet, "the ECtHR knows no *stare decisis*" (Villiger 2017: para. 25), and is not bound by its own decisions either at an earlier procedural stage or in other cases.

From a genre perspective, "it is impossible to identify a fixed structure for it that would suit any and all ECtHR judgments" (Peruzzo 2019b: 66), as this section reflects the core operation of legal reasoning. Some recurrent patterns can be identified also in this part, dedicated to issues of legal reasoning and justification.

From a pragma-dialectical perspective, "the justification is part of a critical discussion between the judge and possible antagonists: the party who may want to appeal the decision and the judge in a procedure in appeal. In the justification, the judge anticipates the critical reactions which may be put forward by these antagonists" (Feteris 2017: 219). While ECtHR decisions are not appealable, the possible antagonists to the decision may be the dissenting judges and the parties, as at least one of the parties will find itself in a "losing" position.

This part is frequently subject to the pigeonhole procedure, as it should represent "the highest common denominator of the Judges' views" (Bedjaoui 1991: 58). The need to find a compromise led to what has been criticized as an "increasingly formulaic style of judicial reasoning in the judgments of the Court" (White & Boussiakou 2009: 60), the textual realization of which is addressed in 7.5, following considerations already presented in 7.3.3 and 7.3.5.

Table 7.6 reports the moves identified in Grand Chamber judgments by Peruzzo (2019b: 62). In RiFT, by virtue of its thematic organization, the upper part of the Law section is typically dedicated to alleged violations of Article 6. The lower part of this section may contain provisions on just satisfaction, i.e. a monetary compensation to be made under Article 41 ECHR, if the applicant made a respective claim.

7.4.4 *The operative part*

As Villiger (2017: para. 18) explains, the operative part of the judgment formulates the points in law mentioned as ratione decidendi as legal conclusions. Curiously, this is the only part of the judgment that enters into legal force. This part of the judgment is also known as the "dispositif" (White 2009: 4), as it carries the performative value of the text.

From a genre perspective, Peruzzo (2019b: 67) defines this section as highly formulaic (see Table 7.7), as it

> opens with the standardised formula "For these reasons, the Court", which may or may not be followed by the adverb "unanimously" in accordance with the decisions taken by the judges in the panel. The

Table 7.6 The Law section from Peruzzo (2019b: 62)

THE LAW (I. THE GOVERNMENT'S PRELIMINARY OBJECTION) [can be further subdivided into subsections] (I. ADMISSIBILITY OF THE APPLICATION) II. ALLEGED VIOLATION OF ARTICLE **no.** OF THE CONVENTION (TAKEN IN CONJUNCTION WITH ARTICLE **no.**) (. . .) The parties' submissions The Court's assessment (XX. ARTICLES 46 AND 41 OF THE CONVENTION/ APPLICATION OF ARTICLES 46 AND 41 OF THE CONVENTION/APPLICATION OF ARTICLE 41 OF THE CONVENTION) A. Article 46 of the Convention B. Article 41 of the Convention	**Law section**

range of verbs that follow this formula is rather limited, with the three most common verbs in the judgments analysed here being "dismisses", "holds", and "joins to the merits", followed by "declares", "decides", and "refuses".

The verbs mentioned in the quote are the so-called verbs with a performative value, already discussed in 6.3.2. They are used in the transposed third person (Austin 1962: 57), as is customary with communication by collegiate bodies and which still satisfies the conditions for the verb to have explicit performative value, i.e. "to do things with words".

The operative part is the part that bestows a legally binding effect to the judgment. From a legal standpoint, the ECtHR judgments are *declaratory* in that they do not repel or revoke national judgments and they invite the Respondent State to undertake general or individual measures.[14] The Inter-American Court of Human Rights (IACtHR) has a wider reach than the ECtHR in this respect as it "may order that the injured party be guaranteed the enjoyment of the particular right that was violated, and may rule that the consequences of the ACHR violation be remedied" (Art. 63(1) ACHR) (Villiger 2017: para. 53).

7.4.5 The closing section

The closing section, similarly to the opening section, forms the formulaic bracketing of judgments, and thus is organized around one of the two most widespread templates (see Table 7.8). If the judgment was delivered at a public hearing, the date and location (e.g., Human Rights Building, Strasbourg)

14 The two types of measures available to remedy a human rights violation.

Table 7.7 The operative part of the judgment (Peruzzo 2019b: 62)

FOR THESE REASONS, THE COURT (UNANIMOUSLY) X. Joins to the merits, unanimously, the respondent Government's preliminary objection with respect to the applicability of Article 6 of the Convention; X. Declares, unanimously, the remainder of the application admissible; X. Holds, unanimously, that Article 6 of the Convention is applicable in the instant case and, consequently, dismisses the respondent Government's preliminary objection; X. Holds, by ten votes to seven, that there has been no violation of Article 6 of the Convention. X. Dismisses the remainder of the applicant's claim for just satisfaction. X. Dismisses the Government's preliminary objection; X. Dismisses the Government's preliminary objection;	**Operative part of the judgment**

Table 7.8 The Closing section

In case the judgment is delivered at a public hearing: Done in English and in French, and delivered at a public hearing in the Human Rights Building, Strasbourg, on date. name surname name surname (Deputy) Registrar President In case the judgment is notified in writing: Done in English and in French, and notified in writing on date, pursuant to Rule 77 §§ 2 and 3 of the Rules of Court. name surname name surname Deputy) Registrar President In case the judgment contains separate, concurring or dissenting opinions: In accordance with Article 45 § 2 of the Convention and Rule 74 § 2 of the Rules of Court, the concurring opinion(s) of Judge(s) XXX is/are annexed to this judgment. initials In accordance with Article 45 § 2 of the Convention and Rule 74 § 2 of the Rules of Court, the following separate opinions are annexed to this judgment: (letter) concurring opinion of Judge XXX (joined by Judge(s) XXX); (letter(s)) (letter) dissenting opinion of Judge XXX (joined by Judge(s) XXX). initials	**Closing section**

Source: Peruzzo (2019b: 63).

are specified. If notified in writing, the date and relevant Rule of Court (e.g., Rule 77.2; 77.3) are indicated. Both versions mention the judgment's language, which includes both English and French for Grand Chamber judgments. If the deliberation was not unanimous, an additional sentence specifies that separate (concurring or dissenting) opinions are annexed, referencing Art. 45.2 of the Convention, and Rule 74.2 of the Rules of Court (see Chapter 8). When there are separate opinions, this sentence is followed by the initials of the President and the Registrar.

7.5 When argumentation meets evaluation: *it is ADJ to-inf/ that* patterns

The Grand Chamber judgment is a product of negotiations, compromise and argumentation. Referring to the composite nature of judgments, Bletsas ascribes argumentation present therein to "a quaestio at least in principle capable of arising a difference of opinion, a text laying out (at least) a quaestio, a decisional standpoint and its motivations, [which] is likely to host various voices" (Bletsas 2015: 80). In addition, as Grand Chamber judgments incorporate multiple legal standpoints and voices (see 7.4.2 and 7.4.3), it is important to remember that "[r]easonable interpretations of valid legal sources predictably go hand in hand with argumentation" (Mazzi 2021: 117). Similarly, Goźdź-Roszkowski (2024: 10) notices how judgments contain expressions of "agreement or disagreement with decisions given by lower courts, opinions expressed by counsel representing the parties and opinions arrived at by fellow judges from the same bench", which inherently translates into a substantial amount of argumentation and evaluation, overt or covert, in judgments. Kloosterhuis (2013), for instance, ponders the covert nature of legal reasoning in the justification of a judicial decision. "Judges may feel compelled to incorporate rhetorical means into their reasoning to explain and justify their decision rather than merely interpreting legal norms in an abstract way. The justification must be crafted so as to make it generally acceptable" (Goźdź-Roszkowski 2024: 12). As the judges "outline the reasons underlying their verdict, judges advance argumentation" (Mazzi 2021: 112).

Argumentation – from the pragma-dialectical vantage point – may take various shapes at a local textual level (Chapter 6). The "stilted" style mentioned in 7.3.3, fruit of compromises at deliberation and drafting stages, coupled with considerations of bilingualism and equal authenticity of both language versions, has led to an increased reliance on a particular marker of legal argumentation and evaluation: the introductory *it*-patterns. Formulated as *it v-link ADJ that* and *it v-link ADJ to-inf*, they could be "selected to obfuscate subjectivity" (Goźdź-Roszkowski 2024: 59), because they introduce elements of evaluation without explicitly mentioning the evaluator. Saying "the Court knows that" focuses the attention on the Court, whereas "it is obvious that" precedes an evaluative legal reasoning sequence in the text of judgments, without specifying the agent.

7.5.1 General overview

A very widespread pattern in RiFT, the bigram "it is" occurs 3,007 times and has skyrocketing log-likelihood[15] value of 15,633; similarly, the bigram "it was" has an absolute frequency of 2,580 and log-likelihood at 10,973,

15 Log-likelihood measures the strength of association in a collocation. Please refer to Chapter 4 for a more detailed explanation of log-likelihood.

Table 7.9 Top 20 collocates of the introductory *it is* pattern in RiFT

Collocates of it is	*Absolute frequency of collocations*	*Log-likelihood*
necessary	294	2396.9
clear	122	1054.4
true	100	937.05
possible	92	654.4
important	65	492.3
impossible	37	299.1
apparent	31	289.6
unnecessary	31	275.0
difficult	33	266.3
sufficient	44	231.1
noteworthy	18	218.5
essential	27	189.4
obvious	20	187.9
incumbent	19	184.7
open (to question, to argue . . .)	27	182.1
appropriate	34	170.4
understandable	14	147.8
(not) disputed	20	128.7
(not) inadmissible	22	126.6
applicable	28	123.2

followed by "it appears" (AF = 134; LL = 900.1). Table 7.9 lists the top 20 collocates of "it is" (5R), arranged by the strength of their association (log-likelihood).

Goźdź-Roszkowski (2024: 37) places the introductory *it*-patterns "among the most common options available for writers intending to express evaluation across different genres and disciplines (Groom 2005)". This pattern collocates with evaluative adjectives (Table 7.9). In addition to performing legal argumentation functions, *it is* patterns function also as stance bundles, as they express emotions, attitudes, value judgments and assessments (Biber et al. 1999).

Stance bundles can be subdivided into *epistemic* and *attitudinal* bundles. Epistemic stance bundles "signal writer comments on the knowledge status of the information contained in the following proposition. Such status can be expressed as certain, uncertain, probable, possible, etc." (Goźdź-Roszkowski 2011: 138). Examples in Table 7.9 would include patterns *it is + true, clear, possible, impossible, apparent, obvious,* to which similar bundles can be added, not reported here. Attitudinal bundles, on the other hand, "express speaker/writer's attitudes towards the actions or events described in the following proposition" (Goźdź-Roszkowski 2011: 140). Examples in Table 7.9 include *it is + applicable, inadmissible, appropriate, understandable, difficult, sufficient, noteworthy, essential, necessary,* as well as others, not reported in the table, but present in RiFT, such as *it is+ natural, legitimate,* etc.

(6) The Court further notes that the threats of deliberate and imminent ill-treatment were made in the context of the applicant being in the custody of law-enforcement officials, apparently handcuffed, and thus in a state of vulnerability. *It is clear that* D. and E. acted in the performance of their duties as State agents and that they intended, if necessary, to carry out that threat under medical supervision and by a specially trained officer. (*Gäfgen v. Germany*[16])

(7) Lastly, while *it is true that* the conduct of the defence is essentially a matter between the defendant and his counsel, whether counsel be appointed under a legal aid scheme or be privately financed [. . .], the ultimate guardians of the fairness of the proceedings – encompassing, among other aspects, the possible absence of translation or interpretation for a non-national defendant – are the domestic courts. (*Hermi v. Italy*[17])

Examples (6) and (7) illustrate how *it is* + *ADJ* + *that* patterns introduce the Court's assessment of the proposition's validity. After contextualizing the factual claim in (6) using the (re)contextualizing function of reported argumentation (Chaemsaithong 2018, see 6.6) introduced by "the Court further notes", which serves as an argumentative premise, the Court advances the conclusion flagged by "it is clear that". In (7) the epistemic assessment sequence *it is true that* is inserted in a concessive clause, which rebuts the validity of the claim by recontextualizing it. While Goźdź-Roszkowski (2011: 140) groups sequences *it is clear that* and *it is true that* with attitudinal stance bundles, I recognize their additional epistemic value, as the Court uses them to comment on the factual components of claims. Indeed, the difference between epistemic and attitudinal stance bundles is subtle and has blurred borders, especially, if they follow the same structural pattern.

Overlaying pattern grammar with reconstruction of legal arguments, Goźdź-Roszkowski (2024: 39) notes how "other adjectives with a meaning associated with the notion of 'validity' will also be found in the *it v-link ADJ that* pattern, and adjectives with a meaning related to the notion of 'appropriacy' will follow the pattern *it v-link ADJ to-inf*". This pattern is indeed confirmed in RiFT.

(8) In the light of the Government's observations and the special circumstances of the case, the Court considers that in the instant case *it is necessary to* take this rule into account when examining the various periods for which the applicant was detained. (*Assanidze v. Georgia*[18])

(9) Furthermore, the ideas, rhetoric, acts and gestures of Jean-Marie Le Pen are accurately described in the novel – as the defendants have claimed, producing cogent evidence to that effect – in relation to the reality of

16 Application no. 22978/05, GC Judgment of 1 June 2010.
17 Application no. 18114/02; GC Judgment of 18 October 2006.
18 Application no. 71503/01, GC Judgment of 8 April 2004.

the various public manifestations of his political activity. Accordingly, *it is appropriate to* examine whether the use of the defamatory comments chosen by the author was preceded by an investigation sufficiently serious to justify the comments in question. (*Lindon, Otchakovsky-Laurens and July v. France*[19])

The pattern *it v-link ADJ to-inf* in (8) and (9) not only evaluates a proposition but also suggests a course of action to be followed with a varied degree of necessity/appropriacy. This pattern indicates an argumentative step where the court pre-empts any possible future counterarguments or, perhaps, replies to some counterarguments advanced during the deliberation stage.

The patterns *it v-link ADJ to-inf/it v-link ADJ that* may coexist or be used with the same adjective, see (10) and (11).

(10) The number of hours appears excessive having regard to the submissions provided and, in so far as *it is possible to* assess the actual work carried out in light of the general breakdown provided, *it seems that* there was some duplication. The Court therefore considers it reasonable to award the sum of 16,000 euros ("EUR") (*Ibrahim and Others v. the United Kingdom*[20])

(11) However, where the domestic remedy has not met all the foregoing requirements, *it is possible that* the threshold in respect of which the amount will still allow a litigant to claim to be a "victim" will be higher. (*Ernestina Zullo v. Italy*[21])

For instance, in (10) the pattern *it is possible to* refers to the feasibility of an action, the assessment of legal assistance in this case. The Grand Chamber panel explains that the documents provided by the party enabled it to assess the actual legal fees, leading it to a conclusion about "some duplication", which was hedged by "it seems that". In (11) – constituting a recurrent routine for Italian cases, where it guided the penmanship of lawyers in nine different cases – *it is possible that* denotes the likelihood or validity of a proposition, in this case a possibility that a threshold for a definition of a victim's status can be higher. This shows the importance of patterning (Pontrandolfo 2023), as aptly remarked by Goźdź-Roszkowski (2024: 39), that the "phraseological whole is semantically much more than the sum of its parts". Pattern grammar (Hunston & Francis 2000) studies the correlation between a given phraseological unit and its sense, "particularly in terms of the prepositions, groups, and clauses that follow the word" (Hunston & Francis 2000: 3). Based on RiFT examples, the different introductory *it* pattern, ending in *to-inf*

19 Application nos. 21279/02, 36448/02, GC Judgment of 22 October 2007.
20 Application nos. 50541/08; 50571/08; 50573/08; 40351/09. GC Judgment of 13 September 2016.
21 Application no. 64897/01, GC Judgment of 29 March 2006.

or in *that*, echoes a different function of a given stance bundle: leaning more towards the epistemic end of evaluation (*it is true that*) or to the attitudinal one (*it is necessary to*). This correlation is not exact, but rather a tendency, where "elements of meaning can be identified via the elements of pattern" (Hunston 2002: 154).

Hunston and Francis (2000: 29), overviewing Francis's (1995) earlier work, identify a limited set of meaning groups in the *it is ADJ to-inf/that* patterns: modality, ability, importance, predictability, obviousness, value and appropriacy, rationality, truth. The evaluative adjectives in these patterns tend to co-occur with a specific clause, though some adjectives, like *possible* (see (10) and (11)), can appear with both. More detailed observations include the finding that the phrase *it is surprising that* is less frequent than its negative counterpart *it is not/hardly surprising that*. Phrases like *it is hard to* are most commonly followed by mental process verbs, as in *it is hard to believe*. In a more recent study, applied specifically to judicial prose and linking elements of legal argumentation with pattern grammar, Goźdź-Roszkowski (2024) identifies four main meaning groups: difficulty, desirability, importance and validity.

In contrast to Goźdź-Roszkowski's (2024: 40) findings pinpointing the prevalence of *it v-link ADJ to-inf* pattern in his corpus of the US Supreme Court judgments, in RiFT these two patterns are used with similar frequency: the *it is ADJ to-inf* pattern totals 418 occurrences versus 416[22] of *it is ADJ that*. As the patterns are used with highly comparable frequencies, both are considered for further analysis, combining quantitative data with qualitative approach, known as Corpus-Assisted Discourse Analysis (Partington et al. 2013).

7.5.2 "It is" *patterns for argumentation: meaning groups*

It is by now a truism that successful pattern analysis is context-sensitive as it combines language inputs with the analysis of the institutional environment. Based on pattern grammar-inspired studies detailed in 7.5.1 and legal argumentation (see 6.4), I grouped different *it is* patterns by their meaning and function, looking at all instances of *it is ADJ* pattern.

The first macro-category is that of *modality* (Francis 1995), further subdivided into *necessity* and *possibility*, see Table 7.10. I group the sequences with the idea of likelihood together with those of possibility, based on their correlation. Degano and Santulli (2022: 4) note that the idea of likelihood (*eikós*) forms a continuum with necessity and truth (validity here).

The patterns performing the discoursal function of necessity in judicial discourse "signal urgency and imply inevitability" (Goźdź-Roszkowski 2024: 59), especially when these apply to the Court's assessment, as illustrated in

22 Goźdź-Roszkowski's (2024: 40) reports 112.26 occurrences of *to-inf* clause versus 79.31 occurrences of *that* clause per million words. Normalizing RiFT data to a million, *to-inf* clause is used 132.1 times as opposed to 130.4 times of *that* clause.

Table 7.10 *It is* patterns in RiFT with discoursal function of modality

Necessity	*AF*	*Possibility*	*AF*
it is necessary (*) to	115	it is possible to	28
it is (not, therefore, thus, strictly, absolutely) necessary (*) to	153	it is possible that	11
it is unnecessary (*) to	25	it is not/hardly possible to	35
it is therefore/consequently unnecessary	4	it is impossible to	32
it is essential to	12	it is not impossible that	1
it is essential that	10	it is irretrievably/virtually/ often impossible	3
it is incumbent (on the Government/State . . .) to	13	it is only/also probable that	4
		it is equally/most improbable that	2
		it is highly/very likely that	6
		it is likely to	4
		it is highly/not unlikely that	11
Total	**332**		**137**

(8) and (12). In (12) *it is essential that* is used as an argumentative premise that legitimizes the Court's conclusion (underlined). Interestingly, the Court's assessment (underlined) is framed in terms of possibility and necessity, reinforcing its position.

(12) The Court considers at the outset that *it is essential* for the proper administration of justice *that* dignity, order and decorum be observed in the courtroom as the hallmarks of judicial proceedings. The flagrant disregard by a defendant of elementary standards of proper conduct neither can nor should be tolerated (see Ananyev v. Russia, no. 20292/04, § 44, 30 July 2009). (*Idalov v. Russia*[23])

The combination of phraseologies of necessity and possibility is characteristic of legal discourse, since it provides a gradient of action (13). By arguing the (im)possibility of a given course of action, the Court can further introduce a deontic operator and acquire more argumentative power by activating the so-called deontic logic (Feteris 2017: 27). In (13), an example of reported argumentation referring to the UN Assembly, such a combination is used twice: first in the binomial *can and must*, then echoed by *it is possible (for X) to* and *it is necessary to*, with the latter inviting action. The phraseologies of possibility and necessity tend to co-occur in this order: first the possibility prepping the argumentative ground, then the necessity that introduces the Court's conclusion.

23 Application no. 5826/03, GC Judgment of 22 May 2012.

(13) In it the Assembly reaffirms that terrorism *can and must* be fought effectively with means that respect and preserve human rights and the rule of law. It considers that international bodies such as the United Nations and the European Union ought to set an example in this respect. While strongly criticising the imposition of targeted sanctions by those organisations, it observes that *it is both possible and necessary* for States *to* apply the various sanctions regimes in conformity with their obligations under the European Convention on Human Rights and the United Nations ICCPR. (*Al-Dulimi and Montana Management Inc. v. Switzerland*[24])

(14) In carrying out this assessment, *it is necessary to look beyond* the appearances and the language used and to concentrate on the realities of the situation (see Van Droogenbroeck v. Belgium, 24 June 1982, § 38, Series A no. 50, and Roche, cited above, § 121). (*Boulois v. Luxembourg*[25])

As (14) illustrates, necessity is invoked as an analytical approach, placing this pattern in an argumentative frame. Legal commentators note that the ECtHR increasingly engages in the so-called proportionality analysis in Article 6 cases "by considering if measures restricting the rights of the defence are 'strictly necessary' and there are adequate compensating measures taken to protect the accused at trial" (Jackson 2022: 103). The cases dealing with the proportionality test may also express the underlying idea of necessity through the pattern *the Court V-mental it necessary to-inf*, e.g. "the Court considers it necessary to".

The patterns with the discoursal function of modality are at times difficult to discern from the patterns grading the importance of a given action because they have a "close connection" (Goźdź-Roszkowski 2024: 66). In fact, while *it is essential to* conveys the sense of necessity and invites action, *it is essential that* (12) could be grouped with phraseologies of importance, too: the line is blurred.

The phraseologies of importance emphasize the Court's supporting arguments, often aiming "to explain a legal choice and to persuade the reader" (Goźdź-Roszkowski 2024: 59). In (15) the problematic issue is topicalized and explained (signalled by "as illustrated", "may raise an issue under"), and the Court's assessment is conveyed using the importance pattern *it is crucial to*. Likewise, in (16) after introducing its point using deontic logic ("should be secured"), the Court proceeds by detailing the point ascribing importance to the preferred interpretation of legal norms (*it is fundamental . . . that*), further reiterated by "a crucial function". Worth noting is the co-occurrence of these patterns with an explicit mention of the Court followed by either verbal or mental processes verbs ("reiterates", "emphasizes", "notes", etc.).

(15) Nevertheless, *as illustrated* in Procola (cited above), the consecutive exercise of advisory and judicial functions within one body *may*, in

24 Application no. 5809/08, GC Judgment of 21 June 2016.
25 Application no. 37575/04, GC Judgment of 3 April 2012.

certain circumstances, raise an issue under Article 6 § 1 of the Convention as regards the impartiality of the body seen from the objective viewpoint. In this context the *Court reiterates* that *it is crucial* for tribunals *to* inspire trust and confidence (see paragraph 191 above). (*Kleyn and Others v. The Netherlands*[26])

(16) The *Court emphasises* that the object and purpose underlying the Convention, as set out in Article 1, is that the rights and freedoms *should be* secured by the Contracting State within its jurisdiction. *It is fundamental* to the machinery of protection established by the Convention *that* the national systems themselves provide redress for breaches of its provisions, the Court exerting its supervisory role subject to the principle of subsidiarity. In that context, Article 13, which requires an effective remedy in respect of violations of the Convention, takes on a *crucial function*. (*Z and Others v. the United Kingdom*[27])

Phraseologies of importance run in tandem with phraseologies of validity (see Table 7.11), as both revolve around grading and ranking a given fact or a course of action as more or less important and valid, in the exercise of legal reasoning. The phraseologies of validity incorporate patterns belonging to the meaning group of truth (*it is true/undisputed/inconceivable that*, etc.) and obviousness (*it is clear/evident/obvious that*, etc.) (Francis 1995). The latter, from an argumentative standpoint, signal that the following conclusion is "irrefutable" (Degano & Santulli 2022: 37).

Example (17), although excelling in its length, is highly emblematic of how typified the local grammar of legal argumentation can be. It shows five consecutive paragraphs from the Grand Chamber judgment in the case *Grzęda v. Poland*.[28] The paragraphs are taken from the section "Relevant legal framework", detailing European law and, specifically, a CJEU judgment[29] in its justification part.

(17) 103. *It is true that*. . . the Court has previously held that the fact that a body, such as a national council of the judiciary, which is involved in the process for appointing judges is, for the most part, made up of members chosen by the legislature cannot, in itself, give rise to any doubt as to the independence of the judges appointed at the end of that process (see, to that effect, judgment of 9 July 2020, Land Hessen, C272/19, EU:C:2020:535, paragraphs 55 and 56). However, *it is also apparent* from the case-law of the Court and, more specifically, from the

26 Application nos. 39343/98, 39651/98, 43147/98, 46664/99. GC Judgment of 6 May 2003.

27 Application no. 29392/95, GC Judgment of 10 May 2001.

28 Application no. 43572/18, GC Judgment of 15 March 2022.

29 Judgment of 15 July 2021 in *Commission v. Poland* (Disciplinary regime for judges), C-791/19, EU:C:2021:596.

Table 7.11 *It is* patterns in RiFT with discoursal functions of importance, validity and difficulty

Importance	*AF*	*Validity*	*AF*
it is (also/crucially/further) important (*) to	38	it is true that	92
it is (also/most/particularly) important (*) that	16	it is also/not true	7
it is noteworthy that	22	it is clear that	93
it's (therefore) immaterial whether	6	it is not clear that	12
it is crucial that/of crucial importance that	6	it is (absolutely) unclear that	8
it is crucial to	1	it is thus/very/also/quite/ moreover/abundantly clear	12
it is fundamental/of fundamental importance that	3	it is apparent from . . . that	21
it is (also) significant that	8	it is not/therefore/perfectly/ readily apparent	10
Total	**100**	it is obvious that	18
		it is also/quite obvious that	2
Difficulty	**AF**	it is disputed that	1
It is difficult to	23	it is not disputed . . . that	17
it is extremely/very/therefore/ particularly difficult to	7	it is undisputed that	10
it is hard to	8	it is evident (from) that	8
it is easy to	2	it is further/also evident that	3
it is not easy to	2	it is certain that	11
Total	**42**	it is objectively/not certain that	2
		it is self-evident that	4
		it is inconceivable that	7
		It is undeniable that	5
		Total	**343**

judgments in A. K. and Others and A.B. and Others, *that* the situation may be different where that fact, combined with other relevant factors and the conditions under which those choices were made, leads to such doubts being raised.

104. In that regard, *it should be noted*, first, that . . .[. . .].

105. Secondly . . . *it is apparent* from Article 6 of the Law of 8 December 2017. . .*that* the thus newly constituted [NCJ] was established through the shortening of the existing four-year term of office, provided for in Article 187 § 3 of the Constitution, of the members which had, until that point, made up that body.

106. Thirdly, *it is important to point out* that the legislative reform which thus governed the process whereby the [NCJ] was established in that new composition took place at the same time as the adoption of the new Law on the Supreme Court [. . .].

> 107. *It is, accordingly, common ground that* the premature termination of the terms of office of certain then-serving members of the [NCJ] and the reorganisation of the [NCJ] in its new composition took place in a context in which it was expected that numerous posts would be soon be vacant within the Supreme Court [. . .]. (*Grzęda v. Poland*)

Although example (17) is not a direct formulation of the ECtHR, but instead reports argumentation of a different court, it shows how phraseologies of importance (*it is important to point out*) are bracketed by multiple instances of phraseologies of validity (*it is true . . . that, it is apparent that, it is . . . common ground that*), illustrating the machinery of legal argumentation. The abundant reliance on the meaning group of validity activates the so-called evidential legal reasoning (Jackson 2022), as it follows "an indication of some evidential statement which provides a logical basis for the claim" (Goźdź-Roszkowski 2024: 63). As Jackson (2022: 102) observes, "the ECtHR would seem to be increasingly considering the reliability of the evidence in determining whether in individual instances the applicant received a fair trial", which is textually realized using the above patterns.

Goźdź-Roszkowski (2024: 63) outlines that evidential legal reasoning textually realized through *it is* patterns most frequently follows the following schemes:

Evidential basis + *it is clear/undisputed* + claim.
Argumentative proposition + *it is clear/undisputed* + claim + clarification

This scheme is evident in example (17) as well as in examples (18) and (19), belonging to the autochthonous ECtHR discourse. In (18) the evidential basis is summarized by "the above" (not reproduced here for reasons of space), and the *it is clear that* introduces the claim followed by the clarification (underlined). In (19) the pattern is repeated twice, with small variation between the impersonal construction and the construction specifying the agent ("The Court deems it equally obvious").

(18) Having regard to the above, *it is clear that* the domestic authorities did not interpret the Operational-Search Activities Act as requiring prior judicial authorisation in the circumstances of the case at hand, since the case was found not to involve the applicant's "home" or the use of wire or mail services within the meaning of section 8 of the Act. The measure was considered to be an investigative step within the domain of the investigating authorities' own discretion. (*Bykov v. Russia*[30])

(19) On the one hand, *it is self-evident that* it is incompatible with the immunities under consideration to base a conviction solely or mainly on the accused's silence or on a refusal to answer questions or to give evidence

30 Application no. 4378/02, GC Judgment of 10 March 2009.

himself. On the other hand, *the Court deems it equally obvious* that these immunities *cannot and should not* prevent that the accused's silence, in situations which *clearly* call for an explanation from him, be taken into account in assessing the persuasiveness of the evidence adduced by the prosecution. (*John Murray v. the UK*[31])

(20) Furthermore, *the Court is not persuaded that* the nature of tax-surcharge proceedings is such that they fall, or should fall, outside the protection of Article 6. *Arguments to that effect have also failed* in the context of prison disciplinary and minor traffic offences (see, among others, Ezeh and Connors and Öztürk, both cited above). While *there is no doubt as to the importance* of tax to the effective functioning of the State, *the Court is not convinced* that removing procedural safeguards in the imposition of punitive penalties in that sphere *is necessary to* maintain the efficacy of the fiscal system or indeed can be regarded as consonant with the spirit and purpose of the Convention. In this case the Court will therefore apply the Engel criteria as identified above. Turning to the first criterion, *it is apparent that* the tax surcharges in this case were not classified as criminal but as part of the fiscal regime. This is however not decisive. (*Jussila v. Finland*[32])

In (20), *it is apparent that* is preceded by a lengthy argumentative proposition. It incorporates negation for argumentation purposes (see 6.7), and the explicit reference to "arguments" as well as citing other cases activating argument from authority. The Court refutes that argument by evaluating it as not convincing ("the Court is not persuaded", "is not convinced") and instead introduces its own assessment after *it is apparent that* (underlined).

Is it possible to speak about a local grammar of evidential legal reasoning? Example (17) comes from the CJEU, Goźdź-Roszkowski's (2024) findings trace it in the US Supreme and the Polish Constitutional Court's judgments and examples (18) and (19) are the ECtHR penmanship. Naturally, more contexts have to be considered, but the findings so far seem to confirm the trend that evidential legal reasoning coincides with patterns of validity.

A similar use of evaluation emerges in the *difficulty* group (Table 7.11), especially when the difficulty expressions collocate with verbs like "see", "accept" or "imagine".

(21) Although this is not expressly mentioned in paragraph 1 of Article 6, the object and purpose of the Article taken as a whole show that a person "charged with a criminal offence" is entitled to take part in the hearing. Moreover, sub-paragraphs (c), (d) and (e) of paragraph 3 guarantee to "everyone charged with a criminal offence" the right "to defend himself in person", "to examine or have examined witnesses" and "to have the

31 Application no. 18731/91, GC Judgment of 8 February 1996.
32 Application no. 73053/01, GC Judgment of 23 November 2006.

free assistance of an interpreter if he cannot understand or speak the language used in court", and *it is difficult to see* how he could exercise these rights without being present (see [. . .]). (*Sejdovic v. Italy*[33])

(22) However, *the Court observes* that this approach is not consistent with the fact that although the Government Commissioner attends the deliberations, he has no right to vote. *The Court considers* that by forbidding him to vote, on the ground that the secrecy of the deliberations must be preserved, domestic law considerably weakens the Government's argument that the Government Commissioner is truly a judge, as a judge cannot abstain from voting unless he stands down. Moreover, *it is hard to accept the idea* that some judges may express their views in public while the others may do so only during secret deliberations. (*Kress v. France*[34])

(23) In the plaintiff's opinion, the way in which the court interpreted the substantive legal rules is in conflict with the ideas and principles of the functioning of the rule of law . . . Taken to the point of absurdity, *it is easy to imagine* a situation where a great number of commercial companies (or legal entities in general) are destroyed by the State on the technical grounds that they lack *locus standi* in compensation proceedings. When a criminal prosecution is brought against the governing body of a commercial company, the company itself is never a party to the criminal proceedings . . ., but this *by no means* rules out the possibility that the company will sustain damage as a result of those criminal proceedings. (*Fu Quan, S.r.o. v. the Czech Republic*[35])

Example (21) approaches something close to irony by outlining the applicant's impossibility to take part in national proceedings and the conclusion that he did not have a fair trial because "*it is difficult to see* how he could exercise these rights without being present". Personal opinions lurking behind impersonal constructions are rare in RiFT – these resurface instead in judges' separate opinions (see Chapter 8) – yet, when these transpire in judgments, it is through the use of difficulty patterns. In (22) the rejection of Government's arguments is framed using value judgment of the Court finding it "hard to accept". In (23) the mirror sequence *it is easy to imagine* is preceded by "taken to the point of absurdity", which loads the statement with additional evaluation elements. In pragma-dialectics, this constitutes a type of "pragmatic argument" (Perelman & Olbrechts-Tyteca 1969: 266) with a consequentialist logic: *argumentum ad absurdum*. As absurdity is the other side of

33 Application no. 56581/00, GC Judgment of 1 March 2006. This routine appears in two others cases in RiFT: Zana v. Turkey, Application no. 18954/91, GC judgment of 25 November 1997, and Hermi v. Italy, Application no. 18114/02, GC Judgment of 18 October 2006.

34 Application no. 39594/98, GC Judgment of 7 June 2001.

35 Application no. 24827/14, GC Judgment of 1 June 2023.

Table 7.12 It is patterns in RiFT with discoursal function of appropriacy and value

Appropriacy	*AF*	*Value*	*AF*
it is appropriate to	18	it is (wholly) understandable that	14
it is not appropriate	5	it is not unreasonable that	1
it is therefore/thus/more appropriate to	7	it is correct that	3
it is inappropriate to	9	it is desirable that	1
it is reasonable to	7	it is not/therefore acceptable that	2
it is thus/therefore reasonable to	2	it is (widely/thus) accepted that	7
it is not unreasonable to	1	it is deemed useful	2
it is justified to	2	**Total**	**30**
it is correct to	1		
it is desirable to	2		
Total	**54**		

reasonableness, this argument is also known as argument from reasonableness, and it "is used when a judge starts from the hypothetical consequences of application of a legal rule in a specific case and argues that application should not take place because of the absurdity, unacceptability or unreasonableness of the consequences" (Feteris 2017: 10).

The consequentialist logic may be invoked also in the desirability patterns (Goźdź-Roszkowski 2024), including patterns of appropriacy and value (Francis 1995), see Table 7.12.

(24) Members not appointed or elected by the judiciary should not represent the executive or legislature but should be appointed on the basis of their personal standing and in their own right. *It is desirable that* the membership of a judicial council should not include persons who hold their position de facto by virtue of an executive office or position in the legislature. (*Grzęda v. Poland*)

(25) The Court has also stated that *it is inappropriate to* require an individual who has obtained judgment against the State at the end of legal proceedings to then bring enforcement proceedings to obtain satisfaction.

In (24) a general legal rule is outlined as a premise (underlined), followed by the Court's assessment as to the desirable outcome of this rule's application, forming the so-called systemic argument (Feteris 2017: 11). In (25) the Court expresses an opinion on the inappropriate course of action following a sequence of events. Remarkably, example (25) is an established routine in the ECtHR discourse: it appears in nine cases in RiFT.

7.6 Conclusions

This chapter was born to cast some light on the "European human rights style" (Villiger 2017: para. 22) of the ECtHR judgments. Forged in over 75 years of its existence and incorporating multiple legal and linguistic negotiations, today it results in an identifiable formulaic profile. The multi-stakeholder participation framework, typical of supranational case-law, along with internal dynamics aimed at finding a "common denominator" for the majority reasoning fuelled the replication of standardized formulae and routines, which nowadays can be associated with the Court's style.

Despite a shift towards alternative bilingualism and resource optimization, Grand Chamber judgments remain defiantly bilingual, with both English and French versions standing shoulder to shoulder in legal authenticity (Rule 76 (1), Rules of Court). This dual authenticity, while admirable in theory, places a significant burden on translators who must ensure that both versions say the same thing – no small feat when legal implications hang in the balance (Brannan 2018: 171). The de facto translated nature of Grand Chamber judgments is another factor contributing to the crystallization of this discourse. Specific linguistic constructs and routines, once created after lengthy negotiations, have a life of their own, reappearing verbatim from year to year and from judgment to judgment. A case in point are the ubiquitous *it is*-patterns (e.g., *it is ADJ that* and *it is ADJ to-inf*). Laden with evaluative adjectives, these patterns play a dual role in argumentation and stance expression (Goźdź-Roszkowski 2024: 37; Biber et al. 1999). A peculiar correlation emerged between *it is*-patterns with the meaning of validity that co-occur with evidentiary reasoning patterns, in the ECtHR context, but also in other judicial prose, making it possible to hypothesize about a local grammar of evidentiary legal reasoning. Yet, the discourse of human rights is not circumscribed to judgments, and judges who wish to express their views without the formulaic constraints of the judgment may append a separate opinion, which is the topic of Chapter 8.

8 Separate opinions

Legal, linguistic and pragmatic insights

8.1 Introduction

Judicial discourse in supranational courts is by no means a monolithic construct. As Epstein et al. (2013: 267) stated overviewing separate opinions in national courts, "the likelihood of disagreement grows with the size of the panel". In the ECtHR context, despite the increased need for legal certainty, insisting on a single, unanimous opinion within a judicial formation consisting of up to 17 judges could amount to a quixotic pursuit as it would need to silence the other voices. Similarly, legal literature posits that when a case concerns individual rights and freedoms or socially and politically salient issues, the room for divergence among judges increases (Bentsen 2018: 194), and the Grand Chamber of the ECtHR meets all three criteria: numerous judicial panel, individual nature of rights and their socio-political salience (Helfer & Voeten 2020: 807).

Separate opinions represent a type of legal writing that is used by judges to convey their individual views on a legal case. Unlike the majority opinion, which represents the official decision of the court, a separate opinion conveys the views of a single judge or a group of similar-minded judges that diverge from the majority opinion – those judges "who lost their case in camera" (Bruinsma 2006: 360), and might want to disagree or simply wish to clarify or expand on a particular point. Conceptualized as *votum separatum* (Goździ-Roszkowski 2020: 381), a separate opinion allows the judges to place distance between the majority voice and their own, promoting and managing the re-emergence of separate identities.

This chapter reconciles legal and linguistic perspectives on separate opinions at the ECtHR. Section 8.2 outlines the genesis of separate opinions and their legal implications. Section 8.3 proceeds with the description of study materials – an ad hoc corpus of separate opinions attached to Grand Chamber judgments – conceptualizing separate opinions as a genre that is distinct from the collegiate judgment. Next, I analyse the style, length, organization typology and linguistic regime of separate opinions, as well as the rationale behind their creation (8.4), to contextualize this "separationist" discourse. The linguistic focus of the chapter shifts to the domain of pragmatics, specifically

DOI: 10.4324/9781003434788-11

studying the correlation between genre conventions, discourse community and (im)politeness (8.5). The findings – proposing a tripartite classification into patterns of politeness, neutral non-politeness and impoliteness (8.6) – may be of interest to both linguists and lawyers.

8.2 Separate opinions: legal implications

8.2.1 Separate judicial opinions across institutions

Separate opinions have been part of professional and discursive practices at the ECtHR "since its earliest days" (White & Boussiakou 2009: 37) as they enshrine the right of judges to feel represented by the majority reasoning or decision.[1] The communicative goal of separate opinions at the ECtHR is set forth in Art. 45.2 of the ECHR and Rule 74.2 of the Rules of Court.

> If a judgment *does not represent*, in whole or in part, the unanimous opinion of the judges, any judge *shall be entitled* to deliver a separate opinion. (Art. 45.2, ECHR, emphasis added)

> Any judge who has taken part in the consideration of the case *shall be entitled* to annex to the judgment either *a separate opinion*, concurring with or dissenting from that judgment, *or a bare statement of dissent.* (Rule 74.2, Rules of Court, ECtHR, emphasis added)

Separate opinions stem from misalignment or disagreement with the majority, i.e. the judgment (Chapter 7). They diverge from other types of legal opinions, such as advisory opinions (issued before the judgment) or expert opinions (issued by outsiders), up to the point where they were equalled with the so-called "genre of judicial dissent" (Langford & Ferguson 2009). Other international courts of human rights, similarly to the ECtHR, allow separate opinions (see Rule 65.2[2] Rules of Court for the IACtHR; Rule 70[3] Rules of Court for the ACtHPR). This practice is framed as a *right*: mind the modal verb "may" ("*may* append the text of his/her separate or dissenting opinion", Rule 70.1, Rules of Court, ACtHPR) or the expression "to be entitled to"

1 White (2009: 1, note 4) refers to former Article 51 of the Convention, which mirrored Article 57 of the Statute of the International Court of Justice to illustrate how this practice has been always part of the Court functioning.

2 Rule 65.2 "Any Judge who has taken part in the consideration of a case is entitled to append a separate reasoned opinion to the judgment, concurring or dissenting. These opinions shall be submitted within a time limit to be fixed by the Presidency so that the other Judges may take cognizance thereof before notice of the judgment is served. Said opinions shall only refer to the issues covered in the judgment."

3 Rule 70 (Separate Opinions, Dissenting Opinions or Declarations) "1. Any Judge who heard the case may append the text of his/her separate or dissenting opinion. 2. A separate or dissenting opinion shall be published along with the decision of the Court. 3. A Judge who wishes to differ with the majority without providing the reasons thereof may do so in the form of a declaration."

(see Rule 74.2, Rules of Court, ECtHR above, or Rule 65.2, Rules of Court, ACtHPR, note 187). This right to feel represented correlates with the indication of judges' names: incidentally judgments rendered by the anonymous three-judge Committee do not envisage separate opinions (Keller & Heri 2018: para. 68).

However, not all institutional contexts allow the practice of separate opinions. The rules on providing a minority opinion vary across domestic high courts[4] and international courts. Some courts frown on the practice and ban separate opinions, while others delight in "separatist" thinking and generate separate opinions with (almost) every judgment (Helfer & Voeten 2020: 806; see also Kelemen 2018; Dunoff & Pollack 2017). The demarcation line does not coincide with national/international contexts: contrary to expectations, some international courts still prefer a single (majority) opinion, i.e. the judgment (e.g. the Court of Justice of the European Union). The dilemma of allowing or disallowing separate opinions has systemic origins rooted in the differences of socio-institutional contexts, judicial cultures and even the professional backgrounds of judges as vastly acknowledged in the literature (see, e.g. White & Boussiakou 2009: 39; Bentsen 2018; Goźdź-Roszkowski 2020: 382; Helfer & Voeten 2020: 806; McKeown 2021: 225). While common law courts are typically reticent "to mask internal debate" (McKeown 2021: 225) for the considerations of transparency, the civil law courts lean towards "the nameless, stylized judgment, and the disallowance of dissent [which] are thought to foster public perception of law as stable and secure" (Goźdź-Roszkowski 2020: 382).

8.2.2 Separate opinions in the literature

Most studies on separate judicial opinions today are dedicated to this practice in domestic settings, with much of research being US-oriented (Dunoff & Pollack 2017). As Kowalski (2023: 27) observes, building on Kelemen's work in 2013, the American strand of research on separate judicial opinions addresses several key aspects. These include investigating the issue of the precedent value of decisions rooted in pluralism, such as decisions lacking justification supported by the majority of judges. Additionally, this line of research explores the role of judges and separate opinions in shaping policy, as well as the economically recognized costs and benefits associated with separate opinions. Finally, there are essays accompanying collections of separate opinions by prominent judges and justices. By contrast, the European branch of research on separate judicial opinions, where the legal order is of a continental civil-law type, is less developed on account of systemic differences: it does not "allow for the disclosure of disagreements among judges so easily and introduces the principle of secret voting" (Kowalski 2023: 27).

4 For an overview of separate opinions in national constitutional courts, see the report by the ECtHR Research Division and the European Commission for Democracy Through Law (Venice Commission), Opinion No. 932/1018, 17 December 2018, CDL-AD(2018)030rev.

Like all international courts, the ECtHR follows a hybrid system, featuring compromises between the common and civil law mechanisms; yet for the practice of separate opinions it leans more on the common law–oriented approach "of permitting multiple opinions in contrast to the civil law tradition of delivering a single reasoned opinion, and permitting no separate opinions, the latter being the system that is more often, though not universally, met in constitutional courts" (White & Boussiakou 2009: 39; see 3.1.1 for the constitutional court analogy).

Separate opinions are

> a valuable tool to ensure the transparency of the ECtHR's decision-making as they disclose the positions of the judges in the particular case: he or she either supports, together with the majority, albeit with nuances, the reasoning and outcome of the judgment or will explain his or her dissent. Separate opinions enable judges, during their terms of office, to compare their views in respect of ECHR guarantees with those of all other judges.
>
> (Villiger 2017: para. 38)

The professional practice – and right – of judges to append their separate opinions has been widely recognized in legal literature (to quote just a few studies focused on the separate opinions of the ECtHR judges: Rivière 2005; White & Boussiakou 2009; Letsas 2011; Vandenhole 2019; Kowalski 2023). Most frequently, these works collect opinions of a given judge or on a given topic and provide legal commentary. The few non-legal-commentary studies on separate opinions in the ECtHR context analyse correlations between the profile of the drafting judge and the so-called "judicial voting patterns", looking at whether national judges "dissent more often than their colleagues when the Court rules against the state that nominated or appointed them" (Helfer & Voeten 2020: 807; see also Voeten 2008), or correlations between the previous career of a judge and their inclination to append a separate opinion (Bruinsma 2006, see also section 8.3.4). Helfer and Voeten (2020: 808) conclude that besides the above topics, legal scholars "have paid little attention to the role of separate opinions on the ECtHR".

Although separate opinions do not produce legal effects in that they merely voice departure from the majority opinion and honour "the pluralism, tolerance and broadmindedness that the Court has repeatedly stated are the characteristics of a democratic society" (White & Boussiakou 2009: 59), they still may have legal repercussions, even if not immediate. For instance, in their innovative analysis of taxation through the prism of human rights protection, Attard and Pinto de Albuquerque (a former judge of the ECtHR) comment on a situation when

> Subsequent judgments of the ECtHR appear to *have taken the advice of the dissenting judges* in Burden in their stride. Thus, in the 2016

> judgment in the case of Guberina v. Croatia, ***the approach adopted was that suggested by the dissenting judges*** in Burden.
>
> (Attard & Pinto de Albuquerque 2023: 145, emphasis added)

Despite the above optimistic analysis of the potential legal consequences of separate opinions, these remain, essentially, devoid of legal validity as they "carry little authoritative legal force and, generally, have no precedential value" (Goźdź-Roszkowski 2020: 381).

Commenting on what may be subsumed under the heading of a communicative purpose of separate opinions, Bruinsma (2006: 360) observes, "[n]ot bound by the straightjacket of the majority judgement and its legal validity, separatists feel free to speak their mind and follow their heart and soul". Separate opinions represent the intellectual diversity and multifaceted nature of the human experience, demonstrating that the pursuit of justice is not a monolithic endeavour, but a complex and nuanced journey. This journey, as Helfer and Voeten (2020: 806–807) analyse, has both ups and downs. Among the former, the scholars list

> improving the quality of a court's reasoning; enhancing judicial independence, transparency and accountability; demonstrating judicial deliberation, including by revealing to the parties that their arguments have been carefully considered; and providing information to other judges, future litigants, compliance constituencies and the public about the errors of the majority's approach, alternative future trajectories of the law or the need for legislation or treaty revisions
>
> (Helfer & Voeten 2020: 806)

However, the practice of having both a majority opinion (judgment) and one or more minority opinions (separate opinions) may also have disadvantages, as it can potentially undermine collegiality and become thus detrimental to the court's authority (Rivière 2005: 24), as well as reduce legal certainty and predictability, and increase the risk of noncompliance (Helfer & Voeten 2020: 806–807). As Judge Paulus (2019: 5) aptly noted, separate opinions "expose, for better or for worse, the relativity of the judicial enterprise".

8.3 Separate opinions: genre considerations

Separate opinions have been defined as "one of the most intriguing and least researched types of judicial expression related to the process of making and justifying judicial decisions" (Goźdź-Roszkowski 2020: 381). At the same time, as a *discursive practice*, separate opinions have remained underresearched. The discourse of separate opinions has received scant scholarly attention from a legal linguistics standpoint in general, with few notable exceptions (Goźdź-Roszkowski 2020; McKeown 2021). Separate opinions "often provide further insight into the discussions that took place inside the Court when deciding a case and the arguments that were tabled in this regard, and therefore represent an important source of further information about the deliberations" (Keller & Heri 2018: para. 71).

This section describes the study materials (8.3.1), outlines separate opinions at the ECtHR as a genre (8.3.2), set against the professional and discursive practices of the institution in terms of their positioning and time of delivery, main categories (8.3.3), participation framework (8.3.4), length and organization (8.3.5), style (8.3.6) and linguistic regime (8.3.7).

8.3.1 Separate Opinions Corpus

To describe this discursive practice, an ad hoc *Separate Opinions Corpus* was created, "SOC". SOC collects opinions appended to the Grand Chamber judgments drafted between 2013 and July 2023, without any thematic limitation, retrieved via the HUDOC database. The temporal criterion was applied based on a number of factors. As White wrote in 2009, crediting the judges of the ECtHR for their willingness to draft separate opinions, there was next to no formal support in this endeavour and "Judges choosing to write a separate opinion are very much on their own" (White 2009: 5). Starting from 2012, Yale Law School, followed by other university law faculties, initiated the practice of sending recent graduates to serve as judicial clerks, thus enhancing the capacity of judges to draft separate opinions in a court which was notoriously overloaded with cases (Helfer & Voeten 2020: 810). I set the initial period for the corpus collection at 2013, when the practice of judicial clerks became more consolidated. The final cutoff was dictated by the drafting period of the chapter, July 2023. Table 8.1 reports the main statistical data on the SOC composition.

The number of separate opinions exceeds the number of judgments by almost three times. This correlation confirms data previously reported by Kowalski (2023: 31) in his analysis of tax-related separate opinions annexed to the ECtHR judgments: his corpus featured 16 opinions to seven judgments of the Grand Chamber (2.3 opinion per judgment on average).

In SOC, the number of separate opinions per judgment ranged from one to nine, with a mean of 2.9 opinions per judgment. Table 8.2 reports the number of judgments[5] per year in correlation to the number of separate opinions in SOC.

White and Boussiakou (2009: 50) analysed the incidence of separate opinions in the general decision-making process of the ECtHR. In their dataset covering 166 Grand Chamber judgments delivered over the nine-year period between 1 January 1999 and 31 December 2007, only 24 (14.5%) were

5 As the retrieval of separate opinions was a highly time-consuming process, involving sorting through all judgments manually, saving the opinions into separate files and coding them respectively, SOC does not include the totality of all separate opinions attached to the Grand Chamber judgments published between 2013 and 2023, but a representative sample.

Table 8.1 Separate Opinions Corpus (SOC)

Number of separate opinions	*Number of judgments*	*Tokens in SOC*	*Types in SOC*
236	84	901,760	42,151

Table 8.2 Separate Opinions Corpus by year and the number of opinions

Year	*Judgments*	*% out of 84*	*Opinions*	*% out of 236*	*Ratio opinions to judgments*
2013	4	4.8	12	5.1	3.0
2014	9	10.7	24	10.2	2.7
2015	10	11.9	32	13.6	3.2
2016	14	16.7	36	15.3	2.6
2017	8	9.5	32	13.6	4.0
2018	10	11.9	22	9.3	2.2
2019	6	7.1	16	6.8	2.7
2020	7	8.3	20	8.5	2.9
2021	6	7.1	22	9.3	3.7
2022	3	3.6	6	2.5	2.0
2023	5	6.0	15	6.4	3.0
Total	84		236		

unanimous, in a sense that no separate opinion was annexed to them. Helfer and Voeten (2020) analysed a larger dataset of Grand Chamber judgments, covering 400 texts delivered between 1999 through 2018, with 83% producing at least one separate opinion (Helfer & Voeten 2020: 800). A reasonable question arises: if 83%–85.5% of Grand Chamber judgments are followed by separate opinions, shall we consider them a structural element of the judgment genre or a distinct (sub-)genre?

8.3.2 *A genre or not a genre?*

Analysing the ICJ context, Bedjaoui (1991: 58–59) argues that separate opinions "act as a foil to the Court's reasoning, one can extract the full substance of the judicial decision and grasp the entire scope of its contribution to the jurisprudence". Foil, moil or broil, separate opinions undoubtedly share a number of characteristics with the judgment. Yet they also possess a different subset of features, which makes it possible to conceptualize them as a distinct genre. First, their communicative goal diverges from the communicative goal of the judgment. The judgment pursues the goal of "subsum[ing] difference in an act of explanation and a moment of decision" (Ferguson 1990: 205), but separate opinions aim at underscoring differences in either the reasoning or the final decision.

Second, from a purely legal standpoint, separate judicial opinions produce no legal effects, making them again distinct from the judgment. Third, whereas judgment is a typified document with stable and legally prescribed structural elements (see 7.4), the generic structure of minority opinions is not clearly defined anywhere. Peruzzo (2019b: 69) posits that separate opinions "are typical of Grand Chamber judgments", yet she excludes them from her empirical study dedicated to the analysis of Italian system-bound elements in ECtHR Grand Chamber judgments, based on (1) their different authorship status (separate opinions "express the view of single judges rather than the ECtHR"), (2) lack of "a fixed structure" and (3) differences in "style and tone" (Peruzzo 2019b: 69). Similarly, Senden (2011: 21) notes how separate opinions are more personal than the judgment.

It makes sense to treat them as a separate genre, also because the judgment is a product of legal and linguistic compromise. Its draft is heavily influenced by the discursive practices of the Registry case lawyers, either from the very beginning as it happens for Chamber judgments or after a round of deliberation, especially if the pigeonhole procedure (see Chapter 7, Keller & Heri 2018: para. 61) has been applied. By contrast, separate opinions are written by judges, in their undiluted style, and they "generally make for interesting reading" (Gerards 2017: 269). Brannan (2021: 223) notes the stylistic assortment in separate opinions, with some being "erudite, with abundant use of Latin; others are more entertaining, with quotations from Shakespeare (dissenting opinion of Judge Zupancic in *Khan v. Germany*, 23/04/2015) or from the lyrics of Bob Dylan (dissenting opinion of Judge Kuris in *Selahattin Demirtas v. Turkey*, 23/06/2015)".

The genesis of separate opinions is also distinct from the judgment in terms of time of drafting/delivery. Having announced their intention to diverge from the majority at the judgment deliberation stage, the "separatist" judges in Grand Chamber formations "have three weeks from the moment of agreement on the final version of a judgment at the second deliberations until separate opinions are due; in the Chamber, this limit is usually two weeks" (Keller & Heri 2018: para. 73).

In the ECtHR context, separate opinions can be appended only to judgments and are not envisaged for decisions on purely procedural matters, such as the issue of admissibility, where only the majority opinion is allowed. Despite the words "appended", "attached" or "annexed" being used in the literature on separate opinions in a relatively consolidated way (see, e.g. White & Boussiakou 2009: 52, see also example (1)), separate opinions – somewhat oxymoronically – do not exist as an independent category in HUDOC, but are instead placed on the margins of judgments. This renders impossible their automatic retrieval and potentially raises a question as to the applicability of the label "genre" to these texts.

Their positioning does not vouch clearly in favour of classifying them as a distinct (sub-)genre: they are always placed after the closing section of the main judgment and do not exist in the HUDOC database as a separate category. However, it is easy to separate them from the judgment, the building blocks of which are very formulaic (Peruzzo 2019b: 68). When a separate opinion is drafted, it is preceded by the formula delineating the perimeter of the judgment (the majority opinion), separating it from minority opinions. This formula is followed by the initials of the President and the Registrar, after which a lettered or numbered list of opinions comes, if more than one opinion is annexed. The opinion type and its authors are always mentioned, thus clearly indicating that these are not part of the main judgment and their authorship is indeed different.

(1) In accordance with Article 45 § 2 of the Convention and Rule 74 § 2[6] of the Rules of Court, the following separate opinions *are annexed* to this judgment [. . .] (emphasis added)

(1a) Au présent arrêt *se trouve joint*, conformément aux articles 45 § 2 de la Convention et 74 § 2 du règlement, l'exposé de l'opinion séparée [. . .] (emphasis added)

While genre-oriented research mentioned separate opinions in the macro-structure of the judgment (Caliendo 2004: 297–298; Peruzzo 2019b: 63), none of the above studies actually analysed them, on account of their apparent divergence from the main judgment.

8.3.3 Types of separate opinions

There are two main types of separate opinions in the ECtHR system – concurring opinions and dissenting opinions – and their variants: partly concurring opinions, partly dissenting and the combination of both (Figure 8.1). "Concurring opinions generally allow judges in the majority to explain the majority's reasoning or to indicate the reasons for their disagreement with that reasoning. Dissenting opinions allow judges in the minority to explain why they voted against the majority and to provide their own alternative account of how they believe that a case should have been decided" (Keller & Heri 2018: para. 71). Alternatively, a judge may append only a declaration of vote, without providing motivation; however, the latter is a relatively rare case. The taxonomy in Figure 8.1 is based on SOC but is also corroborated by one of the pioneering and probably the most complete studies on separate opinions by Rivière (2005).

As Levy and Levy (1971: 302) mentioned more than 50 years ago, judicial opinion should typically provide "the rationale for the decision, the grounds accounting for it, an exposition of the reasons which justify it". The dotted line in Figure 8.1 divides the separate opinions into two groups in terms of the moves expected to be present in these texts. The "full-fledged" separate opinions in the left column typically contain

6 Prior to changes introduced by Protocol no. 14, the articles mentioned in this formula were different and it started with "In accordance with Article 51 para. 2 of the Convention (art. 51–2) and Rule 55 para. 2 of Rules of Court . . .".

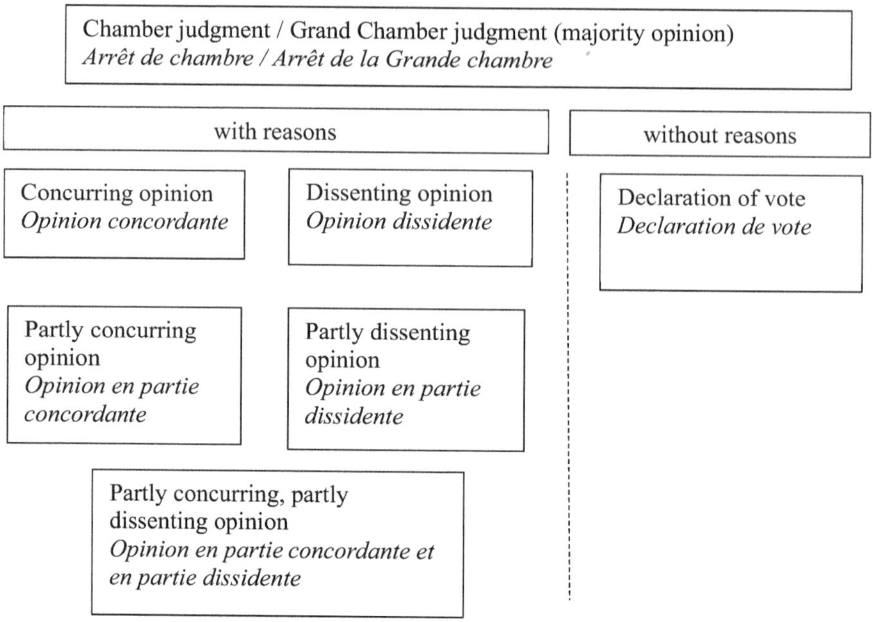

Figure 8.1 Main categories of separate opinions at the ECtHR

1 A move/speech act evaluating the majority opinion and expressing either concurring or dissenting position, wholly or in part;
2 An explanation or motivation of filing a separate opinion, i.e. the so-called *justification*, the core function of which "is to reveal the motives and the reasoning of those judges who have provided the disposition of a particular case in order to convince the legal community and the public that the disposition is correct" (Goźdź-Roszkowski 2024: 20; see also 7.4.3);
3 Conclusions.

The right-column opinions are limited to "a bare statement of dissent" (Rule 74.2, Rules of Court, ECtHR), which is most frequently expressed as a declaration of a different vote. "It is a widely accepted – although unwritten and not always observed – practice at the Court that judges who do not vote with the majority in a judgment should append such a statement of dissent to disclose how they voted" (Keller & Heri 2018: para. 69). All judgments have to be reasoned (Art. 45 ECHR), i.e. contain an explanation of the judicial decision-making, so the choice to provide a reasoned separate opinion may be construed as the judicial aspiration to approach the standard required of the judgment. After all, the case-law of the ECtHR, besides its effective legal value, serves also the representational purposes: the voices of judges are "first and foremost an ideological beacon in the symbolic field of human rights lawyering" (Bruinsma 2006: 362).

In one of the few previous studies which analyses the typology of separate judicial opinions at the ECtHR, Rivière (2005) analysed 908 separate opinions[7] delivered between 1960 and 1998, out of which 413 (45.5%) were dissenting opinions; 204 (22.5%) were concurring opinions (inclusive of 3 partly concurring opinions); 170 (18.7%) were partly dissenting opinions; 95 (10.5%) were marked just as separate opinions; and only 26 (2.8%) were bare statements of dissent; see also Bruinsma (2006: 359).

Table 8.3 compares SOC with Rivière's data shedding light on both convergent and divergent tendencies. First, there is a potential shift in the dynamics of separate opinions over the period between 2013 and 2023 as the number of dissenting and concurring opinions is equal (78, or 33.1%), rather than the former prevailing over the latter as it used to be in Rivière's data. Second, there is an increase in the "partly" categories. Rivière reported only three partly concurring opinions out of 908, i.e. 0.3%, whereas SOC features seven such texts, amounting to 3%, which signals a ten times increase. If fully and partly dissenting opinions are combined, SOC still shows a decrease in dissent with 55.1% as compared to 64.2% in Rivière (2005). Most previous legal studies on separate opinions focussed specifically on dissenting opinions (see, e.g. Langford & Ferguson 2009; Helfer & Voeten 2020; Stone Sweet et al. 2021), somewhat overlooking the practice of concurring opinions. Given the SOC data, is it still relevant to talk about the culture of dissent? Or is there room for a culture of concurrence? And what should be understood by concurrence, if it still implies distancing one's opinion from the majority? While dissenting opinions are expected of judges who do not vote with the majority, concurring opinions "are voluntary" (Villiger 2017: para. 36). The rise of concurring opinions and the implications for the discursive practice of separate opinions will be further discussed in 8.4. There is an apparently new category of "partly concurring, partly dissenting opinions", which might be replacing the unspecified label

Table 8.3 Separate opinions in the Separate Opinions Corpus and in Rivière (2005)

Corpus and reference period	*SOC (2013–2023)*		*Rivière (2005) (1960–1998)*	
Category of separate opinions	*Texts*	*Percentage*	*Texts*	*Percentage*
Dissenting	78	33.1%	413	45.5%
Concurring	78	33.1%	201	22.1%
Partly dissenting	52	22.0%	170	18.7%
Partly concurring	7	3.0%	3	0.03%
Partly concurring, partly dissenting	16	6.8%	n/a	n/a
Separate (unspecified)	3	1.3%	95	10.5%
Declaration of vote	2	0.8%	26	2.8%
Total	236		908	

7 Rivière (2005) does not indicate the number of judgments to which these opinions were attached.

"separate opinion", now on the decrease. In any case, a convergent trend is clear: unspecified separate opinions and the mere declaration of vote remain the least numerous categories.

8.3.4 Participation framework

After analysing 4,000 cases which generated 30,000 separate opinions, White and Boussiakou (2009: 59) did not arrive at a clearcut analytical explanation underlying the decision of single judges to append a separate opinion, other than their "judicial temperament". Besides judges' personas, judicial temperament frequently taps into their pre-ECtHR careers: academics, practicing lawyers, national judges, administrative staff or a combination of the above (Bruinsma 2006). Former trial judges and litigators focus on the case specifics and often view themselves as part of a cohesive judicial body. For them, the act of filing separate opinions holds limited significance, as they prioritize achieving a unified stance. In contrast, former administrators and academics bring an academic and administrative perspective to their roles as judges, broaching broader perspectives on human rights jurisprudence. While these observations offer valuable insights into potential correlations, they should not be taken as absolute truths.

Judges can draft separate opinions either individually or collectively. In cases where a single judge authors the opinion, it begins with a heading indicating its type, followed by the judge's surname. When separate opinions are drafted collegially, i.e. by at least two judges, they are termed "joint" (*commune* in French). These joint opinions bear a heading that specifies the multi-authorship status, the type of opinion, and the surnames of all contributing judges, thereby acknowledging the collaborative nature of the text. A hybrid scenario arises when an opinion is initially drafted by one judge or a group of judges (although less common), and after internal discussion – although its details remain veiled – other judges decide to join in. In this case, the opinion is labelled by its type, followed by the name of the judge who initiated the opinion, after which "joined by" (*à laquelle se rallie*) is added with the names of joining judge(s). Judges may file several separate opinions: "a judge might file a partly dissenting opinion of his or her own, and join in a partly concurring opinion put forward by other judges" (White & Boussiakou 2009: 48). Draft separate opinions are not circulated before the deliberations, but the intention to append an opinion is announced (Keller & Heri 2018: para. 72).

Table 8.4 reports on the authorship status of separate opinions in SOC, encompassing three principal categories of authorship, namely *individual*, *joint*, and *joined*, presented vertically, crossed with the typological attributes of opinions, presented horizontally. Most opinions are drafted by individual judges (135 texts; 57.2%) totalling 552,346 tokens, i.e. 61.3% of the total number of tokens in SOC. If opinions marked as *joined* are added to this dataset, amounting to 66.9% of all texts and 70.1% of all tokens, a clear preference towards individual authorship emerges. Remarkably, single authors produce more concurring opinions (52 out of 135, i.e. 38.5%) than dissenting (42 out of 135, i.e. 31.1%), whereas this tendency is reverted for joint authorship. Joint concurring opinions amount to 19 out of 75, i.e. 25.3%, leaving the lead position to joint dissenting opinions with 25 out of 75, i.e. 33.3%. It would appear that filing a dissenting opinion as a joint venture is a more recurrent practice than filing a "lone wolf" dissenting opinion. The same pattern emerges if one looks at the number of partly dissenting opinions, amounting to 20% for individual opinions and 29.5% for joint opinions. This mirrors the observation by Helfer and Voeten in their 2020 study of "walking back dissents", a label used to indicate separate (minority) opinions declaring that the Grand Chamber "has overturned prior rulings or settled doctrine in a way that favours the respondent government" (Helfer & Voeten 2020: 799) as opposed to "walking forward dissents", which accuses the majority of a similar overturning of the previous case-law but in favour of the applicant. For walking back dissents in the post-Brighton[8] period (2012–2018) that partially overlap with SOC, 56 texts were joint separate opinions against only 19 single-authored texts (Helfer & Voeten 2020: 815), with a ratio of 2.95. Many of these were drafted by a group of "serial dissenters": Judges Tulkens, Rozakis, Sajó, Spielmann and Pinto de Albuquerque, who all authored or joined at least 15 such separate opinions (Helfer & Voeten 2020: 815).

Table 8.4 data may provide indirect insight into the much discussed dichotomy between judicial activism or judicial restraint (Voeten 2008). These concepts pertain to the role of courts and judges in interpreting and applying the law, often in relation to the Constitution in domestic settings or the Convention in supranational settings, and the degree of deference or assertiveness they exhibit in making legal decisions. Since the Convention has been repeatedly conceptualized as a living instrument (Letsas 2011, see 3.1.2), its interpretation caters to the changing realia. In this context, judicial restraint

Table 8.4 Authorship of different opinions in the Separate Opinions Corpus

Authorship	*Individual*		*Joint*		*Joined*	
	Texts	*Tokens*	*Texts*	*Tokens*	*Texts*	*Tokens*
Concurring	52	211,761	19	62,347	8	33,881
Dissenting	42	199,158	25	80,342	9	35,152
Partly concurring	2	9,369	5	4,761	5	9,274
Partly dissenting	27	94,537	23	82,247	0	0
Partly concurring, partly dissenting	9	31,029	4	38,261	1	614
Separate	2	5,579	1	2,123	0	0
Declaration of vote	1	913	1	110	0	0
Total	135	552,346	78	270,191	23	78,921
Total as % SOC	57.2%	61.3%	33.1%	30%	9.7%	8.8%

8 High Level Conference on the Future of the European Court of Human Rights, resulting in the so-called Brighton Declaration (20 April 2012) and the subsequent reform of the Court.

stands for exercising caution and granting the Member States "a wide margin of appreciation when deciding whether a violation of the Convention has occurred" (Voeten 2008: 422), which correlates with the "age of subsidiarity" (Spano 2018). Judicial activism then revolves around making bold and expansive interpretations of the Convention, allowing the Member States less room for manoeuvre "to hide behind national customs or interests" (Voeten 2008: 422).

It would be simplistic to assert any straightforward correlation between the quantitative data and the concepts of judicial activism and judicial restraint; to do that, a qualitative legal analysis of the content of these opinions would need to be conducted, much like what Helfer and Voeten (2020)[9] did. Still, the very incidence of separate opinions can be a factor to consider in future studies.

Recipients of separate opinions coincide with those of judgments (see 7.3.2). Whenever the opinion is attached to Chamber judgments (seven judges), and goes on appeal to the Grand Chamber, the appealing party tends to include separate opinions in their argumentations, thus it is virtually certain that all ECtHR judges will read them. Separate opinions reach also the parties to the dispute and the community at large, as they offer insights into the judicial reasoning and highlight potential areas of legal development. When the case is concerned with socially and/or politically salient issues, such as medically assisted procreation, euthanasia or same-sex marriage, the media would often quote separate opinions as much as the judgment. As Goźdź-Roszkowski (2024: 12) observed, "[m]odern judicial opinion provides a unique opportunity to reach out to these audiences".

8.3.5 Length and organization

The length and organization of separate opinions vary considerably, tying into the judges' prior experiences and/or the possibility to rely on judicial clerks. As Keller and Heri (2018: para. 74) disclose, "[t]here is no general limit to the length of separate opinions. However, overly lengthy opinions require a lot of the Court's translation and language check resources, and thus create delays with regard to the publication of judgments". In SOC, the shortest opinion (2) counted 36 words,[10] followed by 71 and 79 words in (3) and (4), respectively.[11]

(2) I *voted in favour of* finding a violation of Articles 6 and 13, *for the reasons set out* in part 2 of the separate opinion of Judge Pinto de Albuquerque.

9 Their work was criticized in a rebuttal research paper by Stone Sweet, Sandholtz and Andenas in 2021, based on the characterization of what counts as a "walking back dissent" done by Helfer and Voeten's "student research assistants" (Stone Sweet et al. 2021: 902). The independent coding by Stone Sweet et al. "even in the most generous reading" does not reach the same results, with only 21.7% agreement rate between the two studies.

10 Including the heading, not reported here.

11 Unless otherwise specified, emphasis has been added in all examples.

(partly dissenting opinion of Judge Vučinić in *De Tommaso v. Italy*, GC, 2017)

(3) To my regret *I could not follow the majority, for the reasons expressed* in the separate opinion of Judge Paulo Pinto de Albuquerque. Even assuming that "compassionate grounds" may mean anything a judge finds reasonable in the United Kingdom, it certainly cannot provide the specific guidance to the prisoner that was stipulated in *Murray v. the Netherlands* ([GC], no. 10511/10, § 100, ECHR 2016) a mere six months ago. (separate opinion of Judge Sajó in *Hutchinson v. UK*, GC, 2017)

(4) I respectfully *disagree with the majority* that there has been a violation of Article 14 of the Convention read in conjunction with Article 8, and in this respect *I concur with the views* expressed by Judges Villiger, Mahoney and Kjølbro in their joint dissenting opinion (see paragraphs 2–45 of that opinion). However, *I voted with the majority* that there was no need to examine the application separately under Article 8 of the Convention. (partly dissenting opinion of Judge Jäderblom in *Biao v. Hungary*, GC, 2016)

Brevity nonetheless, these are *opinions* and not a mere declaration of vote, and the presumption for an opinion is that it is reasoned. Examples (2)–(4) contain clear indications of the judges' positions: "I voted in favour of", "I could not follow the majority", "I respectfully disagree with the majority". These are followed by intertextual grounds, referring to other sources. Example (3) contains a prototypical dissenting pattern "I could not follow the majority", yet its author labelled it simply as *separate opinion*. Besides the two main moves mentioned above – expressing dissent and motivating dissent – the contents of separate opinions are quite varied, and the variation increases with the length of the opinion.

Little is known about the drafting process underlying the creation of separate opinions. Already at the drafting stage of the main judgment, "a certain minority trend or trends will come to light" (Bedjaoui 1991: 50). If the judges fail to integrate their reservations in the text of the judgment, these may take the form of separate opinions. As Brannan (2023) observes, "Opinions leave judges free to structure the text as they see fit, so even the formatting may at times be different".[12]

The longest opinion in SOC totalled 30,149 words (dissenting opinion of Judge Pinto de Albuquerque, joined by Judge Dedov in *Ilnseher v. Germany*, GC, 2018), preceded by another opinion by the same author of 26,746 words (partly dissenting, partly concurring opinion of Judge Pinto de Albuquerque in *G.I.E.M. S.r.l. and others v. Italy*, GC, 2018) and an opinion of 21,003 words (dissenting opinion of Judge Serghides in *Nait-Liman v. Switzerland*, GC, 2018), not reproduced here for reasons of space.

12 From a personal interview with James Brannan, Reviser and Head of English Language Division 2 at the Registry of the ECtHR, June 2023.

Table 8.5 Length of separate opinion in the Separate Opinions Corpus

Range	*Length in words*	*Number of opinions*	*%*
Short	<500	30	12.7%
Medium-short	500–1,000	35	14.8%
	1,001–1,500	19	8.1%
Medium	1,501–2,000	21	8.9%
	2,001–2,500	22	9.3%
	2,501–3,500	24	10.2%
Medium-long	3,501–4,500	19	8.1%
	4,501–5,000	12	5.1%
	5,001–6,000	13	5.5%
Long	6,001–9,000	18	7.6%
	9,001–13,000	12	5.1%
Very long	13,001–16,000	4	1.7%
	16,001–18,000	4	1.7%
	21,000–30,100	3	1.3%

As Table 8.5 shows, in the vast majority of cases (151 out of 236 texts, i.e. 64%) the length of separate opinions did not exceed 3,500 words (short to medium range). Only 23 out of 236 (9.7%) of opinions were longer than 9,001 words, with 20 (8.5%) of these being authored by Judge Pinto de Albuquerque. On average, a separate opinion would total 3,820 words, and if the outliers of the shortest and the longest opinion are excluded, the mean becomes 3,723 words.

Differences in "judicial temperament" could tie into the length of opinions, partly confirming previous research by Bruinsma (2006). For example, not only did the "serial dissenter" Judge Pinto de Albuquerque produce more opinions than his colleagues, his opinions were also significantly longer and presented different structural elements, such as a table of contents, organization into sections and subsections with headings, extensive list of references and footnotes, as well as a fully developed argumentation part. These discursive practices are associated with a research paper (e.g. addressing the history and development stages of a legal principle) and the judgment (case-law overview, organization in parts and sections). Since the pre-ECtHR career of Judge Pinto de Albuquerque covers both roles of a legal practitioner (trial judge and lawyer) and an academic (a doctorate in law and both tenured and visiting professor positions), it is not surprising to see traits of a research paper and a judgment in the organization of his separate opinions. On the whole, it is not unusual for medium and medium-long separate opinions to be organized in ordered sections and subsections.

8.3.6 *Style*

Judicial opinions "offer examples of the best judicial thought and language under maximal pressure" (Ferguson 1990: 204), as they open a window into the reasoning, perspectives and experiences of individual judges when interpreting the law. Moreover, separate opinions contribute indirectly to honing the main judgment style as the majority is allowed to "suffer to a lesser extent from the need to reach an agreement with all judges, which might result in vague and opaque reasoning" (Senden 2011: 21).

Judicial prose bears clear imprints of "judges' personal values and ideologies" (Goźdź-Roszkowski 2024: vii). The personal style of separate opinions is notoriously acknowledged in the literature (Pontrandolfo 2016: 63–68; Peruzzo 2019b: 69). While the judgment undergoes "a subtle osmosis" tending to what can be termed a "house style" (Bedjaoui 1991: 50), separate opinions are allowed greater stylistic freedom. However, what is intended by the vague label "personal style"?

In stark contrast to stylized judgments, some separate opinions contain epigraphs (yet it functions as an idiosyncratic embellishment rather than a structural element). Example (5) shows the beginning of a dissenting opinion by Judge Yudkivska in the case *Bédat v. Switzerland*, GC, 2016, dealing with the right to freedom of expression.

(5) "[F]ree speech and fair trials are two of the most cherished policies of our civilisation, and it would be a trying task to choose between them." Justice Black in *Bridges v. California*.

Other markers of personal style of judges include a separate opinion starting with an almost journalistic headline, see (6), which opened with a question summarizing the position of the judge.

(6) Do States' negative obligations, in terms of jurisdiction, go beyond Article 1 of the Convention, therefore being wider than their positive obligations? – An important question not addressed in the present case. (partly concurring opinion of Judge Serghides in the interstate case *Georgia v. Russia (II)*, GC, 2021)

While (rhetorical) questions are not rare in some more ornate separate opinions, this is a peculiar case of their topicalization, which bears a striking resemblance to media discourse with concise headlines of news reports or press releases. Separate opinions in politically resonant cases, as in (6), are deemed to be put under mediatic scrutiny, which may explain the organizational choice of the drafting judge to pre-pack some information for further dissemination (see 9.4 on institutional press releases).

Peculiarly, statements of dissent/declaration of vote are not the shortest texts in SOC. Example (7) features the statement of dissent by Judge Kjølbro in the case *Halet v. Luxemburg*, GC, 2023 (totalling 205 words), emphasis added.

(7) *I voted against* the finding of a violation of Article 10 of the Convention (point 1 of the operative provisions).

> *On two points, I distance myself from the Court's reasoning in the judgment.*
>
> Firstly, I do not support the Court's further development of the general principles in respect of the so-called "second Guja criteria", namely "the public interest in the disclosed information" (see paragraphs 131 to 144), where the Court extends the protection granted to whistle-blowers to cover not only (i.) "illegal conduct" (the term used in the Guja judgment) or "unlawful acts" (the term used in the present judgment) and (ii.) "wrongdoing" (the term used in the Guja judgment) or "reprehensible acts" (the term used in the present judgment), but also to cover (iii.) "a matter that sparks a debate giving rise to controversy as to whether or not there is harm to the public interest" (see, in particular, paragraphs 138 and 140 of the present judgment). Secondly, and in consequence, *I cannot agree with the majority* when this new general principle is applied to the specific circumstances of the present case. *Despite my disagreement of principle, I will refrain from further developing my legal arguments. I have therefore limited myself to this "declaration of vote".*

In (7) the judge's divergent standpoint is clearly stated, along with a brief reasoning (underlined). The latter, apparently, did not classify as a legal argument for the judge, who defined his text as a "declaration of vote" in the text and as a "statement of dissent" in the label. Compared to the shortest opinions in SOC (see examples (2)–(4)), no particular structural differences emerge, and yet examples (2)–(4) were labelled as opinions, whereas example (8) was defined as a "statement of dissent". Judges enjoy a wide discretion in defining and denominating the types of documents that they produce based on their own perceptions, and what is labelled as a "separate opinion" or a "declaration of vote" may indeed be a "dissenting opinion". Similarly, in line with what Helfer and Voeten (2020) found, an opinion labelled as "concurring" may be qualitatively defined as a "walking back dissent". The self-perception of judges as producing opinions that concur or disagree with the majority is a remarkable trait of the court's dialectical dynamics and an indicator of fuzzy borders across different opinion types. When judges are asked to label their opinions, it "is not an easy question to answer where the Judge has voted 'yes' to some parts of the operative clause and 'no' to others" (Bedjaoui 1991: 56). In other words, misalignment or disagreement with the majority will "always be subject to nuances" (Bedjaoui 1991: 50), reflecting the complexity of the judgment which generated the discord.

8.3.7 Linguistic regime

Grand Chamber judgments are bilingual, and the separate opinions appended to these judgments are likewise bilingual. In contrast to judgments, where both language versions are equally authentic, separate opinions are drafted by individual judges in either English or French, based on their preferred working language. Consequently, to attach such an opinion to a bilingual judgment, a translation into the other official language is performed, typically by the Registry's translation division, and subsequently approved by the judge in question. These opinions are also marked as "translation" or *traduction*, shifting direct responsibility further away from the Court.

In cases of multi-authored opinions, these may be labelled as "partial translations" because some judges write in English and others in French. In SOC, there are 29 translated opinions (12.3%), indicating that the drafting judges initially wrote them in French and then submitted them to the translation department. This indirectly supports the observations in Section 7.3.5, which note the increased reliance on English as the preferred working language of the Court.

What happens to an opinion attached to a monolingual Chamber judgment? Typically, judges have two weeks (as opposed to two to three weeks for Grand Chamber cases) to draft their opinions. If their working language differs from the Chamber's drafting language, no in-house translation is envisaged. When a Chamber issues a judgment in English, a separate opinion written in French remains in French at the publication stage.

8.4 Separate opinions: the rationale

It is not uncommon to talk about separate opinions in terms of complementarity and tensions with the judgment (Paulus 2019). Dissenting opinions challenge the prevailing legal interpretation and introduce an element of disagreement and divergence in legal deliberations, leading to a heightened sense of uncertainty. Paulus (2019: 5) notes that separate opinions should "serve a function beyond demonstrating disagreement". Reasons to write a dissenting opinion include "to sharpen the rhetorical bite of their critique, heighten its political implications, or invite new cases from future litigants" (Helfer & Voeten 2020: 799).

Concurring opinions reflect a shared perspective among judges, generating a relatively unified legal viewpoint. A logical question arises. Why do judges write concurring opinions? US Supreme Court Justice Scalia famously declared that concurring opinions issued "only to say the same thing better than the court has done, or worse still, to display the intensity of the concurring judge's feelings on the issue" represented an abuse (Entrikin 2017: 219). Separate opinions "should not be used to demonstrate who is the better judge, but rather what would have been the better judgment" (Paulus 2019: 5).

The distinction between concurring and dissenting opinions might not always be as clear-cut as it seems. Judges might concur on a particular outcome for different reasons, highlighting subtle variations in their legal reasoning that cannot be neatly categorized as a unified viewpoint. Conversely, dissenting opinions might hold a diverse range of objections, spanning from minor reservations to fundamental disagreements. The complex nature of judicial opinions and the inherent categorization subtleties led to the creation of a gradient (partly concurring or partly dissenting) and mixed categories (partly concurring and partly dissenting). As illustrated in 8.3.5, the label attached to an opinion seems to be left to the discretion of the drafting judges. In Helfer and Voeten's (2020) study, the formal labels are also disregarded:

> We identify minority opinions asserting that the Grand Chamber has overturned prior rulings or settled doctrine in a way that favours the respondent government. We label such minority opinions as 'walking back dissents'. The large majority of these minority opinions (85%) are denominated as dissents; the remainder are concurring opinions that agree with the outcome of the case but nonetheless charge the majority with overturning prior case law or doctrine. For convenience, we label all minority opinions containing such assertions as "walking back dissents".
> (Helfer & Voeten 2020: 799)

Further classification and subdivisions are possible and have been advanced in the existing literature. For example, Rivière (2005) highlights such possible reasons: underscoring differences of perspectives focused on the fundamental rationale behind the Court's judgment and divergences centred on critiques regarding coherence within its jurisprudence (cf. with walking back and walking forward dissents in Helfer & Voeten 2020). Another possible type of reasons concerns divergence between viewpoints dealing with matters of admissibility and fact-finding and those tackling substantial rights; and yet another between opinions driven by varying methods of interpreting the Convention, notably a meticulous textual analysis versus a more comprehensive purposive understanding.

Goźdź-Roszkowski (2024: 20) lists the following functions of justification, which is one of the moves in separate opinions, illustrating indirectly a variety of reasons underlying their creation.

> formal (courts are bound by law to provide a justification), descriptive (how the judges arrived at a particular outcome of a reasoning process), rationalizing (rationalize the outcome of the decision-making process), persuasive (to convince that the decision is correct), educational and cultural (promoting specific developments of law; propagating a certain vision of the state and law within the broad framework of a legal culture; appealing to the axiological and ideological dimensions of a particular legal culture with a view to ensuring the legitimacy of a decision) and controlling (enabling mechanisms of reviewing a given decision).

Table 8.6 summarizes the main reasons underlying the genesis of separate opinions, supplemented by examples from SOC (emphasis added). These categories are not meant to be exhaustive, but rather to function as a broad-brush synopsis.

Table 8.6 Typical reasons underlying the creation of separate opinions

	Dissenting opinion	*Concurring opinion*
Definition	A dissenting opinion is a separate judicial opinion written by a judge or a group of judges who disagree(s) with the outcome or reasoning of the majority judgment.	A concurring opinion is a separate judicial opinion written by a judge or a group of judges who agree(s) with the outcome of the majority judgment but wishes to express a different or additional legal reasoning or perspective.
Reasons	1. **Legal Disagreement**: Judges who dissent believe that the majority's legal analysis is incorrect or that the decision violates established legal principles. They may use a dissenting opinion to present their own interpretation of the law. E.g. We regret that *we cannot share the view of the majority* that there has been a violation of Article 1 of Protocol No. 1 to the Convention. *In our opinion, that provision is not applicable* in the circumstances of the present case. (Belany Nagy v. Hungary, GC, 2016, Joint dissenting opinion of Judges Nussberger, Hirvelä, Bianku, Yudkivska, Møse, Lemmens and O'Leary)	1. **Clarification or Emphasis**: A judge might write a concurring opinion to clarify or emphasize a particular point of law, ensuring that the reasoning behind the decision is more comprehensive and nuanced. E.g. *I agree with* the way this judgment lays down the general principles governing expulsion cases under Article 3 of the Convention. *I think it was high time, indeed,* to do so. *I also agree* with the way in which these general principles were applied in the concrete circumstances of the case, leading to the finding of a potential violation. *I would add, however, the following.* [. . .] (J.K. and Others v. Sweden, GC, 2016, concurring opinion of Judge Bianku)
	2. **Future Precedent**: Dissenting opinions can lay the groundwork for future challenges or revisions of the law. They provide alternative viewpoints that may gain traction in subsequent cases. E.g. The majority misunderstand this fact. But their findings of the case must also be seen against the background of the Court's minimalist understanding of the principle of legality and *the current slippery slope in which the Court has embarked regarding criminal law.* (Ilnseher v. Germany, dissenting opinion of Judge Pinto De Albuquerque, joined by Judge Dedov, §89.)	2. **Alternative Legal Grounds**: Judges may concur to propose alternative legal reasoning for reaching the same decision as the majority, based on different legal principles or precedents. E.g. While *I have joined in the finding* of a violation of Article 14 of the Convention in conjunction with Article 8 in the present case, *I cannot fully share the reasoning in the judgment leading to such a finding.* (Biao v. Denmark, 2016, concurring opinion of Judge Pinto De Albuquerque)

(*Continued*)

Table 8.6 (Continued)

	Dissenting opinion	*Concurring opinion*
	3. Legal Discourse: Dissents contribute to the ongoing legal discourse by presenting differing viewpoints and encouraging a robust exploration of legal issues. E.g. When a case that has *sharply divided a Chamber is referred to the Grand Chamber, it usually means that some important principles need to be clarified*. The present case provided an opportunity to nuance an approach to the weighting of the conflicting interests of the media in reporting on ongoing trials, on the one hand, and protection of the private life of an accused and the interests of justice, on the other. (Bédat v. Switzerland, 2016, dissenting opinion of Judge Yudkivska)	**3. Specific Concerns**: A judge might have specific concerns about aspects of the case not fully addressed in the majority opinion. Writing a concurring opinion allows them to highlight these concerns without breaking from the majority's conclusion. E.g. I agree with the dissenting judges that, had the Grand Chamber found that the *Engel* criteria had been met, the two questions related to Article 7 of the Convention would be of real interest in the present case. [. . .] *The Court has not so far had an opportunity to deal with these questions*. Since the Chamber *addressed this important matter only briefly*, in just one paragraph, without any deeper analyses [. . .], and *Grand Chamber did not have an opportunity to deal with it*, I should like *merely to flag the principles* that, in my opinion, *should guide the Court in deciding these complicated issues*. (Gestur Jónsson and Ragnar Halldór Hall v. Iceland, 2020, concurring opinion of Judge Turković)
	4. Policy Considerations: Judges may dissent to underscore specific policy considerations or societal implications related to the case, offering their unique perspective on the matter. E.g. To my regret, I have to dissent with regard to the finding of a violation of the Convention. I could not vote with the majority. *I can agree with the majority that this case is about freedom. But what is freedom?* (Baka v. Hungary, 2016, dissenting opinion of Judge Pejchal)	**4. Policy Considerations:** Judges may concur to underscore specific policy considerations or societal implications related to the case, offering their unique perspective on the matter. e.g. I share both the conclusion and the reasoning in the present judgment. However, *given this case's more general importance from the perspective of the independence of the judiciary, I should like to make the following observations* with regard, more specifically, to the scope of this principle under Article 6 § 1 of the Convention. (Baka v. Hungary, GC, concurring opinion of Judge Sicilianos (translation))

8.5 "Separatist" discourse: pragmatic considerations

8.5.1 A no-compromise land: between dissent and disrespect?

Paulus (2019: 2), a judge of the German Constitutional Court, admits to enjoying reading dissents on account of their clear reasoning – "unforgiving of what they perceive as mistakes within the majority findings" (Paulus 2019: 2) – and captivating style:

> They do not seek to build a consensus, but to declare why compromise is impossible. Phrases such as my former colleague Gertrude Lübbe-Wolff's "One ought to refuse being sent on grand desert tours that will not lead to any spring", or Law Lord Hoffmann's "The real threat to the life of the nation . . . comes not from terrorism but from laws such as these", are still ringing in our ears.
>
> (Paulus 2019: 2)

Separate opinions are thus the linguistic land of no compromise. Paulus (2019: 4) juxtaposes the rhetoric of "a compromise" in the majority opinions and their "serene tone" to the frequently more convincing and forceful tone of separate opinions, which, however, "may run the risk of merely expressing vanity and personal offence rather than sober and rational argument" (Paulus 2019: 4). James Brannan comments that the ECtHR judges are "free to express themselves as they wish, although there is an unwritten principle that if they dissent they should not be too critical of the majority" (Brannan 2023).

Costa (2021: 403) defines the drafting of separate opinions as "a delicate exercise", wherein the judges have to explain their positions, "but it is customary and good practice to do so with courtesy and moderation, without any unpleasant or excessive criticism of the majority". Similarly, Paulus (2019: 5) observes, "dissents should be clear and concise but not offensive, and be based on legal argument, not hyperbole".

The Venice Commission and the ECtHR Research Division overviewed the practice of separate opinions in national constitutional courts and made an important distinction between "dissent, which is important, and disrespect, which is to be avoided" (Venice Commission 2018: 13, § 42). As concerns provisions on the wording and style of separate opinions, the report mentions only a few countries where such provisions exist. Ironically, no formal provisions on the wording and content of separate opinions exist at the ECtHR.

The distinction between respectful and disrespectful dissent is also raised by Entrikin (2017), who analyses the US Supreme Court Justice Scalia's "vitriolic" dissents reflecting "uncloaked scorn for the majority" (Entrikin 2017: 202) and marking the turning point in the practice of separate opinions at the US Supreme Court. In the early days of the US Supreme Court, separate opinions were rare, reluctant and even apologetic in their style. In the case *Brown v. State of Maryland* (1827) the dissenting Justice Thompson introduced the following formula in his dissent: "with some reluctance, and very considerable diffidence".[13] Then in the 1950s their rhetoric can be defined as respectful, until the arrival of Justice Scalia in 1986, whose opinions are renowned for their caustic style,[14] up to the introduction of the distinction between "respectful dissent"[15] for collegial disagreement and "disrespectful dissent" that appears antithetical to the Court's collegiality. Entrikin's (2017) work draws a fascinating picture of Scalia's career and opinion writing, without providing a clear linguistic commentary on what makes them disrespectful.

8.5.2 *Separate opinions: politeness theory*

The discourse of judicial dissent or misalignment – respectful or disrespectful – finds a compelling parallel in the principles of *politeness theory*. Just as politeness theory provides a framework for managing interpersonal interactions while safeguarding individuals' *face* (Goffman 1967), i.e. the public image and representation of self, the expression of separate judicial opinions requires a delicate balance between asserting divergent legal viewpoints and upholding the dignity of the court and its members. Costa (2021: 455–457) posits that if the opinion is too "sharp, or even lacking in courtesy or collegial spirit, the President will have to persuade their authors to redraft them or tone them down – but cannot force them to do so". The dichotomy of respectful/ disrespectful language and style of separate opinions, raised by legal scholars, can find a systematic explanation through the linguistic paradigm of *politeness*.

Originally developed in the seminal work by Brown and Levinson (1987), *politeness theory* has been applied to the study of the pragmatic dimension of courtroom interaction in a number of works focussing predominantly on oral interaction (Lakoff 1989; Fraser 1990; Harris 2011; Ridao Rodrigo 2016), with a few exceptions dealing with written judicial discourse (Kurzon 2001; Zejnilović et al. 2022). Brown (2017: 383) offers the following broad definition of politeness: "the feelings and expectations of those one is interacting with so that social interaction proceeds smoothly". Yet what counts as impolite or lacking in courtesy in a judicial context? Building on conceptualizations of politeness in Brown and Levinson (1987), Lakoff (1989) and Fraser (1990), Kurzon (2001: 62) problematizes how politeness is challenging to analyse in legal discourse. In other words, what is considered impolite in one community

13 *Brown v. State of Maryland*, 25 U.S. (12 Wheat.) 419 (1827), 449–50 (Thompson J, dissenting).

14 As Entrikin (2017: 219–220) describes, "By the end of his judicial career, his separate opinions had been variously described as 'harshly worded', 'sarcastic and divisive with a cutting writing style', 'acid', 'corrosive', 'belligerent', 'hostil[e]', 'caustic', 'invective', 'degrading', 'brutal', 'outside the boundaries of judicial discourse', 'strident and contentious', 'bold vitriol', a 'torrent of outrage', 'prone to stylish stabs', 'vituperative', and even 'nasty'. They were perhaps written as much to garner attention and entertain as to enlighten readers" (internal citations omitted).

15 Entrikin (2017: 2016, note 81) specifies that Justice Whittaker is credited for the phrase "respectful dissent" in this meaning.

of practice may be quite the norm in another, amounting to what Archer called some time later "systematic impoliteness" (Archer 2008: 181–182).

The ECtHR judges form a community of practice as well as a discourse community (see 1.3), wherein they engage in certain discursive practices as developed to perform in a common task: judicial deliberation and drafting, in this case. It is natural to expect some form of disagreement in separate judicial opinions, as they stem from the desire to place some distance between a minority and a majority opinion. To wit, not every form of disagreement – or misalignment and partial agreement for concurring opinions – should be automatically considered impolite. Whereas some more recent theories on (im)politeness proposed more intricate taxonomies,[16] featuring such categories as "verbal aggression" (Archer 2008) and "reasonable hostility" (Tracy 2008), all of these appear to be applied to oral interaction with only Kurzon's (2001) taxonomy applied to judicial opinions. The latter is used here.

Kurzon (2001) delineated between the categories of *politeness*, *impoliteness* (*rudeness* in Lakoff 1989) and the third neutral category of *non-politeness.*

Politeness strategies in separate opinions would typically include using deferential language ("my learned friend"), acknowledging counterarguments, and employing hedging techniques; it can be harnessed by judges to mitigate the potential face-threatening nature of dissent or misalignment in concurring opinions. The neutral category of *non-politeness* may be realized through a typical formula of dissent: "I do not agree"/"I cannot agree with" (Kurzon 2001: 71). As expressing one's viewpoint regarding agreement/disagreement in separate opinions is one of the established moves in this genre, the mere statement of it cannot amount to being impolite. This resonates with Fraser's (1990) conceptualization of politeness as something expected and taken for granted, and impoliteness as a violation of the norm, which makes it noticeable. Studying politeness as social practice, Kádár and Haugh (2013: 66) explain how it "involves evaluations occasioned by social actions and meanings that are recognisable to participants". So, what makes some judicial opinions recognizably impolite to members of judicial community? What Entrikin (2017) indirectly equalled to the linguistic realization of *impoliteness* in Scalia's vitriolic dissents was typically associated with wit and sarcasm (see also Harris 2011), which provided a general derisive reading of the majority's opinion, as well as explicitly denigrating evaluative language.

Based on the above, I conceptualize *impoliteness* as a deviation from the non-polite neutrality or polite mitigation which are structurally expected to be present in separate opinions. Impoliteness occurs when face is threatened or undermined (Brown & Levinson 1987). It is appropriate to mention here the notion of "social harm" (Tedeschi & Felson 1994: 171) lowering the "power or status" of the majority judges. Explicit verbal aggression is not typical of supranational separate opinions. Instead, impoliteness can be associated here with implicatures achieved through irony and sarcasm, because of a mismatch between the outwardly polite formulation and the intended criticism, where

16 See, e.g. Harris 2011 for an overview.

"a polite interpretation is not sustainable [and thus] could end up exacerbating the impoliteness of the message" (Culpeper 2011: 168).

Other markers of impoliteness include deliberately aggressive style and excessively harsh language, frequently ascribed to American judges (Kurzon 2001; Entrikin 2017). In linguistic terms, these issues can be addressed through the concept of *evaluation* (Hunston 2011). Evaluation can be explained as "the broad cover term for the expression of the speaker's or writer's attitude or stance towards, viewpoint on, or feelings about the entities or propositions that he or she is talking about" (Thompson & Hunston 2000: 5). Evaluation in judicial discourse has been the object of a number of studies (Mazzi 2010; Pontrandolfo & Goźdź-Roszkowski 2014; McKeown 2021), but – to the best of my knowledge – no studies so far have applied this notion in combination with politeness theory to the discourse of separate opinions at the ECtHR. As Mazzi (2010: 384) observes, evaluation in judicial writing is closely intertwined with persuasion and argumentation, and the skilful use of evaluation enhances the ability to influence the reader's perspective. However, as problematized above, the line between respectful and disrespectful dissent is a fine one, and the following sections pursue also an applied goal: to highlight the discursive tools routinely employed by legal professionals in crafting their reasoning and to raise awareness among judicial operators of different available strategies that could help "shape their discourse in an arguably 'legally grammatical' way" (Mazzi 2010: 384).

In the absence of any style and content-related provisions, separate opinions at the ECtHR may tap into both creative criticism with some more or less explicit evaluative language (Pontrandolfo & Goźdź-Roszkowski 2014) interspersed with politeness markers (Kurzon 2001) along with other conventional linguistic means of placing distance between the majority and the opinion drafter, which all contribute to what I call here the discourse of dissent. The following sections address the most characteristic markers thereof.

8.6 The (im)politeness continuum in SOC

8.6.1 Non-politeness markers across different opinion types

As previously mentioned, each judicial opinion commences with the addresser's declaration of (mis)alignment with the majority viewpoint (the first move). Commenting on the evaluative function of the couplet *agree/disagree*, Mazzi (2010: 378) defines it as "straightforward". Despite its overt evaluative nature, this statement of agreement or disagreement is, within the confines of generic structure and customary conventions of separate opinions, devoid of inherent politeness or impoliteness; therefore, it is categorized here as non-polite. It is a formulaic performative. As Kecskes (2017: 13) observed, "no act is inherently polite or impolite, but such a condition depends on the context or speech situation", and the speech situation of separate opinions vouches for the expression of disagreement, misalignment and critique of the majority, thus legitimizing the existence of these acts.

Frequently, this (mis)alignment is linguistically realized through specific formulaic expressions (as outlined in Table 8.7).

As Table 8.7 recaps, the same verb can be used in the positive meaning ("I agree with the majority") and in the negative meaning, either by placing some negation markers before it ("I cannot agree with") or by changing the addressers ("I agree with the dissenting judges" rather than with the majority). The negative formula can be hedged, by making the negative part longer ("I am unable to agree") and by de-personalizing the addressees ("We cannot share the conclusion that"). As the language of judicial opinions belongs to the formal register (Kurzon 2001: 64) and legal discourse in general is renowned for its inclination towards nominalization and impersonal constructions (Crystal & Davy 1973; Bhatia 1993), these slight variations do not really impact the enunciation, which remains neutrally non-polite as it merely implements the communicative goal of the opinion – to dissent or to concur – in a formal context of judicial writing for a supranational court. Considerations of general markers of legal discourse apart, it is acknowledged that not mentioning explicitly the majority (judges) and mentioning instead the judgment or its parts can be interpreted as a face-saving strategy, when we deal with dissent.

Similarly, for the second move in separate opinions, i.e. explaining the grounds for its writing, it is natural to find some critique of the majority's reasoning, as in (8).

(8) While we fully agree with the outcome in the instant case, we have serious reservations as to the manner in which the judgment was reasoned. The reasoning reveals, in our view, all the weaknesses and inconsistencies in the approach adopted to date by the Court in Article 8 cases. (*Paradiso and Campanelli v. Italy*, 2015, joint concurring opinion of Judges De Gaetano, Pinto De Albuquerque, Wojtyczek and Dedov)

It is admittedly more difficult to remain in the neutral non-politeness zone when the speech act to be performed is to explain the grounds for divergence, i.e. to criticize implicitly the majority judgment or parts thereof. What makes it relatively neutral is avoiding directly addressing the people responsible for the judgment, as well as avoiding strongly evaluative language. Following Pontrandolfo and Goźdź-Roszkowski (2014: 72), this study adopts "a rather

Table 8.7 Typified non-polite linguistic realizations of the first move across different opinions

Addresser	*Negative*	*Positive*	*Addressees*
I/we	cannot	agree/disagree with voted with/against	the majority the minority/dissenting judges
	am/are unable to	share/subscribe to/follow (the conclusion, the view, etc.) of/in	the (part of the) judgment in X/up to X . . .

reductionist and dualistic sense of evaluation [. . .], according to which evaluation refers to the good or bad dichotomy, disregarding other aspects such as significance, (un)certainty, (un)expectedness, etc." This dualistic outlook is placed against the theory of context-based politeness. It is one thing to talk about "weaknesses and inconsistencies" – which might sound impolite outside of the separate opinion context, but is in fact a neutral explanation of grounds for disagreement within this particular context and community of practice – and it is quite different to call the Court's statutory interpretation "sheer applesauce"[17] (Entrikin 2017: 221 referring to Justice Scalia's rhetoric).

(9) *To our regret, however, we are unable to join the majority* in concluding that no further just satisfaction is to be awarded [. . .]. In our opinion, *the Court should have* awarded compensation in respect of non-pecuniary damage. Moreover, we believe that the costs and expenses *should have* been reimbursed in a more generous way. (Abdi Ibrahim v. Norway, 2021, joint partly dissenting opinion of Judges Lemmens and Motoc)

Example (9) demonstrates another neutral non-politeness marker: the bigram "should have" (note also hedging the disagreement by using both "to our regret" and the adversative "however"). This bigram occurs in 108 out of 236 separate opinions, i.e. 46% of all texts, 238 times (26.4 occurrences per 100,000 words). To the left, it collocates predominantly with "the Court", "the Grand Chamber", "the majority", "the judgment" (or its aspects as "costs and expenses" in (9)). To the right, it collocates with past participles. Grammatically, *should have* followed by a past participle marks the nonfulfillment of an obligation (Quirk et al. 1985: 235). Pragmatically, it functions as a critique of the majority's operation, providing an alternative solution.

Curiously, this marker is more widespread in dissenting and partially dissenting opinions, occurring in 63 out of 130 (48.5%) opinions collectively, as opposed to only 33 out of 75 (44%) in concurring and partially concurring texts.[18] What is crucial, based on the data presented in Table 8.8, is that this marker is present across all types of opinions. Additionally, the concordance analysis demonstrates that it is consistently employed to express criticism of the majority opinion in a neutral manner. General principles of politeness, as elaborated in other contexts, do not apply here due to the genre conventions of separate opinions. Consequently, the utterances containing this bigram in separate opinions are characterized as non-polite: neither polite nor impolite.

17 Note 120 in Entrikin 2017: 221, referring to the case Zuni Pub. Sch. Dist. No. 89 v. Dep't of Educ., 550 U.S. 81, 113 (2007) (Scalia, Thomas & Souter, JJ., & Roberts, C.J., dissenting).

18 It is essential to exercise caution when interpreting these frequency normalization (NF) figures, as they are predictions and may deviate from actual data, especially when the corpus size significantly differs from other subcorpora. This is particularly relevant in the case of partially concurring and, especially, unmarked separate opinions in SOC. In essence, NF values of 53.6 and 48.0 should be considered with care, but the respective ranges do indicate the extensive use of this bigram marker.

Table 8.8 Occurrences of non-polite marker *should have* across different corpora expressed as absolute frequencies (AF), normalized frequencies (NF; normalization base 100,000 word[19]) and simple range.

should have	*Tokens*	*AF*	*NF*	*Range*
SOC	901,458	238	26.4	108/236
Concurring	228,995	52	22.7	28/78
Dissenting	379,348	101	26.6	41/78
partly concurring	22,381	12	53.6	5/7
partly dissenting	153,152	45	29.4	22/52
partly concurring, partly dissenting	113,444	29	25.6	11/16
Separate	4,165	2	48.0	1/3

The following subsections will address the deviations from the non-politeness baseline towards more or less polite discourse of dissent.

8.6.2 *Politeness markers across different opinion types*

When a dissent formula is hedged, or a concurrence formula is boosted, the politeness level of such formulae increases, making it possible to rank such enunciations as pragmatically polite. Brown and Levinson (1987) distinguished between negative and positive politeness strategies. The former aimed at saving the face of the addressee and included such strategies as indirect language, deferential expressions, apologies, hedging, impersonal language, and nominalization. Positive politeness is employed to boost the addressee's sense of self-esteem, in situations of an established familiarity between the communicators, such as judges working in the same court. In addition to employing hedging techniques and efforts to steer clear of conflicts, positive politeness encompasses actions like expressing collegiality, demonstrating solidarity and offering compliments.

As (10) illustrates, the adverb of intensity "wholeheartedly" or the prepositional phrase "without hesitation" in (11) increase convergence with the majority, and represent a clearly positive evaluation of their operation. It is worth noting how (10) is a concurring opinion, while (11) is a dissenting one. Example (10) uses "clarify" instead of any disagreement verb (note also how it reflects Reason 1 behind the creation of concurring opinions in Table 8.6: clarification and emphasis), hedging it by "respectfully" to mitigate divergence from the Court's reasoning, thus increasing the general level of politeness.

Remarkably, there are 7 instances of "disagree" per 100,000 words in concurring opinions, and 69% of them are hedged by "respectfully", against 11 instances of "disagree" per 100,000 words in dissenting opinions with 36% of them collocating with "respectfully", see (12). This shows that the bigram

19 As the number of words in the subcorpora of different opinion types vary, whenever a comparative perspective is adopted, relative frequencies are reported, i.e. not the actual number of instances but the number of instances normalized to 100,000 words.

"respectfully disagree" is part of the discourse of polite dissent/misalignment and is more typical of concurring opinions (69% of all "disagree" collocates) than of dissenting opinions (36%).

(10) *We wholeheartedly agree* with the majority's finding that Article 3 has been violated in this case. We would, however, *respectfully clarify* the reasoning by which we arrive at this conclusion. (*Svinarenko and Slyadnev v. Russia*, GC, 2014, Joint concurring opinion of Judges Nicolaou and Keller)

(11) *I can without hesitation agree with the judgment*, up to and including the first sentence of paragraph 40, and *with the majority's conclusion* [. . .]. *However, in my view* the Grand Chamber *should have continued* the examination of the application [. . .]. (*V. M and Others v. Belgium*, 2016, Dissenting opinion of Judge Ranzoni, joined by Judges López Guerra, Sicilianos and Lemmens, translation)

(12) I *respectfully disagree* with the majority in their finding that there has been no violation of Article 10 in this case. *I take this position with some unease*. (*Sanchez v. France*, 2023, GC, Dissenting opinion of Judge Bošnjak)

(13) *It is not so easy for me to agree* with the conclusion of the Court in paragraph 155 of the judgment that [. . .]. (*Albert and Others v. Hungary*, GC, 2020, concurring opinion of Judge Dedov)

As (12) illustrates, dissent can be mitigated by "respectfully", to which a further personal note is added. It signals the dissenting judge's reluctance to dissent, reminiscent of the early US Supreme Court dissents, discussed in 8.5. Example (13) manifests a similarly reluctant flavour: here a hedged agreement (in italics) functions pragmatically as disagreement. In fact, Judge Dedov criticizes the majority, despite marking his opinion as concurring. Out of 72 instances of the verb "agree" to express the judges' position[20] in concurring opinions, 9 (12.5%) were used to express dissent with the majority, blurring the line between concurrence and dissent.

Other positive politeness strategies include mentioning explicitly the direct addressees, either by their names (see examples (2)–(3) and (15)) or by using the terms of deference, such as "esteemed" or "learned" colleagues, etc., see (14) and (15).

(14) Although we, like all *our esteemed colleagues*, *voted for* a finding of a violation of Article 4 of Protocol No. 7, *we cannot subscribe* to *some of the reasoning* set out in the judgment, and in particular paragraphs 110 et seq. thereof. (*Mihalache v. Romania*, GC, 2019, Joint concurring

20 Instances of the verb "agree" that do not refer to the addressing judge's position were excluded from the analysis.

opinion of Judges Raimondi, Nussberger, Sicilianos, Spano, Yudkivska, Motoc And Ravarani, translation)

(15) Having had *the benefit of reading Judge Sajó's opinion*, I must state that I share some of *my learned colleague's* thoughts in this respect, especially on Hungarian constitutional case-law and the incompatibility of the Supreme Court decision with that case-law. (*Károly Nagy v. Hungary*, GC, 2017, Dissenting opinion of Judge Pinto de Albuquerque)

Interestingly, the term "colleague", modified or not, is used more frequently in concurring opinions (10 instances per 100,000 words) than in dissenting opinions (4.2 instances per 100,000 words), which shows that this politeness strategy is more typical of concurring opinions.

The "respectful" rhetoric is intertwined with mentions of regret, see (16)–(18). Kurzon (2001: 69) remarks on how dissent may be "clothed in words of regret, to tone down the disagreement", which is quite typical of the discourse of separate opinions.

(16) *We regret* that the majority rejects these issues simply on the ground that the applicant's situation is not similar enough to that of cissexuals [. . .]. (Hamalainen v. Finland, 2014, joint dissenting opinion of Judges Sajó, Keller and Lemmens §19)

(17) *We regret* that the reasoning refrained from clarifying these notions. (*Paradiso and Campanelli v. Italy*, 2017, joint concurring opinion of Judges De Gaetano, Pinto De Albuquerque, Wojtyczek and Dedov, §5)

(18) *It is with regret that I find myself in deep disagreement with* the Grand Chamber judgment in the present case and cannot subscribe to either the reasoning or the conclusions of the majority for several reasons. (*Chiragov and Others v. Armenia*, 2015, dissenting opinion of Judge Gyulumyan)

Instead of a more straightforward statement that the majority is wrong, "which to an extent threatens the addressee's face, the addresser mitigates his disagreement by virtually apologizing ('I regret') for opposing his colleague on the bench" (Kurzon 2001: 69). A version of a more straightforward performative with a first-person deixis is found in (18), which instead hedges the disagreement with two prepositional phrases: "with regret" and "in deep disagreement with".

While the rhetoric of regret is widespread across all opinion types (see Table 8.9), it seems to be more prominent in dissenting and partly dissenting opinions, where the criticism is inherently harder by the very label "dissent" and requires more mitigation to appear polite. Kurzon (2001: 81) posits that mitigating disagreement with *regret* is more typical of English judges than of their American colleagues. Similarly, Entrikin (2017) defines Scalia's legacy *regrettable*, but he does not report on the use of this politeness marker in Scalia's rhetoric.

Table 8.9 Frequencies of *regret* and *regrettably* across the subcorpora, normalized to 100,000 words.

Opinion types	*Regret*	*Regrettably*
Concurring	6	4
Dissenting	8	2
partly concurring	0	5
partly dissenting	14	3
partly concurring, partly dissenting	6	0

Other ways of mitigating disagreement include narrowing it down to the addresser's personal standpoint. It is emblematically expressed by using the first person pronoun followed by mental verbs ("we think", "I believe", etc., see (20)) and by using the opinion expressions ("in my view", "in my humble opinion", etc.), see (19).

(19) The opinion expressed by the Court in the current case, however, is a new and – *in my opinion* – regrettable tendency. (*Chiragov and Others v. Armenia*, 2015, dissenting opinion of Judge Gyulumyan)

(20) *For good or ill, and I believe for ill more than for good*, with the present judgment the *Strasbourg Court has just opened the gates for an electronic "Big Brother"* in Europe. *If* this is the new normal that *my learned colleagues* in the majority want for Europe, I cannot join them, and *this I say with a disenchanted heart*, with the same consternation as that exuding from Gregorio Allegri's *Miserere mei, Deus.* (*Big Brother v. the United Kingdom*, 2021, partly concurring and partly dissenting opinion of Judge Pinto de Albuquerque)

Examples (19) and (20) feature also the so-called "embedded evaluation", i.e. "items of intrinsically favourable evaluation which are found embedded in expressions of overall unfavourability" (Partington et al. 2013: 61–62). In (19) the judge inserts a hedge "in my opinion" in a negative evaluation of the Court's "new and regrettable" policy. In (20), although Judge Pinto de Albuquerque calls his colleagues "learned" and hedges his negative assessment with "I believe", his overall evaluation is clearly negative, yet not impolite. This shows the complexity of balancing negative evaluation with politeness expectations. By mitigating criticism, judges implement the so-called "positive politeness" (Brown & Levinson 1987), i.e. making efforts to express collegiality and show appreciation for the addressees of their critique.

Table 8.10 gathers normalized frequencies of personal opinion expressions across the subcorpora. It was created using "in my" and "in our" as search parameters in #LancsBox 6.0 (Brezina et al. 2021), and excluding instances where the search expression did not refer to personal views (e.g. "in our times") or where it referred to a document ("in my separate opinion"). The vast majority of immediate collocates to the right were "view" and "opinion". Sometimes

Table 8.10 The use of "in my/our" followed by personal standpoint expressions (view, opinion, etc.) as a hedge across the subcorpora.

Type of opinion	*In my *, NF*	*In our *, NF*
Concurring	28	13
Dissenting	28	20
Partly concurring	27	27
Partly dissenting	27	19
Partly concurring, partly dissenting	25	34
Separate	0	0

these were premodified by "humble" or "respectful" to increase the level of politeness; however, these instances were insignificant frequency-wise. These hedges are used comparably across all opinion types, with slight variation in "in my" and "in our" explained by the authorship distribution of opinions between single-authored and multi-authored texts. Other ways of expressing evaluation included the already discussed *it v-link ADJ that* and *it v-link ADJ to-inf* patterns (Goźdź-Roszkowski 2024; see 7.5), which were used more frequently in separate opinions (NF = 190) than in judgments (NF in RiFT = 95, see Chapter 7) and collocated with a wider range of evaluative adjectives. It is important to remember that the use of evaluation is indicative of legal reasoning and does not amount to politeness or impoliteness on its own.

8.6.3 Impoliteness markers across different opinion types

While judges are expected to maintain a neutral and objective tone, and a degree of evaluation is to be expected in this discourse community, instances of sarcasm, ridicule or overly emotional language can be perceived as impolite and unprofessional, or a "regrettable legacy" in Entrikin's (2017) words. And yet, within the judicial community it is the strong-worded opinions that frequently "are still ringing in our ears" (Paulus 2019: 2). "Behaviours and expressions considered impolite are more noticed and discussed than politeness" (Watts 2003: 5). The close reading of SOC revealed that most judges follow the non-polite or polite approach in formulating their divergence with the majority. Entrikin (2017) defined Scalia's dissents disrespectful on account of the colourful wording the Justice chose to express his opinions. Yet where can we draw the line between linguistically expressive or creative and impolite or disrespectful?

Kurzon (2001), in probably the only work dealing with politeness in judicial opinions, does not provide a clear classification of what counts as impolite, also because his work problematizes the additional aspect of cultural embeddedness (American vs. English norms) besides the community of practice, and the cross-cultural dimension of impoliteness with different lexicalization strategies is a well-established fact (Kecskes 2013). The ECtHR is a *European* court, so do pan-European norms of judicial politeness apply or even exist?

Research on intercultural (im)politeness for users of English as a lingua franca is an "almost unchartered territory" (Kecskes 2017: 8). The Court's discourse community is diverse, multilingual and multicultural, and the judges working there may have been exposed in the course of their careers to multiple legal cultures, including the American one. To wit, it is challenging to come up with a clearcut, on-the-shelf definition of what should count as pragmatically impolite in separate judicial opinions at the ECtHR. Drawing on Fraser (1990), who conceptualized impoliteness as a deviation from the norm, the norm being the established baseline of non-politeness and politeness, there are few cases of potential impoliteness in SOC.

(21) In this regard the majority ***attempts*** to demonstrate (***in our view, and with all due respect, in a strained way***) that a positive obligation to protect, and prevent the ill-treatment of, children at school through an appropriate framework of regulations encouraging complaints was clearly established under the Convention in 1973. (*O'Keefe v. Ireland*, 2014, joint partly dissenting opinion of Judges Zupančič, Gyulumyan, Kalaydjieva, De Gaetano and Wojtyczek)

(22) I cannot subscribe to this ***uninspiring judgment***. [. . .] For ***reasons that remain in the realm of the unknown***, the majority of the Grand Chamber have ***chosen*** to pursue neither of these avenues.

Instead, the most difficult decisions are taken by ***cutting corners*** in order to arrive at ***a foregone conclusion***. (*Karoly Nagy v. Hungary*, 2017, dissenting opinion of Judge Pinto de Albuquerque, §1–2)

If we compare (21) and (22), we notice that both express disagreement with the majority, but they differ in politeness. In (21) the dissenting judges use the conventionalized politeness formula to mitigate their criticism, and this is an expected linguistic behaviour for separate opinions. Trying to establish whether impoliteness can be conventionalized, Culpeper (2011: 175) discussed the pattern ***I hate to be rude, but*** and ***no offence, but***, which bears a striking pragmatic resemblance to ***with all due respect*** in (21). These phrases are conventional politeness markers, but nonetheless they introduce a negative evaluation afterwards, paying a "blatantly superficial lip-service [. . .] to politeness" (Culpeper 2011: 176) and constituting the so-called mixed message devices. ***With respect to*** has been analysed by Harris (2001) in the legal field, specifically in British Parliamentary debates. Harris (2001: 403) concluded that this pattern, despite its superficial politeness tended to introduce "deliberate threats to the hearer's positive face, i.e. acts which are clearly intended to be impolite". Yet, healthy criticism in separate opinions is sanctioned, and the degree of impoliteness depends on the load of the following evaluative lexis. "Strained" in (21) is clearly negative, but not necessarily impolite as it still can be perceived as expressing solidarity with the majority struggling to find a compromise.

Example (22), next to conventionalized non-politeness formula of dissent "I cannot subscribe to this judgment", features pragmatically loaded lexis with clear negative evaluation, which sways it closer to the impoliteness pole. The adjective "uninspiring" was not necessary to convey the generic move of disagreement, hence it is not sanctioned by the genre. The judge goes on sarcastically to attack the reasoning of the judgment in a creative way, implicitly accusing the judges of lacking diligence in their work as they "chose to pursue" (intentionally) a certain avenue, "cut corners" and left their reasoning "in the realm of unknown" to arrive at a "foregone conclusion". Whereas none of the above is scandalous or offensive, the overall rhetorical bite of the paragraph is impolite on account of its poetic deviations from the norm.

(23) *The measure of confusion* of the majority's reasoning can be perceived in the way *they mix law and facts and equate sentencing and enforcement of penalties*, in the *pivotal* paragraph 207 of the judgment. [. . .]

There is only one, *very unsatisfactory justification* for the "rarity argument" to be used here by the majority: they know that they are entering uncharted, dangerous territory in paragraph 207 and want as far as possible to limit the scope of the proposed interpretation and the ensuing collateral damage caused to the basic foundational principles of modern criminal law and the principle of legality [. . .]. The limited scope of applicability of the interpretation proposed in paragraph 207 does not detract from the fact that it constitutes *a heresy* in criminal law. (*Ilnseher v. Germany*, dissenting opinion of Judge Pinto De Albuquerque, joined by Judge Dedov §107)

In (23), the language and tone used by Judge Pinto de Albuquerque could be potentially construed not only as dissenting, but also as sarcastic. He begins by criticizing the majority for their "confusion", which, on the surface, may appear as a milder way of suggesting they are wrong. Defining paragraph 207 of the judgment as "pivotal" represents a clear case of mismatching (Culpeper 2011: 168) between the surface organization of the phrase and its context-enabled interpretation, which excludes interpreting "pivotal" as a positive evaluation. As the passage unfolds, the judge intensifies his critique, characterizing the majority's argument as a "very unsatisfactory justification" and eventually labelling it "a heresy in criminal law". This progression from apparent politeness to increasingly negative evaluation reflects the use of sarcasm.

Haiman (1998: 20) defines sarcasm as "overt irony intentionally used by the speaker as a form of verbal aggression", drawing the line between irony and sarcasm in the intentionality of the latter as opposed to the fact that irony can be unintentional and unconscious. Intentionality is frequently mentioned among factors contributing to impoliteness. For Culpeper (2005: 38) impoliteness occurs when "(1) the speaker communicates face-attack intentionally, or (2) the hearer perceives and/or constructs behaviour as intentionally face-attacking, or a combination of (1) and (2)". By building up the legal argument in such a way as to partially ridicule the opposition (a face-threatening act), while using an absolutely reasonable amount of negatively evaluated lexis, the sarcastic effect is created, which leads to the perception of impoliteness. Frequently, besides semantically negative lexis, the sarcastic effect is achieved also through the use of metaphors and similes in the culminating points, as (24) illustrates (compare it with Scalia's "sheer applesauce").

(24) The majority now hold that it is sufficient for all the elements of the offence to be made out, thus making it possible for a criminal court to find a person "liable" even if the criminal proceedings are discontinued because of the application of a statute of limitations (see paragraph 261 of the judgment). *This is, for us, a plaster on a wooden leg.* It remains to be seen whether this adaptation of the Court's case-law will be sufficient to allow the Italian judiciary to take effective action against unlawful site development. (*G.I.E.M. S.r.l. and Others v. Italy*, 2018, joint partly dissenting, partly concurring opinion of Judges Spano and Lemmens)

The examples reported in this subsection demonstrate how sarcasm can be subtly infused into legal arguments, exploiting mismatches and mixed message devices, potentially leading to a perception of impoliteness.

8.7 Conclusions

Chapter 8 emerged from my reflections on the use of norms and conventions in judicial prose, serving as the chapter's *fil rouge*. The crystallized norms and conventions of judgments clash with the personal and idiosyncratic style of separate opinions, due to their independent nature and different legal status. Despite the challenges of capturing and schematizing individuality, separate opinions appeared as a different genre, distinct from a judgment.

The very existence of separate opinions in the ECtHR represents another type of convention, promoting independent judicial prose that contributes to jurisprudence. Corpus-adduced evidence highlighted that separate opinions in the ECtHR are as much about concurrence – and hence voicing individual lines of judicial reasoning – as they are about dissent. However, their nomenclature must be approached with caution, as what is labelled concurrent may essentially be dissenting, not to mention the variety of mixed types.

Conventions and norms also resurfaced when examining the language of separate opinions. Their generic makeup draws on prior contextual experiences of judges and their judicial temperaments (White & Boussiakou 2009), resulting in more or less stable repertoires. These were particularly evident from a pragmatic standpoint, as I examined the spectrum of politeness/impoliteness conventions used to distance the "separatist" judge from the majority.

As Kecskes (2017) observed, in the socio-cognitive approach, conventions, norms and expectations deriving from a writer's previous experience are as important as immediate evaluation. Moreover, "[p]rior experience with politeness and impoliteness expressions is especially important for non-native speakers in intercultural communication" (Kecskes 2017: 18), which is a typical linguistic milieu for supranational courts. Judges drafting separate opinions in one of the court's official languages – statistically rarely their mother tongue – rely on a repertoire of conventionalized politeness/impoliteness patterns borrowed from English- (or French-)speaking judicial contexts or imported from their native languages. While politeness formulae, such as hedges, the rhetoric of regret and respect, deferential mentions of the majority or minority colleagues, were consonant, the other end of the continuum was more problematic to trace.

Separate opinions sanction healthy criticism because of their communicative goal: to place distance between the opinion writer and the majority, explaining reasons for doing so. Hence, not every face-threatening act amounts to impoliteness. Building on Kurzon's (2001) taxonomy, I overview patterns expressing politeness, neutral non-politeness and impoliteness. In a context where criticism is sanctioned, there is no watertight distinction between what is non-polite because it is expected in a given professional practice and what is impolite because it oversteps the boundaries of generic conventions. The latter seems to coincide with the use of sarcasm coupled with negative evaluation and mixed message devices, which could be perceived as "mock politeness" when they coexist with sarcasm. Judicial writers may have to balance the desire of writing a memorable opinion with considerations of impoliteness, or at least make a linguistically informed choice.

Part IV

The life of cases beyond and after the ECtHR

9 Beyond case-law

Disseminating convention-related knowledge

9.1 Introduction

The ECtHR judge and former president Robert Spano (2018: 489, original emphasis) stated,

> the effective implementation of human rights requires a *culture of human rights* at all levels of government as well as in society in general. Here, drawing on literature in the field of sociology of human rights, I am referring to the claim that for human rights to have social meaning, they must become institutionalised socially and become embedded in peoples' mindsets as well as in the day-to-day workings of societal institutions such as the judiciary, the legislature, the schooling and healthcare systems, and the family.

How can a culture of human rights permeate peoples' mindset and the daily operation of our societies? The answer may be both simple and complex. Not only has the digitalization of law transformed the circulation of information about human rights, it has also revolutionized the accessibility of human rights knowledge to laypeople, effectively contributing to the propagation of a human rights culture.

In the past, legal texts were often confined to libraries, court archives and communities of legal professionals. The lack of physical accessibility added to the overall challenges of the general public in understanding legal discourse. Legal English is notorious for its conceptual, lexical and syntactic complexity, observed both by lawyers (see, e.g. the pivotal work by Mellinkoff 1963: 11–29) and linguists alike (Crystal & Davy 1973; Maley 1994; Mattila 2013), as well as by scholars who combine both professional outlooks (Tiersma 1999, 2015).[1] In practical terms, the convoluted nature of legal discourse hindered the general public's full understanding of their rights and legal protections. These attested difficulties of the conventional discursive practices within the

1 For an overview of Legal English features, see Nikitina 2018a.

DOI: 10.4324/9781003434788-13

legal profession led to the rise of various plain language movements, whose aim was to eradicate "legalese" (see 4.6).

From a more general perspective, the Internet has democratized access to legal information under what has been defined as the ***digital (r)evolution of legal discourse*** (Anesa & Engberg 2023). As Bondi (2015: 7) comments,

> Knowledge can no longer be hemmed in by neatly-packed and restricted communicative products: today's globalized and digital environment has increasingly destructured the élitarian fences of knowledge communication and knowledge communication is gaining centrality in a plurality of contexts, from the strictly specialized ones to the more general lay milieus.

Today, most international courts and many domestic ones render their case-law accessible online enabling laypeople from any country with Internet access to read and download court rulings free of charge. However, the question remains: how comprehensible are such texts to a layperson? Whereas the physical barriers of accessibility have been abated, at least in the developed countries, the contents of legal texts have not yet completely shed user-unfriendly lexicogrammar or syntax that might impinge on the public's understanding of human rights issues.

Communication to vaster audiences involves overcoming inter- and intra-linguistic barriers of knowledge asymmetry. Section 9.2 presents the theoretical framework of knowledge communication and dissemination, focussing specifically on the phenomenon of popularization, i.e. transformation of specialized knowledge for lay audiences. In order to tackle knowledge asymmetry (outlined in 9.2), inherent in the communication from specialists to non-specialists, some international organizations set up digital platforms with resources that provide guidance on navigating the legal system in question. Section 9.3 details the ECtHR initiatives promoting the knowledge on the Convention and human rights case-law, ranging from translation into non-official languages (9.3.1) to the operation of the Press Service (9.3.2). Often, knowledge dissemination, understood here as "the spread of knowledge within and across settings, with the expectation that the knowledge will be used conceptually, as learning, enlightenment, or the acquisition of new perspectives, attitudes and behaviours" (Salvi & Bowker 2015: 11), is accompanied by certain strategies of knowledge transformation that cater for different background information of a variety of stakeholders in the modern digital domain, known as popularization practices (Salvi & Bowker 2015; Garzone 2020; Anesa & Kulbicki 2022). Within the ECtHR system of genres, a strategically important genre in this regard is the institutional legal press release, addressed in 9.4. Subsection 9.4.2 explains the criteria of newsworthiness, and subsection 9.4.3 addresses the general methodological considerations of press releases functioning as vehicles of legal knowledge. Subsections 9.4.4 and 9.4.5 reflect on their specificities in the ECtHR context using an ad hoc corpus of press releases overviewing Grand Chamber judgments.

9.2 Knowledge asymmetry, specialized communication and popularization

To conceptualize the communication of legal knowledge across multiple stakeholders involved in the mechanism of human rights protection, Cloître and Shinn's (1985) model may offer a useful framework. While undoubtedly dated, this model remains a functional tool for describing, categorizing and differentiating various types of texts, particularly focusing on their accessibility and specialization levels.

Building on this model[2] and applying the Critical Genre Analysis (Bhatia 2015, 2017) perspective, I propose to identify six distinct levels of specialized exposition.

1 *Monodisciplinary intra-specialist exposition* involves communication from one legal specialist to another with the same legal specialism and within the same field. In the ECtHR context this level applies to communication among lawyers specializing in human rights and the European Convention protection mechanisms. By virtue of sharing the same professional disciplinary culture and being exposed to the same discursive practices, specialists coming from the same branches of law may use highly technical and specialized language, which might render their communication inaccessible to out-group members. In the system of genres of the ECtHR, judgments and decisions, as well as separate opinions, when these are read by other judges and lawyers representing clients before this supranational court, would fall under this category.
2 *Monodisciplinary inter-specialist exposition*[3] involves communication from one legal specialist to another within the general discipline of law, but having different legal specialties or operating in different branches of law. While many fundamental legal concepts will be shared (e.g. the difference between material and procedural law, the way legal sources are interpreted), other, field-specific, concepts may be new. For example, a lawyer specializing in family law in domestic settings may not necessarily be familiar with the concepts *subsidiarity* or *margin of appreciation*, used in the ECtHR context (see 2.4). When lawyers coming from different jurisdictions or legal domains are exposed to the procedural genres of the ECtHR, this communication amounts to monodisciplinary inter-specialist exposition.
3 *Interdisciplinary exposition* entails specialists communicating across different fields. For example, a lawyer may communicate with a medical practitioner or a bioethicist. Whereas both have advanced degrees in their respective

2 Originally, Cloître and Shinn's 1985 model focussed on scientific exposition and identified four levels of scientific exposition: (1) intra-specialist (among the specialists in the same field); (2) inter-specialist (among specialists coming from different fields); (3) pedagogical (from specialist to non-specialist) and (4) popular (targeting the widest possible audience).

3 Level 1 (monodisciplinary intra-specialist exposition) and Level 2 (monodisciplinary inter-specialist exposition) were originally subsumed under "intra-specialist" exposition in Cloître and Shinn (1985).

disciplines, they typically will not share methodological approaches or domain-specific terminology. As the ECtHR deals with complex societal and bioethical issues, sometimes a degree of interdisciplinary exposition is ingrained in its procedural genres. For instance, Nikitina (2019a, 2019b) outlines a degree of cross-fertilization between legal and bioethical terminology in the ECtHR case-law, with bioethical notions entextualized into the legal matrix of judgments without altering the generic structure of the latter.

4 *Didactic/pedagogical exposition* focuses on conveying specialized knowledge from a specialist to a non-specialist, requiring a more pedagogical approach to make complex concepts understandable. This is a usual situation for a university context, where lecturers address a public of future specialists. They would typically expose their students to professional and discursive practices of a given discipline and domain, but will provide explanations for learning purposes. This type of exposition is hybrid: it features both highly specialized terminology and less complex explanations. Pedagogical exposition, which aims to make complex concepts understandable to non-specialists, can be applied in various contexts beyond the university setting. For example, in the corporate world, employees often need to acquire specialized knowledge or skills relevant to their job roles. In this context, pedagogical exposition can be used to ensure that employees can grasp and apply these specialized concepts effectively.

5 *Popularized exposition* aims to reach the widest possible audience with simplified language and explanations, distilling complex notions into meaningful information that is made accessible to the general public. Exposition from specialists to non-specialists does not necessarily pursue didactic goals, but rather raises public awareness of a given specialized concept or phenomenon, be it scientific or legal literacy. Legal literacy and exposure to popularized exposition of human rights issues are essential for individual empowerment, access to justice, the prevention of abuses, citizen engagement, social change, conflict resolution and promoting a sense of global responsibility and empathy. The discursive and conceptual transformation that specialized knowledge undergoes in this process is known as ***popularization***. Whenever knowledge is transformed and recontextualized on the "specialized-lay" continuum (Calsamiglia & van Dijk 2004: 370) addressing the vastest possible non-specialized audience (Gotti 2014: 16), it is referred to as popularized exposition. In the ECtHR context, press releases and other genres pertaining to media communication by the Press Office (see 9.3) fall under this category. Legal blogs could also be included in this category if they are aimed at a vaster public.

6 *Popularized intergenerational exposition* is similar to popularized exposition, but it takes into account popularization to younger audiences. Similarly to Level 5, i.e. popularized exposition to unspecified adult audiences, it encompasses a set of discursive practices that enhance children's understanding of specialized knowledge involving "'mediation' between experts and

non-experts having a different stage of cognitive development" (Diani & Sezzi 2019: 203). While there is a growing body of research dedicated to popularizing legal knowledge to children (see Diani 2018; Diani & Sezzi 2019), it is worth noting that, to the best of my knowledge, none of these studies have specifically addressed the discourse of human rights for children. This gap in the literature underscores the need for further exploration and development of effective communication strategies to impart human rights concepts to younger generations.

From a linguistic standpoint, the exploration of specialized communication across various levels of exposition can be traced back to the 1980s. Since then the field has witnessed significant growth generating journal special editions, monographs (e.g. Garzone 2020), and edited collections (e.g. Bongo & Caliendo 2014; Salvi & Bowker 2015).

Whereas in previous chapters, the first two (and potentially three) levels of exposition were addressed, Chapter 9 looks predominantly at the discursive practices aimed at reducing knowledge asymmetry and promoting the Convention-related knowledge dissemination, hence Level 5 takes on a particularly prominent role, discussed in the following subsections.

9.2.1 ***Popularization of law***

Earlier studies on popularization, characterized by the so-called culturally dominant view, primarily focused on translating specialist knowledge into a format accessible to non-specialist audiences, often in a one-way manner, simplifying it for laymen who were presumed to be ignorant and divided from the professional community by a nearly unsurmountable knowledge gap. Later research shifted away from this unidirectional and polarized approach and introduced a more interactive perspective on popularization. This perspective emphasized the active role of the public in engaging with and processing knowledge, making popularization a two-way street of information exchange. Modern studies on popularization (Garzone 2020) emphasize re-contextualization of specialist knowledge (see also Engberg 2020 on knowledge communication). This process involves complex linguistic and discursive adaptation to suit the interests and backgrounds of the audience. Today the emphasis is placed "on the ways language shapes conceptualization and the co-construction of epistemological frameworks for specific modalities, audiences and interactions" (Salvi & Bowker 2015: 13).

One of the most famous definitions of popularization was provided by Calsamiglia and van Dijk (2004: 371) in their seminal work that outlined the tenets of this line of research:

> Popularization is a social process consisting of a large class of discursive-semiotic practices, involving many types of mass media, books, the internet, exhibitions and other genres of communicative

events, aiming to communicate lay versions of scientific knowledge, as well as opinions and ideologies of scholars, among the public at large.

Most recent studies on popularization have revolved around the popularization of science through mass media (Garzone 2020; Nikitina 2019a) following the new developments of science in a variety of domains, ranging from physics to genetics. Legal science is not an exception: a substantial body of modern research is devoted to the dissemination of legal knowledge (Engberg 2020; Anesa & Engberg 2023), driven by the overarching goal of enhancing the legal consciousness of citizens, if not their legal acumen.

The popularization of law is not a novel concept, as historical records and texts from various civilizations demonstrate the existence of efforts to make legal principles and regulations accessible to the general public dating back centuries. Throughout history, societies have recognized the significance of ensuring that legal knowledge is comprehensible and readily available to promote a more informed and engaged citizenry. As early as in 1756, Blackstone defined the laws and constitution of England as "a species of *knowledge*, in which the gentlemen of England have been more *remarkably deficient* than those of all Europe besides" (1756: 4, quoted in Cairns 1942: 562, emphasis added), aiming to resolve knowledge deficit with his famous *Commentaries*. Somewhat later, in 1942, Cairns problematized the idea of popularizing law as opposed to the popularization of science: "Legal popularization is without the aid of two characteristics that mark the current attempts to popularize science: novelty and intellectual gratification" (Cairns 1942: 562). Cairns' criticism predates the arrival of mass media and the Internet, with their vast potential of knowledge dissemination, enabling any user to self-educate or self-illude. Discussions of the popularization of law developed along with criticism of legal discourse's obscure nature, and were frequently framed in terms of the need to increase legal literacy (Robertson 1982). These legal studies used the concept of popularization in a relatively general way. Here, the term *popularization* will be used in a linguistically oriented way, as a set of discursive strategies aimed at increasing the accessibility of legal information to wider public.

9.2.2 Popularization mechanisms

Given the inherent complexity of legal discourse, it becomes imperative for the process of popularization to involve deliberate efforts on the part of the writer. The aim is to convey facts and concepts in a manner that remains engaging and comprehensible to a broad readership, including individuals without any specialized background in law. To achieve this objective, legal popularizers must use linguistic and discursive strategies that render specialized legal knowledge accessible to readers who possess minimal or no domain-specific knowledge. In essence, popularizing discourse aims to bridge this knowledge gap.

Garzone (2020: 158) explains popularization mechanisms as follows:

> If one compares popularizing discourse with specialized communication it becomes obvious that the semiotic coordinates change radically. The basic difference regards the participation framework: in popularization, communication participants are specialized journalists and/or popularizers on the one side (only rarely do scientists materially take care of writing for the general public) and non-specialized readers on the other.
>
> This involves specific relations of power between writers and addressees, and a gap between them in terms of pre-existing knowledge, beliefs and shared values.
>
> (Garzone 2020: 158)

By addressing the existing knowledge asymmetry (Engberg 2020), popularizers carry out the process of *recontextualization*. As the term suggests, this process involves extracting information and knowledge from one context or domain (such as that of a supranational court or human rights) and subsequently repositioning it in a different context (for example, that of a digital ecosystem with a variety of stakeholders). As Salvi and Bowker (2015: 2013) observe, recontextualization shows how "discourse is re-shaped and re-written for changing recipients with different purposes, and may reflect popularization or simplification of expert knowledge, or, on the other hand, switches between discourse communities, domains or fields". In other words, recontextualization underlines the dynamic nature of discourse as it adapts to cater to diverse audiences and contexts. Calsamiglia and van Dijk (2004: 372) posit, in fact, that "popularization discourse must always adapt to the appropriateness conditions and other constraints of the media and communicative events, e.g. those of the daily press or specialised magazines, in which they appear".

Recontextualization is frequently used interchangeably with the notion of *entextualization*. Originally introduced in anthropology, the latter is used in modern studies on popularization (Garzone 2020; Nikitina 2019c) to describe the extraction of meaning from one discourse and its subsequent incorporation into another through a process involving de-centering and re-centering of knowledge in different contexts. This transformation naturally includes changes in the reliance on authoritative sources, shifts in reference, and shifts in indexical frames, among other aspects (Garzone 2020: 172). It can involve quoting, paraphrasing or reusing linguistic elements (such as words, phrases or discourse) to convey a different meaning or to adapt the communication to a new audience or purpose. In general, *entextualization* or *recontextualization* are applied in linguistics to understand how language is flexible and adaptable, allowing speakers and writers to convey ideas in various contexts and for different communicative goals, or to re-use or rework the previous *textualizations*.

In legal scholarship, *textualization* stands for the transformation of legal norms into written texts, "writing down the law in an authoritative way"

(Tiersma 2007: 1188), while in linguistics, recontextualization transforms linguistic elements by placing them in new communicative contexts. Legal scholars often analyse the textualization process, examining how legal norms and principles are articulated, codified and modified through written legal texts, raising the question as to how close a given interpretation should be to the written text, which can be especially problematic for common law systems with their tradition of orality (Tiersma 2007: 1189). While *textualization* and *recontextualization/entextualization* have different primary uses in their respective fields, they share the transformation of content, as both language and legal norms are not static but are subject to adaptation and reinterpretation.

Legal scholars explore how recontextualization of legal texts occurs when legal precedents or statutes are applied to new cases or situations (e.g. the "living instrument" doctrine). Linguists study how legal documents are constructed and how language originally textualized in one domain is adapted – and recontextualized – in a different field, to which the digitalization of communication should be also added.

Popularization implies a degree of knowledge migration or transfer. As Garzone (2020: 172) observes,

> Recourse to the notion of entextualization enables the researcher to reconstruct the "natural history of texts" (borrowing the title of Silverstein and Urban's 1996 book), seeing them as the last stage of trajectories (Catenaccio et al. 2011) where other texts opposition on which the current textualization relies one way or another.

Tracing the path or trajectory of texts is particularly pertinent to popularizing content, as it often emerges through the assemblage, compilation and synthesis of elements from both content and form drawn from previous or concurrent textualizations.

9.2.3 Popularization strategies

The conventional approach to linguistically and discursively analysing popularizing discourse is rooted in Calsamiglia and van Dijk's 2004 framework. Their influential model serves as a cornerstone in the majority of popularization studies, and is a fundamental aspect covered in specialized communication manuals that adopt the perspective of popularization and Discourse Analysis, as illustrated by Garzone in 2020.

Calsamiglia and van Dijk (2004: 372) delineate five popularization strategies that elucidate specialized concepts, also recognized as popularization techniques found "on the surface of discourse" (Garzone 2020: 162–165).

a) *Denomination,* or *designation*, introduces new terms with specific meanings. In the legal context, it is frequent to place such specific denominations in inverted commas. These can be preceded by such markers as "called", "known as", "meaning", "so-called", and "in other words", see the parts in italics in example (1).

(1) Its activities include preparing tax returns on behalf of its clients and requesting advance tax rulings (*"ATAs"*) from the tax authorities. These rulings, *also known as "advance tax agreements", "tax rulings" or "tax rescripts"* concern the application of tax legislation to future transactions. (GCPR, *Halet v. Luxemburg*, 2023)[4]

b) *Definition* provides an explanation/description of specialized terms. In example (1) the underlined part corresponds to the functional definition that explains the essence of the denomination "tax rulings". Example (2), similarly, defines the multiword term "relinquished jurisdiction", but uses a footnote for the purposes of extensive explanation. It is somewhat difficult to distinguish between definition and explanation in this context, as there are multiple types of definitions[5] identified in the literature. For the purposes of this study, these two strategies are treated as a macro-category.

(2) On 28 January 2014 the Chamber to which the case had been assigned *relinquished jurisdiction* in favour of the Grand Chamber[3].

Under Article 30 of the European Convention on Human Rights, where a case pending before a Chamber raises a serious question affecting the interpretation of the Convention or the Protocols thereto, or where the resolution of a question before the Chamber might have a result inconsistent with a judgment previously delivered by the Court, the Chamber may, at any time before it has rendered its judgment, relinquish jurisdiction in favour of the Grand Chamber, unless one of the parties to the case objects. (GCPR, *Parrillo v. Italy*, 2015)

c) *Reformulation,* or *paraphrase,* alters the way a specific portion of text is presented to make it easier for the intended audience to understand. This is often indicated by using metalinguistic expressions like "that is", "that is to say", "i.e.", or "in other words" before or after a term. Reformulation can also be visually marked, for example, by enclosing the paraphrase in brackets. For instance, in (3) the importance of the date is explained through the explanatory paraphrase and in (4) the term "temporal jurisdiction" is reformulated and defined.

(3) Mr Fábián had raised the complaint for the first time in his observations of 9 February 2015, *that is to say, after the expiry of the six-month time-limit for lodging complaints.* (GCPR, *Fábián v. Hungary*, 2017)

4 All examples are taken from the ad hoc corpus of press releases dealing with the Grand Chamber judgments (GCPR), the details of which are reported in 9.4.4. Unless specified otherwise, emphasis has been added.

5 See, for example, Nikitina 2023a on the types of legal definitions as opposed to medical and popular ones from a qualitative and quantitative perspectives.

(4) At the same time, the Court joined to its examination of the merits of the complaint the issue of its temporal jurisdiction, *in other words, whether the Court could examine the adequacy of an investigation into the events which had occurred before Russia ratified the Convention.* (GCPR, *Janowiec and Others v. Russia*, 2013)

d) *Generalization* introduces a general term or expression instead of a specific one, frequently using for this purpose a superordinate term. For instance, in (5) a specific legislative document is referred to as "the new legislation" using the general term for a smoother discursive organization.

(5) The applicant shareholders essentially complained that *the new legislation* had restricted their right to influence the operation of the banks in which they held shares. (GCPR, *Albert and Others v. Hungary*, 2020)

e) *Exemplification* represents the opposite strategy to generalization: it explains a given legal concept using specific examples. In (6) the concept of serious crimes under international law is exemplified by the different types of these crimes.

(6) This might be the situation of serious crimes under international law, such as war crimes, genocide or crimes against humanity. (GCPR, Janowiec and Others v. Russia, 2013)

The surface level strategies are supplemented by the so-called *cognitive* (Calsamiglia & van Dijk 2004: 376) or *pragmatic-level* strategies (Garzone 2020: 166) introduced through 'analogy' or 'association'. This category encompasses *similes*, which are distinguished by linguistic cues that indicate comparison, such as "like", "such as", "similar to" and so forth. It also includes *metaphors*, which conceptualize "one type of thing in terms of another" (Lakoff & Johnson 1981: 5) without relying on any explicit linguistic markers, see (7).

(7) The Grand Chamber therefore upheld the Chamber's finding that in the circumstances of the present case there were no elements capable of providing *a bridge from the distant past into the recent post-entry-into-force period.* (GCPR, Janowiec and Others v. Russia, 2013)

Salvi and Bowker (2015: 13) advanced a more wide-ranging taxonomy of "generalizable discursive strategies", subdivided into recontextualization, re-conceptualization, and trans-mediation. In their taxonomy, *recontextualization* was intended as the re-shaping and re-writing of discourse for a different type of recipients with different purposes, and *reconceptualization* stood for "a re-working of cognitive representations and mental models, through re-framing and re-scripting, these representations constituting the intrinsic epistemological components of knowledge" (Salvi & Bowker 2015: 13). Finally, trans-mediation was mentioned together with entextualization, already addressed in the previous section, as "movement across different channels and modalities, from visual to oral modes, for example, which involves describable reformulations and intertextual affiliations" (Salvi & Bowker 2015: 13).

9.3 Knowledge dissemination at the ECtHR

Previous sections have overviewed the process of popularization, which is frequently compared with translation, in that it involves rewriting of knowledge using the same national language, i.e. intralingual translation (Jakobson 1959). Translation proper, or interlingual translation, also may play a pivotal role in the dissemination of knowledge, as it breaks down language barriers. Whereas popularization, which typically occurs within the same language, allows information, ideas and insights to be shared across professional and lay communities, interlingual translation typically tackles linguistic and cultural boundaries. The European Court of Human Rights employs both types of knowledge dissemination practices, facilitating the global exchange of human rights knowledge and fostering cross-cultural understanding.

To provide some historical background, three significant conferences that explored the future of the Court, respectively, in Interlaken in 2010, İzmir in 2011 and Brighton in 2012 should be mentioned. These conferences emphasized the importance of improving accessibility, understanding, and dissemination of key Convention principles and standards to facilitate their implementation at the national level, primarily through clear and consistent case-law. They aimed to enhance accessibility and comprehension of the Convention principles, and led to multiple interlingual and intralingual mechanisms of knowledge dissemination.

9.3.1 Translation and knowledge dissemination at the ECtHR

With regard to interlingual knowledge dissemination endeavours, several initiatives have to be mentioned. As explained in 3.5, the linguistic regime of the Court is that of an alternative bilingualism, where it can operate either in English or in French (Rule 76.1, Rules of Court). The HUDOC database, which serves as a critical repository of ECtHR case-law, was originally available only in English and French, too. However, following the Court's increased attention to knowledge dissemination dynamics and the three conferences mentioned above, it has undergone a transformation. No longer confined solely to English and French, it has expanded to include interfaces in four additional languages spoken by Council of Europe Member States: Turkish in 2013, Russian in 2014, Spanish in 2017 and, finally, Georgian in December 2018.

In contrast to the text of the Convention, which is always translated into national languages of the Member States of the Council of Europe upon the adoption, even if only for information purposes, the ECtHR judgments were, until recently, notably absent in languages other than the official English and French. Translation services into non-official languages were neither offered, supported, nor even acknowledged at the European level (Kjær 2022: 192).

The burden of translating case-law into national languages relied on the Member States. In 2002, the *Recommendation on the publication and dissemination in the Member States of the text of the European Convention on Human Rights and of the case-law of the European Court of Human Rights* specified:

> It is important that governments of the member states . . .
> ii. ensure that judgments and decisions which constitute relevant case-law developments, or which require special implementation measures on their part as respondent states, are rapidly and widely published, through state or private initiatives, in their entirety or at least in the form of substantial summaries or excerpts (together with appropriate references to the original texts) in the language(s) of the country, in particular in official gazettes, information bulletins from competent ministries, law journals and other media generally used by the legal community, including, where appropriate, the Internet sites.
> (Recommendation CM/Rec(2002)13, no. ii)

The Interlaken reform process, which resulted in the adoption of Protocols nos. 14, 15, and 16 (see 3.2.3–3.2.4), as well as five Declarations concerning the ongoing operation and efficacy of the Court, highlights the importance of translating the Court's judgments into the languages of the Member States, emphasizing their necessity and desirability.

Peruzzo (2019b: 38) reports on how the ECtHR (2014: 3) acknowledged that:

> Ensuring that the Court's leading cases are made available in all official languages of the member States would enable judges, prosecutors, legal practitioners, public officials and civil society to better understand the leading Convention principles, thereby reinforcing the principle of subsidiarity. In addition, such translations would be of assistance when considering the conclusions to be drawn from a judgment finding a violation of the Convention by one State, where the same problem of principle exists in other member States as well.

Recognizing the importance of making its jurisprudence accessible to as many people as possible, including "those who are not well-versed in either English or French but who may nevertheless turn to the Court's Internet site for guidance" (Press Release n. 982 (2009) of 21 December 2009; see also Kjær 2022: 204–205), the ECtHR launched the Case-Law Translation Programme in 2010. It resulted in the first 500 translations into non-official languages of some of the Court's key judgments being added to the HUDOC database.

In 2012, Registry's Case-Law Information and Publications Division initiated the project "Bringing Convention standards closer to home: Translation and dissemination of key ECHR case-law in target languages". What has been defined as an "ambitious" (Peruzzo 2019b: 38) project, lasted four years

(2012–2016) and attracted significant funding, with a lion's share provided for by the Human Rights Trust Fund (HRTF). As the report of the project[6] states, "over 3,500 translations were commissioned from some 70 vetted external translators, [. . .] principally the cases which the Court's Bureau had selected for publication in the Court's official series Reports of Judgments and Decisions (about 30 cases per year)" (ECtHR 2017: 2).

The Court also encouraged non-official translations from various entities, including Governments, judicial training centres, legal professional associations, NGOs, publishers, and other partners, for case-law to which they held rights. This collaborative effort resulted in the collection of approximately 17,000 translations in nearly 30 languages, apart from English and French, which were subsequently made accessible through the HUDOC portal. The substantial number of non-official translations contributed by Governments and partners underscores the widespread interest in Convention principles and ECtHR case-law, highlighting the necessity for their dissemination in languages beyond English and French. Moreover, the report mentions a survey conducted in 2016 among stakeholders, which yielded positive results, with 90% of respondents expressing satisfaction with translation quality, and well over 90% respectively reporting the practical use of translations in legal practice, education and training. (ECtHR 2017: 2; see also Peruzzo 2019b: 38–39 for an overview).

While the case-law translation programme has undoubtedly raised awareness of the importance of knowledge dissemination dynamics through translation into non-official languages, Kjær (2022: 190) argues that it was fuelled by political agenda as the Court strived to legitimize its existence against the backdrop of growing criticism, even from liberal democracies that established it. After an overview (Kjær 2022: 196–204) of the Court's reforms and their impact on language and translation practices in the perspective of knowledge dissemination dynamics, ranging from *travaux preparatoires* to the latest declarations, Kjær (2022) contends that while the translation issue is framed as "access to the Court's case law" bolstering the effectiveness of the Court system, an underlying narrative centres around promoting the national interests of Member States over the continued Europeanization of human rights protection, with Declarations from Member States increasingly emphasizing the concepts *subsidiarity* and *margin of appreciation* (3.2.4) as part of the reform process (Kjær 2022: 190). She observes the significant variation in the amount of translated case-law among Member States and notes that some Member States, described as "translation-reluctant", have the discretion to decide what case-law is deemed "necessary" to translate. In many cases, this results in the translation of only the case-law relevant to their specific state (Kjær 2022: 206).

The Court showed a steadfast commitment to multilingual knowledge dissemination. Minor translation initiatives continued in 2017 and 2018,

6 Available at https://rm.coe.int/168070c5c7.

alongside contributions from NGOs and various national sources, the HUDOC database now offers an impressive collection of over 26,400 texts in 31 languages apart from English and French (as reported in 2018; see also Kjær 2022: 207–208).

The Court's website features the following disclaimer under the section "case-law translation" (emphasis added)[7]:

> Unless otherwise indicated, translations into non-official languages are not produced by the Registry of the Court and *the Registry does not check their accuracy or linguistic quality.* These translations are published in HUDOC *for information purposes only* and the Court accepts no responsibility for their quality or content. All translations are copyright protected and may not be reproduced or republished electronically, in print or in any other form without prior approval by the copyright holder. Should you wish to reproduce or republish a translation which contains no specific copyright mention, please contact the HUDOC team for the details of the rights holder (using the contact form in the link further below).
>
> Please note that *more than one translation of a particular judgment or decision into a given language may exist.*

While a substantial body of case-law is now accessible in non-official languages, concerns regarding the quality and reliability of these translations remain unaddressed. Additionally, the disclaimer acknowledges the existence of multiple translated versions of the same judgment in some national contexts,[8] potentially giving rise to situations of ambiguity when local judges are tasked with applying Convention-related principles.

Despite the possible political underpinnings behind the various case-law translation initiatives, the ECtHR's commitment to greater linguistic inclusivity is apparent. Today, "a simplified version of the Convention is available in 33 languages and 'The European Convention on Human Rights – A Living Instrument' was published to mark its 70th anniversary, while the 'Applicants' pages' can be accessed in 36 languages" (Brannan 2021: 220). By offering access to its case-law, guides and other resources in multiple languages, including HUDOC interfaces in additional languages, the Court demonstrates a dedicated effort to overcoming language barriers and promoting a more extensive dissemination of human rights jurisprudence.

7 Available at https://www.echr.coe.int/case-law-translations, last accessed 4 October 2023.

8 For example, in some prominent cases up to 11 different translated versions of the same judgment were reported to circulate in Russia, when it was still a member of the CoE (personal communication with Russian lawyers at the conference "Successful application to the European Court of Human Rights: from theory to practice", held in Strasbourg in September 2018).

9.3.2 *Knowledge dissemination and popularization at the ECtHR: the Press Service*

As concerns the general – intralingual – knowledge dissemination practices, including popularization, the Court's Press Service[9] has to be mentioned. As former ECtHR President Costa (2021: 435, original emphasis) said, "*communication* in a court such as that of Strasbourg is crucial". Despite its very public nature, little is known about the internal mechanisms behind the Press Unit's operations. The importance of the Press Service seems to have gone unnoticed both in the ECtHR's Rules of Court and in academic literature, with probably the only exception being the article by Patrick Titiun[10] in 2015.

It is remarkable how Titiun repeatedly defines the work of the Press Service a "pedagogical" endeavour, far from the reductionistic copy-paste philosophy, stressing the outreach activities of the press officers and their strive towards ensuring increased "clarity and intelligibility" (Titiun 2015: 130, my translation). Despite the word "pedagogical" is used consistently in Titiun's article, according to the framework outlined in 9.2, the Press Unit's operation falls under the category of popularized exposition, as its intended audience includes journalists, but also "academics, governments, and a range of individuals who are concerned, to varying degrees, by the Court's judgments" (Titiun 2015: 129–130, my translation). Whereas in classical science popularization contexts there is no link between the original authors and the external popularizers, in the ECtHR context the press officers are *part* of the Registry and they have direct access to the lawyers who draft the original judgment, or the judges who give interviews, and thus can guarantee high precision of information.

The Press Service's work originally focussed on the creation of press releases, which are discussed in more detail in 9.4, but it is open to new technological and societal developments as concerns knowledge dissemination outlets. Following the Interlaken conference, the Court undertook many important steps to render its case-law more accessible. To enhance communication and the spread of information via social media, an X (Twitter) account was launched in 2012. In 2015 it was still perceived as a relatively "new communication form" acting as a bridge to reach new public (Titiun 2015: 135, my translation). A new multilingual X (Twitter) account was added to the existing one in 2015. The original account shares tweets featuring direct links to the Court's press releases found on HUDOC, while the newer multilingual account focuses on providing updates about the latest publications in various languages, additions to HUDOC, and other relevant information pertaining to the ECtHR case-law. A typical tweet includes the case title and a brief description, with an enclosed image of the first page of a press release and a link to where it can be downloaded.

9 Available at https://www.echr.coe.int/press-service, last accessed 4 October 2023.
10 Head of the Cabinet of the Presidency of the European Court of Human Rights.

Thematic factsheets and national factsheets were also a novelty created in 2012, following Interlaken. These derived genres represent another notable aspect in the work of the Press Service, as they allow the public at large and journalists alike to consult the national situation or a topic that interests them most in a targeted way (Titiun 2015: 134). These factsheets and case-law guides are typically multilingual. They are produced by the press unit and the research department and "are aimed at lawyers and laypersons alike" (Brannan 2021: 220). These documents possess both the monodisciplinary and pedagogical potential, covering each Convention Article, and since they are constantly updated, they could be "particularly useful for applicants and their legal representatives in preparing an application before the Court (see Villiger 2019: 457, 461) and also for students of law" (Brannan 2021: 220).

The Court's website also contains audiovisual knowledge representation under the form of webcasts of hearings that ensure visibility and accessibility to the hearing by the vastest possible audience.

A significant milestone was achieved on 18 October 2022, with the launch of the *Knowledge Sharing platform* (https://ks.echr.coe.int/). This platform represents a groundbreaking effort by the ECtHR to further disseminate information on its case-law. It offers an innovative and user-friendly interface for accessing and exploring the Court's jurisprudence, enhancing transparency and accessibility. "Its mission is to share Convention case-law knowledge, complementing the existing information tools such as HUDOC. The ECHR-KS is maintained by the Registry and its content does not bind the Court" (ECHR-KS, online).

ECHR-KS Gateway page explores multimodal communication, in that it employs different modes. The concept of *mode* refers here to the use of language, image, layout, video and their combination as resources for making and exchanging meanings. The transformation of knowledge involving multimodal means has been referred to as trans-mediation in Salvi and Bowker (2015), and it is part of the general knowledge dissemination effort. The Gateway page, in fact, does not contain much text; it explores instead infographics. The main portion of the page features large orange icons with the number of the Convention Article, which open to different pages containing case-law guides organized around key themes.

The infographics immediately below the articles visually represent the so-called "transversal themes". The same information is also available in the classical navigation bar at the top of the page (drop-out lists). This shows the intention to re-shape and represent the same information in a new way, which could be more attractive and user-friendly to a variety of stakeholders. The right column of the Gateway page contains a number of sections with useful links, materials as well as a "news" section with changing photos representing the latest news. When clicking on the latter, a new page opens with a brief summary of the event and a link to a full press release (see 9.4). This visual re-elaboration of knowledge demonstrates the adaptation of communicative practices within the domain of international human rights.

9.4 Press releases

9.4.1 Institutional press releases at the ECtHR

The pinnacle genre in the operation of the Press Service[11] is the institutional legal press release. Its *raison d'être*, above all, is to "introduce the case to the external world" (Titiun 2015: 129, my translation).

The Press Service's webpage[12] states

> We aim to help media professionals with questions about the work of the Court in general, to provide information which is publicly available about cases, and guide you in the use of our database of previous cases and those which have been notified to Governments.

Press releases, thus, are positioned as a key communication tool for supranational courts, serving the dual purpose of promoting transparency and advancing the cause of human rights. They allow the public, legal experts and stakeholders to understand the Court's decisions and raise awareness about significant human rights cases and their implications, facilitating informed discussions on these critical issues.

While classical corporate press releases are renowned for their hybrid informative-promotional character (Catenaccio 2008), legal institutional press releases serve the additional purpose of law popularization, breaking down complex legal matters and making them accessible to non-legal experts. In essence, press releases have emerged as powerful tools that bridge information, communication and law, shaping public perceptions.

In the ECtHR context, press releases are prepared by the so-called press officers, who form part of the Court, and who are able to draft a press release as closely and loyally to the judgment as possible (Titiun 2015: 130). There is significant collaboration among the press officers and the Registry lawyers who drafted the judgment (Titiun 2015: 130). It is impossible for the press release to be published and disseminated without prior validation by the registry lawyer who drafted the respective judgment. A typical press release is thus the result of a dialogue. First, the press officers prepare a draft, next the registry lawyer would make modifications aimed at increasing the legal and informational precision of the press release and would supplement the press officer with any additional information that is required. Titiun (2015: 130) stresses how the press release creation is a concerted effort, both on the part of the registry lawyers who need to accept the simplification of their initial

11 It has to be specified that there are three Press Units at the Council of Europe: the CoE Press Unit, the ECtHR Press Unit and the General Assembly Press Unit. The professional profiles and modus operandi of their press officers are consonant and the units liaise with each other; however, typically there is no overlap in their operation. This section is dedicated predominantly to the operation of the ECtHR Press unit.

12 https://www.echr.coe.int/press-service, last accessed 11 October 2023.

project within the spirit of popularization, and on the part of the press officers who need to make their writing clear, intelligible and appealing to widest possible audience, maintaining at the same time a high fidelity of contents to the original.

The press officers serving at the Court's Press service have a double professional profile: with expertise both in journalism/PR and international relations. As the ECtHR has a very high workload, not all of its cases are covered by the Press Office. It is a must to issue a press release for all Grand Chamber judgments, but with regard to Chamber judgments a selection is necessary. Even if the Press Service regularly issues press releases (typically on Thursdays, every week), the knowledge transformation dynamics involved in the press release creation is so complex and time-consuming that it does not allow a 100% coverage. Out of 704 cases heard at the Chamber level in 2012, Titiun (2015: 131) observes, only 204 cases (29%) were covered by press releases.

This natural selection stems from a number of factors. First, the Chamber may simply request a press release to be issued. This is standard practice, when a section judge approaches the Press Service to request a press release be issued on a case they are dealing with. However, the Press Service effects their own analysis, and frequently the cases that are being signalled by the judges have been already earmarked by the Press Service. The earmarked cases may not necessarily spark the journalists' curiosity. Sometimes these are cases with legally innovative elements, in other words, their primary relevance is jurisprudential and not popular. For example, if the case explores the exhaustion of new domestic remedies that are deemed effective by the Court, this may not elicit any particular passion in the general public, but it will nonetheless be covered by the press release as being highly relevant for the Court, Titiun (2015: 132) explains.

The other category of cases selected by the Press Office include cases that are expected to have mediatic resonance, i.e. to be newsworthy. Before proceeding with outlining the generic structure of press releases, it is important to comment on how and why certain cases are chosen for press coverage and the inherent popularization purposes and why others are not, which can be done using the notion of newsworthiness.

9.4.2 Newsworthiness

News and newsworthiness are concepts used in media discourse studies to denote how news reports – including here also press releases – are "disseminated by news organizations" (Bednarek & Caple 2017: 6), including considerations of their target audiences.

In her analysis of science popularization, Garzone (2020: 177–178) overviews the mechanisms underlying the selection of certain scientific news to be disseminated, drawing on works in journalism/communication studies by Gregory and Miller (1998: 111–114) that incorporates Galtung and Ruge's (1965) pivotal ideas. She defines a number of newsworthiness factors, which is reported below, adapted to the context of law popularization and supplemented, where possible, by Titiun's (2015) insider information. This framework is supplemented by Bednarek and Caple's (2017) conceptualizations of newsworthiness[13] in their analysis of discursive mechanisms employed by news agencies and institutions to create news values.

1 **Threshold**: Events become newsworthy when they reach a significant scale of interest. As Galtung and Ruge originally explained it, "the bigger . . . the more violent [the event is] the bigger the headlines it will make" (1965: 66). As concerns the human rights case-law, by virtue of exhausting the national remedies and getting into the ECtHR case-law, all cases would seem to meet the criterion of threshold.
2 **Meaningfulness, relevance and consonance**: Legal stories must hold meaning for readers to grasp and be relevant enough for them to invest time in reading. Cultural and geographical proximity play vital roles. In fact, Bednarek and Caple (2017: 3) define this parameter as "proximity (nearness to the audience)". From a less linguistic perspective, Titiun comments on the journalistic syndrome to be majorly interested in what happens in "one's own backyard", overlooking cases that do not concern one's state (Titiun 2015: 133, my translation). Hence, the press unit tries to raise awareness of national media agencies also for cases that do not concern directly that particular state (Titiun 2015: 133). For example, they may try to reach out to the Polish news outlets for a case concerning the United Kingdom or vice versa. Most national news outlets would focus predominantly on cases concerning that particular jurisdiction, not deeming relevant or newsworthy enough rulings against another respondent state, mirroring the situation with translation of case-law into non-official languages.

   Alignment with existing beliefs and attitudes also increases a story's weight. For example, a case concerning the use of veil, such as *S.A.S. v. France* (application no. 43835/11), will resonate more in a country whose population is exposed to veil-wearing citizens, than in a country where this is not part of the citizens' daily life.
3 **Co-option and composition**: In the realm of law popularization, co-opting a story, i.e., connecting it to an ongoing one, can boost its chances of being covered. In fact, Titiun comments that journalists frequently ask whether a given case is the first of its sort or placed in a series of similar events (Titiun 2015: 134). In order to address these frequently asked questions, the Press Service compiles thematic factsheets (case-law organized around ca. 50 different topics) and national factsheets (case-law sorted by jurisdiction). Other derived genres prepared by the Press Service contribute to the co-option of its press releases.

13 Newsworthiness and news values have been addressed in a variety of studies with some varying and overlapping classifications. For an overview of different taxonomies, see Chapter 2 in Bednarek and Caple (2017).

Additionally, when talking about press coverage, it is important to analyse where a legal article is placed (composition), such as in a law section or general news page, as the placement affects its competition with other stories.

4 **Frequency, unexpectedness and continuity**: Frequent legal events can be anticipated, allowing journalists to prepare in advance. For instance, the so-called "clone" cases deriving from the same systemic problem (e.g. the length of court proceedings in Italy) could amount to be newsworthy simply because they used to be very frequent and numerous. However, the element of surprise ("unusuality" in Bednarek and Caple (2017)) often works in favour of law-related stories, as it adds news value. Continuity, or how long a story unfolds, is valuable in journalism as it engages the public and fosters familiarity with key figures. As Galtung and Ruge (1965: 67) posited, "once something has hit the headlines and been defined as 'news', then it will continue to be defined as news for some time". Since proceedings at the ECtHR level are only possible after the case has been already addressed domestically, it is reasonable to expect a high level of continuity. It is not uncommon for local news outlets to report on the case as being lodged or accepted at the ECtHR, which lays basis for the factor of news continuity.

5 **Competition**: Similarly to science, scoops are infrequent in law, and yet news outlets may compete to be the first to cover specific legal events or facts, especially if these cover socially or bioethically challenging topics. For example, cases related to end-of-life (assisted dying) or beginning-of-life (donating embryos to science) situations are frequently overviewed by multiple news agencies, thus becoming the object of competition.

6 **Unambiguity and negativity**: Similar to science popularization, legal stories with clearly indicated – positive or negative – aspects are more newsworthy. Negative news tends to garner more attention than positive news, often being reported in dramatic tones. Bednarek and Caple (2017: 2) refer to this feature in terms of "major negative consequences". Legal events involving problems, risks or adversities attract substantial coverage.

7 **Facts, sources and reliability**: Factual accuracy enhances news value, a crucial aspect that institutional legal press releases, created as a result of collaboration among press officers and lawyers, can provide.

8 **Elite and personalization**: Legal events with relevance to elite nations, social groups, or prominent individuals tend to be more captivating. For example, inter-state applications could typically raise the public's interest. Similarly, high-profile cases lodged by or involving public personas, such as *Berlusconi v. Italy* (Grand Chamber 2018:[14] strike-out decision) or *Von Hannover (no. 2) v. Germany*[15] could spike up the public's attention.

14 Application n. 58428/13, GC decision of 27 November 2018.

15 Cited by Titiun (2015: 132) as an example of media interest that led, inter alia, to an exceptional edition of a German version of the press release.

9.4.3 Press releases: literature review

Press releases play a significant role in contemporary communication, serving as versatile genres with hybrid informational and promotional features (Catenaccio 2008). As illustrated in 9.4.1, they have a multipurpose nature and are "meant for different audiences" (Jacobs 1999: 22), and their "intended primary readership has been recently shifting to the general public" (Catenaccio 2008: 11).

Multiple studies in the fields of Discourse Analysis, genre analysis, and public relations have delved into their nature and impact (e.g. Jacobs 1999, 2006; Catenaccio 2008; Lindholm 2008; Tessuto 2021). One key principle in understanding press releases from a linguistic perspective is the concept of "preformulation", as described by Jacobs (1999, 2006). Press releases are crafted to require minimal reworking by journalists who receive them (Jacobs 2006: 201). This prefabricated character of press releases has been referred to as generating "churnalism". Blending the words "churning" and "journalism" or "chunk" and "journalism", it denotes "a practice in which pre-packaged stories provided by news agencies and press releases are adapted for publication instead of reported news" (Barel-Ben David et al. 2020: 10, cf. Jacobs 1999, 2006). As a press release is conventionally prepared in such a way that chunks of its text can be taken out and re-inserted into a news story, it has become a vital genre for disseminating information quickly and effectively across a number of contexts, including the legal one.

In the legal context, press releases have been used to pre-announce legislative changes, which became known in the literature as "legislation by press release". For example, Chen (2015) examined this phenomenon in Singapore, explaining how it "involves an announcement (or press release) by the government notifying the public that an existing statute will be amended and that the amendment, upon legislative approval, will be made retrospectively effective from the announcement date". Despite the absence of any formal legal impact in the announcement, the introduction of the term "legislation" mirrors the real-world consequences of the announcement. Private entities are expected to promptly adjust their actions in accordance with the modified law following the announcement date. It underscores the influence that press releases can wield in shaping public opinion and understanding of legal matters, even in the realm of international law, and opens new stimulating research avenues, also from a Critical Discourse Analysis perspective, exploring the interaction of language and power.

Press releases may be said to have blurred the lines between journalism and public relations. Scholars like Sissons (2012) and Lindholm (2008) have explored this cross-fertilization, particularly in the context of institutions like the European Commission.

Interestingly, despite their significance, institutional legal press releases in international courts remain somewhat underresearched. While studies like Tessuto (2021) have examined the European Court of Justice (ECJ), there are no linguistic studies on this genre within the ECtHR context. This gap suggests the need for further exploration into the role and impact of press releases within the operation of international courts in general and ECtHR, in particular.

9.4.4 *Types of press releases at the ECtHR*

Press releases at ECtHR can be accessed either through the respective section of HUDOC (Press Collection) or through the Knowledge Sharing platform. The former retrieval mechanism has been used here.

In September 2023, there were altogether 17,644 press releases available through HUDOC, covering the period starting from 1 January 1999.

There are different types of institutional legal press releases in the ECtHR context (Table 9.1). These have different statistical weight in the daily operation of the Press Service, ranging from press releases overviewing Chamber judgments (50.44%), as the most prominent category or subgenre, to press releases dealing with referrals with only 0.03%. Some press releases represent a brief announcement of forthcoming judgments (ca. 12%) with factual summaries and, as the name suggests, there is typically more than one judgment that is going to be overviewed. Others contain more elaborate data that incorporate a summary of the Court's reasoning, typically to be disseminated on the day of delivery (Brannan 2021: 219). As explained in 9.4.1 and 9.4.2, not every case and not every operation of the Court becomes the object of a press release. Yet, this distribution largely corresponds to the Court's operations after the communication stage (Chapter 5). In fact, there are press releases announcing communicated cases, which lays the ground for the co-option of a news story (see 9.4.2): first a mediatic prepping occurs with the announcement of

Table 9.1 Press release categories

Category	*Number of texts*	*Percentage*
Chamber judgments	8,899	50.44
Committee judgments	42	0.24
Communicated cases	53	0.30
Decisions on admissibility	949	5.38
Forthcoming hearings	341	1.93
Forthcoming judgments	2,109	11.95
General	2,809	15.92
Grand Chamber judgments	740	4.19
Hearings	1,043	5.91
Interim measures	108	0.61
Referrals	5	0.03
Referrals to Grand Chamber	466	2.64
Relinquishments to Grand Chamber	80	0.45
Total	**17,644**	**100%**

a communicated case, and then the following press releases may take up the story overviewing the other genres along the procedural flow (see 3.4.2).

Press releases are typically prepared by the Registry in one of the official languages and can be translated by the Court's Translation Department into the other official language, English or French (Brannan 2021: 219). Exceptionally, some press releases may be translated into national languages to facilitate their dissemination in national press. For example, the press release concerning the first domestic violence case brought against Russia, *Volodina v. Russia* (application 41261/17, Chamber judgment rendered in 2019) was translated into Russian. Similarly, the press release concerning declaration of the case *Ukraine and the Netherlands v. Russia*[16] as partly admissible by the Grand Chamber (application nos. 8019/16, 43800/14 and 28525/20) was translated into both Russian and Ukrainian. Little is known about the way these translations are made except that sometimes the Registry lawyers who were involved in the judgment drafting contribute to their creation.

Press releases covering decisions on (in)admissibility represent a moderately large category (5.38%). The function of these texts is most probably "to dissuade would-be applicants from bringing unmeritorious cases" (Brannan 2021: 219): by publishing an additional document, stating in a clear and accessible way that a given claim is inadmissible enhances the chances of preventing an avalanche of inadmissible "clone" cases.

Besides the typological classification, press releases can be further filtered and organized either thematically or using a Convention Article as a search parameter, along with a set of other possible filters available in HUDOC. As press releases are issued for all Grand Chamber judgments, and these are admittedly among the longest and the most detailed documents within the system of genres at the ECtHR, I decided to focus on this type to assess their knowledge dissemination algorithms and potential. Table 9.2 shows some general statistical data about the Grand Chamber Press Release corpus (GCPR).

The GCPR was created setting a simple temporal parameter to include press releases published between 2013 and 2023, dealing with Grand Chamber judgments. Only English versions were gathered, using the Press Collection on HUDOC. The texts were all static .pdf files, so I had to optically recognize them to transform them into a text-searchable format. Finally, as

Table 9.2 The Grand Chamber Press Release corpus composition

Texts	*Tokens*	*Types*	*Ave. length*	*Timeframe*
149	351,169	10,943	2,356	2013–2023

16 "The case concerns complaints related to the conflict in eastern Ukraine involving pro-Russian separatists which began in spring 2014 [. . .] [and the] shooting down of Malaysia Airlines flight MH17 in eastern Ukraine on 17 July 2014, which resulted in the deaths of 298 people, including 196 Dutch nationals" (Press release ECHR 026 (2023) 25 January 2023).

every press release ended with the press officers' contact details, I eliminated those parts along with boilerplate descriptions. The next subsection details the generic composition of the GCPR texts.

9.4.5 GCPR: generic structure

The GCPR texts have a clearly identifiable generic structure, summarized in Table 9.3.

Press releases encompass elements from both journalistic and legal institutional realms. For instance, in Move 1 (Press release identification), there are distinct signals of the press release's institutional and legal origins, such as the official logo and protocol numbers. Simultaneously, Move 2 (Headline) embodies journalistic discourse, highlighting the hybrid nature of this genre. It illustrates how contextual and text-external resources are incorporated within and across professional genres and practices.[17]

The Press Service aims to make press releases appealing to the general public by crafting concise yet compelling headlines that summarize the case in a single sentence (Titiun 2015: 131). This approach enables journalists, who often contend with vast amounts of information, to identify the most newsworthy aspects and navigate through the relevant case-law. The same headline is used for the corresponding X (Twitter) post, accompanied by the case name, a link to access the full press release, and an image of its first page.

There is yet another journalistic marker. Each press release is saved as a .pdf file in the system, and the file name contains both the official case name and a brief alternative title. For instance, examples (8) and (10) illustrate the full-fledged headline in the main file, and examples (9) and (11) show an abridged version in the file name, which is visible in HUDOC, but is physically outside of the .pdf file.

(8) No breach of Portugal's duties in the case of a voluntary psychiatric inpatient who committed suicide; civil proceedings for damages lasted too long.

(9) Grand Chamber judgment Fernandes de Oliveira v. Portugal – mentally ill patient who committed suicide.

(10) French ban on the wearing in public of clothing designed to conceal one's face does not breach the Convention.

(11) Grand Chamber judgment S.A.S. v. France – ban on wearing in public clothing concealing one's face.

The file name must contain the name of the case, but the Press Service additionally exposes the public/journalists to an alternative, content-based, title, providing them with a sort of a synopsis, in a fashion similar to the 18th-century

17 See Bhatia's (2010) interdiscursivity.

Table 9.3 Generic structure of a press release in the Grand Chamber Press Release

Move	*Steps/Examples*
Move 1: PR identification	1a: Fixed steps • the ECtHR logo • Label "Press Release" • Indication of the text producer: "issued by the Registrar of the Court" 1b: Variable steps • PR number, e.g. ECHR 409 (2018) • Date (Note: different from corporate context "for immediate release")
Move 2: Headline	E.g. "The Berlusconi case is struck out of the list" or "No breach of Portugal's duties in the case of a voluntary psychiatric inpatient who committed suicide; civil proceedings for damages lasted too long"
Move 3: Lead	3a: Clear indication of the GC case (name, hyperlink, number) followed by its topic 3b: "In today's Grand Chamber judgment* in the case, the European Court of human rights held" + majority quantification (e.g. "by eleven votes to six", "unanimously", "by majority") 3c: A popularizing footnote (a fixed formula): *"Grand Chamber judgments are final (Article 44 of the Convention). All final judgments are transmitted to the Committee of Ministers of the Council of Europe for supervision of their execution. Further information about the execution process can be found here: www.coe.int/t/dghl/monitoring/execution" 3d: Summary of the judgment • Violation Y/N, article and its name, e.g. "that there had been a/no violation of Article 8 (right to respect for private and family life) of the European Convention on Human Rights" • Summarized majority opinion
Move 4: (Principal) Facts	Represents a summary of the Judgment section "The circumstances of the case"
Move 5: Complaints, procedure and composition of the Court	5a: "The application was lodged with the European Court of Human Rights on [date]" 5b: The Applicant's complaints 5c: Description of procedural steps (application, case communication, the parties observations (optional), jurisdiction issues (e.g. relinquishment; optional), hearings, third party comments (optional), "A Grand Chamber hearing on the case was held in public in Strasbourg on [date]" 5d: "Judgment was given by the Grand Chamber of 17 judges, composed as follows: [name surname (Country)] President, [name surname (Country)]. . ."

(*Continued*)

Table 9.3 (Continued)

Move	*Steps/Examples*
Move 6: Decision of the Court	6a: Article X 6b: Article Y
Move 7: Just satisfaction (optional)	"The Court held that [state] was to pay [the Applicant] [the amount] euros (EUR) in respect of pecuniary and non-pecuniary damage and EUR [the amount] in respect of costs and expenses".
Move 8: Separate opinions (optional)	E.g. "Judges [surname] and [surname] expressed a joint concurring opinion. Judge [surname] expressed a concurring opinion. Judges [surname] and [surname] each expressed a dissenting opinion. These opinions are annexed to the judgment."
Move 9: Specification of linguistic regime	"The judgment is available in English and French" (a fixed formula)
Move 10: Boilerplate disclaimer	"This press release is a document produced by the Registry. It does not bind the Court. Decisions, judgments and further information about the Court can be found on www.echr.coe.int. To receive the Court's press releases, please subscribe here: www.echr.coe.int/RSS/en or follow us on Twitter @ECHRpress." (a fixed formula)
Move 11: Contact information	Press contacts
Move 12: Boilerplate description of the Court	"The European Court of Human Rights was set up in Strasbourg by the Council of Europe Member States in 1959 to deal with alleged violations of the 1950 European Convention on Human Rights".

literary titles.[18] Peculiarly, both headline alternatives in the GCPR tend to be under the 140-character length, to facilitate the press release dissemination via X (Twitter), before it abolished its signature character-limit in 2023. The abridged title, already containing the case name, was used if the headline was too long for the original X (Twitter) setting.

Move 3, the Lead, is the quintessential preformulated move, meant for journalists to adopt as is, with no or minor modifications. Its function combines informative, persuasive and instructive elements. It is easy to identify

18 For example, the famous works by Jonathan Swift, *Gulliver's Travels*, and by Daniel Defoe, *Robinson Crusoe*, published in the 18th century, originally were titled as *Travels into Several Remote Nations of the World, in Four Parts. By Lemuel Gulliver, First a Surgeon, and then a Captain of several Ships* and *The Life and Strange Surprising Adventures of Robinson Crusoe of York, Mariner: Who lived Eight and Twenty Years, all alone in an un-inhabited Island on the coast of America, near the Mouth of the Great River of Oroonoque; Having been cast on Shore by Shipwreck, wherein all the Men perished but himself. With An Account how he was at last as strangely deliver'd by Pyrates. Written by Himself.* A relatively lengthy content-oriented title was necessary to boost book sales. A potential reader was provided with a kind of a story synopsis, the function that can be found in modern film trailers and news headlines, including, as it appears, institutional legal press releases.

graphically, as it is placed within a light grey box. It represents the apogee of the entextualization process as it transforms a hundred-page long judgment into a half-page exposition meant for a wider public. As Table 9.3 reports, it starts with a clear case identification by its name and the application number, including a hyperlink to the judgment. Next it summarizes the topic of the case, typically introduced by "The case X concerned . . .", which in earlier press releases was placed after specifying the decision of the court, but now precedes it. Next, the ruling of the court is announced with an indication whether it was unanimous or by majority, followed by a brief summary thereof. Move 3 contains also a clearly popularizing step (3c), where a fixed formula is used to explain that the Grand Chamber judgments are final, providing a link to the Committee of Ministers website dealing with the execution of judgments. This step shows the press release's intent to be clear to different audiences, including those that are not familiar with the Court's practices.

Moves 4 and 5 contain additional details for journalists who can dedicate more space to the story and outline its facts (Move 4, based on the judgment subsection "circumstances of the case"), the Grand Chamber composition, complaints and procedure (Move 5). While Move 5 is quite formulaic as it repeats some portions of the judgment verbatim (e.g. the court composition section), Move 4 is a complex summary of facts. It is worthwhile noticing how facts precede legal details in the press release, following the so-called inverted pyramid model, according to which information is structured and ordered in such a way as to allow the readers to grasp its gist without detailed deviations. In other words, press release readership is expected to be more interested in the factual matrix of the case than in its legal intricacies that are left to Move 6.

Table 9.4 illustrates the Press Service's approach to the restructuring of facts as this knowledge is de-centred from the original judgment (right column) and re-centred in the GCPR "Facts" section (left column). On average, this section was eight times shorter in the GCPR corpus than in the judgments. In addition to the reduced length, which can be interpreted as a clear sign of entextualization and simplification, the text format was adapted to a different context: section markers, paragraph numbering and headings were eliminated (underlined in Table 9.4), as these pertain to the generic makeup of judgments, and not journalistic discourse. In general, the GCPR texts employ various popularizing strategies: many technical details are omitted (underlined) or paraphrased, and at the same time, the text contains clarifying additions (in italics). For example, while the judgment talks about "the Applicant", which is the standard term of reference, the press release specifies his name and refers to him throughout the whole text as "Mr Baka". A clear marker of legalese is replaced by the lay equivalent, as part of the popularization process. In a similar vein, "legal duty" replaced "statutory obligation". Besides these lexical popularization strategies, press release writers rely on syntactic simplification: as Table 9.4 illustrates, selected passages from the judgment were kept very close to the original but in a syntactically streamlined way (in bold). In general, Move 4 presents features of popularized exposition.

Table 9.4 Comparison of the facts description in the Grand Chamber Press Release and in the Grand Chamber Judgment in the case *Baka v. Hungary*

GCPR, Baka v. Hungary	*GC Judgment, Baka v. Hungary*
The applicant, *András Baka*, is a Hungarian national who was born in 1952 and lives in Budapest (*Hungary*). *Mr Baka*, a former judge at the European Court of Human Rights (1991–2008), **was elected on 22 June 2009 by the Parliament of Hungary as President of the Supreme Court of Hungary** ("the Supreme Court"). **He was due to serve a six-year term, due to expire on 22 June 2015**. In that capacity, he was also the Head of the National Council of Justice and was under a *legal duty* to express his opinion on parliamentary bills affecting the judiciary.	THE FACTS I. THE CIRCUMSTANCES OF THE CASE 11. The applicant was born in 1952 and lives in Budapest. A. Election of the applicant as President of the Supreme Court and his functions 12. **On 22 June 2009**, after seventeen years of service (from 1991 to 2008) as a judge at the European Court of Human Rights and, subsequently, more than one year's service as a member of the Budapest Court of Appeal, **the applicant was elected** by the Parliament of Hungary, by decision no. 55/2009 (VI. 24) OGY, **as President of the Supreme Court for a six-year term, until 22 June 2015.** 13. In that capacity, [. . .] As the head of the National Council of Justice, *the applicant* was under an explicit *statutory obligation* to express an opinion on parliamentary bills that affected the judiciary, after having gathered and summarised the opinions of different courts via the Office of the National Council of Justice (see paragraph 44 below).

Move 6 ("Decision of the Court") offers a summary of the legal side of the matter. It is organized by the Convention articles, and generally operates with legal terminology and phraseology, which counteract the popularizing purposes of the text, see (12) and (13).

(12) As regards the house arrest decisions, in spite of the courts finding that there were no reasons for his continued detention such as his *absconding* or *interfering with* the investigation, the courts nevertheless ordered his house arrest in June and July 2007. [GCPR, *Buzadji v. the Republic of Moldova*]

(13) The Court also noted that, while the limitation period had not been interrupted and could therefore have been considered to have expired following the Court of Cassation ruling of 10 October 2002, that fact had not yet been established by a judicial decision, still less one with res judicata effect. [GCPR, *Vegotex International S.A. v. Belgium*]

Examples (12) and (13) are indicative of the general lexicogrammatical organization of Move 6, with markers of legal discourse, specialized terminology, unexplained Latin terms, embedded clauses, nominalization and lengthy sentences in general. Such textual organization testifies to the mixed target audience of press releases, which includes also legal professionals. Move 6 appears to be tacitly targeted at them, as it remains at the level of monodisciplinary intra- and inter-specialist exposition.

(14) The present application was not therefore an *actio popularis*[19]
(15) In particular, the Court considered that, notwithstanding *the discretion left to the respondent State (its "margin of appreciation")*, there had not been a reasonable relationship of proportionality between the measure complained of and the legitimate aim pursued. [GCPR, *Magyar Helsinki Bizottság v. Hungary*]
(16) It concluded that the Supreme Court's application of the rules concerning the statutory minimum for lodging an appeal had not disproportionately hindered Ms Zubac's right of access to a court, nor gone beyond *the State's room for manoeuvre ("margin of appreciation")* to regulate the rules on access to court and the application of those rules. [GCPR, *Zubac v. Croatia*]

Some elements of popularization are occasionally evident. For instance, in (14), a Latin expression is clarified with a definition in a footnote. In (15) and (16), the specialized term "margin of appreciation" is first explained through a paraphrase and then formally introduced within brackets. The inconsistent approach to popularization in Move 6 can be tentatively attributed to the human factor. As previously mentioned, press releases are collaborative efforts of various press officers and Registry lawyers. Consequently, the legal style may at times overshadow the journalistic one, and vice versa. It seems that there are no specific guidelines or a style sheet advising press release drafters on how to bridge the knowledge gap between the creators of the text and the public.

Moves 7 and 8 are optional as they depend on the presence or absence of, respectively, just satisfaction claims and separate opinions. These moves rely on the recurrent formulae reported in Table 9.3. Remarkably, separate opinions (Chapter 8) are only mentioned without any content-related details, which stresses the line between the majority and minority opinions. The former are associated with the Court, and thus deserve a complex entextualization, and the latter – while encouraging transparency and judicial independency – are never objects of institutional press releases.

Moves 9, 10, 11 and 12 are the so-called boilerplate descriptions: they follow a preformulated template reported verbatim in every press release. The only variable element concerns Move 11 (contact information), as officer names and contact details may vary. Move 10 is a disclaimer necessary for authorship attribution and responsibility limitation; it also contains links to

19 Action by which an individual challenges in abstract terms the law or legal practice of a State in the collective interest. [GCPR, *S.A.S. v. France*]

other channels of knowledge dissemination, inviting the readership to acquire more information, if necessary. Move 12 serves the goal of knowledge dissemination about the Court in the spirit of popularization of law.

9.5 Conclusions

Chapter 9 stretched considerations on the discourse of human rights beyond the procedural flow of the ECtHR. The digital age offers unprecedented opportunities for widespread access to legal information, but the challenge remains in making this information understandable to the general public. For human rights to gain meaningful social traction, they must transcend formal legal frameworks and become ingrained in societal norms, behaviours and institutions. This chapter analysed strategies, initiatives and mechanisms of knowledge dissemination and popularization. Communication of human rights knowledge, as I strived to problematize in this chapter, has to overcome barriers in both content and form, ensuring that human rights information reaches diverse audiences effectively.

The ECtHR has made significant strides in enhancing multilingual access to its jurisprudence, which originally operated exclusively in English and French, reinforcing indirectly the principle of subsidiarity as multilingual case-law supports the integration of ECtHR knowledge into national legal systems. The intra-linguistic mechanisms rely on knowledge recontextualization through press releases, as well as other outlets, such as X (Twitter) or multimodal Knowledge Sharing platform, to communicate key decisions. A legal institutional press release derives from a complex interweaving of journalistic and legal discourses, balancing elements of popularization with those of legal precision, and its creation requires significant time and collaborative human resources.

Despite the effectiveness of press releases in making legal information more accessible, the inherent complexity of legal language remains a challenge. The generic structure of press releases often retains elements of legal discourse, which can alienate lay audiences. However, efforts to streamline content through popularization strategies, such as simplifying technical terms and providing contextual explanations, demonstrate a commitment to clarity. The mixed approach, while occasionally inconsistent, generally succeeds in addressing the diverse informational needs of these audiences, enabling both efficient knowledge dissemination and informed public discourse.

Titiun (2015: 138, my translation) observes how the Press Service is in "continuous adaptation" to technological and societal evolution, so it is interesting to reflect on what the future horizons and frontiers of its operation could be. Against the backdrop of a high workload and limited resources, a selection of cases destined for press releases is made. It is physically impossible to elaborate and entextualize all judgments. What if part of the knowledge transfer from judgments to press releases could be effected in a machine-assisted way relying on the fresher possibilities of AI? Experiments carried so far (Nikitina 2023b) suggest that current AI-algorithms are not yet fully capable of understanding contextualization cues, i.e. markers of professional jargon, balancing levels of intra- and inter-specialist exposition and supplying popularizing insights. Only time – and perhaps more cases and press releases – will show whether this is the path forward for the most productive supranational human rights court, the ECtHR.

References

Acosta Lopez, J. I., & Maya Calle, M. C. (2009). The right of individual petition in the Inter-American system of human rights, and its relation with interim and provisional measure. *Estudios de derecho (Medellín)*, 66(148): 13–40.

Agha, P. (2017). *Human Rights Between Law and Politics: The Margin of Appreciation in Post-National Contexts.* Hart Publishing.

Alcaraz Varó, E., & Hughes, B. (2002). *Legal Translation Explained.* Manchester: St. Jerome.

Allan, K. (2019). Taboo words and language: An overview. In K. Allan (ed.), *The Oxford Handbook of Taboo Words and Language.* Oxford University Press, 1–27.

Anesa, P., & Engberg, J. (eds.). (2023). *The Digital (R)Evolution of Legal Discourse: New Genres, Media, and Linguistic Practices.* Berlin-Boston: de Gruyter.

Anesa, P., & Kulbicki, L. (2022). The impact of digitalization on legal communication: Introduction. *International Journal of Law, Language & Discourse*, 10(2): 5–8.

Anscombre, J.-C., & Ducrot, O. (1983). *L'argumentation dans la langue.* Brussels: Mardaga.

Archer, D. E. (2008). Verbal aggression and impoliteness: Related or synonymous? In D. Bousfield & M. Locher (eds.), *Impoliteness in Language: Language, Power and Social Processes Series.* Mouton de Gruyter, 181–207.

Attard, R., & Pinto de Albuquerque, P. (2023). *Taxation at the European Court of Human Rights.* Alphen aan den Rijn: Wolters Kluwer Law International.

Austin, J. L. (1962). *How to Do Things With Words.* Cambridge: Harvard University Press.

Avila-Cabrera, J. J. (2023). *The Challenge of Subtitling Offensive and Taboo Language into Spanish: A Theoretical and Practical Guide.* Bristol-Jackson: Multilingual Matters.

Baker, M. (1996). Corpus-based translation studies: The challenges that lie ahead. In H. Somers (ed.), *Terminology, LSP and Translation: Studies in Language Engineering in Honour of Juan C. Sager.* Amsterdam, Philadelphia: John Benjamins, 175–186.

Bakhtin, M. (1981). Discourse in the novel. In M. Holquist (ed.), *The Dialogic Imagination.* Austin: University of Texas Press, 259–421.

Bakhtin, M. (1984). *Problems of Dostoevsky's Poetics*, edited and translated by Caryl Emerson. Minnesota: University of Minnesota Press, Vol. 8.

Barel-Ben David, Y., Garty, E. S., & Baram-Tsabari, A. (2020). Can scientists fill the science journalism void? Online public engagement with science stories authored by scientists. *PLoS One*, 15(1): e0222250.

Bassnett, S., & Lefevere, A. (1990). Introduction: Proust's grandmother and the thousand and one nights: The 'cultural turn' in translation studies. In S. Bassnett & A. Lefevere (eds.), *Translation, History and Culture.* London: Printer Publishers, 1–13.

Bates, E. (2011). The birth of the European Convention on Human Rights – and the European Court of Human Rights. In *The European Court of Human Rights Between Law and Politics*. Oxford University Press.

Bazerman, C. (1994). Systems of genres and the enhancement of social intentions. In A. Freedman & P. Medway (eds.), *Genre and New Rhetoric*. London: Taylor and Francis, 79–101.

Beaupré, R. M. (1986). *Interpreting Bilingual Legislation*. Toronto: Carswell.

Bedjaoui, M. (1991). The "manufacture" of judgments at the international court of justice. *Pace International Law Review*, 3(1): 29–61.

Bednarek, M., & Caple, H. (2017). *The Discourse of News Values*. Oxford University Press.

Beitz, C. R. (2009). *The Idea of Human Rights*. Oxford University Press.

Bentsen, H. L. (2018). Court leadership, agenda transformation, and judicial dissent: A European case of a "mysterious demise of consensual norms". *Journal of Law and Courts*, 6(1): 189–213.

Berger, V. (1992). La confection des arrêts de la Cour européenne des droits de l'homme et le rôle du Greffe. *Bulletin d'information du CREDHO*, 2: 6–9.

Berkenkotter, C., & Huckin, T. (1995). *Genre Knowledge in Disciplinary Communication: Cognition/Culture/Power*. Hillsdale: Lawrence Erlbaum.

Bhatia, V. K. (1983). *An Applied Discourse Analysis of English Legislative Writing*. Birmingham: University of Aston.

Bhatia, V. K. (1993). *Analysing Genre: Language Use in Professional Settings*. London, New York: Longman.

Bhatia, V. K. (1998). Intertextuality in legal discourse. *The Language Teacher*. Available at http://www.jalt–publications.org/tlt/files/98/nov/batia.html

Bhatia, V. K. (2006). Legal genres. In K. Brown (ed.), *Encyclopedia of Languages and Linguistics*. Oxford: Elsevier, Vols. 1–14, 1–7.

Bhatia, V. K. (2010). Interdiscursivity in professional communication. *Discourse and Communication*, 4(1): 32–50.

Bhatia, V. K. (2014). *Worlds of Written Discourse: A Genre-Based View*. London: Bloomsbury.

Bhatia, V. K. (2015). Critical genre analysis: Theoretical preliminaries. *Hermes*, 27(54): 9–20.

Bhatia, V. K. (2017). *Critical Genre Analysis: Investigating Interdiscursive Performance in Professional Practice*. London: Routledge.

Biber, D., Conrad, S., Finegan, E., Johansson, S., & Leech, G. (1999). *Longman Grammar of Spoken and Written English*. Harlow, Essex: Pearson Education Ltd.

Biel, Ł. (2014). Phraseology in legal translation: A corpus-based analysis of textual mapping in EU law. In L. Cheng, K. Kui Sin, & A. Wagner (eds.), *Ashgate Handbook of Legal Translation*. Aldershot: Ashgate, 177–192.

Biel, Ł. (2024). Linguistic approaches. In M. Siems & P. J. Yap (eds.), *The Cambridge Handbook of Comparative Law*. Cambridge Law Handbooks. Cambridge University Press, 91–112.

Biel, Ł., & Engberg, J. (2013). Research models and methods in legal translation. *Linguistica Antverpiensia. New Series – Translation Studies*, 12: 1–11.

Biel, Ł., & Kockaert, H. J. (eds.) (2023). *The Handbook of Terminology: Legal Terminology*. Amsterdam, Philadelphia: John Benjamins.

Biel, Ł., Koźbiał, D., & Wasilewska, K. (2019). The formulaicity of translations across EU institutional genres: A corpus-driven analysis of lexical bundles in translated and nontranslated language. *Translation Spaces*, 8(1): 67–92.

Bletsas, M. (2015). The voices of justice: Argumentative polyphony and strategic manoeuvring in judgement motivations: An example from the Italian Constitutional Court. In F. H. van Eemeren and B. Garssen (eds.), *Scrutinizing Argumentation in Practice*. John Benjamins, 79–97.

Bondi, M. (2015). Preface. In R. Salvi & J. Bowker (eds.), *The Dissemination of Contemporary Knowledge in English*. Lausanne: Peter Lang Verlag, 7–10.

Bongo, G., & Caliendo, G. (eds.). (2014). *The Language of Popularization: Theoretical and Descriptive Models*. Bern: Peter Lang.

Boot, E. (2017). *Human Duties and the Limits of Human Rights Discourse*. Cham: Springer Verlag.

Borja Albi, A. (2013). A genre analysis approach to the study of the translation of court documents. *Linguistica Antverpiensia New Series*, 12: 33–53.

Borja Albi, A., García Izquierdo, I., & Montalt, V. (2009). Research methodology in specialized genres for translation purposes. *Interpreter and Translator Trainer*, 3(1): 57–77.

Bourcier, D., & Bruxelles, S. (1995). Une Approche Sémantique de l'Argumentation Juridique. *Dire et C'est-à-dire, Revue Française de Sociologie*, 36: 35–57.

Bowker, L. (2019). Terminology. In M. Baker & G. Saldanha (eds.), *Routledge Encyclopedia of Translation Studies*. London, New York: Routledge, 579–583.

Brannan, J. (2013). Coming to terms with the supranational: Translating for the European Court of Human Rights, *International Journal of Semiotics of Law*, 26: 909–925.

Brannan, J. (2018). Specificities of translation at the European Court of Human Rights: Policy and practice. In F. Prieto Ramos (ed.), *Institutional Translation for International Governance: Enhancing Quality in Multilingual Legal Communication*. London: Bloomsbury, 170–180.

Brannan, J. (2021). Conveying the right message: Principles and problems of multilingual communication at the European Court of Human Rights. In S. Goźdź-Roszkowski & G. Pontrandolfo (eds.), *Law, Language and the Courtroom*. London: Routledge, 217–230.

Brannan, J. (2023). From the domestic to the supranational: The terminology of "expulsion" as used at the European Court of Human Rights. In Ł. Biel & H. J. Kockaert (eds.), *The Handbook of Terminology: Legal Terminology*. Amsterdam, Philadelphia: John Benjamins, Vol. 3, 327–350.

Bres, J. (1999). "Vous les entendez?". Analyse du Discourse et Dialogisme. *Modèles Linguistiques*, 20: 71–86.

Bres, J. (2001). Article «dialogisme». In C. Détrie, P. Siblot, & B. Verine (eds.), *Termes et Concepts pour L'analyse du Discours*. Champion: Paris.

Bres, J. (2005). Savoir de quoi on parle: Dialogue, dialogal, dialogique, dialogisme, polyphonie . . . In J. Bres, P. P. Haillet, S. Mellet, L. Rosier, & N. Hennig (eds.), *Dialogisme, Polyphonie: Approches Linguistiques*. Brussels: Duculot, 47–61.

Bres, J. (2020). Binarité syntaxique rhématique et dialogisme interdiscursif. *L'Information grammaticale (Paris)*, 164: 40–45.

Bres, J., & Nowakowska, A. (2005). Dis moi avec qui tu 'dialogues', je te dirai qui tu est . . . de la pertinence de la notion de dialogisme pour l'analyse due discours. *Marges Linguistiques*, 9: 137–153.

Brezina, V. (2018). *Statistics in Corpus Linguistics: A Practical Guide*. Cambridge University Press.

Brezina, V., Weill-Tessier, P., & McEnery, A. (2021). *#LancsBox v. 6.x*. [software package].

Brown, P. (2017). Politeness and impoliteness. In Y. Huang (ed.), *Oxford Handbook of Pragmatics*. Oxford University Press, 383–399.

Brown, P., & Levinson, S. C. (1987). *Politeness: Some Universals in Language Use*. Cambridge University Press.

Bruinsma, F. (2006). Les opinions séparées des juges à La Cour Européenne des Droits de l'Homme. *Netherlands Quarterly of Human Rights*, 24(2): 358–362.

Cairns, H. (1942). The popularization of law: The requirements of popularization. *Michigan Law Review*, 40(4): 560–573.

Caliendo, G. (2004). Intercultural traits in legal translation. In *14th European Symposium on Language for Special Purposes (LSP 2003)*. University of Surrey, 296–301.
Calsamiglia, H., & van Dijk, T. (2004). Popularization discourse and knowledge about the genome, *Discourse & Society*, 15: 369–389.
Cameron, I. (2013). The court and the member states: Procedural aspects. In A. Føllesdal, B. Peters, & G. Ulfstein (eds.), *Constituting Europe: The European Court of Human Rights in a National, European and Global Context*. Cambridge University Press, 25–61.
Cao, D. (2007). *Translating Law*. Clevedon, Buffalo, Toronto: Multilingual Matters Ltd.
Catenaccio, P. (2008). Press releases as a hybrid genre: Addressing the informative/promotional conundrum. *Pragmatics*, 18: 9–31.
Chaemsaithong, K. (2018). Use of voices in legal opening statements. *Social Semiotics*, 28(1): 90–107.
Chaemsaithong, K., & Kim, Y. (2018). From narration to argumentation: Intertextuality in two courtroom genres. *Lingua*, 203: 36–50.
Chen, J. (2015). Tools for immediate regulatory tax implementation: Subsidiary legislation vs legislation by press release. *Singapore Journal of Legal Studies*: 1–25.
Cheng, L., Cheng, W., & Sin, K. (2014). Revisiting legal terms: A semiotic perspective. *Semiotica*, 202: 167–182.
Clapp, J., Ghornburg, E., Galanter, M., & Shapiro, F. (2011). *Lawtalk: The Unknown Stories Behind Familiar Legal Expressions*. New Haven, CT: Yale University Press.
Cloître, M., & Shinn, T. (1985). Expository practice: Social, cognitive and epistemological linkages. In T. Shinn & R. Whitley (eds.), *Expository Science: Forms and Functions of Popularization*. Dordrecht/Boston/Lancaster: Reidel, 31–60.
Cohen, M. (2016). On the linguistic design of multinational courts: The French capture. *International Journal of Constitutional Law*, 14(2): 498–517.
Costa, J.-P. (2009). Opening speech. In *Ten Years of the "New" European Court of Human Rights. 1998–2008 Situation and Outlook. Proceedings of the Seminar*, 13 October 2008, Strasbourg, 11–15.
Costa, J.-P. (2011). Preface. In *Quel filtrage des requêtes par la Cour européenne des droits de l'"homme?* Strasbourg: Council of Europe, 7–9. https://book.coe.int/en/european-court-of-human-rights/4856-quel-filtrage-des-requetes-par-la-cour-europeenne-des-droits-de-l-homme.html
Costa, J.-P. (2021). *Judges for Freedom* (English translation by James Brannan). In *Encyclopaedia of the European Court*. Moscow: iRGa 5, Vol. 4, Book 1.
Coulthard, C. (1994). On reporting reporting: The representation of speech in factual and factional narratives. In M. Coulthard (ed.), *Advances in Written Text Analysis*. London: Routledge, 295–308.
Crystal, D., & Davy, D. (1973). The language of legal documents. In D. Crystal & D. Davy (eds.), *Investigating English Style*. Bloomington: Indiana University Press, 193–217.
Culpeper, J. (2005). Impoliteness and entertainment in the television quiz show: The weakest link. *Journal of Politeness Research*, 1(1): 35–72.
Culpeper, J. (2011). *Impoliteness: Using Language to Cause Offence* (1st ed.). Cambridge University Press.
Culpeper, J., & Hardaker, C. (2017). Impoliteness. In J. Culpeper, M. Haugh, & D. Kadar (eds.), *Palgrave Handbook of (Im)politeness*. Basingstoke: Palgrave, 199–225.
Culpeper, J., Haugh, M., & Sinkeviciute, V. (2017). (Im)politeness and mixed messages. In J. Culpeper, M. Haugh, & D. Kadar (eds.), *Palgrave Handbook of (Im)politeness*. Basingstoke: Palgrave, 323–355.
Cutting, J. (2000). *Analysing the Language of Discourse Communities*. Elsevier.
de Salvia, M., & Remus, M. (2011). *Ricorrere a Strasburgo: presupposti e procedura*. Milano: Giuffré Editore.

Degano, C., & Santulli, F. (2022). *Agreement in Argumentation: A Discursive Perspective.* Cham: Springer.

Degener, R. (2020). Pilot-judgment procedure: European Court of Human Rights (ECtHR). In *Max Planck Encyclopedia of International Procedural Law*, online. Available at https://opil.ouplaw.com/display/10.1093/law-mpeipro/e1961.013.1961/law-mpeipro-e1961, last accessed on 5 March 2024.

Dendale, P. (2006). Three linguistic theories of dialogism/polyphony: An external point of view and comparison. *Sprogli Polyphony Arbeitspapiren*, 5, February 2006. Roskilde: Institut for Sprog og Kultur, Roskilde Universitetscenter. Available at http://webh01.ua.ac.be/dendale/Articles/Dendale2006PolyphonyRoskilde.pdf

Deppermann, A. (2014). "Don't get me wrong": Recipient design by using negation to constrain an action's interpretation. In S. Günthner, W. Imo, & J. Bücker (eds.), *Grammar and Dialogism: Sequential, Syntactic, and Prosodic Patterns Between Emergence and Sedimentation.* Berlin: de Gruyter.

Devitt, A. J. (2004). *Writing Genres.* Carbondale: Sothern Illinois University Press.

Diani, G. (2018). Popularization of legal knowledge in English and Italian information books for children. In J. Engberg, K. Luttermann, & S. Cacchiani (eds.), *Popularization and Knowledge Mediation in the Law: Popularisierung und Wissensvermittlung im Recht.* Münster: LIT Verlag, Vol. 9, 291–316.

Diani, G., & Sezzi, A. (2019). The EU for children: A case of web-mediated knowledge dissemination. In S. Maci & M. Sala (eds.), *Representing and Redefining Specialised Knowledge: Variety in LSP.* University of Bergamo, 203–222.

Driedger, E. A. (1982). Legislative drafting style: Civil law versus common law. In J.-C. Gémar (ed.), *Langage du Droit et Traduction/The Language of the Law and Translation.* Montréal: Linguatech/Conseil de la Langue Française, 63–81.

Ducrot, O. (avec la collaboration de M. C. Barbault et J. Depresle). (1974). *La Preuve et le Dire. Langage et Logique.* Paris: Mame.

Ducrot, O. (1984). *Le dire et le dit.* Paris: Minuit.

Dunoff, J. L., & Pollack, M. A. (2017). The judicial trilemma. *The American Journal of International Law*, 111(2): 225–276.

Dworkin, R. (1986). *Law's Empire.* Harvard University Press.

ECtHR. (2020). *European Convention on Human Rights. A Living Instrument.* Strasbourg: Council of Europe. Available at https://edoc.coe.int/en/european-convention-on-human-rights/8528-the-european-convention-on-human-rights-a-living-instrument.html

Engberg, J. (2016). Conceptualising corporate criminal liability: Legal Linguistics and the combination of descriptive lenses. In G. Tessuto, et al. (eds.), *Constructing Legal Discourses and Social Practices: Issues and Perspectives.* Cambridge Scholars Publishing, 28–56.

Engberg, J. (2020). Comparative law for legal translation: Through multiple perspectives to multidimensional knowledge. *International Journal for the Semiotics of Law*, 33: 263–282.

Engberg, J. (2022). Looking for knowledge in language for law: Preliminaries for a knowledge communication approach to comparative law. *Comparative Law and Language*, 1(2): 74–86.

Engberg, J. (2023). Frame approach to legal terminology: What may be gained from seeing terminology as manifestation of legal knowledge? In Ł. Biel & H. J. Kockaert (eds.), *The Handbook of Terminology: Legal Terminology.* Amsterdam, Philadelphia: John Benjamins, Vol. 3, 16–36.

Entrikin, J. L. (2017). Disrespectful dissent: Justice Scalia's regrettable legacy of incivility. *The Journal of Appellate Practice and Process*, 18(2): 201–295.

Epstein, L., Landes, W., & Posner, R. (2013). *The Behavior of Federal Judges: A Theoretical and Empirical Study of Rational Choice.* Harvard: Harvard University Press.

Etxabe, J. (2022). The dialogical language of law. *Osgoode Hall Law Journal*, 59(2): 429–515.

Evans, T. (2005). *The Politics of Human Rights: A Global Perspective*. London: Pluto Press.
Fairclough, N. (1992). *Discourse and Social Change*. Oxford: Polity Press.
Fairclough, N. (2003). *Analysing Discourse: Textual Analysis for Social Research*. London, New York: Routledge.
Fawcett, J. (1967). The international protection of human rights. In D. D. Raphael (ed.), *Political Theory and the Rights of Man*. Bloomington: Indiana University Press, 119–133.
Felberg Radanović, T., & Šarić, L. (2017). Interpreting impoliteness: Interpreters' voices. *FLEKS-Scandinavian Journal of Intercultural Theory and Practice*, 4(1): 1–17.
Ferguson, R. A. (1990). The judicial opinion as literary genre. *Yale Journal of Law & the Humanities*, 2(1): 201–219.
Feteris, E. T. (2015). A pragma-dialectic approach of legal argumentation: The role of pragmatic argumentation in the justification of judicial decisions. In F. van Eemeren & B. Garssen (eds.), *Scrutinizing Argumentation in Practice*. Amsterdam/Philadelphia: John Benjamins, 99–119.
Feteris, E. T. (2017). *Fundamentals of Legal Argumentation: A Survey of Theories on the Justification of Judicial Decisions*. Dordrecht: Springer.
Flikschuh, K. (2011). On the cogency of human rights. *Jurisprudence*, 2: 17–36.
Foster, S. (2011). *Human Rights & Civil Liberties* (3rd ed.). Harlow: Longman.
Francioni, F. (2007). *Access to Justice as a Human Right*. Oxford University Press.
Francis, G. (1995). Corpus-driven grammar and its relevance to the learning of English in a cross-cultural situation. In A. Pakir (ed.), *English in Education: Multicultural Perspectives*. Singapore: Unipress.
Fraser, B. (1990). Perspectives on politeness. *Journal of Pragmatics*, 14: 219–236.
Freixa, J. (2006). Causes of denominative variation in terminology: A typology proposal. *Terminology*, 12(1): 51–77.
Fuglinszky, Á., & Somssich, R. (2020). Language-bound terms – Term-bound languages: The difficulties of translating a national civil code into a lingua franca. *International Journal for the Semiotics of Law – Revue Internationale de Sémiotique Juridique*, 33(3): 749–770. https://doi.org/10.1007/s11196-020-09704-x
Galdia, M. (2017). *Lectures on Legal Linguistics*. Berlin: Peter Lang.
Galtung, J., & Ruge, M. H. (1965). The structure of foreign news: The presentation of the Congo, Cuba and Cyprus crises in four Norwegian newspapers. *Journal of Peace Research*, 2: 64–91.
Garlicki, L. (2009). Judicial deliberations: The Strasbourg perspective. In N. Huls, M. Adams, & J. Bomhoff (eds.), *The Legitimacy of Highest Courts' Rulings: Judicial Deliberations and Beyond*. The Hague: TMC Asser Press, 389–397.
Garner, B. (2013). *Legal Writing in Plain English: A Text With Exercises*. University Press of Chicago.
Garzone, G. (2013). Variation in the use of modality in legislative texts: Focus on *shall*. *Journal of Pragmatics*, 57: 68–81.
Garzone, G. (2015). *Le traduzioni come fuzzy set. Percorsi teorici e applicativi*. Milan: LED.
Garzone, G. (2016). Polyphony and dialogism in legal discourse: Focus on syntactic negation. In G. Tessuto, et al. (eds.), *Constructing Legal Discourses and Social Practices: Issues and Perspectives*. Cambridge Scholars Publishing, 2–27.
Garzone, G. (2020). *Specialized Communication and Popularization in English*. Rome: Carocci.
Garzone, G., & Catenaccio, P. (2022). *Ethics in Professional and Corporate Discourse*. Berlin: Frank and Timme.
Gerards, J. (2017). The European Court of human rights. In A. Jakab, A. Dyevre, & G. Itzcovich (eds.), *Comparative Constitutional Reasoning*. Cambridge University Press, 237–276.

Goffman, E. (1967). *Interaction Ritual: Essays on Face-to-Face Interaction.* Aldine.

Goffman, E. (1981). *Forms of Talk.* Philadelphia: University of Pennsylvania Press.

Gotti, M. (2014). Reformulation and recontextualization in popularization discourse. *Ibérica*, 27: 15–34.

Goźdź-Roszkowski, S. (2011). *Patterns of Linguistic Variations in American Legal English: A Corpus-Based Study.* Frankfurt: Peter Lang.

Goźdź-Roszkowski, S. (2020). Communicating dissent in judicial opinions: A comparative, genre-based analysis. *International Journal for the Semiotics of Law = Revue Internationale de Sémiotique Juridique*, 33(2): 381–401.

Goźdź-Roszkowski, S. (2024). *Language and Legal Judgments: Evaluation and Argument in Judicial Discourse.* London, New York: Routledge.

Goźdź-Roszkowski, S., & Pontrandolfo, G. (2013). Evaluative patterns in judicial discourse: A corpus-based phraseological perspective on American and Italian criminal judgments. *International Journal of Law, Language and Discourse*, 3(2): 9–69.

Gregory, J., & Miller, S. (1998). *Science in Public: Communication, Culture, and Credibility.* New York: Plenum Trade.

Grove, T. L. (2020). Which textualism? *Harvard Law Review*, 134(1): 265–307.

Groves, M., & Mundt, K. (2021). A ghostwriter in the machine? Attitudes of academic staff towards machine translation use in internationalised higher education. *Journal of English for Academic Purposes*, 50: e100957.

Haiman, J. (1998). *Talk Is Cheap: Sarcasm, Alienation, and the Evolution of Language.* Oxford University Press.

Hale, S., Martschuk, N., Goodman-Delahunty, J., Taibi, M., & H. Xu. (2020). Interpreting profanity in police interviews. *Multilingua*, 39(4): 369–393.

Hampson, F., Martin, C., & Viljoen, F. (2018). Inaccessible apexes: Comparing access to regional human rights courts and commissions in Europe, the Americas, and Africa. *International Journal of Constitutional Law*, 16(1): 161–186.

Hardaker, C. (2020). Pranksters, provocateurs, propagandists: Using forensic corpus linguistics to identify and understand trolling. In M. Coulthard, A. May, & R. Sousa-Silva (eds.), *The Routledge Handbook of Forensic Linguistics.* London, New York: Routledge, 694–708.

Harris, D., O'Boyle, M., Bates, E., & Buckley, C. (2014). *Harris, O'Boyle, and Warbrick Law of the European Convention on Human Rights* (3rd ed.). Oxford University Press.

Harris, S. (2001). Being politically impolite: Extending politeness theory to adversarial political discourse. *Discourse and Society*, 12(4): 451–472.

Harris, S. (2011). The limits of politeness re-visited: Courtroom discourse as a case in point. In Linguistic Politeness Research Group (ed.), *Discursive Approaches to Politeness.* Berlin: De Gruyter Mouton.

Hart, H. L. A. (1961). *The Concept of Law.* Oxford University Press.

Hart, J. (2010). The European Human Rights system. *Law Library Journal*, 102: 533–559.

Hart, J. (2017). Update: International Human Rights. *GlobaLex.* Available at https://perma.cc/TA4N-WTKX

Helfer, L. R., & Voeten, E. (2020). Walking back human rights in Europe? *European Journal of International Law*, 31(3): 797–827.

Horn, L. (2001). *A Natural History of Negation.* Chicago: University of Chicago Press.

Horn, L. (ed.). (2010). *The Expression of Negation.* Berlin/New York: De Gruyter Mouton.

Huddleston, R., & Pullum, G. K. (2002). *The Cambridge Grammar of the English Language.* Cambridge: Cambridge University Press.

Hunston, S. (2002). *Corpora in Applied Linguistics.* Cambridge University Press.

Hunston, S. (2011). *Corpus Approaches to Evaluation: Phraseology and Evaluative Language. Routledge Advances in Corpus Linguistics.* Routledge.

Hunston, S., & Francis, G. (2000). *Pattern Grammar: A Corpus-Driven Approach to the Lexical Grammar of English*. Amsterdam: John Benjamins.

Husa, J. (2017). Translating legal language and comparative law. *International Journal for the Semiotics of Law*, 30(2): 261–272.

Ioriatti, E. (2021). Comparative law and EU legal language: Towards a European restatement? *Global Jurist*, 21(2): 305–340.

Jackson, J. (2022). Common Law Evidence and the Common Law of Human Rights: Towards a harmonic convergence? In J. Ferrer Beltrán & C. Vázquez (eds.), *Evidential Legal Reasoning: Crossing Civil Law and Common Law Traditions*. Cambridge University Press, 98–122.

Jacobs, G. (1999). *Preformulating the News: An Analysis of the Metapragmatics of Press Releases*. John Benjamins.

Jacobs, G. (2006). The dos and don'ts of writing press releases (and how learners act upon them). In P. Gillaerts & P. Shaw (eds.), *The Map and the Landscape: Norms and Practices in Genre*. Bern: Peter Lang, 199–218.

Jakobson, R. (1959). On linguistic aspects of translation. In R. Brower (ed.), *On Translation*. Harvard University Press, 232–239.

Janis, M., Kay, R., & Bradley, A. (2008). *European Human Rights Law: Text and Materials* (3rd ed.). Oxford University Press.

Jopek-Bosiacka, A. (2023). Definitions in law across legal cultures and jurisdictions. In Ł. Biel & H. J. Kockaert (eds.), *The Handbook of Terminology: Legal Terminology*. Amsterdam, Philadelphia: John Benjamins, Vol. 3, 37–71.

Kádár, D. Z., & Haugh, M. (2013). *Understanding Politeness*. Cambridge University Press.

Kecskes, I. (2013). Politeness and impoliteness. In *Intercultural Pragmatics*. Oxford University Press.

Kecskes, I. (2017). Context-dependency and impoliteness in intercultural communication. *Journal of Politeness Research: Language, Behaviour, Culture*, 13(1): 7–31.

Kelemen, K. (2018). *Judicial Dissent in European Constitutional Courts: A Comparative and Legal Perspective*. London, New York: Routledge.

Keller, H., & Heri, C. (2018). Deliberation and drafting: European Court of Human Rights (ECtHR). *Max Planck Encyclopedias of International Law [MPIL]*, online.

Kjær, A. L. (1990). Context-conditioned word combinations in legal language. *Terminology Science & Research, Journal of the International Institute of Terminology Research – IITF*, 1(1–2): 21–32.

Kjær, A. L. (2007). Phrasemes in legal texts. In H. Burger, D. Dobrovol'skij, P. Kühn & N. R. Norrick (eds.), *Phraseology: An International Handbook of Contemporary Research*. Berlin: Mouton de Gruyter, 506–516.

Kjær, A. L. (2011). European legal concepts in Scandinavian law and language. *Nordic Journal of International Law*, 80: 321–349.

Kjær, A. L. (2022). Translation of judgments of the European Court of Human Rights into non-official languages: The politics and practice of European multilingualism. In A. L. Kjær & J. Lam (eds.), *Language and Legal Interpretation in International Law*. New York: Oxford University Press, 189–220.

Kloosterhuis, H. (2013). The rule of law and the ideal of a critical discussion. In C. Dahlman & E. Feteris (eds.), *Legal Argumentation Theory: Cross-Disciplinary Perspectives*. Dordrecht: Springer, 71–83.

Kosař, D. (2015). Selecting Strasbourg judges: A critique. In M. Bobek (ed.), *Selecting Europe's Judges*. Oxford University Press, 120–161.

Koskinen, K. (2014). Institutional translation: The art of government by translation. *Perspectives*, 22: 479–492.

Kowalski, P. (2023). Statistical picture of the European Court of Human Rights' tax-related cases containing separate opinions. *EC Tax Review*, 32(1): 26–37.

Kurzon, D. (2001). The politeness of judges: American and English judicial behaviour. *Journal of Pragmatics*, 33(1): 61–85.

Lakoff, G., & Johnson, M. (1981). *Metaphors We Live By*. University of Chicago Press.
Lakoff, R. T. (1989). The limits of politeness: Therapeutic and courtroom discourse. *Multilingua Journal of Cross-Cultural and Interlanguage Communication*, 8: 101–130.
Lambert-Abdelgawad, E. (2010). The execution of decision of international human rights jurisdictions: Towards a harmonization of regional systems. *Anuario Colombiano de Derecho Internacional*, 3: 9–55.
Lambert-Abdelgawad, E. (2018). The practice of the European Court of Human Rights when striking out applications. *Netherlands Quarterly of Human Rights*, 36(1): 7–23.
Langford, C. L., & Ferguson, R. A. (2009). Toward a genre of judicial dissent: *Lochner* and *Casey* as exemplars. *Communication Law Review*, 9(2): 1–12.
Lanius, D. (2019). *Strategic Indeterminacy in the Law*. Oxford University Press.
Legg, A. (2012). *The Margin of Appreciation in International Human Rights Law: Deference and Proportionality*. Oxford University Press.
Lemmens, K. (2018). General survey of the convention. In P. van Dijk & G. J. H. Van Hoof (eds.), *Theory and Practice of the European Convention on Human Rights* (5th ed.). Antwerp: Intersentia, 1–78.
Lester, A. (1998). Universality versus subsidiarity: A reply. *European Human Rights Law Review*, 3: 73–77.
Letsas, G. (2011). Judge Rozakis' separate opinions and the Strasbourg dilemma. Available at SSRN: https://ssrn.com/abstract=1872384
Levy, B. H., & Levy, B. F. (1971). On justification of judicial decisions: Some American contributions. *Logique et analyse*, 14(53/54): 301–312.
Lindholm, K. (2008). A community text pattern in the European commission press release? A generic and genetic view. *Pragmatics*, 18(1): 33–58.
Lo Cascio, V. (2009). *Persuadere e convincere oggi. Nuovo manuale dell'argomentazione*. Milan: Academiauniversa Press.
Maass, C. (2020). *Easy Language, Plain Language, Easy Language Plus: Balancing Comprehensibility and Acceptability*. Frank & Timme.
MacKenzie, I., & Kayman, M. (2016). Introduction: Formulaicity and creativity in language and literature. *European Journal of English Studies*, 20(1): 1–14.
Madsen, M. R. (2018). Rebalancing European Human Rights: Has the Brighton declaration engendered a new deal on Human Rights in Europe? *Journal of International Dispute Settlement*, 9(2): 199–222.
Madsen, M. R. (2021). "Unity in diversity" reloaded: The European Court of Human Rights' turn to subsidiarity and its consequences. *Law & Ethics of Human Rights*, 15(1): 93–123.
Malblanc, M. (2019). *La technique des notions autonomes en droit de la Convention européenne des droits de l'Homme*. Doctoral dissertation, Lyon 2 University.
Maley, Y. (1994). The language of the law. In J. Gibbons (ed.), *Language and the Law*. London: Longman, 11–50.
Martin, J. R., & White, P. R. R. (2005). *The Language of Evaluation: Appraisal in English*. London: Palgrave Macmillan.
Mateo, J., & Yus, F. (2000). Insults: A relevance-theoretic taxonomical approach to their translation. *International Journal of Translation*, 12(1): 97–130.
Matoesian, G. (2000). Intertextual authority in reported speech: Production media in the Kennedy Smith rape trial. *Journal of Pragmatics*, 32(7): 879–914.
Mattila, H. E. S. (2013). *Comparative Legal Linguistics: Language of Law, Latin and Modern Lingua Francas* (2nd ed.). Aldershot: Ashgate.
Mazzi, D. (2007a). "The rhetoric of judicial texts": The interplay of reported argumentation and the judge's argumentative voice. In G. Garzone & S. Sarangi (eds.), *Discourse, Ideology and Specialized Communication*. Frankfurt am Main: Peter Lang, 379–399.

Mazzi, D. (2007b). The construction of argumentation in judicial texts: Combining a genre and a corpus perspective. *Argumentation*, 21(1): 21–38.
Mazzi, D. (2010). "This argument fails for two reasons. . .": Linguistic analysis of judicial evaluation strategies in us supreme court judgments. *International Journal for the Semiotics of Law*, 23(4): 373–386.
Mazzi, D. (2011). "In other words, . . .": A corpus-based study of reformulation in judicial discourse. *HERMES*, 46: 11–24.
Mazzi, D. (2021). Without proof of negligence or a causative connection: On causal argumentation in the discourse of the Supreme Court of Ireland's judgments on data protection. In S. Goźdź-Roszkowski & G. Pontrandolfo (eds.), *Law, Language and the Courtroom*. London: Routledge, 112–125.
McAuliffe, K. (2015). Translating ambiguity. *Journal of Comparative Law*, 9(2): 65–87.
McAuliffe, K. (2016). Hidden translators: The invisibility of translators and the influence of lawyer-linguists on the case law of the Court of Justice of the European Union. *Language and Law/Linguagem e Direito*, 3(1): 5–29.
McAuliffe, K. (2017). Behind the scenes at the Court of Justice: A story of process and people. In B. Davies & F. Nicola (eds.), *EU Law Stories*. Cambridge University Press. Available at SSRN: https://ssrn.com/abstract=3808094
McAuliffe, K. (2020). Creating multilingual law: Language and translation at the Court of Justice of the European Union. In M. Coulthard, A. May, & R. Sousa-Silva (eds.), *The Routledge Handbook of Forensic Linguistics*. London and New York: Routledge, Vol. 2, 64–78.
McEnery, T. (2006). *Swearing in English: Bad Language, Purity and Power From 1586 to the Present*. London: Routledge.
McKeown, J. (2021). A corpus-based examination of reflexive metadiscourse in majority and dissent opinions of the U.S. Supreme Court. *Journal of Pragmatics*, 186: 224–235.
Mellinkoff, D. (1963). *The Language of the Law*. Boston: Little Brown & Co.
Merrills, J. (1993). *The Development of International Law by the European Court of Human Rights*. Manchester University Press.
Miller, C. (1984). Genre as a social action. *Quarterly Journal of Speech*, 70: 151–167.
Molbæk-Steensig, H. (2023). Subsidiarity does not win cases: A mixed methods study of the relationship between margin of appreciation language and deference at the European Court of Human Rights. *Leiden Journal of International Law*, 36(1): 83–107.
Mossop, B. (1988). Translating institutions: A missing factor in translation theory. *TTR: Traduction, terminologie, rédaction*, 1(2): 65–71.
Mouritsen, S. (2023). Ordinary meaning in common law legal interpretation. In Ł. Biel & H. J. Kockaert (eds.), *The Handbook of Terminology: Legal Terminology*. Amsterdam, Philadelphia: John Benjamins, Vol. 3, 72–89.
Nikitina, J. (2018a). *Legal Style Markers and Their Translation: Written Pleadings at the ECtHR*. Beau Bassin-Riga: Edizioni accademiche italiane.
Nikitina, J. (2018b). *Written Pleadings before the ECtHR. Genre Description and Text-Organising Patterns*. Vicalvi: Key Editore.
Nikitina, J. (2019a). Discourse on medically assisted procreation: From legal institutions to blogs. *Textus*, XXXII(1): 55–74.
Nikitina, J. (2019b). New balance of conventionality: Phraseological patterns in L2 translations of written pleadings before the European Court of Human Rights. In V. Bonsignori, G. Cappelli, & E. Mattiello (eds.), *Worlds of Words: Complexity, Creativity, and Conventionality in English Language, Literature and Culture*. Pisa: Pisa University Press, Vol. 1, 313–324.
Nikitina, J. (2019c). Representing gene-editing in newspapers: Between science dissemination and fantasy. In G. De Riso, R. Doerr, & G. Garzone (eds.), *Representing,*

Disseminating, and Debating Controversial Bioethical Issues in Popularised Discourse, special issue of *Anglistica AION*, 23(1): 43–56.
Nikitina, J. (2019d). The discourse of bioethics in the ECtHR case-law: A corpus-based perspective. *Lingue e Linguaggi*, 27: 269–289.
Nikitina, J. (2021). Exploring ideological messages in newspaper editorials and news reports on the first human gene-editing case. *Lingue e Linguaggi*, 42: 101–122.
Nikitina, J. (2022a). Case communication at the ECtHR: Genre-based and translation perspectives. *Lingue e Linguaggi*, 52: 229–248.
Nikitina, J. (2022b). The discourse of the European Court of Human Rights: The role of case communications in the introduction of system-bound elements. In L. Ločmele (ed.), *Language for International Communication: Linking Interdisciplinary Perspectives: Language for Specific Purposes in the Era of Multilingualism and Technologies.* Riga: University of Latvia Press, Vol. 4, 91–106.
Nikitina, J. (2022c). The Covid-19-related cases before the European Court of Human Rights: A multiperspective approach. *Languages Cultures Mediations*, 9(2): 101–122.
Nikitina, J. (2023a). On the definitory crossroads: Legal, medical and popularized definitions of (human) gene editing. In K. Ackerley, et al. (eds.), *Thinking Out of the Box in English Linguistics, Language Teaching, Translation and Terminology.* Padua University Press, 309–331.
Nikitina, J. (2023b). Evolving patterns of knowledge dissemination and digital communication of law: Institutional press releases at the European Court of Human Rights. Presentation delivered at the annual conference of the *Italian Association of English Studies AIA XXXI: Future Horizons: New Beginnings in English Studies*, 14 September 2023, University of Calabria, Rende (CS).
Nikitina, J. (2025, forthcoming). Dialogical reasoning in separate judicial opinions: The path of negation. In S. Goźdź-Roszkowski & G. Pontrandolfo (eds.), *In the Minds of Judges. Argumentative Discourse at the Intersection of Law and Language.* De Gruyter.
O'Boyle, M. (2010). The future. In E. Myjer, et al. (eds.), *The Conscience of Europe: 50 Years of the European Court of Human Rights.* London: Council of Europe, Third Millennium Publishing Limited.
Office of the High Commissioner for Human Rights & the International Bar Association. (2003). *Human Rights in the Administration of Justice: A Manual on Human Rights for Judges, Prosecutors and Lawyers.* New York, Geneva: United Nations.
Ondelli, S., & Pontrandolfo, G. (2016). Multiple negatives in legal language: The case of English, Italian and Spanish. In G. Tessuto, V. Bhatia, G. Garzone, R. Salvi, & C. Williams (eds.), *Constructing Legal Discourses and Social Practices: Issues and Perspectives.* Cambridge: Cambridge Scholar Publishing, 146–171.
Parks, T. (2014). *Where I'm Reading From: The Changing World of Books.* London: Harvill Secker.
Partington, A., Duguid, A., & Taylor, C. (2013). *Patterns and Meanings in Discourse: Theory and Practice in Corpus-Assisted Discourse Studies (CADS).* Amsterdam, Philadelphia: John Benjamins.
Paúl, A. (2017). The American convention on human rights: Updated by the Inter-American Court. *Iuris Dictio*, 20: 53–87.
Paulus, A. (2019). *Judgments and Separate Opinions: Complementarity and Tensions*, speech delivered at the Opening of the Judicial Year on January 25, 2019. Strasbourg: Council of Europe.
Pedersen, J. (2005). How is culture rendered in subtitles? In *MuTra 2005 – Challenges of Multidimensional Translation: Conference Proceedings*, Saarbrücken: Marie Curie Euroconferences. 1–18. https://www.translationconcepts.org/pdf/MuTra_2005_Proceedings.pdf
Perelman, C., & Olbrechts-Tyteca, L. (1969). *The New Rhetoric: A Treatise on Argumentation.* Paris: University of Notre Dame Press.

Peruzzo, K. (2012). Secondary term formation within the EU: Term transfer, legal transplant or approximation of Member States' legal systems? *The Journal of Specialized Translation*, 18(2): 175–186.

Peruzzo, K. (2019a). When international case-law meets national law: A corpus-based study on Italian system-bound loan words in ECtHR judgments. *Translation Spaces*, 8(1): 12–38.

Peruzzo, K. (2019b). *National Law in Supranational Case-Law: A Linguistic Analysis of European Court of Human Rights Judgments in English*. Trieste: EUT Edizioni.

Peruzzo, K. (2023). Legal terms that travel: Constraints to presenting national legal terminology to international audiences. In Ł. Biel & H. J. Kockaert (eds.), *The Handbook of Terminology: Legal Terminology*. Amsterdam, Philadelphia: John Benjamins, Vol. 3, 152–172.

Peruzzo, K., & Scarpa, F. (2023). Making national immigration and asylum case law accessible to a non-Italian audience: The role of intra-lingual translation. In P. Anesa & J. Engberg (eds.), *The Digital (R)Evolution of Legal Discourse: New Genres, Media, and Linguistic Practices*. Berlin, Boston: de Gruyter, 121–142.

Pisillo Mazzeschi, R. (2021). *International Human Rights Law: Theory and Practice*. Springer.

Plantin, C. (1996). *L'Argumentation*. Paris: Seuil.

Plantin, C. (2005). *L'Argumentation. Histoire, Théorie et Perspectives*. Paris: PUF.

Plantin, C. (ed.). (2022). *Argumentation Through Languages and Cultures*. Springer.

Pontrandolfo, G. (2016). *Fraseología y lenguaje judicial. Las sentencias penales desde una perspectiva contrastiva*. Roma: Aracne.

Pontrandolfo, G. (2023). The importance of being patterned: Old and new perspectives on legal phraseology. In Ł. Biel & H. J. Kockaert (eds.), *The Handbook of Terminology: Legal Terminology*. Amsterdam, Philadelphia: John Benjamins, Vol. 3, 124–150.

Pontrandolfo, G., & Goźdź-Roszkowski, S. (2014). Exploring the local grammar of evaluation: The case of adjectival patterns in judicial discourse. *Research in Language*, 12(1): 71–91.

Popović, D. (2007). Le Droit Comparé dans l'Accomplissement des Tâches de la Cour Européenne des Droits de l'Homme. In L. Caflisch, et al. (eds.), *Droits de l'Homme. Regards de Strasbourg, Liber Amicorum Luzius Wildhaber*. Kehl: N.P. Engel Verlag, 371–386.

Prakken, H. (1993). *Logical Tools for Modelling Legal Argument*. Amsterdam: Dissertation Amsterdam.

Prakken, H. (2005). AI & law, logic and argument schemes. *Argumentation*, 19: 303–320.

Prakken, H., & Sartor, G. (1996). A dialectical model of assessing conflicting arguments in legal reasoning. *Artificial Intelligence and Law*, 4: 331–368.

Prieto Ramos, F. (2014a). Legal translation studies as interdiscipline: Scope and evolution. *Meta: Translators' Journal*, 59: 260–277.

Prieto Ramos, F. (2014b). Quality assurance in legal translation: Evaluating process, competence and product in the pursuit of adequacy. *International Journal for the Semiotics of Law*, 28: 11–30.

Prieto Ramos, F. (2014c). Parameters for problem-solving in legal translation: Implications for legal lexicography and institutional terminology management. In *The Ashgate Handbook of Legal Translation*. Farnham: Ashgate, 121–134.

Prieto Ramos, F. (2020). Translation at international organizations: The legal and linguistic hierarchies of multilingualism. In M. Ji & S. Laviosa (eds.), *The Oxford Handbook of Translation and Social Practices*. Oxford University Press, 455–477.

Prieto Ramos, F. (2021). Translating legal terminology and phraseology: Between inter-systemic incongruity and multilingual harmonization. *Perspectives*, 29(2): 175–183.

Prieto Ramos, F., & Guzman, D. (2018). Legal terminology consistency and adequacy as quality indicators in institutional translation: A mixed-method comparative study. In F. Prieto Ramos (ed.), *Institutional Translation for International Governance: Enhancing Quality in Multilingual Legal Communication.* London: Bloomsbury, 81–101.

Quirk, R., Greenbaum, S., Leech, G., & Svartvik, J. (1985). *A Comprehensive Grammar of the English Language.* London: Longman.

Rachovitsa, A. (2019). On new "judicial animals": The curious case of an African court with material jurisdiction of a global scope. *Human Rights Law Review*, 19(2): 255–289.

Rachovitsa, A. (2020). Balancing test (ACtHPR). In H. Ruiz-Fabri (ed.), *Max Planck Encyclopedia of International Procedural Law.* Oxford University Press, 2020 (forthcoming) – Unedited Version. Available at https://pure.rug.nl/ws/portalfiles/portal/136163960/Balancing_Test_ACtHPR.pdf

Rainey, B., Wicks, E., & Ovey, C. (2017). *Jacobs, White, and Ovey: The European Convention on Human Rights* (7th ed.). Oxford University Press.

Rappaport, B. (2014). A lawyer's hidden persuader: Genre bias and how it shapes legal texts by constraining writer's choices and influencing readers' perceptions. *Journal of Law and Policy*, 22(1): 197–263.

Richardson, P. J. (ed.). (2006). *Archbold 2006: Criminal Pleading, Evidence and Practice.* London: Sweet &Maxwell.

Ridao Rodrigo, S. (2016). Between truth and lies: (Im)politeness strategies in trials. *Revista de llengua i dret*, 65: 59–75.

Rietiker, D., 2013. The European Court of Human Rights from a comparative law viewpoint: A logical example of a "mixed jurisdiction" court. *Cyprus Human Rights Law Review*, 2(1): 36–52.

Rivière, F. (2005). *Les opinions séparées des juges à la Cour européenne des droits de l'homme.* Bruxelles: Bruylant.

Robertson, M. K. (1982). Popularization of law. *The Comparative and International Law Journal of Southern Africa*, 15(2): 158–188.

Roitman, M. (2015). Constructing one's arguments based on refutations of the other's discourse. A study of the traditional presidential debate: Chirac/Jospin (1995) versus Sarkozy/Royal (2007). *Argumentation*, 29(1): 19–32.

Rosulek, L. (2010). Legitimation and the heteroglossic nature of closing arguments. In D. Schiffrin, A. De Fina, & A. Nylund (eds.), *Telling Stories: Language, Narrative, and Social Life.* Washington, DC: Georgetown University Press, 181–194.

Rowe, N., & Schlette, V. (1998). The protection of human rights in Europe after the eleventh protocol to the ECHR. *European Law Review*, 23: 3–16.

Sager, J. (1990). *A Practical Course in Terminology Processing.* Amsterdam: John Benjamins.

Sager, J. (1998). Terminology: Theory. In M. Baker (ed.), *Routledge Encyclopedia of Translation Studies.* London, New York: Routledge, 258–262.

Sala, M. (2014). Plain language in legal studies: A corpus-based study. *The European Journal of Law Reform*, 16(3): 651–668.

Salojärvi, J. (2020). The rise of human rights discourse, 1965–1980. In *Human Rights Redefining Legal Thought: Studies in the History of Law and Justice.* Cham: Springer, Vol. 16.

Salvi, R., & Bowker, J. (2015). Introduction. In R. Salvi & J. Bowker (eds.), *The Dissemination of Contemporary Knowledge in English.* Lausanne: Peter Lang Verlag, 11–18.

Šarčević, S. (1985). Translation of culture-bound terms in laws. *Multilingua*, 4(3): 127–134.

Šarčević, S. (1997). *New Approach to Legal Translation.* The Hague: Kluwer Law International.

Šarčević, S. (2007). Making multilingualism work in the enlarged Europe Union. In K. Kredens & S. Goźdź-Roszkowski (eds.), *Language and the Law: International Outlooks*. Frankfurt am Main: Peter Lang, 35–54.
Šarčević, S. (2018). Challenges to legal translators in institutional settings. In F. Prieto Ramos (ed.), *Institutional Translation for International Governance: Enhancing Quality in Multilingual Legal Communication*. Bloomsbury: London, 9–24.
Sartor, G. (2002). Teleological arguments and theory-based dialectics. *Artificial Intelligence and Law*, 10: 95–112.
Schäffner, C., Tcaciuc, L. S., & Tesseur, W. (2014). Translation practices in political institutions: A comparison of national, supranational, and non-governmental organisations. *Perspectives*, 22(4): 493–510.
Scheinin, M. (2009). Impact on the law of treaties. In M. T. Kamminga & M. Scheinin (eds.), *The Impact of Human Rights Law on General International Law*. Oxford University Press, 23–36.
Schmitt, P. (2017). *Access to Justice and International Organizations: The Case of Individual Victims of Human Rights Violations*. Edward Elgar Publishing.
Senden, H. (2011). *Interpretation of Fundamental Rights in a Multilevel Legal System: An Analysis of the European Court of Human Rights and the Court of Justice of the European Union*. Antwerp: Intersentia.
Shelton, D. (2016). Significantly disadvantaged? Shrinking access to the European Court of Human Rights. *Human Rights Law Review*, 16: 303–322.
Shuy, R. W. (2007). Language in the American courtroom. *Language and Linguistics Compass*, 1(1–2): 100–114.
Sicilianos, L.-A. (2018). *The Reform and Current Challenges in the Work of the European Court of Human Rights*. Strasbourg: Council of Europe.
Sicilianos, L-A., & Kostopoulou, M.-A. (2019). *The Individual Application Under the European Convention on Human Rights. Procedural Guide*. Strasbourg: Council of Europe.
Siems, M. (2022). *Comparative Law* (3rd ed.). Cambridge: Cambridge University Press.
Sissons, H. (2012). Journalism and public relations: A tale of two discourses. *Discourse & Communication*, 6(3): 273–294.
Solan, L., & Tiersma, P. (2012). Introduction. In P. Tiersma & L. Solan (eds.), *The Oxford Handbook of Language and Law*. Oxford University Press, 1–9.
Solan, L. M. (1993). *The Language of Judges*. University of Chicago Press.
Sousa Domingues, J. (2017). The multilingual jurisprudence of the Court of Justice and the idea of uniformity in European Union Law. *UNIO – EU Law Journal*, 3(2): 125–138.
Spano, R. (2018). The future of the European Court of Human Rights – Subsidiarity, process-based review and the rule of law. *Human Rights Law Review*, 18(3): 473–494.
Spielmann, D. (2012). *Allowing the Right Margin: The European Court of Human Rights and the National Margin of Appreciation Doctrine – Waiver or Subsidiarity of European Review?* Cambridge: Centre for European Legal Studies Working Paper Series.
Stein, D. (2015). Words, words, words – But what's in a legal text? In L. Solan, J. Ainsworth, & R. Shuy (eds.), *Speaking of Language and Law: Conversations on the Work of Peter Tiersma*. Oxford University Press, 51–55.
Stone Sweet, A., Sandholtz, W., & Andenas, M. (2021). Dissenting opinions and rights protection in the European Court: A reply to Laurence Helfer and Erik Voeten. *European Journal of International Law*, 32(3): 897–905.
Swales, J. (1990). *Genre Analysis: English in Academic and Research Settings*. Cambridge University Press.

Swales, J. (1996). Occluded genres in the academy: The case of the submission letter. In E. Ventola & A. Mauranen (eds.), *Academic Writing: Intercultural and Textual Issues*. Amsterdam: John Benjamins, 45–58.

Tedeschi, J. T., & Felson, R. B. (1994). Coercive actions and aggression. In J. T. Tedeschi & R. B. Felson (eds.), *Violence, Aggression, and Coercive Actions*. American Psychological Association, 159–176.

Tessuto, G. (2021). Making sense of web-based European Court of Justice institutional press releases: Context, structure and replicable genres. *Ibérica*, 42: 219–244.

Thompson, G., & Hunston, S. (2000). Evaluation: An introduction. In G. Thompson & S. Hunston (eds.), *Evaluation in Text: Authorial Stance and the Construction of Discourse*. Oxford University Press, 1–27.

Tiersma, P. (1999). *Legal English*. Chicago University Press.

Tiersma, P. (2007). The textualization of precedent. *The Notre Dame Law Review*, 82(3): 1187–1278.

Tiersma, P. (2008). The nature of legal language. In J. Gibbons & M. T. Turrell (eds.), *Dimensions of Forensic Linguistics*. Amsterdam, Philadelphia: John Benjamins, 14–25.

Tiersma, P. (2015 [2006]). Some myths about legal language. In L. Solan, J. Ainsworth, & R. Shuy (eds.), *Speaking of Language and Law: Conversations on the Work of Peter Tiersma*. Oxford University Press, 27–34.

Titiun, P. (2015). La création d'un service de presse de la Cour à Strasbourg: Enjeux passés, présents et futurs. In E. Lambert-Abdelgawad & P. Dourneau-Josette (eds.), *La Cour européenne des droits de l'homme dans la presse*. Brussels: Nemesis, 129–136.

Toury, G. (1986). Monitoring discourse transfer: A test–case for a developmental model of translation. In J. House & S. Blum–Kulka (eds.), *Interlingual and Intercultural Communication: Discourse and Cognition in Translation and Second Language Acquisition Studies*. Gunter Narr: Tübingen, 79–94.

Toury, G. (1995). *Descriptive Translation Studies – And Beyond*. Amsterdam: John Benjamins.

Tracy, K. (2008). "Reasonable hostility": Situation-appropriate face-attack. *Journal of Politeness Research: Language, Behaviour, Culture*, 4: 169–191.

Valoti, G. (2023). *The Linguistic Regime of the Inter-American Court of Human Rights the Challenges of Translating and Interpreting in a Multicultural Environment*. Unpublished BA Degree Thesis (Supervisor J. Nikitina). University of Milan.

van de Meene, I., & van Rooij, B. (2008). *Access to Justice and Legal Empowerment: Making the Poor Central in Legal Development Co-Operation*. Leiden University Press.

van Els, T. J. M. (2001). The European Union, its institutions and its languages: Some language political observations. *Current Issues in Language Planning*, 2(4): 311–360. https://doi.org/10.1080/14664200108668030

Vandenhole, W. (2019). Of principles and values: An explorative reading of separate opinions of Judge Paul Lemmens. In K. Lemmens, S. Parmentier, & L. Reyntjens (eds.), *Human Rights with a Human Touch: Liber Amicorum Paul Lemmens*. Cambridge, Antwerp and Chicago: Intersentia, 41–62.

van Eemeren, F. H. (2010). *Strategic Maneuvering in Argumentative Discourse: Extending the Pragma-Dialectical Theory of Argumentation*. Amsterdam, Philadelphia: John Benjamins.

van Eemeren, F. H., & Grootendorst, R. (1992). *Argumentation, Communication, and Fallacies: A Pragma-Dialectical Perspective*. Hillsdale, NJ: Erlbaum.

van Leeuwen, T. (2005). *Introducing Social Semiotics*. London, New York: Routledge.

Viljoen, F. (2012). *International Human Rights Law in Africa* (2nd ed.). Oxford University Press.

Villiger, M. (2017). Judgment: European Court of Human Rights (ECtHR). *Max Planck Encyclopedias of International Law [MPIL]*, online.

Villiger, M. (2019). The research division of the European Court of Human Rights and its relevance for the court's case-law. In K. Lemmens, S. Parmentier, & L. Reyntjens (eds.), *Human Rights with a Human Touch: Liber Amicorum Paul Lemmens*. Cambridge, Antwerp and Chicago: Intersentia, 449–466.

Voeten, E. (2008). The impartiality of international Judges: Evidence from the European Court of Human Rights. *The American Political Science Review*, 102(4): 417–433.

Waldock, C. M. H. (1958). The European Convention for the Protection of Human Rights and fundamental freedoms. *XXXIV British Year Book of International Law*, 356.

Watson, A. (1974). *Legal Transplants: An Approach to Comparative Law*. Scottish Academic Press.

Watts, R. (2003). *Politeness*. Cambridge University Press.

Weston, M. (1988). The role of translation at the European Court of Human Rights. In F. Matscher & H. Petzold (eds.), *Protecting Human Rights: The European Dimension. Studies in Honour of Gerard J. Wiarda* (2nd ed.). Koln: Carl Heymanns Verlag, 679–689.

Weston, M. (2005). Characteristics and constraints of producing bilingual judgments: The example of the European Court of Human Rights. In J.-C. Gémar & N. Kasirer (eds.), *Jurilinguistics: Between Law and Language*. Brussels: Bruylant, 445–459.

Weston, M. (2010). Speaking unto nations: The language dimension of the Court's work. In J. Sharpe (ed.), *The Conscience of Europe: 50 Years of the European Court of Human Rights*. London: Third Millennium Publishing, 77–79.

White, R. (2009). *Judgments in the Strasbourg Court: Some Reflections*. Available at https://papers.ssrn.com/sol3/papers.cfm?abstract_id=1435197

White, R., & Boussiakou, I. (2009). Separate opinions in the European Court of Human Rights. *Human Rights Law Review*, 9(1): 37–60.

Williams, C. (2007). *Tradition and Change in Legal English: Verbal Constructions in Prescriptive Texts* (2nd ed.). Bern: Peter Lang.

Williams, C. (2011). Legal English and plain language: An update. *ESP Across Cultures*, 8: 139–151.

Woolf, H., et al. (2005). *Review of the Working Methods of the European Court of Human Rights*. Strasbourg: Council of Europe. Available at https://www.echr.coe.int/documents/d/echr/2005_lord_woolf_working_methods_eng

Wright, S. (2018). The impact of multilingualism on the judgments of the EU Court of Justice. In F. Prieto Ramos (ed.), *Institutional Translation for International Governance: Enhancing Quality in Multilingual Legal Communication*. London: Bloomsbury, 141–156.

Zeijlstra, H. (2004). *Sentential Negation and Negative Concord*. Amsterdam: University of Amsterdam.

Zeijlstra, H. (2023). *Negation and Negative Dependencies*. Oxford University Press.

Zejnilović, L., Tripković Samardžić, V., & Knežević, Ž. (2022). Pragmatic aspects of judicial discourse: Zooming in on a nuanced language use. *Folia linguistica et litteraria*, XIII(42): 261–278.

Legal and institutional sources

ACtHPR. (2020). *Rules of Court*. Arusha: African Union. Available at https://www.african-court.org/wpafc/wp-content/uploads/2021/04/Rules-Final-Revised-adopted-Rules-eng-April-2021.pdf

African Union. (1981). *African Charter on Human and Peoples' Rights*.

Australian Government. (2011). *Federal Plain Language Guidelines*. Available at https://www.plainlanguage.gov/media/FederalPLGuidelines.pdf

Council of Europe. (1950). *Convention for the Protection of Human Rights and Fundamental Freedoms.* Council of Europe Treaty Series 005.

Council of Europe. (2004). *Explanatory Report to Protocol No. 14 to the Convention for the Protection of Human Rights and Fundamental Freedoms, Amending the Control System of the Convention.* Available at https://rm.coe.int/16800d380f

Council of Europe & EctHR. (2024). *Guide on Article 6 of the European Convention on Human Rights. Right to a Fair Trial (criminal limb).* Available at https://ks.echr.coe.int/documents/d/echr-ks/guide_art_6_criminal_eng

Drafting Techniques Group (DTG). (2008). *Shall. Paper 19.* Available at http://www.writerguy.co.uk/wp–content/uploads/2015/02/shall.pdf

ECtHR. (2009). *Pilot-Judgment Procedure.* Available at https://www.echr.coe.int/documents/d/echr/pilot_judgment_procedure_eng

ECtHR. (2014). *The Court's Case-Law Translations Programme: Aims, Achievements and Remaining Challenges.* Available at http://www.echr.coe.int/Documents/HRTF_standards_translations_ENG.pdf

ECtHR. (2017). *"Bringing the Convention closer to home" The Court's case-law translations project (2012–2016): Achievements and remaining challenges.* Available at https://rm.coe.int/168070c5c7

ECtHR. (2021). *The ECtHR in 50 Questions.* Available at https://www.echr.coe.int/documents/d/echr/50questions_eng

ECtHR. (2022). *The European Convention on Human Rights: A Living Instrument.* Available at https://www.echr.coe.int/documents/d/echr/Convention_Instrument_ENG, last accessed on 3 March 2024.

ECtHR. (2023a). *European Court of Human Rights: Finding and Understanding the Case-Law.* Available at https://www.echr.coe.int/documents/d/echr/clip_finding_understanding_case_law_eng

ECtHR. (2023b). *Practical Guide on Admissibility Criteria.* Strasbourg: Council of Europe. Available at https://prd-echr.coe.int/documents/d/echr/Admissibility_guide_ENG

ECtHR. (2023c). *Application Form.* Strasbourg: Council of Europe. Available at https://www.echr.coe.int/apply-to-the-court

ECtHR. (2024). *Rules of Court.* Strasbourg: Council of Europe. Available at https://prd-echr.coe.int/documents/d/echr/rules_court_eng

IACtHR. (2000). *Rules of Procedure of the Inter-American Court of Human Rights.* San José. Available at https://www.oas.org/36ag/english/doc_referencia/reglamento_corteidh.pdf

International Organization for Standardization (ISO). (2020). *ISO 20771:2020(en) Legal Translation – Requirements.* Available at https://www.iso.org/obp/ui/en/#iso:std:iso:20771:ed-1:v1:en

New Zealand's Parliamentary Counsel Office. (2009). *Plain Language.* Available at https://www.pco.govt.nz/plain-language

Organization of American States. (1969). *American Convention on Human Rights.* Treaty Series, No. 36.

Steering Committee for Human Rights. (2004). *Position Paper of the European Court of Human Rights on Proposals for Reform of the European Convention on Human Rights,* 4 April 2003 [CDDH-GDR(2003)024].

Venice Commission (the European Commission for Democracy Through Law) & the ECtHR Research Division. (2018). *Opinion No. 932/1018,* 17 December 2018, CDL-AD(2018)030rev.

Index

Note: Page locators in **bold** indicate a table and page locators in *italics* indicate a figure.

ability 51, 61, 78, 88, 95, 97, 185, 220
absurdity 192–193
accountability 199
ACHPR *see* African Charter on Human and People's Rights
ACHR *see* American Convention of Human Rights
ACtHPR *see* African Court on Human and People's Rights
adaptation: linguistic 138, 230, 239, 242; of system-bound elements 99, 264
admissibility criteria for applications to the Court: compliance 81–82, 85, **174**; observations 127, **128**, 131; procedures 56–57, 63–65, 68, 72, 80–81, 202; reforms 51–52, *54*, 55
advisory opinion 53, 55, 66, 196
African Charter on Human and People's Rights (ACHPR) **16–17**, 18, 22–24, 33–34
African Court on Human and People's Rights (ACtHPR): culture 15–16; genres *23*, 72; jurisdictional reach 24, 33, 35; two-tier/dual system 18–19, 46, 77
African Union (AU) 16–17, 20
American Convention of Human Rights (ACHR) **16**, 22–24, 78, 179
applicant: abuse of right of application 82, 87; administrative liability 146; case referral 46, 78; counter-argument 149–150; increased claims against government 49; linguistic diversity 69; sequence of actions 61, 63, 84, **101**; *significant disadvantage* 52, 82
application: accompanying document list 86; admissibility (ratione) 18, 46, 48, 56, 64, 81–82; application form 80, 84; initial application 79 (*see also* right to a fair trial); modification criteria 52; statement of facts 85; time-limits 82; use of language 85
Arabic language 8, **19**, 21n21
argument: acceptable 137; contrasting/opposing 142–143, 145, 149–150; legal 28, 42, 133; structure 134
argumentation: legal argumentation toolbox 133–134; patterns 158, 181, 185; schemes 147; voicing/reporting 138; what/how of 134; *see also* legal reasoning; pragma-dialectics
argumentation theory 133–134
argumentative: discourse 133–134, 152; premise 140, 149, 183, 186–187; proposition 190–191
argumentative patterns 117, 138
arrêt *see* judgment
Article 10 *see* freedom of expression
Article 45 *see* Rules of Court
Article 6 *see* right to a fair trial
assessment 63, 70, 109, 142, 182–183, 186–187, 191, 226
attitudinal bundle 182–183, 185
Austin, J.L. 133, 179
Australia 85
authentic 117, 157, 162; *see also* equal authenticity; legal authenticity
Avila-Cabrera, J.J. 114

Bakhtin, M. 135, 137, 145
Bates, E. 41n1, 44, 46n11, 47, 78
Bedjaoui, M. 120, 135, 166, 176, 201
Bednarek, M. 253–254
Beitz, C.R. 6
Belgium 88, 168

Bhatia, V. K. 11–13, 15, 22, 58–60, 143, 172–173
Biel, Ł. 28, 30
bilingualism: alternative 12, 20, 152, 170, 194, 245; institutional 8, 20, 69, 71; in judgment translation 170–171; rationing 71
bioethics 34, 43, 237–238, 254
Black's Law Dictionary 65
Blackstone, W. 240
Bondi, M. 236
Bourcier, D. 138
Boussiakou, I. 200, 206
Bowker, J. 241, 244, 250
Brannan, J. 29–30, 37, 69, 83, 94, 166–167, 170–171, 202, 209, 217
Bres, J. 136
Brighton/Brighton Declaration 53, 55, 207, 245
Brown, P. 218, 223
Bruinsma, F. 199, 205, 210
Brussels 53
Bruxelles, S. 138
bundles 30, 182–183
Bureau for the Prevention and Combating of Corruption (Korupcijas novēršanas un apkarošanas birojs, KNAB) 104, **104**, **105**

Cairns, H. 240
Caliendo, G. 172
Calsamiglia, H. 239, 241–242
Canada 17, 85
Caple, H. 253–254
case communication (CC): case determination 73, 83, **102**, 103, **104**, 104–105, **105**, 106; corpus composition **101**; *D'Amico v. Italy* 104; defined scope of 91; goals of 63, 90, 93; *Kramareva v. Russia* 103; *Martynenko v. Ukraine* 101–103, 122; perspectives 91, 93; *Pīlāgs v. Latvia* **104**; procedure *62*, 63, 69, 90–91; reliance on 91, 102, 104–105, 107, 181, 190; study 99, 101–102; system-bound element across different genres (*Pīlāgs v. Latvia*) **104**; translation 94–95, 97, 105, 107–108, 110–111, **111**, 113, 115; verbatim accounting 102–103; *see also* written pleadings
case-law: case-law information note (CLIN) 67; Case Law Translation Programme (ECtHR) 247–248; collocation 36, 38; guide 67–68, 248, 250; informative translation 72, 88; vulgar expressions/vulgarity 109–112, 114; well-established *50*, *54*, 57, 132, 165, 227
caseload 9, 18, 35, 48–49, 51, 71, 125, 162
categorization 60, **173–174**, 176, 213
Catenaccio, P. 6–7
CBEs *see* culture-bound elements
CGA *see* Critical Genre Analysis
Chaemsaithong, K. 139–140
chamber of judges 47, 49, 79; *see also* Grand Chamber; judicial formations
Chen, J. 255
China/Chinese language 8
civil law 172, 197–198
CJEU *see* Court of Justice of the European Union
classifications 88, 96
clone/repetitive cases 51, 57, 80, 254, 257
cognitive causes 27, 59, 109, 239, 244
Cohen, M. 71, 166
colleague 81, 159–160, 198, 210, 217, 224–226, 231
collocates 143–144, 182, 222, 226
commission 18, 78
committee 49, 56–57, 79, 125; *see also* drafting
Committee of Ministers 46, *47*, 49; execution of judgments *50*, 52, *54*, 67, **259**, 261
common law 84, 172, 197–198, 242
communicative: goal 13, 61, 66, 80, 93, 119, 196, 201, 221, 231, 241; purpose 58, 61, 66, 68, 120, 199; situation 61, 65, 69, 119, 141
community: academic 58, 116; discourse 11–12, 21, 27, 28, *50*, *54*, 59, 74, 119, 196, 219, 227–228; discourse community of the Court (ECtHR) 51, 157–158, 165, 169; discursive 34; institutional 60; judicial 28, 219, 227; legal 164, 204, 246; professional 14, 28, 58, 239
community at large: disputes and 208
Community legislation (ECJ judgments) **173**
community of practice 29, 222; ECtHR judges as 219; im/politeness in 218–219, 227
comparative law 3, 6–7, 9–11, 20, 27, 37, 107, 110, 159

Comparative Legal Linguistics 9
complaints 42, 78, 82, 87, 93, 228, 243
complex preposition 30, *31*, 32, 88, 143–144
concept: analytical 13–14, 59, 91, 187, 206; autonomous 37; conceptualization 3, 6, 40–41, 146, 218–219, 239, 244, 253; legal 3–6, 12, 27, 97, 237, 244; linguistic inquiry 27; shared 12, 33, 125, 144, 213, 234, 241, 245; static 24, 118, 242; system-specific 38, 60, 97
concession 117, 138
concurring opinion: joint concurring opinion 207, 221, 224–225, **260**; misalignment 219, 223–225; partly concurring 203, *204*, 205–206, 209
conferences 53, 245
confirmation 85, 138
Constitutional Court and constitutional courts 42, 166, 176, 191, 198, 217; *see also* Supreme Court
contextualization 59, 73, 265; *see also* recontextualization
continuum 26, 107, 185, 220, 231, 238; terminological-phraseological 26, 30, 95–95
Contracting Party 46, 69, 82
convention 33, 36, 81, 230, 235
conventionalized form 61; *see also* generic structure; genre
conversation, recipient design 146
Copenhagen, Denmark 53
corpus-adduced evidence 230
Corpus-Assisted Discourse Analysis 139, 185
corpus linguistics 10, 55, 87n9; absolute or raw frequencies in 87n9, **148**; relative or normalized frequencies in 87n9, **148**; *see also* log-likelihood measures; normalization; normalized frequencies (NF)
Costa, J-P. 56, 81, 95, 217–218, 249
Council of Europe (CoE): ECtHR and **16**, 17, 45, 48, 83, 164; translation service/languages and 71, 83, 172, 174, 245
Court of Justice of the European Union (CJEU) 8–9, 20, 95, 188, 191
COVID-19 73, 117, 123, 137, 144–145
criminal: charge 37; limb (Article 6 ECHR) 164
critères de recevabilité 78, 81; *see also* admissibility criteria
Critical Discourse Analysis (CDA) 14–15
Critical Genre Analysis (CGA) 11–12, 14, 16, 61, 117, 119, 158, 237; *see also* Bhatia, V. K.
Crystal, D. 88
crystallization 28–29, 36, 42, 68, 194, 230
Culpeper, J. 228–229
culture-bound elements (CBEs) 96, 107, 110–111, 115
Cutting, J. 12

data protection 68
Davy, D. 88
decision(s) and decision-making: by domestic courts 37–38, 53, 81, 135, 159, 169; genres of 61–66; judgment (*arrêt*) as distinct from 65; judicial 21, 58, 78, 160, 181, 198–199, 201, 204, 262; regarding admissibility/inadmissibility **17**, 18, 46, 49, *50*, 52, *54*, 56, *62*, 63–64, 72, 79, 91
décision de recevabilité or *décision d'irrecevabilité* 64; *see also critères de recevabilité*
Dedov, D. 209, 224
deliberation: Grand Chamber 160; proceedings 116, 121, 158–159
delivery of judgment: date of 173; positioning and time of 200; pre-delivery stage of 73; public hearing for 116; summary of Court's reasoning disseminated on day of 69, 256; time of drafting/delivery of 202
democracy 40–41, 49
democratization 18, 49
Dendale, P. 137
denomination 59, 242–243
designation 3, 27, 242
dialogical: markers 138; patterns 150; reasoning 137–138
dialogically 138, 148
dialogism 130, 135–139, 144–146, 152; *see also* Bakhtin, M.; heteroglossia// heteroglossic; polyphony
didactic/pedagogical exposition 238
digital: platforms 236; revolution 235
digitalization 164, 235, 242
disagreement 65–66, 136, 145, 159, 181, 195; *see also* separate opinion
discourse: analysis 6, 14, 136, 185, 242, 255; as genre 13; realization *13*; community 11–12, 21, 27, 51, 59,

74, 119, 157–158, 169, 196, 219, 227; transfer 125–127
discursive practices: concepts of 12–13; conventional 85, 235; organizational 22, 25, 29, 107
disrespect 217–218, 220, 227
dissemination 38, 72–73, 240; *see also* knowledge dissemination
dissent: expressing 209; formula of 219, 229; polite 218, 224; statement of 196, 204–205, 211–212
dissenting opinion 180, 203, 205–207, 211–213, **215–216**, 224–228
divergence 32, 195, 203, 213–214, 221, 223, 227
diversity 4, 7; *see also* linguistic diversity
doctrine 34–35, 43, 53, 55, 207, 214, 242
domestic/national: legal system 10, 48–49, 53, 56, 71, 93, 95–97, 264; proceedings 38, 116, 120, 134–135, 139, 169, 192
drafting and deliberation: adoption process 159–160; committee 161, 165; language 72, 170, 213
Ducrot, O. 137, 146
due diligence 171–172
duel/dueling 116–117, 121, 139, 145, 148
Dworkin, R. 3

echoes (linguistic) and echo-utterances 138, 140, 186
ECtHR *see* European Court of Human Rights
Engberg, J. 9, 12, 28
English (language) 8, 71, 112
enlightenment 40, 236
entextualization 102, 241–242, 244, 261, 263
Entrikin, J.L. 217–219, 225, 227
environment 10, 43, 68, 93, 185
epistemic 147, 182–183, 185
Epstein, L. (et al 2013) 195
equal authenticity 7, 11, 65, 71–73, 170, 181, 212
equivalence 11, 28, 98; cultural 98; dynamic 98; functional 98; legal 98; non-equivalence 98
equivalent(s): functional 11, 98–99, **100**, *101*, 103, 104, 106, 110–111, **111**, 112, 114, 172; equivalent target speech act 72; legal 107; legalese replaced by lay equivalents 262; literal **100**; phraseological binary 98; taboo 113; terminological 95
escalation 150–151
European Bill of Rights 41
European Convention on Human Rights (ECHR): Article 10 (freedom of expression) 107; domestic remedies 81; effectiveness 51–52, 55–56; history of 45; inception 40, 43; interpretation 68, 78; linguistics 33–34; old court/new court 46–51; protocol 18, 48; standard procedures 116, 119, 165, 178; violations 62, 145
European Court of Human Rights (ECtHR): Admissibility Guide (the Guide) 80–81; autonomous concepts 37–38; bilingualism 8, 20, 69, 71, 152, 170–171, 181, 194, 245; case law/interpretation 41–42; embedding phase 48–49, 53, 82, 137, 169, 172; historical background 45, 245; judgments, language of 66, 96, 99, **100**, 155, 158, 165, 168, 170, 172, 176, 179, 200, 237, 245; judicial formation/genres 56–58; jurisdiction 15–18; knowledge dissemination 61, 66, 236, 239, 245, 249; Language Department 71, 73; linguistics/phraseology 19, 20–21, 33–35; procedural genre 58–61, 66, 72, 90, 99, 101, 178 237–238; protocols 44, 48, 51–55
evaluation/evaluative: argumentation and 158, 181–182, 185, 191–192; concept of 220, 222; patterns of 135, 158; positive/negative 223, 226, 228–229, 231
exemplification 244
exhaust remedies/exhaustion 34, 81, 135, 252–253
expert/expertise: independent 46; knowledge/legal knowledge 12, 27, 107, 241, 251; linguistics/translations 70, 110, 113, 115, 125; national law 64; opinions 196, 238
expulsion/extradition 37, 67, **215**

factsheets 24, *62*, 67, 94, 250, 253
fair: balance 35, **131**; trial 33, 78, 164, 211; *see also* RiFT
Fairclough, N. 14, 138

fallacy 150
Fawcett, J. 40
Feteris, E.T. 133–135, 137
filtering section/filter 79, 90, 257
Flikschuh, K. 6
forensic linguistics 3, 108, 121
formulaic/formulaicity: bracketing **174**, 178–179; patterns 28, 30, 32, 38, 88, 168; phrases 107, 167, 221, 261; *see also* crystallization
France/French: administrative law 35–36; judgments 71–72, 171–172; language 8–9, **19**, 20, 69–70, 83, 95, 98, 119, 122, 138
Francis, G. 185
Fraser, B. 218–219, 228
free market system 52–53
freedom of expression (Article 10) 36, 107–109, 167, 211
freedom of speech 108
Freixa, J. 27
French Supreme Court 138
full jurisdiction 36, 171

Galdia, M. 4
Gallicism 171
Galtung, J. 252–254
Garlicki, L. 44, 162, 176
Garzone, G. E. 6, 137–138, 149, 241–242, 252
GCPR *see* Grand Chamber Press Release
general legal style markers 30, *31*, 32
generalization 244
generic structure: of GCPR texts 258–264; of legal opinions 220, 238; of press releases 252, **259**, 264
genre 13; core genre 22, 32, *62*; derived genre 22, 24, 60–61, *62*, 66–68, 72, 250, 253; genre knowledge 59; genre set 59–61, 64, 66; Genre Studies 60–61; occluded genre 60–61, 64, 101–102, 117; operational genre 23–24, 60, *62*, 66; placement 59–60; primary genre 22, 24, 60; procedural genre 23–24, 29, 60, 72 (*see also* ECtHR); regional human rights courts 22; system of genres 60, *62*, 69, 71, 74, 94, 116, 157, 236–237, 257; theory 58; *see also* Critical Genre Analysis (CGA)
Gerards, J. 164
German (language) 9
gloss (brief explanation) 110, **111**, 114
Goffman, E. 61
government: agent 6, 94–95, 165; conduct 6, 48, 135, 136, 142, 147, 192; interference 107; observations **101**, **105**, 183; written observations *62*, 63–64, 90, 102; *see also* WOC
Goździ-Roszkowski, S. 134, 164, 181–185, 190–191, 208, 214, 221
Grand Chamber: case transfer 34, 49; judgments 65, 72, 158, 165, *166*, 170, 172, 174, 180–181, 194, 200–202, 212, 252, 257, 261; members 57–58, 159, 161, 165; proceedings 57–58, 91, 118, 121; *see also* judicial formations
Grand Chamber Press Release (GCPR) 257–258, 260–261
Gregory, J. 252
Grootendorst, R. 133
guide *see* case-law

Haiman, J. 229
Hammurabi Code 41
harassment 108
Harris, D. (et al 2014) 42
Harris, S. 228
Hart, H. L. A. 3
Hart, J. 45, 47, 61
Haugh, M. 219
hearsay 138
Helfer, L. R. 198–199, 201, 207–208, 212, 214
Heri, C. 56, 159, 208
heteroglossia/heteroglossic 106, 135–137, 146, 176; *see also* dialogism; polyphony
High Contracting Parties 53, 77
Hoffmann, L. 150, 217
Holmes, O. W. 23
Horn, L. 145–146
House of Lords 150
HRTF *see* Human Rights Trust Fund
HUDOC *see* human rights documentation
human rights: conceptualization 6, 12, 14–15, 27, 40–41, 235; contemporary rights 68; inhuman treatment 44; international legal order 4–5; legal vs utopian 6; protection 35, 37, 70, 109, 187, 192, **216**; regional/supranational courts 12, 15, **16–17**, 19, 22, 24, 30, 33, 60; researchers 5, 165; right of individual

petition 48–49, 77–78, 80, 83, 89, 152; violations 15, 36, 38, 40, 62, 81, 85, 101
human rights documentation (HUDOC) 58, 63–64, 67, 93, 101, 106, 111, 163–164, 200, 202, 245–246, 248
Human Rights Trust Fund (HRTF) 247
Hungary/Hungarian 111, 114, 167–168, **262**
Hunston, S. 185

IACmHR *see* Inter-American Commission on Human Rights
IACtHR *see* Inter-American Court of Human Rights
ICC *see* International Criminal Court
ICJ *see* International Court of Justice
ICTY *see* International Criminal Tribunal for the former Yugoslavia
image (reputation) 107, 218
immediate and simplified communication of application (IMSI) 91–92, *92*, 93, 102, 120, 175
immigration 68, 129, 142
immunity 190–191
impoliteness: intentional 108–109; perception of 227–230; systematic 219–220; unintentional 222, 226–227, 231; *see also* insult
importance: of interpretation 52, 58; of language and communication 3, 91, 95, 104, 134; *see also* phraseology
indeterminacy 55, 84; *see also* vague
individual petition, right of 48–49, 77–78, 80, 83, 89, 152
innovation 42, 119
insult 91, 108–114
integrity 28, 134
Inter-American Commission on Human Rights (IACmHR) **16**, 18
Inter-American Court of Human Rights (IACtHR): context and culture 15–16, **16–17**; judicial composition 21, 24, 35, 46, 48, 179; linguistics/language **19**, 21, 37; parallels 17–18, 77–78, 165
interdisciplinary: exposition 237–238; perspectives 99
interdiscursive dialogism 68, 135–136, 144; *see also* dialogism
interference: government 107; justification 44, 144; linguistic 119, 125–126, 133
Interlaken, Switzerland 53, 245–246, 249–250
interlingual translation 245
interlocutive dialogism 136; *see also* dialogism
international court: multilingualism 9, 58, 157, 170; operation of 7–8, 10, 58, 77, 171, 196
International Court of Justice (ICJ) 8, 116, 120–121, 135, 164, 166, 171, 201
International Criminal Court (ICC) 8–9, 62
International Criminal Tribunal for the former Yugoslavia (ICTY) 8
international law: crimes 244; principles 5, 33, 41, 81
International Organization for Standardization 97
international organizations 7, 9–10, 14, 25, 29–30, 33, 70, 96, 236
Internet: access 63, 66, 236, 240; sites 83, 246, 251
interpretation 12–13, 18, 20, 44, 111; legal 39, 125, 213; polite 220; preferred 187
intertextual/intertextuality: reference 144–145, 209, 245; routines 14, 63, 68, 84, 93, 130; voices/voicing 139–140, 152
intralingual translation 245
Ioriatti, E. 3
irony 84, 138, 140, 145, 176, 192, 219, 229
Italian Source Corpus (ITSC) 118
Italy/Italian 9, 22, 95–96, 99, 102, 117, 167–168
ITSC *see* Italian Source Corpus
Izmir, Turkey 53, 245

Jackson, J. 164, 190
Jacobs, G. 255
judge: Chamber of 47, *50*, *54*, 57, **259**; Committee of 49, 57, 79; judicial opinion re: judgments 210, 212–213, **215**, 218–220, 227; language of 4, 155; rapporteur 49, 57, 64, 95, 158–161, 165, 170, 174; role of 64, 197; *single* (as part of term pattern) 31; single *54*, 56, 63–65, 72, 79–80, 119n4, 125, 195, 202, 206–208
judgment: analysis 162–163; appropriacy and value 183–185, 193, **193**; argumentation 181,

185–186; authenticity 170, 194; case history 174–175, **177**, 178; closing section 172, **174**, 179, **180**, 202; counterarguments 184, 549; definition 157; dispositifs (operative part) 178–179; drafting of 161, 213; introductory unit 173; justification 176, 178, 181; language 167, 179, 183; law section **179**; length 168, 169, *169*; linguistic metaphors 158; majority 66, 199 (*see also* separate opinion); official decision 157, 160, 173, 178, 195; operative sections **180**; overview 181, **182**, 183; participation framework 164–165, **175**; scope of proceedings **173**, 175; separate opinions 164, 194, 202; style 165–166, 172, 211; textual genre 157; validity 164, 183–185, 196
judicial: clerk 200, 208; discourse 4, 133, 152, 167, 185, 195, 218, 220
judicial formation 24, 34, 49, 51, 53, 56, 58, 65, 78–79, 162, 195; Chamber of Judges and 47, 49, *50*, *54*, 57, **259**; Committee of Judges and 49, 57, 79; Grand Chamber 58, 121, 163, 202; single judge and *54*, 56, 63–65, 72, 79–80, 119n4, 125, 195, 202, 206–208
jurisdiction: contentious **16**, 17–19, 21, 24, 45, 48; of the court 23, 45–46, 48, 82; full 36, 171; relinquish 34, *50*, *54*, 58, *62*, 165, 243
jurisprudential creations *31*, 32, 34, 52
justice, right of access to 78
justification 44, 130, 178, 181, 197, 204, 214, 229
just satisfaction 33, *47*, 123, 127, **129**, **131**, 178, **180**, 222, 263

Kádár, D.Z. 219
Kecskes, I. 220, 230
Keleman, K. 197
Keller, H. 56, 159, 208
key case 64–65, 73
Kim, Y. 140
Kjær, A.L. 247
Kjølbro, J. F. 211
Kloosterhuis, H. 181
KNAB *see* Bureau for the Prevention and Combating of Corruption
knowledge: asymmetry 236–237, 239, 241; communication 12, 236, 239; dissemination 235, 245; gap 239–240, 263
Korupcijas novēršanas un apkarošanas birojs (KNAB) *see* Bureau for the Prevention and Combating of Corruption
Kostopoulou, M.-A. 81, 84
Kowalski, P. 197, 200
Kurzon, D. 164, 218–219, 225, 227, 231

Lakoff, R. T. 218, 219
language: adjectives 34, 36, 52, 84, 182–193, 185, 194, 227; insulting or offensive 85, 108–112, 167, 217, 229; of the law 3–4, 10, 24; official vs working languages 7–9, **19**, 20; pivot 8–9; sexually explicit/slang 109–111, 114; use of 12, 69, 71, 250
languages for special purposes (LSP) 3, 61
Latin 30, 82, 86, 88, 202, 262–263
Latvia 102, 105–106, 117
lawyer: access to 78, 168, 249; case lawyer 57, 65, 161–162, 165, 202; *see also* Registry lawyer
legal: argumentation 4, 28, 120, 127, 133, 137, 140, 145, 158, 181–183, 212, 230; authenticity 170, 194; commentary 55, 85, 187, 198, 218; culture 4, 29, 60, 97, 214, 228; interpreting/interpreter 39, 110–111, 113, 125, 213; knowledge 27–28, 39, 94, 125, 236–237, 240; language (legalese) 3–4, 9, 26, 48, 58, 86, 88, 95, 264; linguistics 3–4, 9, 11, 25, 39, 87, 158, 199; literacy 238, 240; literature 6, 36, 158, 195, 198; norm 37, 48, 176, 181, 187, 241–242; philosophy 6; phraseology 26, 28–29, 32; process 58, 72, 107, 135, 151, 193; reasoning 30, 67, 125, 133, 157, 178, 188, 190, 213, **215**, 227; scholars/scholarship 6, 11, 13, 24, 66, 165, 218, 241; style marker 30, *31*, 32, 88, 93, 126–127; style markers 30, *31*, 32, 88, 127, 263; terminology 11, 25–29, 39, 97, 262; transplants 30, 35, 37, 96–97; writing 4, 86, 195
Legal English 235
legal phraseology 28–29; *see also* phraseology
legal reasoning 133–135

legal system: comparability 97; domestic 4, 9–11, 26, 48, 56; national 10, 97, 264; source 98, **100**, 107, 126; supranational 33, 86, 115
Legal Terminology 27–28
legal translation: creativity 107; institutional 10, 91, 107, 110, 115; purpose 10–11, 72–73; research 26, 28, 97–98; services 21
Legal Translation Studies (LTS) 3, 9–11, 27–28, 96, 115; *see also* Translation Studies
legislation: national 38, *62*, 95, 103, 169, **173**; new/reform 199, 244
Levinson, S.C. 218, 223
Levy, B.H./Levy, B.F. 203
lexicogrammar 4, 29, 66, 68, 86, 167, 236
Lindholm, K. 255
linguistic: compromise 10, 167, 171, 202; creativity 107; diversity 7, 11, 20, 69; gap 9; implications 82; inclusivity 20, 248; interference 119, 125–126, 133; precedent 36, 171–172
linguistic regime: authentic language 212–213; influences official language 8; of judgments 172, 195; Rules of Court 19, **19**
living instrument 23, 42–43, 53, 68, 207, 242
loanword/borrowing 99, **100**, 103–106, **111**, 112
log-likelihood values and measures 149, 149n36, 181, 181n15, 182, **182**

machine translation (MT) 71, 123–125
majority opinion 46, 57, 66, 145, 160–162, 195, 197–199, 202, 204, **216**, 217, 219, 222, **259**
Malta/Maltese 117, 132, 145
manifestly ill-founded 36, 87, 91, 132, 167
manipulation 138
margin of appreciation 30, 34–35, 53, 55, 171, 208, 237, 247, 263
marker: negation **148**, 221; politeness/impoliteness 220, 222–223, 225, 227–228; style-marker 30, *31*, 32, 88, 93, 109, 126–127
Martin, J.R. 145
Mateo, J. 109
Mattila, H. E. S. 9
Mazzi, D. 138, 140, 169, 173, 176, 220
media communication 66, 238
Mellinkoff, D. 88
metaphor 6, 111, 135, 158, 230, 244
migration 29, 43, 242
Miller, S. 252
minority: colleagues 231; language 63; opinion 145, 197, 199, 202–203, 207, 214, 263; trend 209
misalignment 145, 160, 196, 212, 218–220, 224
modality 30, 185, **186**, 187
monodisciplinary: inter-specialist exposition 237; intra-specialist exposition 237
monolingual 9, 70, 86, 157, 161, 213
monolithic 27, 157, 195, 199
multilingual: confusion 7, 63, 121, 125 (*see also* bilingualism); factsheets *62*, 67, 250 (*see also* case-law guide); legislation 72; meaning-making 20
multilingualism 8–9, 157, 170; *see also* linguistic diversity
MWT *see* phraseology; terminology
MWU *see* phraseology; terminology

narrative 7, 41, 139, 146, 247
national judge 48, 56–58, 64, 82, 159–161, 166, 198, 206
national language 7, 20–21, 72, 83, 90, 94–95, 108, 113, 115, 122, 152, 245
necessary in a democratic society 34, 44
necessity 167, 184–187, 246–247
negation: syntactic 138; ***descriptive negation*** 146; markers of 148, 221; ***polemic negation*** 117, 146
New Zealand 85
newsworthiness 236, 252–254, 258
NGOs *see* non-governmental organizations
Nikitina, J. 6n3, 73, 90n1, 96n3, 100n6, 107, 129n18, 130, 138, 143–144, 236n1, 238, 244n5
non-governmental organizations (NGOs) 42, 49, 247–248
non-official translation 247
non-politeness 196, 219, 221–222, 228–229, 231
normalization, of number of words in subcorpora 223n19, **226**
normalized frequency (NF) **148**, **223**, 226

objections 87, 102, 130, **174**, **180**, 213
obscene expression 108–109; *see also* taboo words or lexis; vulgarity
obviousness 185, 188
occluded genre 60–61, 64, 101–102, 177
offensive language 108–111, 217
Office of the High Commissioner for Human Rights (OHCHR) 8
opening section 172–174, **175**, 179
Operational-Search Activities Act 190
operative clause **174**, 212
opposition 117, 138, 143, 152, 230, 242
Organization of American States (OAS) 16–18, 21

paraphrase 38, 99, **100–111**, 114, 138, 243, 261, 263
parliamentary 110, **262**
participation framework 59, 61, 66–68, 84, 112, 119, 125, 164–165, 194, 200, 241; participant 60–61, 84, 134, 146, 165, 219, 241
pattern grammar 158, 183, 185
Paúl, A. 24
Paulus, A. 199, 209, 213, 217
performative/performativity 36, 130, 132–133, 141, 178–179, 220, 225
Permanent Court of Arbitration (PCA) 8
Peruzzo, K. 30, 38, 94, 96–97, 99, 103, 107, 112, 126, 172, 176, 178, **179**, 202, 246
petitioner 15, 80
phraseology: adjectival strings in *31*, 34, 36, 38; chunks of texts and 32, 36, 167, 243, 255; human rights terminology and 29–38; importance and validity 188; legal 26, 28–29, 32; multiword terms (MWT) 28, 31, 33, 35–36, 38, 44, 55, 105–106; multiword units 29–30, 44, 97–98, **100**; of necessity and possibility 186; pattern/patterning 189; phraseological continuum 26, 30, *31*, 96, 107; phraseological units 26, 28–30, 37; phrases 11, 26, 28, 32–33, 39, 87, 107, 109, 225, 228, 241; routines 29, 36, 192
pigeonhole procedure/pigeonhole 161–162, 165, 178, 202
pilot judgment procedure 51–52
pinnacle genre of judgment 116, 157, 251
Pinto de Albuquerque, P. 198, 207–210, 226, 229
Pisillo Mazzeschi, R. 42
pivot language 8–9
plain language 77, 85, 89
Plain Language Movement 85, 236
Plantin, C. 133, 137
pleadings: one-sided 120; oral vs written 24, 82, 116, 118, 121, 218–219 (*see also* written observations); statements of case 119
Poland 79, 151, 168, 172
politeness: impolite 218–220, 222, 226–229, 231 (*see also* impoliteness); non-polite/non-politeness 196, 219–222, **223**, 227–229, 231; theory 218, 220
polyphonic discourse 137
polyphonous 139, 152
polyphony 135, 137, 139, 143–144
Pontrandolfo, G. 29, 32, 221
popularization: definition 236, 238; intergenerational exposition 239; of law 239–240, 264; popularized exposition 238, 249, 261; strategies 242, 261, 264
Portugal 168, 258, **259**
pragma-dialectical: approach 133–134; perspective or vantage point 147, 178, 181; theory of argumentation 133–134
pragma-dialectics 133–134, 192
pragmatics 110, 195
Prakken, H. 133, 137
precedent 68, 176, 197, 199, **215**, 242; *see also* legal norm
predictability 185, 199
preformulation/pre-packaged 255
press release: genre 68–69, 211, 238; institutional 236, 251, 263–264
press unit/press service 249–250, 253
presupposition 138
Prieto Ramos, F. 10, 26, 30, 33
private life 43, **216**
proceedings/procedure: procedural embedding 53, 82; procedural flow 24, *50*, *54*, 69, 71, 90, 257, 264
profanity 108
professional: culture *13*, 14–15, **16**, 25–26, 29, 68; practices 12, *13*, 14–15, 26, 60, 68, 74, 162, 198, 231
protocols 44, 55, 58, 66, **131**, 258

Protocols: Additional Protocol (Protocol no. 1) 44, **215**; advisory opinions (Protocol no. 16) 33, 44, 55, 66; court reform (Protocol no. 11) 18, 44–45, 48–49, *50*, 51, 71, 77, 169, **175**; Explanatory Report (Protocol no. 14) 51, 57; procedural amendments (Protocol no. 15) 53, 55, 82–83, 169; resident aliens (Protocol no. 7) 37

Rainey, B. (et al 2017) 61
reasonable hostility 219
reasoning: dialogical 137–138; legal 30, 67, 125, 133, 157, 178, 188, 190, 213, **215**, 227
rebuttal 137–138, 147
recite 10, 27, 44, 59
recontextualization 102, 140–141, 239, 241–242, 244, 264; *see also* entextualization
reform: process 51, 246–247; protocols 44, 48–49, 77
reformulation 138–139, 141, 243
refutation 117, 136, 138, 151, 153
regional human rights courts 15; *see also* genre
Registrar 56–57, 70, 161, 165, 180, 203
Registry lawyers: non-judicial rapporteurs 56, 107; reliance on 91, 93–94, 126, 251; role of 63, 67–68, 71–72, 79, 95, 97, 108, 110, 115
regret/regrettably 209, **215**, 222, 225, **226**
relinquishment 58, *62*, 165, **256**, **259**
report on admissibility 64
reported speech 138–141, 143, 147, 152
repudiatory: escalation 150; functions or patterns 148, **149**
repudiation 148, **149**, 149–150
resolution 19, *50*, 52, *54*, 134, 172, 238, 243
Respondent Government 63, 69, 90, 110, 117, 120, 123, 134, 164
rhetoric 14, 133, 183, 217–218, 225, 231
Rietiker, D. 172
RiFT *see* right to a fair trial corpus
right to a fair trial: Article 6 36n12, 78, 101, 168, 171; standards 164
right to a fair trial corpus (RiFT) 162–164; composition of **163**; *It is* patterns in 185, **189**
Rivière, F. 198, 203, 205, 214
Roitman, M. 136
Romania 79, 95, 168
Rosulek, L. 140–141
Rozakis, C. 207
Ruge, M.H. 252–254
Rules of Court: Article 45 32, 180, 203
Russia/Russian Federation 8, 87
Russian Source Corpus (RUSC) 118

Sajó, A. 207, 225
Salojärvi, J. 6
Salvi, R. 241, 244, 250
sarcasm 219, 227, 229–231
Sartor, G. 133, 137
Scalia, A. 213, 217–219, 225, 227
self-dialogism/interlocutive dialogism 136; *see also* dialogism
Senden, H. 202
senders and receivers 59, 61
separate opinion/separate judicial opinion: authorship 202–203, 206, **207**, 227; communicative purpose 199; concept (votum separatum) 195; drafting/delivery 198, 202, 209, 211, 213–214, 217, 219, 231; judicial temperament 206, 210, 230; justification 197, 199, 204, 214–215, 217, 221, 229; legal implications 194–196; length and organization of 195, 200, 208–210, **210**; main types of 203, *204* (*see also* concurring opinion; dissenting opinion); phraseology 28, 221–222, 227–228; precedent value 197; reasons for 203, *204*, 208–209, 213–214, **215**, 223; as separate genre 164 (*see also* separate judicial opinion); Separate Opinion Corpus (SOC) 200, **201**, **205**, **207**, **210**; style 200, 202, 210–211, 217–218, 220; types/categories 203, *204*
separatist discourse 197, 199, 202, 217, 230
Serghides, G. 209, 211
Sicialianos, L-A. 81, 84, 92, **218**
similes 230, 244
single judges 30, 56, 63–65, 72, 79–80, 125, 195, 202, 206
Sissons, S. 255
South Africa 85
Spanish (language) 8–9, **19**, 20–21
Spano, R. 34, 42, 48, 235
specialized communication 237, 239, 241–242

specialized exposition (monodisciplinary/intra-specialist/inter-specialist/interdisciplinary/diadactic exposition/pedagogical exposition/level of exposition) 67, 237–239
specificity of human rights 10, 25
Spielmann, D. 35, 207
standardization 27, 97, 126
State/Contracting Party 46, 69, 82
Steering Committee on Human Rights 52
Strasbourg, France 16, 34, 40, 45–46, 55, 68, 72, 87
style: of judgments 167, 178, 211; markers, legal 30, *31*, 32, 88, 93, 126; personal 86, 211
subsidiary measures 33
subsidiarity 33, 53, 55, 82, 169, 188, 208, 237, 247
supranational court: accessibility 49, 60; human rights courts 15, 20–21, 46, 72; judgments 164–165; terminology/phraseology 26, 28–29, 33, 98, 106, 152
Swales, J. 11, 60–61, 101
system-bound elements (SBEs) 107, 115; culture–specific 38, 96; movement across procedural genres of 100; terminological variation in 104–106; translation of CBEs and 115; translation couplets with loanwords of 112

taboo words or lexis 108–109, 112–113
taxonomy 14, 26, 60, 141, 203, 219, 231, 244
technology, advancements in 39, 43, 249, 264
terminology: bridges 28, 98; collocations 28, *31*, 32, 34, 38, **182**; decision-making process 29, 160; formulaic patterns 32; lexicogrammatical patterns 12, 30, 52, 61, 86, 138, 262; multiword terms (MWT) 28, 31, 33, 35–36, 38, 44, 55, 105–106; multiword units (MWU) 29–30, 44, 97–98, **100**; term-related units 30
terrorism 43, 68, 187, 217
Tessuto, G. 255
text: characters 102; chunks of 32, 36, 167, 243; internal/external 11–12; of judgments 160, 181, 209; original 41–42, 44, 52
textual fit 126
textualism 12
textualization 241–242
theory: argumentation 133–134; of human rights 41–42; of law 4; politeness 218, 220, 222
Thompson, S. 217
Tiersma, P. 86, 88, 97
Titiun, P. 249, 251–252
Tower of Babel (Genesis 11:1–9) 7
translation: accuracy 171; audiovisual 110; case-law 248; Case Law Translation Programme (ECtHR) 247–248; conventionalization 126–127; covert/third language 94–95, 115, 172; dark side 70, 94; force of law 73; formation-specific 65, 158; informative purposes 72, 122; issue of 247; for general legal or judicial purposes 72–73; general perspectives on legal translation 72; for informative purposes 72; of insults 91, 110, 114; legal 3, 11, 20, 25–26, 72–73, 97–98, 107, 152; legal institutional 10, 93, 110, 115, 152; literal 38, 99, 103–104, 111–112, 123, 127; for normative purposes 72; strategies 99
Translation Studies 10, 91, 98; authentic legal texts as source texts as understood in 170; descriptive 125; Early 125; cultural turn in 96–97; interference as understood in 125; Legal 3, 9–11, 27–28, 96, 115; paradigms of 110; prescriptive 125; terminological equivalents in 98
transparency 28, 197–199, 250–251, 263
travaux préparatoires 247
treaty **16**, 19, 22, 32–35, 44, 199
tribunal 8, 34, 55, 143, 172, 188
trust building 48, 80, 188
truth 142, 185, 188
Tulkens, F. 207
Turin Court of Appeal 126, **262**
Turkey 79, 106, 168, 170, 172

Ukraine 79, 93, 106, 117, 168, 257
United Kingdom (UK) 86, 106, **129**, 138
United Nations 7–8, 35, 186
United Nations High Commissioner for Refugees 142
Universal Declaration of Human Rights (UDHR) 5, 40

universality of human rights 5
US Supreme Court 138, 185, 213, 217, 224

vague/vagueness 10, 55, 84, 211
value: cultural 5; fundamental 42; news value 253–254; performative 130, 132–133, 147, 153, 178; social 108
van Dijk, T. 239, 241–242
van Eemeren, F. 133–134
van Leeuwen, T. 14
variation: subtle 168, 190, 213, 221, 227; terminological 4, 6, 27, 104–105, 118
Venice Commission 217
verbal aggression 219, 229
viewpoints, divergent 16, 21, 35, 84, 162, 169, 205, 212, 218
Villiger, M 166, 168, 173, 178, 209
Voeten, E. 198–199, 201, 208, 212, 214
voices, embedded 135, 137, 139–143, 147, 152, 176, 181
vulgarity 108–114

watershed genre 90–91
whistle-blower 212
White, R. 145, 172, 200, 206
witness 70, 102–103, **131**, 151, 164, 191; *see also* expert
Woolf, (Lord) 63, 80, 119
working language 7–8, **19**, 20, 95, 170, 212–213
World Trade Organization (WTO) 8
World War II 25, 40–41
Written Observations Corpus (WOC): applicant observations 123; contains written pleadings 117–119; embedded voices/collocates 139, 143–144; negation markers 148–149, 151
written observations/written pleadings: applicant introductory section **128**; case communication 63, 69–70, 94, 105, 119–120; dialogical reasoning 137–138; dialogism 130, 135–138, 144–145, 152; explicit deconstruction 147; lexical cues 139, 141; linguistic interference 119, 125–126, 133; main parties 139; occluded/non-accessible to public 64, 101–102, 116–117; procedural order 121–122; reasoned dialogue 133, 135; structure 117, 127–128, **131**, 134–135; submit/submission terminology 141; titling and text 118

X (Twitter) 249, 258, 260, 264

Yale Law School 200
Yudkivska, G. Y. 211
Yus, F. 109

Zupančić, B. M. 202, 228

FSC
www.fsc.org
MIX
Papier | Fördert gute Waldnutzung
FSC® C083411

Kolibri 360 GmbH
Ferdinand-Jühlke-Straße 7
99095 Erfurt, Deutschland
produktsicherheit@kolibri360.de